Pub @ £25.00

£4.95

MONASTIC STUDIES

THE CONTINUITY OF TRADITION

II

Edited by
JUDITH LOADES

HEADSTART HISTORY
1991

Published by   HEADSTART HISTORY
                    PO Box 41, Bangor, Gwynedd LL57 1SB
Set by   LAZERTYPE
                    Bridgegate Pavilion, Chester Business Park
                    Wrexham Road, Chester CH4 9QH
Printed by   THE IPSWICH BOOK COMPANY LTD
                    The Drift, Nacton Road,
                    Ipswich, Suffolk IP3 3QR

ISBN 1 873041 10 1
A CIP catalogue record for this book is available from the British Library

CONTENTS

PREFACE

MONASTIC STUDIES I arose from a conference held in 1989 at Bangor. It was a success both in terms of scholarship and general enjoyment so much so that many requested that a second such meeting be arranged. Luckily the University College of North Wales, Bangor was able to provide accommodation and the papers in this volume refer to that conference held in September 1990.

I was privileged that Professor David Luscombe was able to address us on the first evening. His work on Abelard over the years has made him the leading scholar in the field. Antonia Gransden's research is of enormous importance particularly with reference to Bury St. Edmunds. Emma Mason has recently published an invaluable contribution to our knowledge of William of Worcester and is an established scholar on the study of Wesminster Abbey. David William's work on the mapping of Cistercian lands was published shortly after he spoke on that subject at MONASTIC STUDIES I so it was an honour that such a distinguished scholar of Cistercian studies was able to address the group on this occasion.

To mention the main speakers by name does not lessen the value of other contributors. Readers will recognise other distinguished names including Simon Tugwell of Blackfriars, Oxford who will be a main speaker at MONASTIC STUDIES III to be held at Leicester in September 1992.

Amongst the young scholars in the volume are Jackie Mountain whose work is supervised by Emma Mason and Fiona Robb supervised by Brenda Bolton. I should mention too, Benjamin Thompson, Peterhouse, Cambridge, a young scholar who is quickly establishing a reputation for his excellent work: MONASTIC STUDIES does present such scolars with an opportunity to present their work in an informal atmosphere and to benefit from discussions with distinguished scholars in their field.

I would also like to draw attention to the article by Mary McLaughlin. Just as Joan Greatrex told MONASTIC STUDIES I about the register she was developing so Dr. McLaughlin has written about her data-base on medieval women. She got in touch with me very recently having missed MONASTIC STUDIES and I agreed to include her article in this volume to encourage European scholars to get in touch. You will see her address in Footnote 2 of her article.

Acknowledgment is given to those who assisted Joan Greatrex in her article on Worcester Cathedral Library and indeed to the many other libraries and archives whose staff have contributed to other papers by their help in a myriad of ways.

I apologise once again to my long-suffering husband and thank him for helping to see this volume through. Thanks are also due to Suzanne, Kevin, Rita and Stan at LazerType, and to Roderick Boyd at the Ipswich Book Company, They all have the technical knowledge and artistic skills which I lack. I record my gratitude to all of them.

Judith Loades
Bangor, 1991.

MONASTICISM IN THE LIVES
AND WRITINGS OF HELOISE AND ABELARD
by
David Luscombe

When the name of Heloise is mentioned we immediately think of a clever girl who became a desperately unhappy nun. But when the name of Abelard is mentioned we do not usually associate him with monasticism. He finds little place in our standard histories of the medieval monastic and religious orders. Rather, I suppose, our first thoughts are likely to relate him to Heloise, the girl and pupil he married and whose correspondence with Abelard has enjoyed a wide readership and much celebrity over several centuries.

Or we think first and immediately of Abelard's notoriety as a controversial academic and philosopher. The spur to doing so lies in his autobiographical letter of consolation to an unknown friend known as *The History of My Troubles, Historia calamitatum mearum*. There we find a narrative of his quarrels with the leading masters of the schools in the cities of Paris and Laon, with William of Champeaux on questions of epistemology and logic and with Anselm of Laon over methods to be used in teaching the Bible to students. There too we find an embittered account of how Alberic and Lotulph, two masters in the schools of Rheims, managed by a series of clever manoeuvres to persuade enough bishops in the course of a synod held in Soissons in 1121 to condemn Abelard for heresy, the heresy being concerned with the doctrine of the Trinity. Abelard's first treatise on this subject was ignominiously cast into the fire and publicly burnt. Seen in this light Abelard is often remembered as the teacher who did most in Paris, during the course of what we call the Renaissance of the twelfth century and during a period of precocious urban development, to stimulate argument and to help to turn Paris itself into Europe's first university city. It is he, as the late Paul Henry once said to me, who first taught the West how to think - after the long centuries in which a somewhat obscure tradition of philosophical and theological reflection had been kept ticking over quietly inside the closed environment of scattered monastic communities.

Or, when we turn our minds to Abelard and to what his life was associated with, we think of Saint Bernard of Clairvaux, the austere leader of the Cistercian order which championed the cause of monastic reform during a time of sensational evangelical awakening. Bernard in the late 1130s engaged Abelard in an acrimonious public slanging match and he succeeded in having Abelard condemned as a heretic for the second time, condemned in fact to perpetual silence as a teacher as well as to being excommunicated by none less than Pope Innocent II.

The issues raised by this quite vast dispute have remained controversial to this day. There are those who will tend to view Bernard and his Cistercian friend William of Saint Thierry as the rallying points of a conservative, somewhat obscurantist, monastic tradition of meditation upon Scripture and upon the spiritual teachings of the Fathers of the Church; and there are those who may be inclined to see in Abelard the champion of academic freedom, the freedom to doubt and to pursue rational enquiry for its own sake and whithersoever it may lead, even if the end point is the adjustment of some traditional formulas used to express the Christian faith. But there are other scholars who will credit Bernard with the courage needed to stop dialectical theology from getting out of hand. Seen in this light, perhaps, the conflict between Bernard and Abelard which reached its climax in the year 1140 was almost a necessary conflict between faith and reason, a bloodletting both for monastic and for scholastic culture. Monastic culture consists, we might say, in an ongoing tradition of combining study and prayer within a dedicated community, of reading in order to shape the personal and collective experience of living the Christian life, whereas scholastic culture appears to be the cultivation of the skills of logical argumentation based upon the techniques provided by Aristotle and Boethius which facilitated the critical analysis of any claim through the use of human language. Abelard therefore has no unchallengeable claim to historical importance *as a monk*. His fame is that of a schoolman and a philosopher or, if you like, a philosophical theologian. The monastic establishment of the twelfth century rejected him and brought him down. Yet it was perhaps a Pyrrhic victory: although a heretical master from Paris was destroyed, the Benedictine centuries were then drawing imperceptibly to a close and the new Europe of the towns, the friars and the universities, of well-drilled armies of scholastic masters at work in the great cities of the later Middle Ages, was about to dawn.

All this may easily be thought to be true, at least in broad and simple historical terms. Yet Abelard *was* a monk, no less than Heloise was a nun. He became a monk in about 1119 at the age of 40 or so and was professed in the royal and ancient abbey of Saint Denis to the north of Paris. And at almost the same time Heloise went into the nunnery of Argenteuil where she had been to school as a child and which was only about seven or eight kilometres away from the abbey of Saint Denis. In fact Abelard came to live in four abbeys. In 1121, after his first condemnation for heresy, he was ordered to be confined in the abbey of Saint Médard in Soissons until he was ready to be returned to his own abbey of Saint Denis. In about 1127 he accepted election as abbot of another monastery, that of Saint Gildas which was far away in his native Brittany, in the diocese of Vannes. Then in 1140 following his second condemnation for heresy, having set out on the long journey to Rome to make a personal appeal to his well placed friends close to the Pope against the sentence of the French bishops, Abelard decided to terminate his journey after visiting the great abbey of Cluny. The abbot, Peter the Venerable, persuaded him to stay there as a member of the monastic community.

In addition to inhabiting four abbeys Abelard also lived at various times in a number of priories and hermitages. He apparently left his first monastery in or shortly after 1119 to move to a smaller house belonging to Saint Denis in order to be free to carry on teaching. And when he was returned to the abbey of Saint Denis from Saint Médard after the condemnation in 1121 he again only stayed for a short while. He fled in fact and went secretly to a priory far away in Champagne in the town of Provins. There he negotiated for his release from the strict obligation to live in the abbey of Saint Denis and obtained permission to live as a monk wherever he chose provided that he did not enter into obedience to another abbot. So it was that in 1122 Abelard obtained some land in the parish of Quincey not far from the town of Nogent on Seine. And there he constructed a small oratory and hermitage and lived in retreat for a number of years. And finally, after entering the abbey of Cluny in 1140, as his health deteriorated, Peter the Venerable moved him away from the great abbey to a nearby small dependent priory at Chalon-sur-Saône and there at Saint Marcel on the banks of the river he died. As for Heloise, in 1129 she and her sisters in the convent of Argenteuil were made homeless following the repossession of their property by the abbey of Saint Denis. Abelard, who was then abbot of Saint Gildas in Brittany, offered Heloise the property he had in Quincey. Heloise and some of her sisters moved there and thus there came into being the convent of the Paraclete of which Heloise remained head until her death in 1163. This convent became the head of a small congregation of houses, six in all, and therefore can be said to have done well under Heloise's direction.

These then are the bare external facts about the religious life led by Abelard and also by Heloise. We should bear in mind as well that Heloise had an uncle, Fulbert, who was a canon of the cathedral of Notre Dame in Paris and that both Abelard's father and his mother retired separately and by mutual agreement at the end of their lives into religious houses. If however Abelard used monasteries only as a refuge from the schools after his violent castration and after his rejection of the married life, there might be little left to say that is worthy of discussion here. For we could continue to follow convention and to relegate both Abelard and to a lesser extent Heloise to the margins of the wider history of that vast subject which is medieval monasticism.

But this we cannot do. One reason why we cannot do so is that monasticism looms so very large in Abelard's written output. It is true that his writings on logic, his commentaries on the philosophical textbooks written by Porphyry and by Boethius, his own book on Dialectic, are bulky and have nothing to do with monasticism.[1] They were not included in volume 178 of Migne's Patrology containing Abelard's writings.[2] But in that volume of the Patrology we have other writings by Abelard which are not philosophical as such, but mainly theological and these fill 1616 columns of which more than one third - to be precise, 562 columns - contain works written explicitly for people in the religious life. And not only *for* them, as these are works explicitly about one or other aspect of the religious life as lived by monks and nuns and regular canons. Furthermore, the other works in this volume of the Patrology, include within them long and substantial enquiries into monasticism. These are found in the midst of such writings as the autobiography and the *Christian Theology* and the *Dialogue between the Philosopher, the Jew and the Christian.*

To discover what Abelard and also Heloise tried to say about monasticism, as well as to attempt to assess this historically, it may be helpful to organise some observations

---

[1] For a listing of Abelard's writings, of their editions and of their manuscripts, see J. Barrow, C. Burnett, D. Luscombe, 'A Checklist of the Manuscripts containing the Writings of Peter Abelard and Heloise', *Revue d'Histoire des Textes*, 14-15 (1984-5), pp. 183-302. For earlier discussions of some of the issues reconsidered in this paper see the references contained in Luscombe, 'Pierre Abélard et le monachisme', *Pierre Abélard - Pierre le Vénérable*, ed. R. Louis and J. Jolivet, Centre national de la recherche scientifique. Colloques internationaux, no. 546 (Paris, 1975), pp. 271-8; *Peter Abelard*, The Historical Association, General Series 95 (London, 1979); 'The *Letters* of Heloise and Abelard since "Cluny 1972" in R. Thomas (ed.), *Petrus Abaelardus (1079-1142)*, Trierer theologische Studien, 38 (Trier, 1980), pp. 19-39, and 'From Paris to the Paraclete: The Correspondence of Abelard and Heloise'. Raleigh Lecture on History, *Proceedings of the British Academy*, 74 (1988), pp. 247-83.

[2] J.-P. Migne, *Patrologia Latina*, t. 178 (Paris, 1855).

around a few themes. Firstly, we may ask what were Abelard's views about the monastic tradition, about the origins and purpose of monasticism, both male and female. Secondly, what did he say about monasticism as it existed in his own time? Thirdly, what are we to make of the efforts of this separated couple to live the monastic life, and especially what are we to think of Abelard for all that hopping in and out of religious houses over much of France? And finally what did Abelard do for Heloise and for the convent of the Paraclete and what did Heloise think of that?

So first, to find Abelard's views about traditional monasticism we can hardly do better than read his autobiography, the *Historia calamitatum*. There Heloise is reported as saying that in all the peoples of history, among the Gentiles and Jews as well as among Christians, there have always been some who have left the world in order to seek virtue;[3] and that unquestionably is a fundamental premiss for Abelard also. It is the key to understanding almost all that he stood for during the last two decades of his life. Abelard insists again and again on the universality of the monastic instinct. Among the Jews there were communities of Essenes and Nazarenes and before them there were the followers of Elisha. Among the earliest Christians there was the great figure of John the Baptist and later there were the Desert Fathers. But also among the Gentiles there were philosophers who lived - although they were pagans - a monastic way of life. The lives of the pagan philosophers illustrate many of the exemplary features of the monastic life such as contempt for this world, the love of solitude, the undertaking of manual work, the practice of continence and temperance, the pursuit of study. The truth of so much that the pagan philosophers taught is the fruit as well as the proof of the virtuous lives lived by, among others, Plato and Socrates, Cicero and Seneca. And Diogenes, living in his tub, reminds one of John the Baptist existing merely on locusts and honey. These thoughts are expressed by Abelard again and again and especially in his thirty-third Sermon which is on St. John the Baptist,[4] also in the second book of his Christian Theology[5] and in a letter he wrote to Bernard of Clairvaux shortly after 1130[6], as well as earlier in a work which carries the title of Exhortation to the brothers and the fellow monks of Saint Denis.[7] Abelard was by no means alone in his time in extolling the values of pre-Benedictine monasticism, of the palaeo-Christian monasticism of the Desert Fathers, but where he is somewhat singular is in the emphasis he places on including the pagan philosophers of antiquity within the universal framework of monasticism. To do this and for support he turns especially to two of the western Fathers. The first is St. Jerome who in the first book of his work against Jovinian had used the example of the pagan philosophers to reinforce his own arguments in favour of virginity.[8] The second Father is Saint Augustine who in his City of God had applauded the Platonists for the truth of their teaching on

---

[3] Abelard, *Historia calamitatum*, ed. J. Monfrin, 2nd edition (Paris, 1962) 11. 483 *et seq.*

[4] Sermon 33, PL.178, 582-607.

[5] *Theologia Christiana*, II, 60-115, ed. E.M. Buytaert, *Petri Abaelardi opera theologica*, II, Corpus Christianorum, Continuatio mediaevalis, XII (Turnhout, 1969), pp. 156-184.

[6] *Letter* 10, ed. E.R. Smits, *Peter Abelard. Letters IX-XIV* (Groningen, 1983), pp. 239-247; also PL.178, 335-340.

[7] This now lost work is mentioned in Abelard's *Soliloquium*, PL.178, 1877D-1878A.

[8] Cf. P. Delhaye, 'Le dossier anti-matrimonial de l'*Adversus Iovinianum* et son influence sur quelques écrits latins du XIIe siècle', *Mediaeval Studies*, XIII (1951), pp. 65-86.

ethics, on God, even on the Trinity, although they did not foresee the Incarnation of Christ.

If we now turn, secondly, to what Abelard thought about monasticism in his own time, what do we find? We certainly find a good deal of criticism levelled against contemporary institutions. Much of this is generalised: Abelard denounces the worldliness of contemporary monastic life, the absorption of monks in urban life or in estate management, their craving for preferment to bishoprics or their preference for living away from the cloister in the comfort of a small priory or cell or obedience. For the Cistercian order, however, Abelard in one of his letters reserves a more restricted kind of criticism over its reform of the liturgy which he thought was a half-baked reform which had resulted in impoverishment.[9] But if he is indeed the author of the Sermon which begins *Adtendite a falsis prophetis,* he regarded the whole Cistercian order as immoderate and hypocritical.[10] He was also extraordinarily harsh in his judgements upon reforming regular canons such as St. Norbert, the founder of Prémontré[11] or William of Champeaux when he founded the canonry of St. Victor.[12] While Abelard had monastic friends such as those who received him at Provins around 1122[13] or such as Peter the Venerable himself,[14] and while he found models to admire such as Robert of Arbrissel, the founder of Fontevraud ,[15] and while in general we must compensate for the fact that Abelard was always more discreet when writing about his friends than his enemies, there can be no question but that Abelard was thoroughly disliked by many monks and canons and that he just as thoroughly disliked those monks and canons in return, especially if they were reformed monks and reformed canons. Relations between Abelard and Bernard were not always cold but they certainly went through periods of bitter strain and there was also tension and conflict with other monks at Saint Denis and at Saint Gildas. At Saint Denis quarrels erupted into a polemic concerning the origins of the abbey and the historical character of its patron St. Denis himself.[16] At Saint Gildas Abelard's attempt to make the monks live in the abbey resulted in his being nearly poisoned by them and also in his flight from Brittany.[17] His own attempt to find peace and stability at Quincey was apparently ruined by hostile criticisms from other religious elsewhere,[18] and so on. By 1140, and long after Abelard had abandoned his abbatial responsibilities at Saint Gildas,

---

[9] *Letter* 10, ed. Smits, pp. 239-47 (with commentary, pp. 120-136).

[10] Ed. L.J. Engels, 'Adtendite a falsis prophetis (Ms. Colmar 128, ff. 152VO-153VO). Un texte de Pierre Abelard contre les Cisterciens retrouvé?' in *Corona Gratiarum. Mélanges E. Dekkers,* t.II (Bruges and The Hague, 1975), pp. 195-228.

[11] Sermon 33, PL.178, 605.

[12] *Historia calamitatum,* ed. Monfrin, *11.70 et seq.*

[13] *Historia calamitatum,* ed. Monfrin, *11.985 et seq.*

[14] Peter the Venerable, Letters 98, 115, 167, ed. G. Constable, *The Letters of Peter the Venerable,* t.1 (Cambridge, Mass., 1967), pp. 258-9, 303-7, 400-01.

[15] *Letter* 14, ed. Smits p. 280; PL.178, 357B.

[16] Abelard, *Historia calamitatum,* ed. Monfrin, *11. 941 et seq;* Letter *11,* ed. Smits, pp.249-255.

[17] Abelard, *Historia calamitatum,* ed. Monfrin, *11. 1229 et seq.*

[18] Abelard, *Historia calamitatum,* ed. Monfrin, *11. 1200 et seq.*

Bernard was able to savage him saying that he was an abbot without monks, and a monk without a rule who had nothing of the monk about him except the habit and the name, and a master who was incapable of staying in the order; he was also a dissembler, Herod within but John without, wholly ambiguous.[19] Is there any other monk of the time who was so ill thought of by Saint Bernard?

Yet what are we to make of the attempts Abelard himself made to live the monastic life? Abelard only became a monk because of his shame and confusion on being forcibly castrated by the agents of his wife's uncle who objected to his niece's marriage. He perhaps only became an abbot at Saint Gildas to acquire a status in the church that he had earlier hoped for when he tried to obtain a chair in the cathedral school of Paris. By any standard of judgement, Abelard lived, even as a monk, a very disturbed life. And he acknowledged it frequently; he complained often of the *invidia*, the envy, shown towards him by other men of religion; he presented himself as a persecuted monastic fugitive. But he had a coherent idea of what the essence of monasticism is and this we may summarize as follows. The word monk, *monachus*, as St. Jerome wrote, means to be alone, *solus*, from the Greek word *monos*. The monk must therefore seek to be like a hermit, at least in spirit. And he must be eremitical in purpose, in order to contemplate. The pursuit of virtue creates the conditions for meditation but meditation requires study. And this study brings us to philosophy, philosophy being the love and pursuit of wisdom. The monk therefore should create the conditions in which, by the practice of virtue and of study, he comes to be wise. Thus the good monk is a philosopher. And that was what St. John Chrysostom meant when he wrote that St. John the Baptist philosophised in the hermitage. And that is what is meant when people say that the true philosophy is that of Christ, *vera philosophia Christus*, because Christ is the *Logos*, the Word, or the Wisdom of God. All this underlies Abelard's descriptions of what he set out to achieve in his small oratory at Quincey and also what he tried to do, though with far less success, on the remote Atlantic coastline of Brittany.

But there is another monastic activity or cause in which Abelard engaged, one to which he devoted much time and for which it would be too harsh to judge him a failure. This is his encouragement of the nuns at the Paraclete.

It is now an established view that the convent of the Paraclete under Heloise's direction adopted mainly Cistercian customs.[20] The convent was not accepted into the Cistercian order but like many other contemporary houses of religious women the Paraclete borrowed Cistercian customs. However, Heloise, once installed in the Paraclete, also sought Abelard's own guidance. She does so in Letter 4 of the collection of their letters where she reminds Abelard that he alone after God is the founder of the oratory and the builder of the community, and moreover that he knows far more than do the nuns about the teachings of the holy fathers who had in the past written so much to encourage as well as to console holy women. So Heloise draws attention to her need to have in writing some guidance for the new community, and in Letter 6 she specifies her needs by making requests and putting questions and problems to Abelard to which he

[19] Letters 193, 331, 332, ed. J. Leclercq and H. Rochais, *S. Bernardi Opera* vol. VIII (Rome, 1977), pp. 44-45, 269, 271.

[20] C. Waddell, *The Paraclete Statutes. Institutiones nostrae. Troyes, Bibliothèque Municipale Ms 802, ff. 89r-90v. Introduction, Edition, Commentary,* Cistercian Liturgy Series, 20 (Gethsemani Abbey, Trappist, Kentucky 40051, 1987).

replied in Letter 7, which is a treatise on the feminine religious life, and in Letter 8 which prefaces a Rule which he had written for the convent. One of the main elements found in this exchange of views is the theme that the weaker sex needs the help of the stronger and that a convent of women should be supported by a monastery of men. Abelard himself in his Rule for the Paraclete developed his argument that women should be governed not by a woman but by a man to the point of stipulating that there should be an abbot presiding over the abbess and her sisters.[21]

Another theme consists of exhortations to study Scripture and to follow Jerome's example. And whatever else one may think of the value or otherwise of Abelard's prescriptions for life in the abbey of the Paraclete he was in this respect appreciated there. In Letters 3 and 8 Abelard asked the nuns to collect any questions they had about Scripture and present them to him.[22] And this they apparently did for we have outside the collection of the correspondence of Heloise and Abelard a letter from Heloise saying that she and the sisters were following Abelard's advice to study Scripture and also following the example set by Jerome.[23] This letter presents 42 questions raised by the community in the course of its studies and to these Abelard provided detailed answers which were collected along with the questions to form a small book that has been known in modern times as The Problems of Heloise.[24] The very last question has a personal twist to it: is it ever sinful, Heloise asks, to do what one is commanded to do by one's lord or master?[25] Earlier in Letter 2 Heloise had reproached Abelard for commanding her to enter the religious life, and this she protested she had done not out of choice and not out of love of God but because of Abelard's command, his *iussio*.[26] As Professor Dronke has rightly suggested, 'it is hard to read this final *Problema* without perceiving an echo of the anguished reproach Heloise had made Abelard in her second letter'.[27]

Another valuable fruit of this engagement in the study of Scripture would certainly appear to be Abelard's written Commentary on the opening of the Book of Genesis.[28] For this Commentary is preceded by a personal letter from him to Heloise whom he addresses as sister once dear to him in the world and now most dear to him in Christ.[29] Abelard emphasises that it is she who has pressed him to send the commentary. In it Abelard

---

[21] The best available editions are: J.T. Muckle, 'The Personal Letters between Abaelard and Heloise', *Mediaeval Studies*, 15 (1953), pp. 47-94 (letters 2-6); 'The Letter of Heloise on the Religious Life and Abaelard's First Reply', *Mediaeval Studies*, 17 (1955), pp. 240-281 (letters 6-7); T.P. McLaughlin 'Abelard's Rule for Religious Women', *Mediaeval Studies*, 18 (1956), pp. 241-292 (the Rule). On the question of the abbot see Abelard, Letter 8, ed. McLaughlin, p.259, Cf. Abelard, *Historia calamitatum*, ed. Monfrin, 11.1464-88; Heloise, letter 6, ed. Muckle, pp.243, 253.

[22] Abelard, letter 3, ed. Muckle, p.73; letter 8, ed. McLaughlin, p.292.

[23] PL.178, 677-8.

[24] PL.178, 677-730.

[25] PL.178, 723-30.

[26] ed. Muckle, p.72.

[27] P. Dronke, *Women Writers of the Middle Ages* (Cambridge, 1984), pp. 134-9, here p.137.

[28] PL.178, 731-84.

[29] PL.178, 731-2.

sought to weave together moral and mystical exegesis of the Creation stories inside a literal and historical framework of interpretation. So the six days of creation become a mirror of the six ages of the world and also a mirror of the path of the individual human soul towards salvation.[30]

Nor is this all we have by way of writings undertaken by Abelard on behalf of the convent. In another letter to Heloise Abelard writes that he is sending her Sermons which he has written at her request for her and for her spiritual daughters in the oratory.[31] He explains that the Sermons are arranged to follow the feasts in the church's year from the beginning of the task of redeeming mankind. Surviving copies of Abelard's Sermons have become detached from this letter preface. But the main surviving collection does indeed begin with a Sermon on the Annunciation to the Virgin Mary and in fact the opening words are *Exordium nostrae redemptionis*, The beginning of our redemption ... [32] There are around thirty two sermons that can be probably associated with the collection sent to the Paraclete and a few more besides prepared for other occasions. A copy of the collection was once kept in the convent of the Paraclete although it is now apparently lost. One of the Sermons, one that was not obviously prepared for reading in the Paraclete, consists of an appeal for alms for the convent.[33]

Furthermore, we have surviving today a collection of hymns and sequences composed by Abelard and accompanied by three letters written by him to Heloise.[34] In the first of these letters Abelard quotes some lines from an otherwise unknown communication from Heloise giving her view that the hymns in use in the Latin and in the Gallican church are not satisfactory, that it is necessary to stick to authentic and accurate texts and to dispense with hymns that have corrupt versification or are the work of uncertain authors, and to avoid incorrect translations of the Psalms. So persuaded was he by Heloise's pleading, he writes, that he has written a new collection of hymns to remedy the deficiencies of tradition to which Heloise has drawn his attention.[35]

The collection of hymns survives and it is unusually large. There are 129 newly written pieces and they are carefully arranged in three books, each of which has its own plan and its own letter preface. Book one has hymns for Sundays and for week days; these celebrate the theme of creation and offer parallels with the six days of creation and the seventh day of rest, as this was expounded in the Commentary that Abelard wrote on the Book of Genesis. The night hymns are concerned with what happened during the six days; the day hymns offer allegorical and moralising interpretations of it. The second

---

[30] See E. Kearney, 'Peter Abelard as Biblical Commentator: A Study of the Expositio in Hexaemeron', *Petrus Abaelardus (1079-1142). Person, Werk und Wirkung*. Trierer Theologische Studien, 38 (Trier, 1980), pp. 199-215.

[31] PL.178, 379-80.

[32] PL.178, 379.

[33] See Barrow, Burnett, Luscombe, 'Checklist', no. 304; L.J. Engels, '*Adtendite*', pp.195-228.

[34] The most recent edition is by C. Waddell, OCSO, *Hymn Collections from the Paraclete. Volume 1: Introduction and Commentary. Volume II: Edition of Texts*, Cistercian Liturgy Series, 8 and 9 (Gethsemani Abbey, Trappist, Kentucky 40051, 1989 and 1987).

[35] Ed. Waddell, *Hymn Collections*, II, pp. 5-9.

book contains hymns for solemn feasts concerned, rather like the Sermon collection, with the mysteries of the Redemption. The third book dwells on the joys of heaven, on the Virgin and on the saints who are in glory. These hymns include hymns to saints who had had a special place in Abelard's life, such as St. Denis and St. Gildas and also St. Benedict and St. Ayoul. Moreover, Abelard provided melodies, although only one now survives.[36]

Now, all these texts - the hymns, the Biblical problems, the Genesis commentary, the Sermons, the Rule, and the collected letters between Abelard and Heloise - prove one thing beyond any reasonable doubt. This is that Abelard made a prodigious effort to endow the convent at the time of its establishment with a carefully reasoned programme of prayer and study and also with a choral or sung office. I can think of no other monastic foundation of those times of numerous new beginnings that was accompanied by so much new writing by a single friend or patron.

However, it is far from clear what came of all of this and far from clear whether Abelard's efforts were put to use or were appreciated in the longer term. Professor Christopher Brooke, in his most perceptive commentary on these events and on the correspondence, writes that 'Heloise sets Abelard to work to give her useful advice about the example of holy women from the past, and to provide a Rule for her community; but being a strong-minded woman with a clear view of her own, she takes the precaution of telling him with some rigour what to say ... Abelard dutifully did what he was told, dug out all he could from the New Testament and the early fathers about the devout life of widows and nuns, and lots of good commendable references to holy women; then he finally provided her, at great length, with a Rule. It is fascinating to observe the way in which he picked up every hint in her letter and solemnly carried her own arguments to their logical conclusion .... Heloise was undoubtedly a very masterful woman, and she is not the only wife in history to have ruled over a man she promised to obey. Peter the Venerable likened her to the Queen of the Amazons, and to Deborah. Abelard she would obey, in her own way, to the end; but it was not in her nature to place herself at the disposal of any other man'.[37]

With all this and indeed with much else that Christopher Brooke has written on these matters I readily agree. One should not be lulled into thinking of Abelard as the sole driving force and of Heloise as a clinging violet and a helpless petitioner bringing her requests meekly to her husband without trying to shape the response.

But it does not follow that the Paraclete observed Abelard's prescriptions in every detail or even at all, and as far as can be known the situation was something like this.[38] At an early period in the history of the convent and still during the lifetime of Heloise, a document known as the Institutes was drawn up.[39] The Institutes aim to provide uniform observances that could be followed in all the five houses dependent upon the mother

---

[36] See Waddell, *Hymn Collections*, I, pp. 45-54.

[37] C.N.L. Brooke, *The Medieval Idea of Marriage.* (Oxford, 1989), pp.116-18.

[38] See on this my 'From Paris to the Paraclete', pp. 271-8.

[39] See note 20 above.

house of the Paraclete, so we are in the period following the early expansion of the Paraclete community, probably after Abelard's death but before that of Heloise. The Institutes manifestly make use of the Rule of Abelard on such matters as clothing, beds and bedding. But they do not follow Abelard in his most unconventional ideas such as his permission to the sisters to eat meat and his provision of a male superior set over the abbess. Moreover, the Institutes take in material from the statutes of the Cistercian General Chapter as these existed from about 1136. It would seem therefore that Abelard's Rule was not ignored at the Paraclete; indeed, it was one of the principal texts used for writing the Institutes. At bottom the Rule of St. Benedict was followed but it was followed in the light of a selection of detailed supplementary provisions taken partly from Abelard's guidance but mostly from the then popular Cistercian customs. Further evidence of Paraclete observances survives in the Paraclete Ordinal of the late thirteenth century, and in the Paraclete Book of Burials of the same date,[40] and in the Paraclete Breviary and Calendar which date from around the year 1500.[41] These are all later documents than the Institutes but they tell us something of how much or how little of Abelard's work remained in use in later centuries. Cistercian influences are clearly dominant as always. But we nonetheless find some of Abelard's hymns still in regular use, together with sequences, antiphons and responsories arranged by him. These are found in the offices of Holy Week and on the feast of the Transfiguration. We find also collects that were written by him. We find too that some of his Sermons are required to be read in the Refectory and that the selection of Biblical lessons to be read on feastdays was called the lectionary or *leconnier* of the master and it conforms to what Abelard outlined in his Rule. In total these are just traces and they are dwarfed by more powerful Cistercian influences. But they are there, even in the sixteenth century, the remnants after the passage of many years of a once very powerful impetus.

What Abelard made of the Cistercian influence upon the way of life at the Paraclete we can only conjecture. New as well as old religious foundations in the Middle Ages experienced many tensions and changes in policy. There is some reason to think, in view of the Cistercian influence upon the Paraclete, that the first nuns must have felt some hesitation and uncertainty in deciding between Abelard and Cîteaux, especially since Abelard's own opinion of Cîteaux was so low. In fact, there was a short quarrel between Bernard and Abelard over the Paraclete on which we are informed by means of a letter that Abelard addressed to Bernard between about 1131 and 1135.[42] The occasion was a criticism made by Bernard of the unusual wording of the Lord's Prayer in use at the Paraclete. This wording, supersubstantial bread as in the Gospel of St. Matthew instead of daily bread as in the Gospel of St. Luke, was certainly Abelard's own preference and we know too that Bernard made his criticism of this reading during or following a visit he made to the Paraclete. Abelard's response to Bernard's objection was an outpouring of wide ranging counter-criticism of the usages of the Cistercian order which were, he

---

[40] C. Waddell, *The Old French Paraclete Ordinary (Paris, Bibliothèque Nationale Ms francais 14410) and the Paraclete Breviary (Chaumont, Bibliothèque Municipale Ms 31)*, 3 vols. in parts, Cistercian Liturgy Series 3-7 (Gethsemani Abbey, Trappist, Kentucky, 1985, 1983). The Ordinal is edited in vol. 2 (1983); the Book of Burials and the Ordinal are discussed in vol. 1 (1985).

[41] The Breviary and the Calendar are edited and studied by C. Waddell in the aforementioned work, Vol. 3, in 3 parts (1983).

[42] Abelard Letter 10, ed. E.R. Smits, pp. 239-47, with commentary on pp. 120-36.

claimed, not only novel but bad; moreover, they wholly undermined Bernard's right to accuse Abelard of improper innovation or of taking liberties with the monastic office. It was a sad moment and also an early warning that if Abelard was ever to be brought into a greater difference of opinion with Bernard there would be even more animated and larger scale exchanges of criticism. Possibly Abelard reacted so sharply at this time because he already felt aggrieved that Bernard and the Cistercians were winning a battle for the hearts and minds of Heloise and her companions. Certainly Bernard had made a deep impression upon the nuns during this visit; even Abelard writes that it had provoked great rapture and had been an encouragement to the community. And later in 1150 we find Bernard writing to Pope Eugenius on behalf of Heloise.[43] History is full of unexpected twists and turns. It is ironical that in the very years when Abelard found his last consolations among the Black monks of Cluny, the Paraclete turned for help to the White monks of Cîteaux.

---

[43] Bernard, Letter 278, *S.Bernardi Opera*, vol.8, ed. J. Leclercq and H. Rochais (Rome, 1977), p. 190.

ASCETICISM IN EARLY SYRIAC CHRISTIANITY
by
Leslie W. Barnard

The origins and nature of Christianity in the Syriac area have been the object of detailed study for some decades, especially since the Qumran and Nag Hammadi discoveries revealed that Judaism, at the beginning of the Christian era, had assumed variegated forms which apparently sometimes influenced certain early Christian communities. By the Syriac area is meant Northern Mesopotamia and Adiabene, the frontier province to the East. The Syriac language is a dialect of Aramaic which was the *lingua franca* of a wide area. Syriac as such however is the dialect of the city of Edessa and its province Osrhoene and it is here that we find the cradle of Syriac Christianity.

Edessa was the capital of the small principality of Osrhoene[1] east of the Euphrates and it lay on the great trade route which passed between the Syrian desert to the South and the mountains of Armenia to the North. We possess no contemporary references to Edessa's role on the international scene during the early Seleucid period. For the later period our knowledge comes in the main from Roman historians who only incidentally refer to the city. However whenever Rome intervened in Mesopotamia she was bound to come into contact with Edessa. The first reference to the city during the Christian era is to Abgar V (4 BC - 7 AD and 13 - 50 AD), King of Edessa, who was a member of a delegation which went to Zeugma to receive Meherdates, prince of Parthia and Roman nominee for the throne of his own country. Abgar subsequently entertained Meherdates 'day after day in the town of Edessa' and finally accompanied him on his expedition to the east, although he deserted him on his defeat at the hands of the Parthians. In Roman eyes Abgar V had acted with duplicity. Similar duplicity occurred when the Emperor Trajan visited Edessa in 114 AD. The then King Abgar VII (109 - 116 AD) protested his loyalty but two years later, when Trajan was resting after his conquest of Adiabene, he joined a general insurrection in Mesopotamia. The Romans exacted swift vengeance and Edessa was laid waste by fire and sword. Even in the time of Abgar VIII (177 - 212 AD), usually called the Great, there are indications that the city was willing to play off the Parthians against the Romans. Septimius Severus however had confidence in Abgar and in 197-198 recognised him as 'King of Kings'. He invited Abgar to visit Rome and his reception there was the most lavish accorded to a foreign potentate since the reign of Nero. Edessa's independence was however drawing to its close and soon after Abgar's death in 213 - 214 the city was proclaimed a *colonia*.[2]

Edessa had a considerable Jewish population during the time of the monarchy although the most powerful of the Jewish communities lived in north - east Mesopotamia - in Adiabene the ruling family adopted Judaism in the first century AD. J. B. Segal[3] has shown that the story of Queen Helena of Adiabene and her two sons was widely current and formed the model for the biographies of Helena, mother of the Emperor Constantine

---

[1] The name Osrhoene may be derived from Orhay, the native name of Edessa.

[2] On these developments J. B. Segal, *Edessa - The Blessed City*, Oxford 1970 p. 14.

[3] J. B. Segal, *ibid* p. 41.

three centuries later. In the second century AD the Adiabene Jews were still numerous.[4] The largest Jewish community of this region was at Nisibis where the financial contributions of the Jews to the Jerusalem Temple were stored. Nisibis moreover boasted the existence of a celebrated Jewish academy whose fame spread throughout Mesopotamia and even to Palestine. Tannaite influence was strong in this city. Relations between Edessa, Nisibis and Adiabene were close not only in religious matters but also through commerce. They were linked by a 'silk' road that skirted the mountains by way of Edessa.[5] The Edessan Jews included among their number many wealthy silk merchants. Several synagogues existed, one in the centre of the city near the intersection of two principal streets.[6] Jews did not live in a ghetto but mixed easily with their neighbours even sharing with pagans the cemetery at Kirk Magara - three inscriptions in Hebrew and one in Greek have been found which commemorate Jews who had a mixture of Hebrew, Macedonian, Roman and Parthian names.[7]

The presence of a Jewish population in Edessa was of importance for the spread of Christianity as we will see later. Further evidence for the influence of the Jews there is provided by a passage in a Syriac treatise of the third century AD which states 'the people of Mesopotamia also worshipped the Hebrew Kuthbi, who saved Bakru the patrician of Edessa from his enemies.'[8] Kuthbi is probably derived from the Semitic root *ktb*, 'to write'. We also know that the Nabataens worshipped a deity Kuthbai or Kuthbar and that writing was regarded as a special Nabataen skill. It is possible that the people of Edessa knew the Jewish practice of affixing a biblical text to the doors of a city house or gates of a city (*mezuzah*)[9] and from them derived their regard for the sacred letter.

What type of paganism existed at Edessa in the first two centuries of the Christian era? We know that its inhabitants worshipped the planets like their neighbours in Palmyra, Harran and Hierapolis. Observation of the stars was indeed the link between the popular religion and the cosmological speculations of the philosophers such as Bardaisan. One of the gates of Edessa was called Beth Shemesh after the sun temple which stood there; the moon is also depicted on coins from this period. The planets also appear in personal names in Syriac texts and inscriptions. The *Doctrina Addai*,[10] an important document which records the emergence of Christianity at Edessa, describes the city at that time as abounding in paganism and the worship of astral deities. This was part of a widespread

---

[4] J. Neusner, ' The Conversion of Adiabene to Judaism', *Journal of Biblical Literature* Vol. 83, 1964, pp. 60-66.

[5] J. Neusner, *A History of the Jews in Babylonia*, Vol. I, Leiden 1965 pp.88-93; H.J.W. Drijvers, 'Jews and Christians at Edessa', *Journal of Jewish Studies* Vol. 36, 1985, p. 89.

[6] G.G. Blum, *Rabbula von Edessa*, Louvain 1969, p. 105ff.

[7] The inscriptions are of different dates between the first and fourth centuries AD and contain proper names, such as Joseph, Samuel, Seleucus and Izates, H.J.W. Drijvers *ibid.* p. 90.

[8] 'Oration to Antoninus Caesar' incorrectly ascribed to Melito of Sardis but probably composed in Osrhoene in the third century AD.

[9] The text Deut. 6, 4-9 has been found affixed to the lintels of door-posts at Palmyra; J.B. Segal, *ibid* p. 43.

[10] Ed. G. Howard (Syriac text), Chico, California 1981. The suggestion of H.J.W. Drijvers that Addai is a borrowing from Manichaeism where a missionary named Adda was one of Mani's inner circle seems improbable; *East of Antioch*, London 1984, ch. VI pp. 159-165.

syncretism which incorporated many beliefs of neighbouring cult centres, such as Hierapolis. Yet during the early Christian period over a large area of Syria and Northern Mesopotamia the concept of a single godhead, a 'chief of the gods', who had delegated to the planets the administration of the universe, was much favoured. In considering the emergence of Christianity in this area, and its specific character, we should not neglect this predisposition towards monotheism. It may be that this had already gained the Jews a ready hearing. Both Judaism at Edessa and this trend towards monotheism were powerful influences which paved the way for the triumph of Christianity. However, as in the Roman Empire, pagan beliefs and practices survived long into the Christian era.

We now turn to the question when Christianity was first planted in Edessa and further east of the Euphrates. The Church Historian Eusebius in his *Ecclesiastical History* I, 13 records the story of Thaddaeus or Addai, one of the seventy two disciples of Jesus, who came to Edessa from Palestine in response to a letter from King Abgar to Jesus:

> 'So it came about that when King Abgar, a most illustrious potentate of the nations beyond the Euphrates, being wasted by a terrible bodily disorder, incurable as far as human power goes, heard of the fame of Jesus' name and the unanimous testimony paid by all to his mighty works, he sent him a message of intreaty by a despatch bearer, asking that he might be delivered from his disease. But Jesus did not at that time hearken to his request; howbeit he deemed him worthy of a personal letter, promising to send one of his disciples to heal his disease and, at the same time, bring salvation to him and all who belonged to him. And not long afterwards, it would seem, he fulfilled that which he had promised. At all events, after his resurrection from the dead and his ascent into the heavens, Thomas, one of the twelve apostles, was moved by a divine impulse to send forth Thaddaeus - he too had been reckoned among the seventy disciples of Christ - to Edessa as a herald and evangelist of the teaching concerning Christ. And through him all that our Saviour had promised received its fulfilment. You have the proof of these facts also in writing, taken from the record office at Edessa, then a city and led by Kings. Thus, in the public documents there, which contain ancient matters and those connected with Abgar, these things have been found preserved from that day until now. But there is nothing like hearing the letters themselves, taken by us from the archives and literally translated from the Syriac, as follows.'

Eusebius then quotes at length the letters written by Abgar to Jesus, Jesus' reply and an account, again translated from the Syriac, of Addai's coming to Edessa and the first evangelisation of the city. In a letter Jesus promises that Edessa would be blessed 'and no enemy shall rule over it forever' (Syriac version). This significant detail suggests at least a basis in early tradition as Edessa was incorporated into the Empire in AD 216 and there would have been no point in adding this detail in Eusebius' day or later. However the main bulk of the correspondence is clearly legendary for, if authentic, it is difficult to explain why early Christian writers knew nothing of it. J.B.Segal calls it 'one of the most successful pious frauds of antiquity.'[11] The legend is repeated with additions in a Syriac document, already referred to, known as 'the Doctrine of Addai' which, in its present

---

[11] J.B. Segal *ibid* p.64; also his 'When did Christianity come to Edessa', *Middle East Studies and Libraries*, London 1980, pp.179-191. The correspondence is also referred to in *Peregrinatio Aetheriae* 17, 1; it was known to be a forgery as early as *Decretum Gelasianum* 5, 8.

form, dates from c.400 AD.[12] The Doctrine states that part of the merchant community of Jews in the city was converted at the same public meeting at which King Abgar became a Christian. Indeed, according to the Doctrine, it was a Jew Tobias, the son of a Palestinian Jew, who introduced Addai to the King. In contrast to the Jews of Palestine, who are represented in an unfavourable light as the crucifiers of Jesus, and also to the Adiabene Jews, the Jews of Edessa are represented in the Doctrine as being friendly to Christianity.[13] This may represent a genuine historical reminiscence as later Edessan Christianity was strongly Jewish - Christian in outlook. In support of the belief that early traditions are incorporated into the Christ - Abgar legends is the fact that Eusebius knew that at that time Edessa was outside the Roman frontier.

The early history of the Church in Edessa is by no means clear. In the Doctrine Addai is said to have died in peace; he was succeeded by Aggai who was martyred, and who was himself succeeded by Palut. Palut was not ordained and had to travel to Antioch for ordination by its bishop Serapion (AD 190 -212).At this point the Doctrine contains contradictory traditions, one referring to the first century, another to the late - second or early - third centuries suggesting a subordination to Greek - speaking Antioch. We know from the 'Edessene Chronicle' that a Church building existed in Edessa in 201 when it was damaged by a great flood.

Early Syriac Christianity came to reflect a particular facet of Judaism, viz. the asceticism of Jewish sectarianism. I illustrate this from the writings of Aphrahat (early fourth century), the first Syriac authority of any considerable weight who was uninfluenced by Greek thought. Aphrahat's view of the Church is very different from that prevailing in Greek-speaking Christendom. For him baptism is not the means of Christian initiation for every Christian, but a privilege reserved for celibates, ie the spiritual aristocracy. In the early baptismal liturgy known as the 'Discourse on Penitents' Aphrahat states that marriage should be entered into before thinking of baptism, as baptism is only for virgins and celibates and is incompatible with the married state:

> Anyone who has set his heart to the state of marriage let him marry before baptism, lest he will fall in the struggle and will be killed. And anyone who fears this part of the contest, let him retreat, lest he will break the heart of his brethren like his own heart. Anyone who loves possessions, let him retreat from the army, lest when the battle becomes hard for him, he will remember his possessions and retreat. And anyone who retreats from the struggle shame belongs to him. Everyone who has not chosen himself and has not yet put on armour, if he retreats he is not blamed. But everyone who chooses himself and puts on the armour, if he retreats from the struggle he will be laughed at. To him who empties himself the contest is suitable, because he does not remember something which is behind him and does not retreat to it.'[14]

---

[12] H.J.W. Drijvers denies that the Doctrina contains any early historical material; *ibid* n. 10.

[13] Is it significant that Jews are described as sorrowing at Addai's death? I am unable to agree with Drijvers that the Tobias story is wholly legendary and part of a propaganda drive to convert Jews to Christianity, *ibid*. n. 5 pp. 92-93. Addai is likely to be a historical figure as had the Church c. 400 been looking for a historical founder Judas Thomas, whose tomb was claimed for Edessa in the mid-third century, would have been the most probable candidate. F.C. Burkitt, 'Tatian's Diatessaron and the Dutch Harmonies', *Journal of Theological Studies* Vol. 25, 1924 p. 130 equated Tatian with Addai on the grounds that the Doctrina states that Addai brought the Diatessaron to Edessa. This conjecture is unlikely on philological grounds.

[14] Syriac text ed. W. Wright p. 345; J. Parisot, *Patrologia Syriaca* Vol. I, Paris 1894 (Syriac with Latin translation)

The Church, for Aphrahat, consists of baptized celibates who are the real spiritual athletes, with a larger body of adherents who only remain on the fringes of the Christian communities, much as the non - circumcised godfearers only remained on the fringes of the Jewish synagogues. The view that celibacy was the essential condition for baptism was the normal practice in the Syrian Churches well into the third century AD although it did not survive as late as the fourth century as F.C.Burkitt claimed.[15] Early Syriac Christianity is permeated with asceticism and there is no recognition, in early sources, of the validity of ordinary married life as a viable Christian way of life.

We now turn to the terms *bar Q'yama* and bath *Q'yama* which are frequently found in Syriac literature not usually in the sense 'monk' or 'nun', but referring to the baptized laity of the Church. The translation of these designations presents difficulties and has been widely disputed. A Vööbus held that the term was the equivalent of the Hebrew *berith,* ie 'covenant' or 'pact',[16] and this has been widely followed; it is certainly preferable to the view of P. Nagel that *Q'yama* refers to the resurrection, ie the *b'nai Q'yama* are those who anticipate the resurrection in this life (cf. Luke 20, 30).[17] If we adopt the meaning 'covenant' then the *b'nai Q'yama* are ascetics who have taken an oath or vow to be faithful to the covenant with God and have accordingly renounced the world. These ascetics often lived at home or in small groups, though there were some anchorites.[18] Subsequent to the time of Aphrahat the *b'nai Q'yama* became a kind of monastic community within the Church but this was not the earliest view. It is also significant that Aphrahat, in his address to 'those who have taken up the yoke of the saints' (Discourse VI) states:
'All the children of light are without fear of him, because the darkness flees from before the light. The children of the Good fear not the Evil one, for he has given him to be trampled by their feet. When he makes himself like darkness unto them they become light, and when he creeps upon them like a serpent, they become salt, whereof he cannot eat ... ' The children of light are the baptized ascetics who are constantly fighting a spiritual warfare against the prince of darkness, the devil. The terms uniformly used in early Syriac literature for this conflict are 'struggle', 'fight', 'battle' and 'war'. The Martyrdom of Shamona and Guria which dates from c.297 repeatedly refers to the daughters of the Covenant *(b'nath Q'yama)* as ascetics and applies to Guria the term *M'qadd'sha,* hallowed or holy. The reason why Guria is holy is that she is celibate while Shamona, who has a daughter, is not.[19]

An affinity, although not necessarily a direct link with the Jewish sectarianism of Qumran, as revealed in the Dead Sea Scrolls, is noticeable in the picture of the Syrian

---

[15] See further R. Murray, 'The Characteristics of the Earliest Syriac Christianity', *East of Byzantium*, Washington 1980, pp. 3-16.

[16] A Vööbus, *A History of Asceticism in the Syrian Orient*, Vol. I 1968 pp. 97ff. S.P. Brock, Early Syrian Asceticism', *Syriac Perspectives on Late Antiquity*, ch. I, London 1984, p.7.

[17] P. Nagel, *Die Motivierung der Askese in der alten Kirche und der Ursprung des Monchtums*. Vol. 95, *Texte und Untersuchungen*, Berlin, 1966 p. 41ff; I owe this reference to S.P. Brock *ibid* p.8.

[18] R. Murray, *ibid.* n. 15 p. 8.

[19] F.C. Burkitt, *ibid* pp. 113 - 130.

Church provided by Aphrahat and other early Syriac documents. The Qumran community believed themselves to be the 'sons of the Covenant' and had separated from ordinary Jewish life in order to seek a special holiness. It is interesting that the Qumran 'Manual of Discipline' refers several times to God's Covenant which men enter through embracing an ascetic form of life. So neophytes entering the community 'pass over into the Covenant of the presence of God'. This Covenant was at Qumran also associated with a vow, requiring total commitment, which had to be renewed each year. The community's deepest purpose was 'to establish the Covenant according to the eternal ordinances.'[20] The members were known as the elect, the chosen of God, the Saints who had adopted the name 'children of Light'.[21] They had renounced marriage and social duties and had come apart to seek total purity of life.[22] They believed themselves to be engaged in a great spiritual warfare against the forces of darkness, a struggle which had cosmic repercussions.

It seems reasonable to suggest that Christianity at Edessa had its origin within a Jewish milieu which had close associations with Palestinian sectarianism, and that the earliest converts were, in the main, Jews. These early Jewish Christians stamped the Edessan Christian community with their own brand of asceticism although, as Dr. Robert Murray has reminded us, other influences also contributed to the ethos of that Church.[23] A. Vööbus suggested that an Aramaic - Christian movement, coming from Palestine, mediated this Jewish asceticism to the Syrian Church.[24] Be that as it may it is certain that this primitive form of asceticism continued to be a feature of Syriac Christianity down to the time of Aphrahat and even later. So the *Doctrine of Addai* states that 'all the society of men and women were modest and decorous, and they were holy and pure, and singly and modestly they were dwelling without spot, in the watchfulness of the ministry decorously, in their care for the poor, in their visitations of the sick.[25]

If then we place the origins of Christianity at Edessa within a Jewish - Christian milieu we can explain certain features in the Gospel of Thomas which was discovered at Nag Hammadi shortly after the second world war. This Gospel is to be dated c. 140 and probably emanated from Edessa. Professor Frend has shown the Jewish - Christian character of many of the logia in Thomas.[26] So the virtues stressed in that Gospel are childlikeness, singleness and simplicity, abstinence and world -

---

[20] I Qs 1, 8, 16; 2, 13; 5, 10, 20-22.

[21] I Qs 8,6; I Qh 2, 13.

[22] M. Black, *The Scrolls and Christian Origins*, London 1961 pp. 27-31; A. Guillaumont, 'A propos de célibat des Esséniens', *Hommages à André Dupont-Sommer*, Paris 1971, pp. 395 - 404.

[23] R. Murray, *ibid* pp. 8 - 9.

[24] n. 16 pp. 1-10, 102.

[25] *Doctrina* 47 - 48.

[26] W.H.C. Frend, 'The Gospel of Thomas: Is Rehabilitation possible?', *Journal of Theological Studies* Vol. 18, 1967 pp. 13 - 26.

renunciation.[27] Advance towards spiritual perfection is through the practice of ascetic virtues and repentance: 'Blessed are the single and the elect, for you will find the Kingdom' This Gospel, in common with other Jewish - Christian documents, exalts the position of James the Just. It stresses the attainment of perfection through complete sexual abnegation. Thus in Saying No. 75, which appears to be related to the Parable of the Virgins in Matt. 25, I - 13, the 'many' who are left standing at the bridegroom's door are not reproached for inattention to their duties but merely because they were not single. Only the celibates enter the bridal chamber. The 'elect' alone are complete beings and among them sexual differences have been transcended.[28] It will be noted how closely these sentiments in the Gospel of Thomas fit into the picture of Syrian Christianity drawn by Aphrahat early in the fourth century. It is likely that from the outset the Church in Edessa was permeated by asceticism of a Jewish-Christian type and that this found expression, as early as c.140, in a slightly Gnosticized or dualistic form in the Gospel of Thomas. An ascetic emphasis is also found in the Acts of Thomas, which contains third and second century traditions. This work was popular among the Marcionites and Manichees which, as S. P. Brock points out,[29] guarantees its ascetic character. The Acts takes a very strict view of marriage and prohibits baptized converts from marrying or living as man and wife. The body is corruptible and hinders the soul from attaining incorruptibility. The Christian ascetic is in this world a 'stranger' and 'foreigner', terms frequently found in Syriac Christianity.

How far are we justified in regarding asceticism as the only facet of the Church in the early period? G. Quispel[30] holds that there were no Gnostics in Edessa in the second century. If we are reserving the term 'Gnostic' for a developed Gnostic system then this may be correct. However Gnostic tendencies became allied to Judaism at an early date as the Nag Hammadi documents reveal. A study of the works of Tatian and Bardaisan would appear to confirm that Gnostic or dualistic tendencies were also present in early Syriac Christianity.

Tatian, the brilliant Assyrian, provides our next point of reference. His parents were Syriac speaking[31] and after leaving his Mesopotamian homeland Tatian visited many lands where he was initiated into various Mysteries before becoming converted to Christianity and settling in Rome. He was a somewhat eclectic thinker from the first who was attracted by an ascetic explanation of life. He was not however adverse from adopting a few semi-Gnostic ideas from Valentinus, ideas from the popular philosophy of the day, as well as drawing on earlier Jewish-Christian traditions. After leaving Rome Tatian appears to have settled in Edessa c. 172-173[32] and it was here that he carried his

---

[27] *Sayings 4, 6, 15, 23, 27 inter alia.*

[28] *Saying 22.*

[29] *Ibid* p.8.

[30] In a paper delivered to the *International Conference on Patristic Studies*, Oxford 1967 (unpublished).

[31] Clem. Alex. *Strom.* 3, 12, 81; Epiph. *Pan.* 46, I, II.

[32] L.W. Barnard, 'The Heresy of Tatian Once Again', *Journal of Ecclesiastical History* Vol.19, 1968, pp. 1 -10.

views to extreme lengths. According to Jerome[33] he maintained that the flesh of Christ was imaginary, a view at variance with his earlier view. He rejected marriage and meats and, like Mercion, rejected some of St. Paul's Epistles. And, according to Irenaeus, he seceded from the Church, adopted certain invisible aeons, similar to those found in Valentinus' works, and denounced marriage as defilement and the equivalent of fornication.[34] Such views would have caused raised eyebrows in Rome but not in Edessa, as we have seen. Tatian's composition of the Syriac Diatessaron, or Harmony of the Gospels, which he carried out soon after his return to Edessa, shows how his thought developed. He used not only the four Canonical Gospels, which he had known in Greek in Rome, but also a tradition which had already found literary expression in Edessa about thirty years before in the Gospel of Thomas. Many scholars hold that this was Tatian's fifth source which he drew on when compiling his Harmony.[35]

There is strong evidence that Tatian modified the tradition in the Canonical Gospels in an ascetic and encratite direction. Thus in Luke 2, 36 the ordinary text speaks of the married life which Anna the prophetess lived for seven years with her husband from her virginity. Tatian however corrected the text so that it stated that Anna remained a virgin in her marriage. There are also other changes, some very subtle, which have the effect of degrading the value of the married state - eg Matt. 19, 4 - 9 in the Dutch Diatessaron. Several corrections illustrate Tatian's strict condemnatory attitude towards the use of wine. The word 'vine' in John 15, 1 ('I am the true vine') was changed to ' I am the tree of the fruit of the truth'.[36] This same ascetic strain appears in his handling of the narrative of the Last Supper in Mark 14, 25 and Matt. 26, 29. Tatian also gave a radical, ascetic turn to the Gospel teaching about possessions, family life, and marriage. He also enhanced Jesus' teaching concerning carrying one's cross in Mark 8, 34, Matt. 10, 38 by adding 'on his shoulder'. [37]

The Diatessaron became the Gospel par excellence of Syriac - speaking Christianity and so it remained until early in the fifth century when Rabbula (bishop of Edessa 411-435) suppressed it and substituted a revision of the Old Syriac Canonical Gospels. Theodoret, the partisan of Nestorius, tells how he withdrew over two hundred copies of the Diatessaron from circulation in his diocese and replaced them with the Gospels of the four evangelists. Tatian's Diatessaron was therefore the only version of the Gospels which was used in Syriac - speaking Christianity for nearly two and a half centuries.[38] The reason for this is not far to seek. It appealed to the Edessan Church because its outlook

---

[33] *Comm. in Ep. ad Gal. 6.*

[34] *Adv. Haer.* I, 26.

[35] G. Quispel, 'L' Évangile selon Thomas et le Diatessaron', *Vigiliae Christianae* Vol. 13, 1959 pp. 87 - 117.

[36] *Diatess. persiano* p. 322.

[37] *Liège Diatess.* p. 97; *persiano* p. 134.

[38] The problem of the original language of the Diatessaron has not been solved by the discovery of a Greek fragment at Dura Europos. I incline to favour a Syriac original composed by Tatian soon after leaving Rome, although an original dual edition in Syriac and Greek is not impossible.

was congruous with an ascetic-encratite tradition which was strong in that Church from its foundation.

Our final point of reference in this paper is the remarkable figure of Bardaisan[39] who was born in Edessa c 155 of rich parents; his name 'son of Daisan' came from the fact that his mother had given birth on the bank of the river Daisan which flows near the capital. It was during the last quarter of the second century that he became a Christian and he was active as a savant until his death in 223 by which time he had separated himself from the Edessan Church. Later ages regarded him as a heretic and his writings were not preserved. His original teaching has therefore to be reconstructed from scattered notices and partisan accounts of later chroniclers. According to Eusebius he fought against the Valentinian heresy even after his conversion to Christianity although other writers, such as Hippolytus, regard him as the leader of Oriental Valentinianism. The fragments of his works which have survived, and the 'Book of the Laws of the Land' in Syriac, do not support the view that he was a Valentinian Gnostic. He is, I think, best interpreted as an eclectic thinker who was interested in astrology and cosmogony. His roots were in the native Syrian tradition of Edessa with its ascetic emphasis, although his vision took him beyond this into more speculative areas.

We should be unwise to exaggerate the importance of early Syriac Christianity. The fact that we can now push back the history of the Church in Edessa into the first century does not revolutionize the history of the early Church. But it does show that an early Christian tradition existed in Edessa, having its roots in Palestinian sectarianism, which was non - Greek in outlook and which was permeated at its core by an ascetic outlook independent of, and prior to, the Christian monasticism which arose in Egypt in the third and fourth centuries.[40] However this original branch of Christendom did not succeed in retaining its independence. Rabbula, bishop of Edessa in the early fifth century, chose the anti-Nestorian side in the great controversy then raging. The result was that the Church in Edessa was largely assimilated on the practical level to Antioch and the other major centres of Greek - speaking Christianity. From now on Edessa, and the rest of Syrian Christianity, was no longer cut off from other Churches by its indigenous Syriac Bible, liturgy and doctrine. However Greek theology did not easily fit into the exuberant non - dogmatic Syriac outlook and the Syrian Church, being without first rate intellects, was the loser. From the fifth century it became secondary to Greek Christianity. But that it had an original independent existence with an ascetic tradition of its own should not be forgotten in the study of the origins of the Church and of Christian monasticism.

---

[39] H.J.W. Drijvers, *Bardaisan of Edessa*, Assen 1962 and his 'Bardaisan von Edessa als Repräsentant des syrischen Synkretismus', East of Antioch ibid. ch. XII, pp. 109 - 122.

[40] See further the introduction to R.M. Price, *A History of the Monks of Syria by Theodoret of Cyrrhus*, Kalamazoo 1985.

THE ROLE OF THE SPIRITUAL FATHER IN ORTHODOX MONASTICISM

by
Muriel Heppell

In both east and west, Christian monasticism had its roots in the teaching and practice of the Desert Fathers; and it is this common origin that is responsible for the close affinities between Orthodox and Catholic monasticism. Nevertheless there were (and are) differences. For example, although the cenobitic form of monastic life became the norm in the east as it did in the west, the east had nothing corresponding to the Benedictine Rule. In the east, each monastery had its own foundation charter or *typikon*, which regulated its pattern of worship as well as the daily activities of the monks and the administration of the monastery. In the case of proprietary monasteries (which most of them were), the *typikon* would also itemise the endowments. It is true that most of these *typika* were very similar to each other, and established a way of life very close to that prescribed by the Benedictine Rule. Moreover it was not unusual for several monasteries to use the same *typikon*; for example, the so-called Studite *typikon*, drawn up by Patriarch Alexios the Studite for a monastery he founded c. 1034[1] was adopted by several Russian monasteries. However the absence of a widely applicable rule did introduce an element of greater flexibility into Orthodox monasticism, which had both positive and negative consequences. One result was that, although Orthodox monasticism produced some famous abbots, the authority exercized by the abbot in virtue of his office was never as strong as in the west. Another difference was the importance attached to the individual training of each monk by another monk, older and more advanced in the spiritual life, who was known as his "spiritual father." This might sometimes be the abbot, but did not have to be.

It is difficult to pinpoint a time when the preponderant role of the spiritual father in Orthodox monastic training first becomes apparent, especially as it is discernible from the earliest times, in the lives of the Desert Fathers. But it was certainly flourishing in the monasteries of Palestine from the early sixth century onwards; by that time Palestine had replaced Egypt as the main centre of Christian monasticism.[2] Palestinian monasteries were complex institutions: a typical establishment would consist of a *cenobium* (following a common life rule), together with a group of anchorites loosely attached to it, who attended the Liturgy on Saturdays and Sundays and collected their weekly supply of food and palm leaves (for making baskets); and also a smaller number of hermits living in complete seclusion. The most interesting of these monasteries, from the point of view of the role of the spiritual father, was a community at Thavata, near Gaza, which had two

---

[1] See V. Grumel, *Les regestes des actes du Patriarcat de Constantinople*, i. fasc. 2 (Paris, 1936), No. 841, 255-56. The Greek original of this *typikon* has been lost, and the Old Church Slavonic translation (see A.Gorskii and K. I. Nevostruev, *Opisanie slavyanskikh rukopisei Moskovskoi sinodal 'noi biblioteki* / Description of the Slavonic Manuscripts in the M o s c o w Synodal Library /, Parts 1 and 2, Moscow, 1855, 1857, No. 330) is still unpublished Copious extracts from the text are available in E.E. Golubinskii, *Istoriya russkoi tserkvi* (History of the Russian Church), i , 1, (Moscow, 1901), 611-24.

[2] See Derwas Chitty, *The Desert a City*, (Oxford, 1966), Chapters V, VI, and VII.

famous spiritual directors, the "'Great Old Men" Barsanuphius and John.[3] They gave advice to hundreds of people, laymen as well as monks, on all sorts of subjects, not just the spiritual life. But it was all done by correspondence, and they each employed a secretary; they never saw or spoke to their spiritual children, or to each other.

A comprehensive survey of the role of the spiritual father in Orthodox monasticism lies outside the scope of this short paper.[4] In fact I will concentrate on the evidence of only two relevant sources: *The Ladder of Divine Ascent,*[5] written early in the seventh century by St. John Climacus, who was for some years abbot of St. Katharine's Monastery on Mount Sinai; and a much later work, the *Paterik* of the Monastery of Caves in Kiev,[6] which gives a detailed picture of the most important monastery in Rus' (Russia) during the earliest period of its history before the Mongol invasions.

The title of *The Ladder of Divine Ascent* is derived from the way in which its material is presented. It is divided into thirty sections, or "steps", representing the thirty unknown years in the life of Christ. In fact the arrangement of the material is not strictly progressive, although the theme of ascent, symbolising spiritual progress, does permeate the whole work. The *Ladder* incorporates much of the teaching of earlier monastic literature, especially that relating to the Desert Fathers. The author not only deals with the same topics, such as the vices to be avoided and the virtues to be cultivated by those seeking spiritual "perfection"; he also uses the same literary devices, such as illustrative anecdotes, elaborate metaphors, and more generalised sayings, or apophthegms. However his treatment of his material is different from that of earlier writers; it is much more analytical and at times he shows quite profound psychological insight. Perhaps this explains the widespread and lasting popularity of the *Ladder*. It has a copious and diversified manuscript tradition, in which Greek and Old Church Slavonic manuscripts predominate;[7] it has also been translated into several modern languages, including English,[8]

---

[3] Chitty, *The Desert a City,* 132-40; Eric P, Wheeler, *Dorotheos of Gaza: Discourses and Sayings* (English translation of the Greek text in PG, lxxxviii), Cistercian Studies Series, 33, (Kalamazoo, 1977), 29-34; Simon Tugwell, *Ways of Imperfection,* (London, 1984) Chapter 8; L. Regnault, P. Lemaire and B. Outtier, *Barsanuphe et Jean de Gaza" Correspondence,* (Solesmes, 1972).

[4] For a detailed and analytical treatment of this subject, see 1. Hausherr, *Direction spirituelle en orient autrefois, Orientalia Christiana Analecta,* 144. (Rome, 1955).

[5] For the Greek text, see PG, lxxxviii, cols. 632-1208; P. Trevisan, *Corona Patrum Salesiana,* series graeca, 8-9, (2 vols., Turin, 1941); and the edition of the monk Sophronios of the Holy Mountain, *Ioannis Climaci ... Scala Paradisi ...* (Constantinople, 1883).

[6] See *Kievo-Pecherskii Paterik,* ed. D.I. Abramovich, (Kiev, 1930), reprinted in *Slavische Propyläen,* 2, ed. D. Chyzhevsky, (Munich, 1964); English translation: M. Heppell, *The Paterik of the Kievan Caves Monastery,* Harvard Library of Early Ukrainian Literature, Vol. 1, (Harvard University Press, 1989).

[7] See D. Bogdanovic, *Jovan Léstvichnik u vizantiiskoi i staroi srpskoi knizhevnosti,* (St John Climacus in Byzantine and Old Serbian Literature, Belgrade, 1968), 203-8, where the author lists 78 Greek and 108 Cyrillic (Old Church Slavonic) manuscripts, Other Cyrillic manuscripts have come to light since this work was published.

[8] There are three English translations: (i) *The Holy Ladder of Perfection by which we may ascend to Heaven,* by Father Robert of Mount St. Bernard's Abbey, (London, 1858), which is in places more of a paraphrase than a translation; (ii) Archimandrite Lazarus Moore, *The Ladder of Divine Ascent,* with an introduction by M. Heppell, (London, 1959), reissued, with some revisions, in 1978 by the Holy Transfiguration Monastery, Boston, Massachusetts; (iii) Colm Luibheid and Norman Russell, *John Climacus: The Ladder of Divine Ascent,* with an introduction by Kallistos Ware, (Paulist Press and SPCK, London, 1982). Quotations are from this edition.

French,[9] Spanish,[10] Italian,[11] Russian,[12] and Serbo-Croatian.[13] One of the curious features of the textual history of this influential work is the lateness of a Latin translation, which did not appear until the early fourteenth century.[14] This was the work of a dedicated Spiritual Franciscan named Fra Angelo Clareno da Cingoli, who learnt Greek and translated the *Ladder* into Latin while he was living in a Byzantine monastery in Thessaly, enjoying a brief respite from harassment by the ecclesiastical authorities. This Latin translation is, so far as I know, still unpublished.

It is very clear from the *Ladder* that St. John Climacus attached great importance to the role of the spiritual father in monastic training, and he stresses that no one should embark on his spiritual journey without a guide: 'A man, however prudent,' he writes, 'may easily go astray if he has no guide. The man who takes the road of monastic life under his own direction may easily be lost, even if he has all the wisdom of the world.'[15] Throughout his work there are numerous references to the relationship between a young monk and his spiritual father, and St. John is very emphatic that one of the most important aspects of this relationship, perhaps the most important of all, is that the disciple must obey his spiritual father absolutely, in order to root out his own self-will, thought to be the greatest enemy of spiritual progress. But this was not to be a blind and formal obedience; it was very important for a monk to have the right kind of spiritual father, that is, one who could best help him on his own journey:

> 'We should analyse the nature of our passions and our obedience', he says, 'so as to choose our director accordingly. If lust is your problem, do not pick for your trainer a worker of miracles, who has a welcome and a meal for everyone. Choose instead an ascetic who will reject any consolation of food. If you are arrogant, let him be tough and unyielding, not gentle and accommodating. We should not be on the look-out for those gifted with foreknowledge and foresight, but rather those who are truly humble, and whose character and dwelling-place match our weakness.'[16]

However, once a monk has chosen his spiritual father, he must submit to him completely, as though to Christ Himself:

---

[9] Placide Deseille, *St Jean Climaque: L'Échelle Sainte*, (Abbaye de Béllefontaine, Begrolles-en-Mauges, 1987). There was an earlier French translation in 1675; see R. Arnauld d'Andilly, *Oevres diverses*, I, (1675).

[10] The *Ladder* was evidently a popular work in sixteenth-century Spain, since the British Library catalogue lists eight early printed editions in different Spanish cities between 1504 and 1576. I do not know of any more recent Spanish translation.

[11] The edition of the Greek text by P. Trevisan (see note 5) is accompanied by an Italian translation.

[12] *Lestvitsa … pyatoe izdanie Kozel 'skoi Vvedenskoi Optinoi Pustynii*, Sergiev Posad, 1898.

[13] Dimitrije Bogdanović, *Sveti Jovan Lestvichnik: Lestvitsa* (The Ladder of St. John Climacus, Belgrade, 1963).

[14] See M. Heppell, 'The Latin Translation of the *Ladder of Divine Ascent* of St. John Climacus, '*Mediterranean Historical Review*, iv, 2, (1989), 340-44; J. Gribomont, 'La Scala Paradisi, Jean de Raithou et Ange Clareno, '*Studia Monastica*, ii, (1960), 345-58.

[15] *The Ladder of Divine Ascent*, trans. Luibheid and Russell (here-after cited as *Ladder*), Step 26, 259.

[16] *Ladder*, Step 4, 119.

'Having once entered the stadium of holy living and obedience, we can no longer start criticizing the umpire, even if we should notice some faults in him. After all, he is human, and if we start making judgments, then our submissiveness earns no profit.'[17]

John's conception of the role of the spiritual father is not limited to training in obedience. He is very fond of medical similes and metaphors, and often refers to the relationship between the spiritual father and his disciple as one between a doctor and his patient.[18] The spiritual father must also be a teacher and a guide;[19] and above all, an example, for the disciple will best be able to advance on his spiritual journey by daily seeing what sort of a person his spiritual father is. John also describes an aspect of the relationship for which he uses the term *anadochos*,[20] the word used to signify the sponsor or god-parent in baptism. Here the emphasis is not on guidance or discipline, but on the way in which a more experienced monk can take upon himself the burden of his disciple's sin if it seems to him right to do so. This is illustrated in the following anecdote:

'There was once a zealous monk who was badly troubled by this demon /i.e. pride /. For twenty years he wore himself out with fasting and vigils, but to no avail, as he realised. So he wrote the temptation on a piece of paper, went to a certain holy man, handed him the paper, bowed his face to the ground, and dared not look up. The old man read it, smiled, lifted the brother up and said to him: "My son, put your hand on my neck." The brother did so. Then the great man said: "Very well, brother. Now let this sin be on my neck for as many years as it has been or will be active within you. But from now on, ignore it." And the monk who had been tempted in this fashion assured me that even before he left the cell of this old man, his infirmity was gone.'[21]

It is clear from the first of these quotations from the *Ladder* that a monk could choose his own spiritual father,[22] though probably he would have some guidance from his abbot; in some cases the abbot himself would be the spiritual father.[23] Certainly this freedom of choice seems to have become a well-established practice in Orthodox monasticism, and there are examples of monks making long journeys in order to find the right spiritual father. The Bulgarian monk known as St. Teodosi of Trnovo, who lived in the first half of the fourteenth century, traversed the whole of Bulgaria, from a monastery in Vidin in the north-west of the country (where he was tonsured) to a remote place near the south-

[17] *Ladder*, Step 4, 92.

[18] See, for example, *Ladder*, Step 1, 75: 'We must have someone very skilled, a doctor, for our septic wounds'; Step 4, 93, 112; Step 8, 150; Step 10, 156; Step 26, 236.

[19] See *Ladder*, Step 1, 75, where the spiritual father is compared to Moses leading the children of Israel out of Egypt.

[20] See *Ladder*, Introduction, 41.

[21] *Ladder*, Step 23, 213.

[22] This was the view of St. Basil (see Hausherr, *Direction spirituelle*, 115), though the spiritual father had to be approved by the abbot.

[23] Some *typika* laid down that the abbot had to be the spiritual father (See Hausherr, *Direction spirituelle*, 114 ff.). Theodore the Studite, abbot of the famous monastery of Stoudios in Constantinople in the ninth century, is a good example of an abbot who combined both functions successfully.

eastern frontier, in search of the right spiritual father; his search ended when he found the Byzantine monk Gregory of Sinai, the founder of the fourteenth-century Hesychasts, who was then living in a small community in the Byzantine-Bulgarian borderlands, where he had fled to escape from Turkish raids on Mount Athos.[24] However it is much less clear how the spiritual fathers were chosen. It would seem that there was no formal election or appointment to this ministry; they "emerge" in the pages of the sources with few clues as to how they were selected. The word used to describe a spiritual father is in Greek *geron* literally an "old man", sometimes translated as "elder", because although the spiritual father had to be mature and experienced, he was not necessarily old in years. The corresponding Russian word is *starets*. Obviously they had to be stable, integrated personalities, who had themselves passed through a rigorous training in the spiritual life;[25] otherwise they would be (to quote St. Basil) "blind guides."[26] Above all they had to possess the gift of discernment *(diakrisis)*, to which St. John Climacus devotes one of his longest sections. Many of them seem to have spent some time living as recluses. I think it is quite probable that experienced spiritual fathers encouraged those of their disciples whom they thought suitable to exercise this ministry themselves. There is an example of this in the life of the Palestinian monk Dorotheos of Gaza who lived in the first half of the sixth century.[27] He was for many years the disciple of the "Great Old Man" John, and for some time acted as his secretary. He also acted as spiritual father to at least one novice in the community named Dositheus, a former military page, while at the same time being in charge of the infirmary.[28]

It must be emphasised that the ministry of the spiritual father was not a sacramental one, and he did not have to be a priest.[29] One modern Orthodox writer has described the role of the spiritual father as in essence charismatic: 'The figure of the spiritual father illustrates the two levels on which the Church exists and functions: the hierarchical and the spiritual, the outward and the inner, the institutional and the charismatic. In this sense the "geron" ... exists alongside the apostles. Although not ordained through the episcopal laying on of hands, the spiritual father is essentially a prophetic person who has received his charisma directly from the Spirit of God.'[30]

The other work from which I wish to illustrate, the *Paterik* of the Kievan Monastery

---

[24] See *Zhitie i zhizn' prepodobnago otsa nashego Teodosiya* (The Life of our venerable father Teodosi), ed. V.I. Zlatarski, *Sbornik za narodni umotvoreniya, nauka i knizhina* (Collected studies in folklore, science and literature), Sofia, 1904), 12-13. It is interesting to note that Teodosi's biographer, Patriarch Kallistos of Constantinople, does not criticize him for making this long search, but compares him to an industrious bee, going round different kinds of flowers and collecting their honey.

[25] See Hausherr, *Direction spirituelle*, 56-123 for a detailed description of the qualities required in a spiritual father.

[26] St. Basil of Caesarea, *Regulae Fusius Tractatae*, 25, 2, PG xxxi, col. 985B.

[27] See Wheeler, *Dorotheos of Gaza*, 23-70; *Dorothée de Gaza. Oevres Spirituelles*, edd. L. Regnault, and J. de Préville, *Sources chrétiennes*, 92, (Paris, 1963), 128-145.

[28] Wheeler, 37-44; *Dorothée de Gaza*, 122-43.

[29] Hausherr, *Direction spirituelle*, 105-8.

[30] J. Chryssavgis, 'The Spiritual Father as Embodiment of Tradition' *Phronema* (Annual Review of St. Andrew's Greek Orthodox Theological College, New South Wales, Australia), i, (1986), 20),

of Caves, is much later than the *Ladder*. Most of it was written early in the thirteenth century, though based on earlier source material.[31] Apart from one full-length *vita* (the Life of Feodosi, one of the earliest abbots of the monastery), it consists mainly of short biographical narratives; but there is one item of a quite different type. This is a long letter written, early in the thirteenth century, by Simon, bishop of the see of Vladimir and Suzdal' in northern Rus' to his spiritual son Polykarp, who was then a monk in the Monastery of Caves, as Simon himself had been earlier. This letter gives us a vivid picture of a spiritual father in action, and begins with a stinging rebuke:

> 'Brother, sit down in silence, collect your thoughts, and say to yourself, "You wretched monk!" Did you not leave the world and parents according to the flesh for the Lord's sake? If even here, when you have come to seek your salvation, you neglect spiritual things, why have you been invested in a monastic name? Your black garments will not save you from torment ... You are not living as a monk should, . . . and I am thoroughly ashamed of you!'[32]

Polykarp's faults and misdemeanours gradually emerge in the course of the letter. He was lazy about attending the Office in the monastic church (preferring to read the Psalter in his cell),[33] he grumbled at the food in the refectory;[34] and he was touchy and unable to bear insults and humiliations. This was in fact one of the acid tests of obedience and humility in the Orthodox tradition; the *Ladder* is full of examples. Still worse, he evidently cared more about advancement in the ecclesiastical hierarchy than about saving his soul. He had left the Monastery of Caves in oder to become abbot of another monastery in Kiev dedicated to St. Cosmas and St. Damian,[36] though he had soon returned, probably at Bishop Simon's prompting. However his restlessness and ambition made him want to leave again, in order to become abbot of the ancient and prestigious monastery dedicated to St. Demetrios; but he was prevented from doing this by the combined pressure from Bishop Simon and the Prince of Kiev.[37] 'I have seen you as an ambitious man, who seeks glory from men and not from God,' commented Bishop Simon on this occasion.[38] There were some members of the ruling princely family who would have liked to see Polykarp made a bishop, but Simon prevented this too: 'Knowing your spiritual poverty,' he writes, 'I forbade this.' He explained his reasons in a letter to a member of this family, who was also one of his spiritual children:

---

[31] See Heppell, *Paterik*, Introduction, xxxix - xl iv.

[32] Abramovich, *Kievo-Pecherskii Paterik*, 99; Heppell, *Paterik*, 113.

[33] Heppell, *Paterik*, 113.

[34] Abramovich, 99 -100; Heppell, 114.

[35] Abramovich, 99 - 100; Heppell, 114 - 15.

[36] Abramovich, 100; Heppell, 115.

[37] Abramovich, 101; Heppell, 116.

[38] Abramobvich, 101; Heppell, 116.

'My daughter Anastasia, what you want is not pleasing to God. If he had remained in the monastery and not left it, keeping his conscience pure, obeying the superior and the brethren, and practising temperance in all things, then not only would he have been clothed in priestly garments, but he would have been worthy of the higher kingdom.'[39]

Bishop Simon may seem rather severe in his judgments; but his severity was prompted by a deep concern for Polykarp's spiritual welfare, and in this he showed himself to be a true descendant of the spiritual fathers of earlier times. As Hausherr says, 'Les Vrais pères spirituels sont à la fois sevérès et très bons.'[40]

The tradition of spiritual direction - of lay people as well as monks - continued to flourish in Russian monasteries right up to the Revolution; and during many centuries there were a number of famous *startsi*. One of these was a priest-monk named Feodorit[41] who lived in the sixteenth century. He was tonsured at an early age in the Solovetsky Monastery on the White Sea, and spent many years as a missionary among the Lapps, whose language he learnt. Later he became abbot of a small monastery near Novgorod, and it was during this period of his life that he acted as spiritual father to a number of prominent ecclesiastics and lay people as well as his own monks. One of his lay spiritual children, Prince Andrei Mikhailovich Kurbsky, paid a moving tribute to his spiritual direction: 'And what great calm and meekness did he possess, what wise instruction did he give, and what wondrous sweet converse and what useful apostle-like talk did he treat us to when he happened to discourse with his spiritual children ... '[42] Like many of his contemporaries, Feodorit died as a victim of the violent temper of Tsar Ivan IV. A famous eighteenth-century *starets*, St. Tikhon Zadonsky,[43] is generally thought to have served as a model for Dostoyevsky's fictional character, Father Zosima, in *The Brothers Karamazov*. In the nineteenth century there was a *starets* called Makary whose "letters of direction" were subsequently published; a selection of these is available in English translation.[44]

In conclusion I would like to suggest that the study of the Orthodox tradition of spiritual direction is not just of historical interest, though it has a long history. At the present time counselling of various forms, including spiritual direction, is being more widely practised, and awareness of its value is increasing. The study of an older tradition has therefore some practical relevance to our own times.

---

[39] Abramovich, 102; Heppell, 117.

[40] Hausherr, *Direction spirituelle*, 163.

[41] See M. Heppell, 'Feodorit, a Russian Non-Possessor, priest and martyr, '*Sobornost*',. v, 2, (1983), 22 -34.

[42] M. Heppell, 'Feodorit, a Russian Non-Possessor,' 33.

[43] See Nadejda Gorodetsky, *St Tikhon Zadonsky*, (London, 1951).

[44] See *Russian Letters of Direction*, 1834 - 1860, by Macarius, *starets* of Optino. Selection, Translation and Foreword by Julia de Beausobre, (St. Vladimir's Seminary Press, 1975).

THE BIBLICAL AND MONASTIC ROOTS OF THE SPIRITUALITY OF POPE GREGORY THE GREAT

by
Joan M. Petersen

It is entirely characteristic of Pope Gregory the Great that he left behind him no single treatise on spirituality and ascetic theology. His teachings on these subjects are to be found principally in his writings on the Bible: the *Moralia in Iob,* based on lectures given to a monastic audience in Constantinople during his time as *apocrisiarius* there (c.578-85), which he revised and dedicated to his friend of that era, Leander of Seville, on his return to Rome; and his other expositions of holy Scripture, delivered in Rome to a similar audience of monks, secular clergy and perhaps a few educated laymen, the *Homiliae in Ezechielem,* and the commentaries on the Song of Songs and on 1 Kings (which we normally call 1 Samuel). Even in the early years of his pontificate, in spite of the heavy burdens of office, he was able to produce two more works, which though not specifically written as biblical commentaries, contain a good deal of spiritual teaching, which is based on the Bible: the *Liber Regulae Pastoralis* (590), written primarily as a guidebook for leaders of the Church, and the *Dialogues* (593-4), a collection of stories compiled to illustrate the conviction that Italy was as capable of producing holy men as any other country. To this period also belongs his collection of *Homiliae in Evangelia:* these are principally a series of straightforward expositions of the Bible, which lay stress on the importance of Christian conduct, but also contain some relevant examples of his teaching on prayer.

The reason why Gregory chose to put across his spiritual teachings by means of such writings is that he was very much a man of the book, the Bible. No one who reads any of Gregory's works can fail to be struck by his immense and detailed knowledge of its subject matter and by the way in which its spirit permeates his life and thought. An American scholar has counted at least 485 biblical quotations in the *RP,*[1] and they occur very frequently in the *Dialogues* and elsewhere. We may surmise that Gregory's thoroughly biblical outlook was due to his earlier monastic training.

By tradition Gregory was long regarded as a Benedictine, and of course, the reading and study of Scripture forms an important part of the *Rule* of St Benedict. Whether Gregory was a Benedictine in the modern sense of the term was first questioned by Baronius at the end of the sixteenth century, and from then onwards, the battle was joined. In my opinion, this vexed question was settled once and for all by Kassius Hallinger, who in a famous article written in 1957, replied to the somewhat ill-founded assertions of Olegario Porcel,[2] though he overstates his case and, at times, seems to employ a sledge-hammer to crack a nut. In fairness, however, it must be admitted that

---

[1] D.M. Wertz, "The influence of the *Regula pastoralis* to the year 900," diss., Cornell University, Ithaca 1936, cited by H. Davis, ed. and tr., Gregory the Great, *Pastoral care*, ACW 11, Westminster, Md, and London 1950, 244, 41n.

[2] O. Porcel, *La doctrina monastica de San Gregorio Magno y la Regula monachorum,* Madrid 1950; K. Hallinger, "Der Papst Gregor der Grosse und der heilige Benedikt," *Studia Anselmiana* xlii(1957), 213-319; O. Porcel, "San Gregorio y el monacato: questiones controvertides," Scripta et documents xii, *Studia monastica* i, Montserrat 1960, 1-95. P. Verbraken in a review of the latter in *Studia monastica* ii (1960), 438-40, sums up the arguments in this controversy.

Porcel has performed a useful service to scholarship by listing the correspondences between the Benedictine rule and Gregory's writings. Paul Meyvaert, in his Jarrow Lecture (1964), rightly contends that Hallinger's thesis that Gregory scarcely knew the Benedictine rule and was little influenced by it, cannot seriously be maintained.[3] Whether or not this rule was followed in Gregory's monastery of St Andrew on the Caelian Hill, we may assume from a passage in one of his letters that the monks were expected to pass a certain portion of each day in reading.[4] Private reading in Late Antiquity and the early Middle Ages did not normally take the same form that it does today, but involved some physical activity. The daily *lectio divina* was not only as optical movement, but also involved the movement of the lips as they pronounced the words and the use of the ears as they listened to them. Indeed doctors sometimes ordered patients, who needed a complete physical rest, to refrain from reading. This slow, careful reading of the Bible was known as *legere et meditari.*[5] It would cause the monk to think carefully about the meaning of what he was reading and help him to remember what he had read. Not for nothing were the words of a book known as *voces paginarum.* Gregory's vast knowledge of the Bible must surely be the result of carrying out this practice over a period of many years. He would have been trained in this discipline from the beginning of his time in the monastery and would no doubt have carried it on in the Western monastic enclave, which he established in a Byzantine palace.[6] In Constantinople, and later, when he became Pope. Moreover, when books were scarce, in the days before the invention of printing, there was a greater motive for cherishing them, reading them slowly, and learning passages by heart. As much reliance was then placed on the memory as is nowadays placed on the written word, which perhaps accounts for the discrepancies, which we find in citations of the Bible in the works of the Fathers, including Gregory himself.

The character of Gregory's spirituality is reflected in his method of interpreting the Bible. Not surprisingly his attitude to the Bible was very different from our own. There was no idea of dealing with a book as a whole, or of discovering what the aims of the writer were, let alone of attempting to see it in its historical setting. For Gregory, as for present-day Christians, the Bible was indeed the Word of God, but for him God spoke through a study of history, typology, and allegory.[7] As a contemplative, Gregory preferred the allegorical method of interpretation, practised by the Alexandrian exegetes, to the literal and historical method of the school of Antioch. He was in the line going back through Augustine to Clement and Origen, who in his turn, had probably been influenced by Philo and the Jewish interpreters of the Old Testament in Alexandria.

---

[3] P. Meyvaert, "Bede and Gregory the Great," Jarrow Lecture vii (1964), *Benedict, Gregory, Bede and others,* London, Variorum Reprints, 1977, 1-26 26, 59n. However, I accept as fundamentally correct Hallinger's view that Gregory cannot have been a Benedictine in the modern sense of the term.

[4] S. Gregorii Magni Registrum epistularum [hereafter *Reg.*] iii.3, I, ed. D. Norberg, *CCSL* cxl, 149.

[5] For further information on this subject, see J. Leclercq, *L'amour des lettres et le désir de Dieu,* 2 ed. Paris 1963, 21-5 ET, *The love of learning and the desire for God,* tr. C. Misrahi, London 1974, 18-23; B. Smalley, *The study of the Bible in the Middle Ages,* Oxford 1941, 13-23.

[6] *Moralia in Iob* [hereafter Mor.], *Ep. miss., praef.,* ed. M. Adriaen, *CSL* cxliii cxliiiA, cxliiiB *[pagin. cont.]*,cxliii, 2.

[7] Ibid., *Ep. miss. 3,* cxliii, 4.

All Gregory's works abound in this type of interpretation. Here are three examples. The first is taken from the *Moralia,* where he commenting on Job 1:3. The verse runs, *Et fuit possessio eius septem millia ovium et tria millia camelorum.* Gregory interprets what seems to us to be a straightforward statement of fact in the following way:

> *Servata quippe veritate historiae, imitari spiritaliter possumus, quod carnaliter audimus. Oves enim septem milia possidemus cum cum cogitationes innocuas, perfecta cordis munditia, intra nosmetipsos inquisito veritatis pabulo pascimus.*
>
> *Eruntque nobis in possessione etiamtria milia camelorum, si omne quod in nobis altum ac tortuosum est, rationi fidei subditur et sub cognitione Trinitatis, sponte in appetitu humilitatis inclinatur. Camelos quippe possidemus, si quod altum sapimus, humiliter deponamus ... Possunt etiam per camelos qui ungulam nequaquam findunt, sed tamen ruminant, terrenarum rerum bonae dispensationes intellegi, quae quia aliquid habent saeculi et aliquid Dei, per commune eas necesse animal designare.*[8]

There are also some good examples of this method of exegesis in the *RP.* Here is one from ii:7, where Gregory is interpreting Ezekiel 44:20. Here, speaking of the Jewish priests, the prophet says, *Caput autem suum non radent neque comam nutrient; sed tondentes attondent capita sua.* Gregory interprets the hairs on the heads of the priests as thoughts about exterior matters:

> *Capilli vero in capite, exteriores sunt cogitationes in ments: qui dum super cerebrum insensibiliter oriuntur, curas vitae praesentis designant; quae ex sensu negligenti, quia importune aliquando prodeunt, quasi nobis non sentientibus procedunt.*[9]

He goes on to say that since priests are placed above others, they are rightly forbidden either to shave their heads or to let their hair grow long, so that they neither discard wholly all consideration for the flesh on behalf of the lives of their subjects nor again to allow it to engross them too much.

Finally there is the great metaphor of the Church as the Ark, not Noah's Ark, as in the old baptismal liturgy, but the Church as the Ark of the Covenant, as described in Exodus 25: 12-15. There are to be four gold rings at the four corners of the Ark. Poles are to be made of shittim wood, covered with gold, and are to be passed through the rings and to be kept there permanently. The four rings are the books of the Gospels, placed at the four corners of the earth, and the poles of shittim wood, the strong and persevering teachers that are to be sought out – teachers, who will adhere to the teaching of the sacred books and as it were, carry the Ark by being let through the rings. The poles are to be inserted permanently, because the teachers are never to depart from the tasks of preaching and sacred study. The gold covering of the poles signifies that the sound of the teaching may always go forth to others, and that they themselves may shine in the splendour of their way of life.[10]

---

[8] Ibid., i, 39-40, cxliii, 46; Job 1:3.

[9] *Regula pastoralis* [hereafter *RP*] ii.7, *PL* lxxvii 42.

[10] Ibid. ii.2, PLlxxvii 48-50.

The symbolism of numbers exercised a great fascination over men's minds in Classical and Late Antiquity and in the early Middle Ages; indeed numerology is a study which, in Western Europe, goes back at least to the days of Pythagoras (c.580-504 BC). The ancients saw numbers as having a mysterious significance, almost a life of their own.[11] The tradition of numerological interpretation was carried on by Augustine and Ambrose who, for example, affirmed the value of the number seven, *non Pythagorico et ceterum philosophorum more ... , sed secundum formam et divisiones gratiae spiritalis.*[12] Gregory, following Ambrose, totally rejected the secular meaning of numbers. He, too, had a predilection for the number seven, which he saw as representing not only the sevenfold gifts of the Holy Spirit, but also the Three Persons of the Holy Trinity and the four cardinal virtues. This is but one example of many.[13]

This kind of scriptural exegesis may seem strange to us, but we make a grave mistake if we look upon it simply as something quaint or even comic. Gregory has to be seen against the background of his own times; this kind of interpretation, both allegorical and numerological, was part of the *Weltanschauung* of educated society in his day. However, set against this background of "things temporal" is the Gregory, whose mind and heart were set upon "things eternal". His biblical hermeneutics were but a means of raising the soul to contemplation. Present-day Christians may find it more natural, when using the Bible devotionally, to take a single verse or even a few words to set a train of thought in motion and to let their minds range more freely and simply rather than to work out a complicated allegorical structure; yet both these approaches may lead to the same goal.

For Gregory contemplation was not only a way of prayer, but also a way of life. It was the way of life which he preferred and to which he believed that he had been called, even though he had at first been slightly reluctant to enter the religious life. He had known the turmoil of the world when he had been a layman in the civil service, and had already attained the high office of Prefect of Rome when the call came to him, but he did not respond immediately. In this connection he uses a curious phrase, *quoniam diu longeque conversionis gratiam distuli.*[14] The Latin word *conversio* can, however, be used in a technical sense to signify entry into the religious life. Once he finally renounced the world, he found such immense happiness and fulfilment in the monastic life that it must have been peculiarly painful to him, when be became Pope, to have to return to what he had earlier given up.

Gregory uses his *Homilies on Ezekiel* as a vehicle to convey his teachings on the contemplative and the active life. His own desire for contemplation is not a merely negative longing to exchange for a burden not of his own choosing the monastic life that he loves. On the contrary, he sees contemplation as something dynamic and positive, which enriches all aspects of the Christian life. The autobiographical fragment embedded

---

[11] See G. Cremascoli, "Le symbole des nombres dans les oeuvres de Grégoire le Grand," *Colloque international CNRS Grégoire le Grand* (Chantilly 1982) [hereafter *Chantilly 1982*], Paris 1986, 445-51.

[12] Ambrose, *Ep.* xxxi (xliv). 3, 32-4, ed. O. Faller, *CSEL* lxxxii, 217.

[13] *Mor.* xv. 18, 15, *CCSL* cxliiiA, 758; for the fascination of the number 7, ibid., i.4, *CCSL* cxliii, 27.

[14] Ibid. *Ep. miss.* 1, 1, *CCSL* cxliii, 1.

in these homilies gives us some conception of the stresses and strains of his daily life.[15] It is not surprising that his mind was *scissa ac dilaniata* and that he feels regret for the peace of the monastery of St Andrew.[16] He believes, however, that men may be called by God to the active as well as to the contemplative life; both lives are good, but the contemplative life is the life of greater merit.[17] He follows Augustine in taking Martha as the type of the active life and Mary as the contemplative and points out that though Jesus praises Mary, he does not rebuke Martha. Mary has chosen the *optimam partem*, but the part which Martha has chosen is *pars bona*.[18] Our active life ceases when we die, but the contemplative life, which begins here, will be perfected in heaven. Similarly, he goes on to show how Leah and Rachel also symbolize the two lives. Their names mean "Laborious" and "The sight of the beginning" respectively. By being married first to Leah, who is dim-eyed but fruitful, and then to Rachel, who is beautiful but barren, Jacob follows the right order of living, which is to pass from action to contemplation.[19]

In his teaching about the two lives Gregory follows Augustine closely, though he expresses himself in a rather more simple and condensed style. However, he goes on to deal in a more practical fashion with the claims of the two lives. In the *Moralia* he cites Jesus as uniting both when he became incarnate. He both preached and worked miracles and spent the night in prayer on the mountain. Gregory stresses that it is important for pastors and preachers to combine the two kinds of life.[20] Sometimes, if there is a shortage of active workers to look after the needs of their neighbours, contemplatives should be prepared to engage in active works. Indeed the love of our neighbours may well help to increase our love of God: *quia tanto subtilius superiora penetrat, quanto humilius pro amore conditoris nec inferiora contemnit.*[21] There are even times when Gregory seems to think that contemplation would be eliminated altogether. Gregory interprets *contemplatio* as the *oculus dexter* of Matthew 5: 29, which is to be plucked out if it offends. It is better to pursue a good *vita activa* without contemplation than a life of false contemplation.[22]

It was the high value that Gregory set upon the monastic virtue of obedience that sustained him when the Spirit led him in one direction and the requirements of life in this world in the other. He saw his own obedience as actualizing the monastic ideal of total obedience to Christ.[23] It was this quality of obedience which enabled him to shun the temptation of fleeing to escape the assumption of the high office of the papacy.

---

[15] *Homiliae in Ezechielem* [hereafter *HEz*] i. 11, 5-6, ed. M. Adriaen, *CCSL* cxliii, 17.

[16] *Dialogues* [hereafter *Dial.*], prol. 2, 1, ed. A. de Vogüé, 3 vols. *SC* ccliv, cclx, cclxv, vol. ii (*SC* cclx), 12/13.

[17] *HEz* i.3, 9, 37.

[18] Ibid. ii.2, 9, 230; *Mor.* vi.61, *CCSL* cxliii, 330-31; cf. Augustine, *contra Faustum* xxii. 52, ed. J. Zycha, *CSEL* xxv, 645-7.

[19] *HEz* ii.2, 10-11, 231-2; cf *Reg.* i.5, 5-7, at 6.

[20] *Mor.* v.66, *CCSL* cxliii, 264-6; xx. 54, cxliiiB, 1528-9; *HEz* 1.4, 9, 54.

[21] *Mor.* xix. 45, *CCSL* cxliiiA, 991-2.

[22] *Mor.* vi. 57, *CCSL* cxliii, 326-8; See also *RP* i. 6, *PL* cxxvii 19.

[23] See *Mor.* xxxv. 28-9, *CCSL* cxliiiB, 1792-4; *Dial.* ii.7, vol. ii (*SC* cclx), 156/7 - 160/61.

Altogether the whole problem of the relationship between the active and the contemplative life, which he must have felt with peculiar acuteness when he was called by the Pope from the monastery to pursue an administrative career and still more so, when he was called upon to assume the papacy himself, caused him a good deal of distress. He was still brooding over it when he wrote the *RP*. The first part of this work is really a piece of introspection to justify to himself the rightness of his action in accepting the papacy. In chapter 10 of this section he draws a picture of the ideal ruler of the Church; it shows us the aims and objects, which he set before himself in his inner life.[24] Throughout this section of the treatise we are made aware of the perils and temptations, which may attack anyone in his position. A bishop may know what course to follow, but by failing to follow it, he may give his flock not pure and living water to drink, but water which has been polluted by his own evil example. He also dwells on the perils which prosperity may bring. Jesus came to us in his flesh not only to redeem us by his passion, but also to teach us by his life. He chose an ignominious death in order that we might learn to love adversity for the sake of truth and to shrink in fear from prosperity, which can defile the mind by vainglory.[25]

There is so much emphasis in Gregory's teaching on the spiritual life about the importance of contemplation that one inevitably asks whether it was intended only for monks or whether it was also intended for the secular clergy and the laity. The *Moralia* were certainly addressed in the first place to the group of Italian monks, with whom Gregory had surrounded himself at Constantinople, but there are many references in these writings to the work of *praedicatores* or preachers, which suggests that his audience included secular clergy.[26] We know that his audience at Constantinople included at least one bishop, Leander of Seville, and in the sixth century, it was the bishops who were the principal preachers; but it is probable that the *Moralia* underwent a certain amount of editing in Rome to render the subject matter more appropriate to the audience there. On the other hand, as A. de Vogüé suggests in connection with Gregory's commentary on 1 Kings, he may have regarded preaching as a theme useful for all, "perhaps because of an ecclesiology which attaches the greatest importance to the ministry of preaching".[27] We may conjecture that these commentaries, which were given as lectures in Rome, were addressed to a similar audience, though it has been suggested that we have here Gregory's recollections of conversations with his collaborator, Claudius, abbot of Classis. Thus the comments would be parallel with those of Peter in the *Dialogues*.[28] This, however, does not seem likely. The introduction of Peter into the *Dialogues* is plainly a literary device. The commentary on 1 Kings is certainly very much concerned with the nature of monasticism and the problems of monks, but even so, there are references to *clerici*. Incidentally this work affords further evidence of Gregory's introspection into his own situation: he described his existence as *ordo remotae vitae* and himself as nevertheless

---

[24] e.g., *RP* i.5, *PL* lxxvii 19; ibid. 10, 23.

[25] *RP* i.2 (Ezek. 34: 18-19), *PL* lxxvii 16.

[26] See e.g., *Mor.* xxiv. 41-2, *CCSL* cxliiiB, 1218-19; cf. *RP* i. 7, *PL* lxxvii 20.

[27] See A. de Vogüé, "The views of St Gregory the Great on the religious life in his commentary on the Book of Kings," *Cistercian Studies* i (1982), 40-64, at 42, lln.

[28] See above article at 44-5, esp. 29n. 30n.

having to function as *sanctae ecclesiae doctor.*[29]

The *RP* was certainly intended for a mixed readership. R. A. Markus has shown in an important and interesting article that the *rectores,* to whom it is addressed, may include both the leaders of the Church and secular rulers;[30] yet the spirituality presented in this treatise is no different in character or quality from what is to be found in his other writings. We have already observed that he uses the same methods of biblical exegesis in the *Moralia* and the *RP.*

Gregory does not appear to offer a different form of spirituality to the laity. In the *Homiliae in Evangelia,* which were delivered to city congregations in Rome, though not necessarily in the churches to which they were assigned by the early editors of Gregory's manuscripts and by Migne, we find again the same form of biblical exegesis and spiritual teaching. A good example is furnished by *HEv* 1.2, where Gregory uses the story of the healing of the blind man on the road to Jericho in Luke 16.31-4 as a basis for a discourse on distractions in prayer. The *caecus* or blind man represents Gregory's congregation in their spiritual blindness and the crowds who went in front of Jesus, the evil thoughts which crowd in and hinder prayer. Such teaching would be appropriate to all Christians, whether monastic or secular.[31]

A further argument in favour of Gregory's presenting a spirituality, which was primarily intended for monks, is the absence in any of his writings of any practical directions about contemplative prayer. For example, unlike modern writers on this subject, he does not offer advice on the length of time that should be spent in contemplative prayer, at what time of day it should be practised, or what posture – kneeling, sitting, or standing – should be adopted. This suggests that he knows that his hearers would have received instruction on such matters in the course of their monastic formation. However, he does admit that when outside the monastery, he finds the practice of contemplation difficult.[32]

Gregory indeed seems to have had mixed feelings about the value of the different kinds of Christian spiritual life. His own vocation and inclination alike led him to prefer the contemplative life, and we find him complaining of the heavy burden of administration, as bishops often do today. Though he believed the contemplative form of life was the higher, he admitted that one one in this world can lead a wholly contemplative life.[33] Indeed he proclaimed a truth that was forgotten by the Church for years and years and is only now being recovered. He believed that all Christians, monastic or secular, married or single, men or women, are called upon to imitate the perfection of Christ their Redeemer, which includes the practice of contemplative prayer. In the *Moralia* he suggests a kind of progress of Christians: married people, pious celibates and independent hermits,

---

[29] *In I Reg.* iv. 100-101, ed. P. Verbraken, CCSL cxliv, 345-6.

[30] R.A. Markus, "Gregory the Great's *Rector* and his genesis," *Chantilly 1982,* 137-46.

[31] *Homiliae in Evangelia* [hereafter HEv] i. 2.3, *PL* lxxvi 1078-9.

[32] *HEz* i. II, 6, 171-2.

[33] Ibid. i.3, 9. 39; see also *Reg.* i.4-5, CCSL cxl, 1-7.

cenobites and hermits who are under obedience, and finally those in holy orders, whom he calls *clerici, rectores* or *praedicatores*. In a similar list in the homilies on Ezekiel, the *praedicatores*, represented by the Old Testament type of Noah, are at the head; then come the *continentes* or celibates, typified by Daniel, and lastly, the *coniugati* or married people, typified by Job.[34] For Gregory, as for St John Chrysostom, the *clerici* are those who have achieved the most perfect state in the Church, because they were leading a mixed life of action and contemplation.[35] This, he believes, is not a life that deflects a person, but on the contrary, leads him from contemplation to action. In his opinion, a *clericus* engaged in pastoral work follows the example of Christ, St Paul, Jacob and Moses. In a letter in which he advises Anastasius, patriarch of Antioch, to leave the high places of contemplation to take up the administration of his patriarchate, he points out that the life of the Apostles was the mixed life *par excellence*.[36] Though he could respect the attraction of the contemplative life for certain individuals, he occasionally encouraged the removal of able and useful men from the monasteries, in accordance with a tradition going back to St John Chrysostom and St Augustine.[37]

Unlike later writers on contemplation and mysticism, such as St Teresa of Avila and St John of the Cross, Gregory did not leave behind him any kind of classification or map of the spiritual life, but we can assign the experiences, which he describes, to regions on such maps. This attitude is in keeping with his combining his teaching on contemplation with his interpretation of the Bible rather than writing a specific treatise on the subject, where a classification or chart might be more appropriate.

In Gregory's insistence on the need for penitence and purgation as the preliminaries for contemplation, we can detect the influence of earlier monastic writers, such as John Cassian, who because he was a Greek-speaker writing in Latin, was able to mediate to him the teachings of St Basil, St Gregory of Nyssa, St John Chrysostom and Evagrius Ponticus.[38] Both Gregory and Cassian see compunction as a state in which the soul, stripped of superfluity, is bared and made conscious of its sins. According to Cassian, this consciousness becomes deeper as the soul acquires a more profound *puritas cordis*.[39] A similar stress on purity and purgation is found in at least two passages in the *Moralia*.[40] Gregory's teaching on compunction, with which I have dealt in greater detail elsewhere,[41] performed a valuable function in disseminating the ideas of Eastern Christendom in the West. It may be regarded as an early example of what later writers on spirituality were to

---

[34] *Mor.* xxxii. 41-4, *CCSL* cxliiiB, 1659-61; *HEz* ii.4, 3-6, 260-61; *Dial.* iv. 28, vol. iii (*SC* cclxv), 96/7-98/9; *HEv* ii. 36, *PL* lxxvi 1274.

[35] *Mor.* vi. 57. *CCSL* cxliii, 326-7; John Chrysostom, *de sacerdotio* ii.4, *PG* xlviii 635-6; vi. 2-10, ibid. 679-86.

[36] *Reg.* v. 42 [39], *CCSL* cxl, 325-7; *Mor.* xxxviii.33, *CCSL* cxliiiB, 1420-21; xxxi, 48-50. ibid., 1584-5.

[37] *Reg.* viii.17, 15, *CCSL* cxlA, 536-8.

[38] R. Gillet in *Mor. SC* xxxii bis, 18-102, 72n; J. Pegon in *Dictionnaire de la Spiritualité*, art. *Componction*.

[39] Cassian, *Inst.* iv. 431, rev. text, ed. and tr. J.C. Guy, *SC* cix, 184-5; xii. 52, 470-71.

[40] *Mor.* xxiii. ll, *CCSL* cxliiiB, 1152 cf. iii.53, *CCSL* cxliii, 147-8; v.55, ibid., 256.

[41] See J.M. Petersen, The Dialogues of Gregory the Great in their late antique cultural background, Studies and Texts lxix, Toronto 1984, 160-65.

call the purgative way.

A further condition for contemplation, in Gregory's view, is a tranquil mind. In one of his letters he complains that when his work is done and he is trying to return to his inner self, he is driven away by vain and tumultuous thoughts, a reminder that this common human difficulty afflicts even the saints.[42] Anger, whether derived from evil or from righteousness, destroys our tranquillity. Even righteous anger makes us agitated and obscures our spiritual sight, so that we no longer see those objects above us, which we were able to seen when our minds were calm.[43] When a soul is engaged in contemplation, it is, as it were, asleep though awake. Gregory cites as examples of this condition the Bride in the Song of Songs, *Ego dormio et cor meum vigilat,* and Jacob at Bethel, when he was asleep, but saw angels ascending and descending the ladder.[44] The soul is never induced to contemplate what belongs to the interior life, unless it carefully withdraws itself and is lulled to rest from earthly desires. Jacob's stone pillow represents the mind of Christ; unless we keep our heads on the pillow, that is, unless we hold ourselves steadily in the presence of Christ, we fail to see the angels, though we may be able to sleep. If we wish to contemplate what is within, we must rest from outward activity. We can hear God's voice, when our minds are quiet; then we rest from life's battles and ponder the divine precepts in the deep silence of our hearts.[45]

Above all, the contemplative must ask himself how much he loves, for love is, as it were, a device or machine for raising the soul. *Machina quippe mentis est vis amoris.*[46] The soul can be weighed down by fear, and if love does not rouse the soul in contemplation, torpor and lukewarmness will obscure its powers of seeing. The mind needs training in recollection, that is, in gathering itself to itself, and in introspection, that is, in looking at itself and in stripping itself of bodily images. Only then can it make the effort to contemplate the invisible Creator. Gregory writes frequently of the sweetness encountered by the soul of the contemplative and of the brevity and transience of contemplation.[47] Some mystical and contemplative writers, such as St John of the Cross, find God through penetrating an immense darkness, but for Gregory, the ultimate object of our contemplation is symbolized by light and brightness. We cannot see the actual light, but only a likeness or reflection of it. When we try to look at it, our vision is clouded by its own weakness. Gregory was perhaps the first writer to express an idea, which subsequently became a commonplace among mystical writers, that contemplation is in this world like looking through a mist or cloud at the sun, an idea ultimately derived from Ps. 17-10: *et caligo sub pedibus eius* (18.9 . . . and it was dark under his feet). This idea was to be developed later, probably in the fourteenth century, by the author of *The Cloud of Unknowing.* Even the holiest people, says Gregory, cannot see God as he is, but only as an enigma, a phrase which recalls St Paul's "through a glass darkly", the Latin

---

[42] *Reg.* i.5, *CCSL* cxl, 5-7.

[43] *Mor.* xx.63, *CCSL* cxliiiA, 1048-50.

[44] *Mor.* v.54, *CCSL* cxliii, 255-6.

[45] Ibid. 55, 256-8; see also *RP* ii.5, *PL* lxxvii 3.

[46] *Mor.* vi. 58, *CCSL* cxliii, 328.

[47] e.g., *Mor.* v. 57, *CCSL* cxliii, 258, viii.50, ibid., 421; *HEz* ii.2, 12, 232-3.

for which is, *Videmus nunc per speculum in aenigmate.*[48]

The question is sometimes asked whether Gregory ever experienced any of those phenomena, such as visions, levitation, bilocation and absence from the body, which are often regarded as the hall-mark of the mystic. Various passages are cited, which are alleged to prove that he did for example, *per contemplationem vero quia super nosmetipsos tollimur;*[49] *animus fit super semetipsum,*[50] *carnis claustra transgrediens super semetipsum ire conatur.*[51] There are also passages, which contain various forms of *rapere*, meaning "seized" or "caught up".[52] It seems to me, however, that in all these instances, the words could perfectly well be used figuratively. Further confirmation that Gregory was unaccustomed to be involved in mystical or psychic phenomena is his description of St Benedict's vision of the light of the sun, the whole world gathered in, and the soul of St Germanus of Capua ascending to heaven in a fiery ball. There he represents St Benedict as being his normal self in the body and calling out to the other monks to come and see the wonder.[53] I believe that Dom Cuthbert Butler was right in his comment that Gregory must have been writing of something totally outside his own experience, when he represented St Benedict, the recipient of a remarkable spiritual experience, as conscious of those around him.[54] Of course, the fact that Gregory was probably without experience of paranormal phenomena in no way detracts from the value of his spiritual teaching and writings.

There is a question that we should ask ourselves in conclusion. Was Gregory an original thinker in the field of ascetic theology and spirituality, or were his writings largely derivative? In answer to this question, no one, whether historian, theologian or any other kind of scholar really writes in a vacuum, and it is undoubtedly true that he was influenced by certain earlier writers, particularly Augustine and Cassian. The latter was a particularly valuable influence in Gregory's spiritual formation, in that he introduced him to the spirituality of the Desert and of the Greek Fathers, which in his turn, he was able to mediate to Western Christendom. Gregory, however, went on where Cassian left off and was able to develop teaching on compunction, which we may look upon as his own. A further important feature of Gregory's spirituality is that he explicitly linked contemplation and prayer:

> *Cum eius Spiritus afflatu tangimur et extra carnis angustias sublevati, per amorem agnoscimus auctoris nostri contemplandam speciem, quam sequamur.*[55]

---

[48] e.g., *HEz* i.8, 30, 119-20.

[49] *Ibid.* i.3, 1, 33.

[50] *Dial.* ii.35, vol. ii (*SC* clx), 238/9-242/3.

[51] *Mor.* x.31, *CCSL* cxliii, 559-60.

[52] e.g., *HEz* ii.2, 13, 234; *Mor.* vii. 53, *CCSL* cxliii, 373; x.17, ibid., 550.

[53] *Dial.* ii.35, vol. ii (*SC* cclx), 236/7-242/3.

[54] E.C. Butler, *Western Mysticism*, 3 ed., London 1967, 89.

[55] *Mor.* x. 13, *CCSL* cxliii, 545-6.

Augustine may have implied a connection between prayer and contemplation, but he never brought it out into the open, while Origen in his treatise on prayer, which deals with many kinds of vocal prayer, never so much as mentions contemplation as a prayerful activity.

We have already noticed that much of Gregory's writing on spirituality is intensely personal and introspective. He is often filled with nostalgia for his peaceful life at the monastery, but at the same time, he tries to justify to himself his acceptance of the papacy. The expression of his reluctance to accept it may well owe something to Rufinus's translation of the *de fuga* of Gregory of Nazianzus, but his sentiments were probably real enough.[56] Yet his need for introspection and self-justification does not render his work dated or obsolete. Human nature is unchanging, and Gregory had an immense understanding of it. His great service to Christians today is to remind us that contemplative prayer is open to all. A great modern Benedictine master of prayer, the late Father Henri Le Saulx, who was known in India, where his life's work lay, as Abhishiktananda, has written:

> Prayer is not a part-time occupation for any of Christ's disciples. Indeed there are no part-time contemplatives any more than there are part-time Christians or part-time men ... To live in the presence of God should be as natural for a Christian as to breathe the air which surrounds him.[57]

The language may be that of the twentieth century, but the sentiment which it expresses is truly Gregorian in spirit.

---

[56] See Gregory of Nazianzus, *Orat.* ii, *PG* xxxv 407-514 and Latin tr., *Tyrannii Rufini orationum Gregorii Nazianzeni novem interpretatio*, ed. A. Engelbrecht, CSEL xxxvi (Vienna 1910, repr. N.Y., 1966), 1-10.

[57] Abhishiktananda, *Prayer*, London, SPCK, 1967, 1-2.

WESTMINSTER ABBEY AND ITS PARISH CHURCHES: c. 1050-1216*

by

Emma Mason

estminster abbey was a rich monastery, thanks largely to the endowment of King Edward (1042-66), who intended that the church of St. Peter of Westminster should be his mausoleum.[1] It possessed considerable property in London and of course in Westminster itself; estates in all of the 'home counties', and outlying properties in the east and west Midlands, and in Sussex.[2] Appurtenant to many of these properties were parish churches which were in themselves sources of income. They also afforded the means of financing the abbey's expert secular clerks, and of offering an acceptable *quid pro quo* to those who mattered in high places. This present survey of Westminster's administration of its churches is confined to the century and a half between King Edward's endowment of the abbey and the end of King John's reign, a period which spanned developments in church history from the beginnings of the Gregorian reform movement down to the Fourth Lateran Council. Westminster's splendid collection of muniments includes more than 490 documents emanating from this period.[3] Some 144 of these concern churches and/or tithes, an indication that considerable attention was paid to parochial sources of income, and their administration. Much the same problems in dealing with these were faced by ecclesiastical proprietors throughout England, and to a large extent they responded in similar ways, although local circumstances also gave rise to some divergences.[4]

Analysis of Westminster's charters relating to ecclesiastical property reveals that about twenty-five per cent are concerned solely with tithe income. Conversely several of the abbey's parish churches may comprise the subject of any one document, while some individual churches, usually the richest and therefore the most contested, gave rise to repeated negotiation and hence to frequent documentation. In contrast, poor and remote churches, and small assignments of tithe income, earned a bare mention even in the most all-embracing confirmatory charters of this period. So far as the documentation allows, the present paper will examine the evidence for the geographical spread of parochial revenues; the uses to which they were assigned; the action taken to secure title to

---

[1] *Vita Aedwardi Regis qui apud Westmonasterium requiescit*, ed. and transl. Frank Barlow (London, 1962), pp. 44-6; Barbara Harvey, *Westminster Abbey and its Estates in the Middle Ages*, (Oxford, 1977), pp. 24-5.

[2] Harvey, *Westminster Abbey and its Estates*, pp. 335-64. For the abbey's property in the vill of Westminster itself, see also Gervase Rosser, *Medieval Westminster 1200-1540* (Oxford, 1989), pp. 12-16.

[3] *Westminster Abbey Charters 1066-c.1214*, ed. Emma Mason, assisted by the late Jennifer Bray, continuing the work of the late Desmond J. Murphy (London Record Society, 25, 1988).

[4] For the administration of parish churches and parochial sources of income in various regions of twelfth-century England, see Janet E. Burton, 'Monasteries and Parish Churches in Eleventh and Twelfth-Century Yorkshire', *Northern History*, 23 (1987), pp. 39-50; Christopher Harper-Bill, 'Bishop William Turbe and the Diocese of Norwich, 1147-1174', *Anglo-Norman Studies 7*, ed. R. Allen Brown (Woodbridge, 1985), pp. 142-60; and his 'The Struggle for Benefices in Twelfth-Century East Anglia', *Anglo-Norman Studies 11*, ed. R. Allen Brown (Woodbridge, 1989), pp. 113-32; and B.R. Kemp, 'Monastic Possession of Parish Churches in England in the Twelfth Century', *Journal of Ecclesiastical History*, 31 (1980), pp. 133-60.

parochial income in confirmations obtained from kings, from popes and their agents, and from diocesan bishops; the evidence in charters of the abbots of Westminster, and in those of benefactors, for the administration of individual churches and, in a concluding section, several case-studies will be examined for evidence, on the one hand, of the impact of canon law on parochial administration, and of the growing efficiency of ecclesiastical jurisdiction in the reform era. On the other hand, these case-studies will also reveal the impact of royal intervention and persuasion; pressures from influential *curiales,* and the entrenched rights, or claims, of incumbents.

The reliability of this survey depends on the validity of the evidence. Westminster assiduously retained texts of the grants which it received, and of those charters which were issued by its abbots and chapter - but texts were also kept of those grants which the monks would like to have received - if only someone had granted them. The question of authenticity looms large over royal charters, and in particular those of King Edward, William I and Henry I, but forgers continued at work in the abbey long after these reigns. Many documents were elaborated in order to lend respectability to older grants by adding witness-lists and place-dates, so that the substance of many charters 'improved' in this way contains a strong factual base. Other suspect charters record genuine grants, but augment them with long lists of judicial and financial liberties which the chapter would like to have seen attached to its properties.[5] The churches and tithes recorded in both categories of document can generally be shown from later and genuine charters to be the possessions of Westminster. Only towards the end of the period under discussion can checks be made against royal records, while papal and episcopal records of the transactions under discussion are virtually non-existent, so that the evidence of the Westminster charters must be considered largely as it stands.

Most of Westminster's churches pertained to lands acquired either before the reign of King Edward or in consequence of his own endowment, but early charters rarely if ever mention the church when granting a manor or a vill. Usually the place was granted 'with everything pertaining to it.' The charters of William I are in general scarcely more explicit, while the grandiose forgeries in the names of both kings include sweeping confirmations of estates ' with all churches, tithes, income for lights, dues ...' etc. etc.[6] This may indicate that such documents were consciously designed to show the open-handed generosity which these kings displayed towards a privileged abbey. But there was another reason for the sparse documentation of parish churches in genuine charters of the eleventh century, namely that the movement was only then under way whereby each substantial vill was acquiring a parish church of its own, and assuming in its own locality the functions of the older minster churches.[7] In the transitional period, acrimonious disputes might arise over the revenues formerly due to the old church of the neighbourhood. This is demonstrated in a writ of Abbot Herbert (1121-*c*.1136), in which

---

[5] *Westminster Abbey Charters,* pp. 8-11.

[6] For instance, the so-called Third Charter of William I: Westminster Abbey Domesday (Muniment Book 11), ff. 51-52v.

[7] J. Blair, 'From Minster to Parish Church', in *Minsters and Parish Churches: the Local Church in Transition 950-1200,* ed. J. Blair (Oxford University Committee for Archaeology, Monograph no. 17, 1988), pp. 1-19. See also J. Blair, 'Minster Churches in the Landscape', in *Anglo-Saxon Settlements,* ed. Della Hooke (Oxford, 1988), pp. 35-58.

he ordered the French and English men of Pershore and its hundred to render all rights and customs which the church of Saints Mary and Edburg of Pershore, (i.e. Pershore abbey) the mother church of Pershore hundred (Worcs.), was accustomed to receive in the time of Herbert's predecessors, in tithes, alms and all other services which the tenants owed the church. They were forbidden to contradict or harass any spiritual pastor set over them, nor act in any way which was detrimental to the rights of that mother church. Abbot Herbert's writ in effect confirmed an earlier concession of the major tithes due from the hundred, which had been made by Abbot Gilbert Crispin (c.1085-1117/8), and were later confirmed to Pershore by John of Pagham, bishop of Worcester, in 1151-7.[8]

Early royal grants or confirmation of vills to Westminster rarely mention a church, whereas these same places were normally provided with one by the early twelfth century. While the pre-existence of old 'mother churches' might impede Westminster's efforts to establish fully-fledged parish churches for its tenants on outlying manors, the abbey regarded several of its own churches as 'mother churches', including those at Benfleet (Essex), Bloxham (Oxon.), Hambledon, Oakham, Uppingham and Wardley (all in Rutland), but the term occurs only in suspect charters which are in the name of William I, although they date in fact from the early twelfth century.[9]

Some of Westminster's churches were acquired by the abbey when individuals - probably priests, but occasionally lay proprietors - were admitted as monks of the abbey and brought their churches with them. In Suffolk, the church of St. Bartholomew, Sudbury, was acquired when the royal moneyer Wulfric donated it on becoming a monk at Westminster. The abbey's subsequent right to it was challenged in the royal court, but upheld by the judges, and ratified by King Henry I.[10] This church later became the site of a small cell pertaining to Westminster, and one of its early inmates, Ivo, donated to it the greater tithe from his demesne at Torp when be became a monk of Sudbury.[11] In London, the church of St. Agnes was donated to Westminster by Godric Lobbe when he became a monk there,[12] while the advowson of St. Martin's Ludgate, was surrendered to the abbey by Laurence, surnamed 'the Devil', in return for confraternity in life and in death.[13]

But Westminster was not the goal of all those with a religious vocation. Ranulph the clerk of Feering (Essex), joined the Arroasian canons of Missenden (Bucks.), and unlawfully detained Westminster's church of Feering. As a brother of the late English pope, Adrian IV, and as father of a substantial tenant of St. Albans abbey, he perhaps felt

---

[8] Brian R. Kemp, 'The Mother Church of Thatcham', *Berkshire Archaeological Journal*, LXIII (1967-68), p. 21, note 32. On the dedication of Pershore abbey, see Alison Binns, *Dedications of Monastic Houses in England and Wales 1066-1216*, (Woodbridge, 1989), pp. 81-2.

[9] These churches are enumerated both in the 'First Charter of King William I', printed in *Calendar of Charter Rolls* IV, pp. 330-6, and in the 'Telligraphus' or Land Book of William I (Westminster Abbey Muniment XXVI). On the spurious nature of these texts, see *Westminster Abbey Charters*, notes to nos. 1, 43.

[10] *Westminster Abbey Charters*, no. 72.

[11] Ivo's grant was confirmed by King Henry I, and later ratified by Henry II: *Westminster Abbey Charters*, no. 130.

[12] *Westminster Abbey Charters*, no. 257.

[13] *Ibid.* no. 359.

able to act with impunity. But Abbot Walter of Westminster appealed to the papal *curia*, and Gilbert Foliot, bishop of London, was commissioned as papal judge-delegate in the case. The outcome was that the church was resigned to the bishop, who restored it to the abbot. The bishop then instituted the abbot's clerk, Mr. Maurice, to Feering, which he was to hold of the abbot of Westminster.[14] Occasionally a church might accrue to Westminster while its former possessor prevaricated about his religious vocation. By an agreement dated 1125, Abbot Herbert and the convent granted their manor of Ockendon (Essex) to Henry son of Wilfrid, to hold for life at an annual rent of £10. Henry gave the church of Ockendon to the abbey, but would continue to hold it at an annual rent of £1.

After his death, his heir would continue to render £1 for the church, but £11 for the manor. If Henry asked to be admitted as a monk, he would be received without the need to make a further agreement, and in that eventuality one heir of his would hold manor and church on the above-mentioned terms. And if Henry's heir wanted to become a monk, he would be received by the same agreement by which his father was admitted, and then both manor and church would revert to Westminster, unencumbered, and with all improvements.[15]

The dispersal pattern of Westminster's ecclesiastical sources of income and patronage can be learned from a few key documents, of which the most reliable were those issued by Pope Adrian IV (1154-9) and by two successive bishops of London, Gilbert Foliot (1163-87) and Richard Fitz Nigel (1189-98). In a confirmatory bull dated 1 June 1157, Pope Adrian enumerated the churches, chapels and tithes which pertained to Westminster: in Middlesex, churches and/or chapels in seven named places, with tithe income elsewhere, 'and all ecclesiastical possessions in London - including Newchurch' (to which we return later in this paper); in Surrey, four churches; in Kent, one church; two churches in Sussex; one in Wiltshire; five churches in Hertfordshire, of which one had an appurtenant chapel; six churches in Essex, of which one had appurtenant land, and another a chapel; only one church in Buckinghamshire, but this was Denham, clearly valuable in view of its subsequent history; two churches in Oxfordshire, of which one had a chapel; three churches in Northamptonshire, of which one had appurtenant chapels and another had substantial appurtenant tithes; five churches listed under Rutland, including one in Stamford, and unspecified quantities of appurtenant chapels, tithes, lands and houses; one church in Lincolnshire with its chapels; one church in Staffordshire; two churches and one chapel in Gloucestershire; fourteen churches and seven chapels in Worcestershire, with tithes appurtenant to fourteen of the twenty-one, and tithe income in eleven other places.[16] But these Worcestershire churches and tithes have left little trace in Westminster's archives for the period under discussion. Perhaps there were amicable agreements with the abbey's tenants in that region, since many of the West Mercian properties were let at farm at that time. There was also the possibility that the income

---

[14] *The Letters and Charters of Gilbert Foliot*, ed. Z.N. Brooke, A. Morey and C. N. L. Brooke (Cambridge, 1967), nos. 465-6.

[15] *Westminster Abbey Charters*, no. 247.

[16] *Papsturkunden in England*, ed. W. Holtzmann, 3 vols. (Abhandlungen der Gesellschaft der Wissenschaften in Göttingen phil. -hist. Klasse, Berlin, Göttingen: I = neue Folge XXV, 1930-31; II = 3. Folge XIV-XV, 1935-6; III = 3 Folge XXXIII, 1952), I, no. 70.

from any one of these churches was insufficient to tempt ambitious courtiers and the like to challenge Westminster's rights and thereby leave traces in the abbey's archives.

The churches in London, which received only a glancing reference in Pope Adrian's confirmation, were listed in a confirmation issued by Bishop Gilbert Foliot early in the 1180s. He named 13 churches in London and its suburbs, together with the pension due from each incumbent. Elsewhere in his diocese, he confirmed in Essex the churches of Ockendon, Kelvedon and Feering, the chapel of Little Tey and unspecified tithes in White Roding, but omitted mention of the churches of Benfleet and *Bymton*, and the chapel of Moulsham, which were included in Pope Adrian's confirmatory bull. In Hertfordshire he confirmed the valuable church of Sawbridgeworth, with its pension of £15, but omitted to mention those of Wheathampstead, Aldenham, Stevenage, Datchworth and Ashwell which were included in the papal confirmation. In Middlesex, he confirmed only the church of Hendon, omitting those of Staines, with its chapels; Shepperton, Sunbury, Hanwell, Chelsea, the chapel of Greenford and the tithes in *Edelinton*.[17] The confirmation by Richard Fitz Nigel recited these identical properties.[18] Some of the churches, missing from the episcopal confirmations were mentioned in a bull dated 18 April 1177 addressed by Pope Alexander III to Abbot Walter and the convent. He confirmed the possessions of the abbey and its exemption from the jurisdiction of the bishop of London, but prohibited the alienation of the churches of Oakham (Rutland), Staines (Middlesex), Aldenham, Ashwell and Wheathampstead (Herts.), with their chapels.[19] Evidently a petition had been sent to the *curia* in the course of the ongoing effort to evade the jurisdiction of the bishop of London and the opportunity was taken to counteract the alienation of the churches in question, but whether the initiative in this matter came from the monastic delegation, or from Abbot Walter himself, is conjectural. If the churches had been allocated to senior royal clerks on the king's instructions, Walter's only means of remedying this was perhaps to request the papacy for a mandate on the subject. On the other hand, the monastic delegation might have secured this on their own initiative, to counteract what they regarded as abbatial mismanagement of Westminster's properties. More likely the mandate concerning the churches had some direct link with the jurisdiction of the bishopric of London, since on 20 July 1189 Pope Clement III, in a bull in which he in turn confirmed the abbey's possessions and exempted it from the jurisdiction of the bishop of London, pointedly confirmed Westminster's control over these same five churches, and any others which it might acquire.[20] Rival claims to the possession of these churches by the chapter of St. Paul's perhaps resulting from their occupancy by royal clerks who were also canons of the cathedral, would account for the otherwise unlikely combination of benefits conferred by these two papal bulls. Westminster would be eager to fortify its position before a new bishop was appointed in succession to Gilbert Foliot.[21]

---

[17] *Letters and Charters of Gilbert Foliot*, no. 462.

[18] *Westminster Abbey Domesday*, folio 627 r-v.

[19] *Papsturkunden in England*, I, no. 144; on the date, see *Westminster Abbey Charters*, no. 176.

[20] *Papsturkunden in England*, I, no. 262.

[21] Gilbert Foliot died on 18 February 1187, and Richard Fitz Nigel was elected on 15 September 1189: John Le Neve, *Fasti Ecclesiae Anglicanae 1066-1300 I. St. Paul's London*, compiled Diana E. Greenway (London, 1968), p. 2.

In the period covered by this paper, few of Westminster's churches were formally appropriated. Exceptions include the rectories of Battersea and Wandsworth (appropriated in 1185) and that of South Benfleet (appropriated in 1189-90). Most of Westminster's appropriations date from the mid-thirteenth century and later.[22] On the other hand, it is clear that Westminster was systematically utilizing its parochial income throughout much of the twelfth century. Evidence of formal appropriation from the latter part of the century onwards normally indicated only the date at which the situation was regularized in the eyes of the diocesan bishop concerned, when he ensured that adequate provision was made for a vicar.[23]

From the mid-twelfth century, the income from certain of Westminster's churches was increasingly earmarked for specific monastic offices. For instance, the Almonry received assignments of grants of tithes in Kensington; in Clakelose Hundred, Norfolk (lost to Shouldham nunnery in King John's reign), and in *Buchetuna* (Buckton, Hereford?).[24] In July 1189, Pope Clement III permitted the abbot and convent to appropriate the tithes of the churches of which they were patrons, when vacancies occurred, for the support of the brethren, their guests and the poor, provided that vicarages were ordained and synodals paid.[25] The ecclesiastical sources of income assigned to the abbey's chamber included revenues from the London churches of St. James, Garlickhithe, and from St. Margaret, Fish Street, together with a pension from the rector of the church of Sunbury, Middlesex.[26] The pittancer's assignments of parochial income included that from the church of South Benfleet.[27] In addition, the church of Easthampstead, in Berkshire, was confirmed by successive abbots to Westminster's cell at Hurley, to provide extra food on the feast of St. Edward.[28] One of the earliest documented assignments of parochial income is that made by Abbot Gervase (1138-*c*.1157) from St. Matthew, Friday Street, towards the monks' clothing.[29]

The proper adornment and furnishing of the great abbey church was an expensive business. Abbot Gervase assigned tithes from Roding (Essex) towards the repair of books, and a substantial pension from Bloxham church (Oxon.) to the sacristy[30] Sawbridgeworth (Herts.) was another church from which revenues, of £15, were assigned

---

[22] Harvey, *Westminster Abbey and its Estates*, pp. 402-12.

[23] This point is reinforced by comparison with the dealings of the bishop and monks of Norwich in the twelfth century towards their churches: Harper-Bill, 'Bishop William Turbe and the Diocese of Norwich', pp. 154-5; and his 'The Struggle for Benefices in Twelfth-Century East Anglia', pp. 117-19. See also Kemp, 'Monastic Possessions of Parish Churches', pp. 148-57.

[24] *Westminster Abbey Charters*, nos. 456. 477-8.

[25] *Ibid.*, no. 178.

[26] *Ibid.*, nos. 217, 365, 369.

[27] *Ibid.*, nos. 214, 299, 317.

[28] *Ibid.*, nos. 285, 302.

[29] *Ibid.*, no. 255.

[30] *Ibid.*, nos. 251, 253.

to the sacristy early in the abbacy of Laurence (*c*.1158-1173),[31] an assignment which was confirmed by Popes Alexander III and Innocent III.[32] In the time of Abbot Herbert (1121-*c*.1136) St. Margaret's Westminster contributed £3 annually to the service of the high altar, and to other necessities of the church, both within and without. When Abbot William Postard (1191-1200) allowed the royal chamberlain Robert Mauduit to have a private chapel in his Westminster residence, he required an annual payment of two besants to the sacristy, in lieu of diverted parochial dues.[33] Two further churches in Middlesex, Hendon and Staines, also contributed income to the sacristy. The latter assignment, of £2 annually, was confirmed by the bishop of London in the 1190s, 'on account of the poverty of the sacristy . . . to improve the lighting in the church.'[34] Revenues from the Buckinghamshire church of Denham were assigned to the high altar in the time of Abbot Herbert, as were those of the 'lost' St. Mary Newchurch in London.[35] But the revenues of St. Mary's, and to some extent those of other churches assigned to the sacristy, were not forthcoming in practice. Given the high inflation rate of the late twelfth century, it was not to be expected that the sacristy could function adequately on a fraction of the assignments made some fifty or more years earlier - hence Bishop Richard Fitz Nigel's acceptance of the need to supplement the revenues required by the sacrist.

The monastic infirmary is documented from the latter part of the twelfth century, when the revenues of the Surrey churches of Battersea and Wandsworth were assigned to its support by Abbot Laurence, and confirmed by Popes Alexander III and Lucius III, and additional revenues were assigned from the Rutland churches of Hambleton and Oakham.[36] The hospital of St. James in Westminster received revenues assigned by Abbot Walter (1175-90) from the London church of St. Alban, Wood Street.[37]

Those of the abbey's churches named above are by no means the only ones for which the revenues are known in the twelfth century, but in the other cases, the purposes to which the income was put are uncertain, beyond the fact that an annual pension was due to the abbot from the clerk whom he had presented to the living. Similarly, those revenues which the various monastic offices derived from churches were only a fraction of what each received annually, because each office was also assigned estates and/or rent income.

Since many of the abbey's churches accrued with estates which were granted to Westminster, and were not separately enumerated, it became necessary to obtain royal confirmations when the use of written records grew more commonplace, and the

---

[31] *Ibid.*, nos. 211, 283-4.

[32] *Ibid.*, nos. 170, 185.

[33] *Ibid.*, nos. 244, 312.

[34] *Ibid.*, nos. 216, 459.

[35] *Ibid.*, no. 244.

[36] *Ibid.*, nos. 169, 177, 321, 336.

[37] *Ibid.*, no. 288.

developing canon law made it essential to define Westminster's legal rights and sources of income. Churches and/or tithes are granted or confirmed in thirteen of the 46 charters which survive in the name of William I.[38] Although this group includes several fabrications, it also includes useful evidence of individual donations at manorial level, which were then brought together in one or another of the spurious catch-all confirmations. And while the authenticity of the latter has usually been challenged on grounds of diplomatic or palaeography, a case has recently been made by Dr. Richard Mortimer, Keeper of the abbey's Muniments, for the possibility that kings were on occasion prepared to ratify some confirmatory charters, unorthodox in wording and historically unsubstantiated, which had been composed by monastic petitioners rather than by royal clerks.[39]

Of the ten charters for Westminster surviving the name of William II Rufus, four include confirmation of churches pertaining to the abbey.[40] A wider confirmation of Westminster's ecclesiastical possessions was probably included in the great *pancarte* which he is known - from sculptural evidence - to have issued for the abbey, but which does not now survive, or at least not in his name.[41] Of the 40 charters surviving in the name of Henry I for the abbey, 13 relate to particular churches or tithe income.[42] Most of these are concerned with the administration of individual churches, in contrast to the vaguely-worded confirmations of ecclesiastical property which occur in the spurious general charters of confirmation which survive in Stephen's name (out of a total of seventeen charters issued for Westminster in his reign).[43] Since Stephen's reign was later regarded as time of unlaw, the monks of Westminster were perhaps disinclined to preserve his charters, but this is unlikely, since his genuine grants of secular properties have survived. Charters from the reign of Henry II again relate to individual churches or tithes, which are the subjects of five of his seventeen charters for Westminster.[44] The abbey's churches are generally confirmed in the charter of liberties which survives in the name of Richard I, and which forbids the intrusion of ecclesiastical or secular officials into the churches of the lands of the abbey.[45] Individual churches pertaining to Westminster are the subject of two charters issued by King John.[46] Ecclesiastical sources of income comprised the subject of about thirty percent of Westminster's petitions to the crown. Successive kings were willing to confirm, at a price, the abbey's rights in its

---

[38] *Ibid.*, Nos. 1, 15, 18-20, 28, 33, 35, 37-38, 40, 43, 45-46.

[39] Richard Mortimer, 'The Charters of Henry II: What are the Criteria for Authenticity?', *Anglo-Norman Studies 12*, ed. Marjorie Chibnall (Woodbridge, 1990), pp. 119-34.

[40] *Westminster Abbey Charters*, nos. 49, 54-56.

[41] Frank Barlow, *William Rufus* (London, 1983), pp. 113-4.

[42] *Westminster Abbey Charters*, nos. 67, 70, 72, 77-78, 81, 83-84, 86-87, 90, 92-93.

[43] *Regesta Regum Anglo-Normannorum III. 1135-54*, ed. H.A. Cronne and R.H.C. Davis (Oxford, 1968), nos. 928-29.

[44] *Westminster Abbey Charters*, nos. 123, 127-128, 130, 138.

[45] *Ibid.*, no. 140.

[46] *Rotuli Chartarum in Turri Londoniensi asservati 1199-1216*, ed. T. Duffus Hardy (Record Comm., London, 1837), ff. 139, col. b; f. 165, col. b.

existing ecclesiastical properties, defended the parish churches against predators, and on occasion even increased Westminster's sources of parochial income. Their charters reveal what the abbey held, or aspired to hold, in this category, but only on rare occasions reveal anything about conditions in the parishes.

Papal and episcopal records are more helpful when considering the administration of the abbey's churches. Some eighteen papal documents are concerned with its churches and tithe income, including two spurious bulls in the names of Popes Leo IX and Paschal II, which both contain a generally-worded confirmation of churches, tithes, and other ecclesiastical income.[47] Papal bulls issued for the abbey from the pontificate of Innocent II onwards are more specific in their confirmation of individual churches and tithe revenues. This in turn suggests that the abbot and convent were increasingly aware of the economic potential of each item, now that the development of the English parochial structure was well under way. Ecclesiastical sources of income were likely to be contested not only by neighbouring territorial lords but also by prominent clerks in the royal service, since kings habitually rewarded favoured clerks with grants of churches.[48] Churches, with their appurtenant lands and tithe income, were becoming more valuable in the twelfth century, as the expanding population not only generated growing numbers of those liable to pay tithe and render the customary oblations, but also triggered a rise in land values, and in the profits from the sale of agricultural produce. A parish church, with its glebe and its associated parochial income, was a prize well worth contesting. The pressures on Westminster to present thrusting royal clerks to its richer benefices were probably intensified by the abbey's proximity to the royal residence of Westminster Hall, and the inevitable close contact with royal officers. It is likely that, when the king was petitioned for favours, such as confirmation of particular estates, or the grant of financial or legal exemptions on specific property, the *quid pro quo* comprised not only the customary cash payment (rarely mentioned in the ensuing confirmatory charter), but also, on occasion, the appointment of a high-flying clerk to some lucrative Westminster living. Indeed, to obtain the king's ear at all, it would be as well to 'make friends with the mammon of unrighteousness', by proposing to a confidential clerk that, if he would expedite matters on behalf of the abbey, then a lucrative rectory would soon come his way. The snag with such arrangements was that the richer abbey churches would come to be regarded as the natural perks of office, and it would be progressively more difficult for the abbey to assert its title, a danger which was intensified in that royal courts were disposed to uphold hereditary succession to benefices throughout the twelfth century.[49]

Such curial expectations and pressures would increase when the abbot was the king's son. Prior Osbert de Clare, the reputed mastermind of many of Westminster's forgeries,[50] brought back from the papal court a bull reprimanding Abbot Gervase about alienations

---

[47] *Papsturkunden in England*, I, nos. 2, 9.

[48] For instance King Edward granted to his physician, Baldwin, the church of Deerhurst (Gloucs.), and probably also that of Taynton (Oxon.); F. E. Harmer, *Anglo-Saxon Writs*, 2nd edn., (Stamford 1989), pp. 244, 293.

[49] Harper-Bill, 'The Struggle for Benefices in Twelfth-Century East Anglia', p. 126.

[50] P. Chaplais, 'The Original Charters of Herbert and Gervase, abbots of Westminster (1121-1157), in his *Essays in Medieval Diplomacy and Administration* (London, 1981), pp. XVIII, 89-110; see esp. pp. 91-95.

of lands and other properties made without the consent of the convent.[51] Barbara Harvey considers that this document was probably a forgery concocted by the prior in the wake of his mission to the papal court in 1139, when he failed to secure the canonization of King Edward.[52] But even if the document is forged, it demonstrates that Osbert's criticisms of Gervase included allegations of high-handed alienations of monastic property. Probably Osbert derived his inspiration from one of the genuine bulls issued by Innocent on behalf of Westminster in December that year. This was addressed to Henry of Blois, bishop of Winchester and papal legate, ordering him to hear the complaint of the monks (conveyed to the *curia* by Prior Osbert) about the wrongful seizure of their goods, which had been unjustly detained, and to render them justice.[53] This question of the unjust detention of Westminster's property was evidently a major preoccupation of Prior Osbert's - since even the papal letter conveying Innocent's decision not to canonize King Edward added that instructions were being sent to Bishop Henry to ensure restitution of misappropriated lands.[54] If genuinely violent misappropriation had taken place, then surely restitution would have been ordered by the abbot's father, King Stephen, but there are no surviving writs in his name to this effect. It is likely, therefore, that Osbert's real complaint was that Abbot Gervase had been too compliant in face of pressures upon him to make grants to courtiers upon favourable terms. Barbara Harvey has carefully examined all of Gervase's leases which might support such allegations, which were later made against him. Her conclusion was that, while his judgement can still be challenged in a few cases, most of his leases were made on reasonable terms as regards Westminster's interests and most had the consent of the chapter.[55] Four charters of Gervase survive in which he is shown granting churches, in return for a pension.[56] In three cases, those of Bloxham (Oxon.); St. Agnes, and St. Matthew, Friday Street, both in London, the amount of the pension was identical with that acceptable to the abbey later in the twelfth century.[57] Evidence is lacking on the pension then required from the church of Islip, but the amounts subsequently required from the other three suggest that Gervase fixed their pensions at a rate beneficial to Westminster. Gervase might occasionally oblige an influential clerk by granting him a church, as in the case of Robert de Chesney and Bloxham,[58] but he expected a proper return. Hints of maladministration appear to have subsided as rapidly as they arose, and were not revived when changing circumstances at the papal *curia* might have encouraged them. Pope Eugenius III was not well disposed towards King Stephen, thanks to intensive lobbying at the *curia* by Abbot Bernard of

[51] *Westminster Abbey Charters*, no. 161.

[52] Barbara Harvey, 'Abbot Gervase de Blois and the Fee Farms of Westminster Abbey', *Bulletin of the Institute of Historical Research*, 40 (1967), pp. 128-9.

[53] *The Letters of Osbert de Clare*, ed. E. W. Williamson (London, 1929), p. 88, no. 20; calendared *Westminster Abbey Charters*, no. 159.

[54] *The Letters of Osbert de Clare*, pp. 87-8, no. 19; calendared *Westminster Abbey Charters*, no. 158.

[55] Harvey, 'Abbot Gervase de Blois and the Fee Farms of Westminster Abbey', pp. 127-41.

[56] *Westminster Abbey Charters*, nos. 253, 255, 257 and 270.

[57] *Westminster Abbey Charters*, no. 225; *Letters and Charters of Gilbert Foliot*, no. 462.

[58] *Westminster Abbey Charters*, no. 253.

Clairvaux,[59] but he addressed to Abbot Gervase two generally-worded confirmations of Westminster's property, including its churches and tithe income, and did not hint that anything was amiss in the abbey's administration.[60]

On 1 June 1157, Pope Adrian IV issued two major charters of confirmation for Westminster. One of these confirmed its three monastic cells, of Great Malvern (Worcs.); Hurley (Berks.) and Sudbury (Suffolk), together with the long list of the abbey's churches, chapels and tithe income which is discussed above.[61] Its companion document confirmed the abbey in its dignities, privileges, and estates, and ordered that anything taken by violence from Westminster, or contrary to its interests, was to be restored.[62] Properties had undoubtedly been taken from the abbey's control during the unrest in Stephen's reign[63] so that this bull was not issued in response to revived allegations of mismanagement.

The increasing permeation of Canon Law into England in the decades after 1170, combined with the application of the decrees of the Third Lateran Council (1179), resulted in Westminster's having recourse to the papal *curia* on a widening range of matters concerning its parish churches. These were increasingly subject to demands made upon them by the growing numbers of expert royal clerks employed in the king's *curia*. From the long pontificate of Alexander III, four papal letters specifically relate to Westminster's churches. The delegation charged with the second, and successful, mission to secure the canonization of King Edward evidently included both Walter the sacrist and Roger the infirmarer. With the support of Abbot Laurence, they took the opportunity to obtain papal confirmation of the more valuable, and also the more insecurely-held, of the churches pertaining to their respective offices. On 7 February 1161, the pope confirmed the church of Sawbridgeworth, to provide lights for the sacristy, and the churches of Battersea and Wandsworth for the benefit of the brethren of the infirmary.[64] The pope confirmed the abbey's three monastic cells in 1163,[65] but no further petition was made to him concerning Westminster's ecclesiastical properties until 1177. In April of that year he concluded a general confirmation of the abbey's properties and exempt status by prohibiting the alienation of five churches with their appurtenant chapels: Oakham (Rutland); Aldenham, Ashwell and Wheathampstead (Herts.); and Staines (Mddx.).[66] From the case study given below, it is plain that Oakham was insecurely held, because

---

[59] R.H.C. Davis, *King Stephen 1135-1154*, 3rd edn., (Harlow, 1990), pp. 96, 98-9, 101-3, 113-4. See, however, C. Holdsworth, 'St. Bernard and England', *Anglo-Norman Studies VIII*, ed. R. Allen Brown (Woodbridge 1986), pp. 151-2.

[60] *Patrologiae Latina* 180, cols. 1115-17, no. XC; *Papsturkunden in England* I, pp. 286-8, no. 47; calendared *Westminster Abbey Charters*, nos. 162-3.

[61] *Papsturkunden in England* I, no. 70.

[62] *Ibid.*, no. 69.

[63] A Saltman, *Theobald, archbishop of Canterbury* (London, 1956, reprinted New York, 1969), pp. 507-8, no. 277. See also *Westminster Abbey Charters*, note to no. 195.

[64] *Papsturkunden in England*, I, nos. 85-6.

[65] *Ibid.*, I, no. 101.

[66] *Ibid.*, I, no. 144.

royal clerks clearly regarded it as a prize worth having. The same applies to Battersea and Wandsworth (discussed below), which were consequently confirmed by Pope Lucius III *c.*1185, while in the abbatial vacancy which followed the death of Abbot Laurence in 1173, King Henry II presented his clerk Walter Map to the church of Ashwell, which he held until his death in *c.*1208-10.[67] Notwithstanding the papal ruling, these five churches remained at risk, since Westminster obtained another confirmation of them from Pope Clement III on 20 July 1189. This is found in a bull covering the abbey's wider ecclesiastical interests, since the pope also prohibited archbishops or bishops from saying mass, or holding synods, in St. Margaret's, Westminster; exempted the abbey from the jurisdiction of the bishop of London (a long-standing aspiration of the monks), and confirmed all pensions from churches which the abbey held before the Third Lateran Council.[68] Individual pensions might well be endangered if powerful men developed entrenched claims to occupy particular churches, hence the confirmation of such income, but so far as can be gauged, once a pension had been set at a given rate, no attempt was made to raise it, despite the current inflation. It might be regarded by the incumbent as having the same status as would rent from land, which was fixed by custom. In an effort to mitigate such a consequence the monks also obtained from Pope Clement, on 5 July 1189, permission to appropriate the tithes of their churches, when vacancies occurred, so long as they appointed vicarages (i.e. established a guaranteed income for the resident priest), and paid the synodal dues. These appropriations were permitted by the pope in order to enable the balance of the income to sustain the monks, and to enable them to offer hospitality, and to provide for the poor.[69]

Apparently there was an interval of almost ten years before the monks of Westminster were again in communication with the papacy over the specific issue of ecclesiastical sources of income. Early in 1199, a group of aggrieved monks evidently complained that Abbot William Postard was acting solely in his own initiative in such matters. On 24 April 1199, Pope Innocent III wrote that he had heard that benefices intended for the use of the chapter, and for the poor, had occasionally been assigned, at the instance of certain magnates, to their clerks. He now specifically ordered that the church of Sawbridgeworth, assigned to the sacristy, was not to be diverted to other uses, and that the same applied to any churches which were assigned to hospitality or to other pious uses.[70] Evidently the monastic delegation was dissatisfied with the wording of this mandate, because they obtained another, issued on 30 April 1199, prohibiting Abbot William from alienating the churches or other possessions pertaining to the whole community, without the consent of the chapter, or of the greater and wiser part.[71] But

---

[67] Pope Lucius's confirmation of Battersea and Wandsworth is printed in *Papsturkunden in England*, I, no. 232. For Walter Map and the church of Ashwell, see *Curia Regis Rolls*, VI, p. 93; Walter Map, *De Nugis Curialium*, ed. and transl. M.R. James, revised by C.N.L. Brooke and R.A.B. Mynors (Oxford, 1983), pp. 496-7.

[68] *Papsturkunden in England*, I, no. 262. For the impact of c.7 of the Third Lateran Council upon agreements concerning pensions, see for example *English Episcopal Acta VI, Norwich 1070-1214*, ed. C. Harper-Bill (Oxford, 1990), no. 332, note.

[69] *Papsturkunden in England*, I, no. 261.

[70] *Monasticon Anglicanum*, I, 312a, no. LXXIII. See also *Westminster Abbey Charters*, no. 185 note.

[71] *The Letters of Pope Innocent III (1198-1216) concerning England and Wales: a calendar, with an appendix of texts*, ed. C.R. Cheney and Mary Cheney (Oxford), 1967), p. 203, no. 113.

Abbot William was in a dilemma. After the death of his predecessor, the chapter had fought hard against the justiciar, William Longchamp, in order to secure the free election which resulted in Prior William Postard becoming abbot. In return, a heavy fine was exacted by influential persons, and consequently all Postard's managerial skills were needed to enable him to raise the 1,500 marks which were demanded.[72] From the complaints of the monastic delegation to the papal *curia* in 1199, it seems that presentations of baronial nominees to certain churches had also formed part of the bargain, hence the grievance of the monastic *seniores*. The delegation had set off for Rome with the overt mission of obtaining from the pope a confirmation of its considerable privileges and indulgences, something which was successfully accomplished on 23 April 1199.[73] The complaints of the *seniores* about the diversion to other uses of churches assigned to hospitality or to the infirmary revived from time to time,[74] but the abbey, like many major landholders at this period, was experiencing a prolonged financial crisis, which called for arbitrary solutions.

In those Westminster documents which survive in the names of visiting papal legates *a latere*, there is no mention of the abbey's administration of its ecclesiastical property, whereas Archbishop Theobald, in his capacity as papal legate, restored to Westminster the disputed church of Ockendon (Essex).[75] Another charter which he issued for Westminster in his capacity as legate confirmed the substance of several charters, in the name of King Stephen, which were possessed by the abbey. These alleged royal grants included a virgate of land pertaining to the church of Hanwell (Mddx.). All of the purported royal charters carry Theobald's attestation, but only one is genuine.[76] Towards the end of Stephen's turbulent reign, the abbey would be glad to have his grants confirmed by someone in unchallenged authority, but it is remarkable that Theobald was prepared to ratify grants which bore his attestation when he must surely have recalled that he had not witnessed them.

Suits concerning the abbey's churches occasionally came before papal judges-delegate. Disputes over St. Margaret Eastcheap, in London; Doddington and Thorpe (Lincs.) and Bloxham (Oxon.) were all resolved by compromise,[77] whereas the contest over Feering

---

[72] *Westminster Abbey Charters*, no. 186, note; Harvey, *Westminster Abbey and its Estates in the Middle Ages*, p. 64, note 2.

[73] *Letters of Pope Innocent III*, p. 203, no. 105. For the chief privileges granted before that date, see *Westminster Abbey Charters*, nos. 155, 162-3, 165, 172-5, 179-80.

[74] There is evidence that Innocent III responded in similar vein on 8 January, in some uncertain year of his pontificate. On this occasion, too, the monastic delegation was sent to secure confirmation of Westminster's privileges: *Letters of Pope Innocent III*, p. 189, nos. 1152-53; but cf. *Westminster Abbey Charters*, nos. 184-5, notes. Since these bulls of 8 January survive only as brief memoranda in a late muniment book, it may be that scribal errors were made. The grantor was perhaps actually Pope Celestine III, since a Westminster delegation is known to have been at the papal *curia* on 13 January 1192 (*Westminster Abbey Charters*, nos. 180-82). The antecedent complaints would therefore have been directed against Abbot William Postard. But if Innocent III was indeed the grantor, then the bulls were probably obtained in the course of a Westminster mission later than 1199, in which case the abbot reprimanded would be Ralph Arundel (who was removed from office in 1214).

[75] Saltman, *Theobald, archbishop of Canterbury*, p. 507, no. 276.

[76] *Ibid.*, pp. 505-6, no 275. See also *Westminster Abbey Charters*. no.197, note. King Stephen's grants are printed in *Regesta Regum Anglo-Normannorum III. 1135-1154*, ed. H.A. Cronne and R.H.C. Davis (Oxford, 1968), nos. 938-41.

[77] *Westminster Abbey Charters*, nos. 194, 209, 225.

(Essex) resulted in an outright verdict for Westminster.[78] The more prominent of these judges-delegate included both Gilbert Foliot, bishop of London,[79] and Hugh, bishop of Lincoln.[80]

The diocesan bishops with whom the abbot and monks of Westminster were most frequently in contact were those of London and Lincoln in which sees the abbey held a considerable number of parish churches. In the diocese of London, successive bishops are recorded instituting to the abbey's churches the parsons presented by the abbot and monks: to the churches of Greenford and Hanwell (Mddx.); South Benfleet (Essex); and to the London churches of St. Martin, Ludgate, and St. Magnus the Martyr.[81] From the diocese of Lincoln, records survive of the institutions of Westminster's nominees to the churches of Datchworth (Herts.); Deene (Northants.); Thorpe-on-the-Hill and Doddington (Lincs.) and Launton (Oxon.),[82] and from the diocese of Worcester an institution to the church of Todenham (Gloucs.),[83] one of the infrequent references in the Westminster archives of this period to its ecclesiastical property in the West Midlands. When making such presentations, care was taken to stipulate the pension payable to the abbey by the incumbent.[84] The abbey's main concern regarding its churches was therefore twofold: the preservation of its control over the advowson, and the guaranteed receipt of the annual pension due. Given that some presentations were in fact of compromise candidates, as much the choice of other interested parties as of the abbot and monks, the receipt of the pension was all that could be hoped for, along with a glancing recognition of the abbey's patronal rights.[85] Bishop Richard Fitz Nigel of London, and both Hugh (of Avallon), bishop of Lincoln and his successor Hugh (of Wells), expressed care for the maintenance of the vicarages of the churches to which they made presentations, while Godfrey de Lucy, of Winchester, was concerned that perpetual vicars should observe their obligations.[86] Several charters also emphasised the due observance of the rights of the diocesan bishop.[87]

Westminster is known to have contested rights of advowson in the royal court from the time of Abbot Walter onwards. It was ordained in the Constitutions of Clarendon (1164), Clause 1, that disputes over advowson were reserved for the royal court, and

---

[78] Ibid., nos. 207-8.

[79] The Letters and Charters of Gilbert Foliot, nos. 465-7.

[80] Jane Sayers, Papal Judges-Delegate in the Province of Canterbury 1198-1254: a study in Ecclesiastical Administration (Oxford, 1971), Appendix B, pp.354-5, no. 5; English Episcopal Acta IV: Lincoln 1186-1206, ed. D. Smith (London, 1986), no. 211.

[81] Westminster Abbey Charters, nos. 210, 215, 218, 220.

[82] Ibid., nos. 222-4, 227.

[83] Ibid., no. 233.

[84] Ibid., nos. 209, 217-18, 220, 222, 224, 226-27, 232.

[85] Ibid., nos. 209, 222-23, 315, 368.

[86] Ibid., nos. 214-15, 223, 227, 232.

[87] Ibid., nos. 198, 223-24, 227, 233.

there is evidence from 1184 of the amercement of those who took pleas concerning advowson to the church courts. Westminster's success in such lawsuits heard by the royal justices was variable.[88] Equal rights in the church of St. Magnus the Martyr were accorded to Westminster and to Bermondsey priory, whereas the advowson of Datchworth was lost in the time of Abbot William, although the abbey's entitlement to an annual pension was secured.[89] It proved necessary to defend the advowson of Parham (Sussex) both in the time of Abbot William and again during the abbacy of Ralph Arundel, in order to secure Westminster's title[90] and the abbey's claim to the advowson of Uppingham (Rutland) was also successfully upheld in Ralph's time.[91] This abbot was willing to offer rights of confraternity to litigants who relinquished their claim.[92] When abbots leased land to tenants, or granted estates to the monks, their charters carefully defined whether or not the advowson was being transferred. Increasingly, from the later twelfth century, it seems from final concords and from abbatial charters that there was an unwillingness to concede an advowson. In granting the Lincolnshire manor of Doddington to his knight William Picot, Abbot William excluded the advowson,[93] and he also reserved the advowson of Parham when granting the vill to the monks.[94] Abbot Ralph, on the other hand, included the advowson with his later confirmation to them.[95]

The men presented to the abbey's churches are rarely identified as clerks who were in the service of the abbot, but a few such identifications can be made from the time of Abbot Laurence onwards, since he presented his clerk, Mr. Maurice, to the church of Sawbridgeworth (Herts.), and his physician, Mr. Ralph de Beaumont (who also served King Henry II in this capacity) to the church of Bloxham (Oxon.).[96] Abbot Walter recompensed his clerk, Mr. Nicholas, with tithes in Bulby and Elsthorpe (Lincs.),[97] whereas Abbot Ralph and the convent granted houses in London to their clerk Alexander of Swerford, who can probably be identified with the Exchequer official of that name.[98] Any abbatial clerks who were appointed to Westminster's rural parish churches would be expected to be non-resident. They might have the cure of souls to a vicar, while they themselves continued to make their expertise available to the abbot. And yet the paucity

---

[88] *English Historical Documents II. 1042-1189*, ed. D.C. Douglas and G.W. Greenway, 2nd edn. (London, 1981), p. 767 no. 126. See also *The Treatise on the Laws and Customs of the Realm of England commonly called Glanvill*, ed. G.D.G. Hall (London, 1965), p. 4; Mary G. Cheney, *Roger, bishop of Worcester 1164-1179* (Oxford, 1980), p. 148.

[89] *Westminster Abbey Charters*, nos. 287, 320.

[90] *Ibid.*, nos. 325, 334.

[91] *Ibid.*, no. 338.

[92] *Ibid.*, nos. 334, 338.

[93] *Ibid.*, no.322.

[94] *Ibid.*, no. 326.

[95] *Ibid.*, no. 335.

[96] *Ibid.*, nos. 284, 286.

[97] *Ibid.*, no. 303.

[98] *Ibid.*, no. 327 and note.

of references to the presentation of the abbey's clerks to its livings may have an explanation other than that they wished to avoid episcopal censure for non-residence. The careers of Ralph de Beaumont and Alexander of Swerford illustrate the point that the able and ambitious men who served the abbot were liable to enter the king's service. There was an ensuing risk that the abbey might lose the churches held by such men, as demonstrated in the case of Bloxham, discussed below. A grant of tithes, or better still, of City real-estate held at an annual rent, would be a safer recompense.

Naturally there is no documentation of the pressure which kings might put upon the abbots to present royal clerks to the abbey's livings, or which influential clerks might personally bring to bear. And conversely there is no record of the reasoning which might prompt the abbot and convent, on their own initiative, to present such men to the abbey's livings. Only the results of such pressures and thought-processes can be discerned on occasion. Since the king of England governed a cross-Channel *regnum,* his clerks might well pursue a cross-Channel career. Men who in their earlier years were incumbents of Westminster's churches might later be elected to Continental bishoprics. Froger, bishop of Seez, held the church of St. James, Garlickhithe, in London, but in the mid 1170s he granted it to John, the nephew of the recently-canonized Thomas Becket. John, for his part, undertook to render an annual pension to the chamber of Westminster abbey. The agreement was witnessed by several of the archbishop's other kinsfolk, including his sister Mary, abbess of Barking. Since the bishop had twice acted on behalf of Henry II in negotiations involving Becket, his concession to John was perhaps made by way of expiation for injuries which the Becket family perceived that Froger himself had committed against the new saint.[99]

On occasion, Continental clerics could be positively helpful to Westminster. When Abbot Walter had trouble in asserting the abbey's claim to Ockendon church against the tenant of the manor, he wrote to Bartholomew, archbishop of Tours, to enlist his help. Bartholomew obligingly sent a letter addressed jointly to Archbishop Richard and to the justiciar, Ranulf Glanville. In this he gave evidence on behalf of Westminster, stating that he was a former incumbent of Ockendon church, to which he had been presented by Abbot Laurence at the request of Queen Eleanor.[100]

Property rights, rather than parochial administration, form the contents of virtually all Westminster's charters concerning its churches. There are in the archives a few charters of archdeacons, of London and of Huntingdon, concerning the induction of clergy to churches held by the abbey, but there are fewer such documents than might be expected from the later twelfth century. These have evidently been preserved because in each case there had either been some prior dispute between claimants or else a pension to define.[101]

In King John's reign, Stephen, parson of Hendon (Mddx.), was nearing the end of a long incumbency, during which the abbey's right to the advowson had not been asserted. No doubt on the prompting of the abbot and monks, he issued a charter to safeguard

---

[99] *Ibid.,* no. 365 and note.

[100] *Ibid.,* no. 463.

[101] *Ibid.,* nos. 368-9, 468.

Westminster's rights. This stated that his father Ralph possessed the church peacefully for several years, on the presentation of Abbot Laurence and the convent. When Ralph died, the abbot and monks, as true patrons, presented Stephen himself to that church, and he was instituted by Bishop Gilbert Foliot. Since then he had possessed the church of Hendon peacefully and prosperously for 43 years, rendering two marks annually to the sacristy of Westminster.[102] It is conjectural whether the bishop was aware that he was perpetuating a hereditary incumbency, but so far as the abbey was concerned, the security of its advowsons and parochial pensions was of more consequence that taking a stand on clerical celibacy among secular priests, or the ending of hereditary succession to benefices. Contemporaries elsewhere in England might share the abbey's financial priorities, although not all would have agreed that Westminster was pursuing its own best interests by relying on the old-style pension instead of appropriating the church and appointing a vicar.[103] A pension fixed some forty three years earlier could scarcely be bringing in a proper return, in view of the rate of inflation in King John's reign.

Many of Westminster's parish churches have left little trace in its twelfth-century records, but a few recur disproportionately often in the muniments of this period, usually because they were wealthy churches, prized by others besides the abbot and convent. A few brief case-studies will serve to illustrate the range of problems with which Westminster was faced.

The church of Bloxham (Oxon.) was assigned by Abbot Gervase, at the petition, and with the assent, of the chapter, to provide lights and other necessities for the sacristy. The incumbent, Robert de Chesney, would pay a pension of five marks annually. If he died, or changed his manner of life (i.e. if he became a monk), or if he was promoted to a higher dignity, then the church of Bloxham would revert to the abbey.[104] In fact, Robert (already archdeacon of Leicester in 1145/6) was elected bishop of Lincoln in December 1148.[105] The church presumably reverted to Westminster, but Abbot Laurence granted it to his physician, Mr. Ralph de Beaumont. The pension due to the sacristy was set at the old rate of five marks, perhaps because Laurence felt bound by precedent, or because he wanted to oblige an influential man, or because Ralph himself insisted on preferential terms. It appears that Laurence had suspicions as to his intentions, because his charter stated that Ralph was not to give this church to anyone, nor to alienate it in any way, except by permission of the abbot. If he died, or became a monk, or was promoted to the rank of bishop, then the church would revert to Westminster. In fact Ralph was drowned in the Channel in March 1170, when the royal entourage was crossing from Normandy. Bloxham should again have reverted to the abbey, and perhaps did so.[106] But some six

---

[102] *Ibid.*, no. 459.

[103] Harper-Bill, 'The struggle for benefices in twelfth-century East Anglia', pp. 126-8.

[104] *Westminster Abbey Charters*, no. 253.

[105] John Le Neve, *Fasti Ecclesiae Anglicanae 1066-1300 III. Lincoln*, compiled by Diana E. Greenway (London, 1977), pp. 2, 33.

[106] *Westminster Abbey Charters*, no. 286 and note. Seffrid, archdeacon of Chichester (1176-8), and dean (1180) was rector of Bloxham, possibly in succession to Ralph de Beaumont. (R.A.R. Hartridge, *A History of Vicarages in the Middle Ages*, (Cambridge, 1930), p. 209.

years later, Henry II's mistress, Rosamund Clifford, was buried in the nunnery of Godstow (Oxon.). Wishing to make a donation to this house, the king granted it the church of Bloxham, a benefaction which was severally confirmed by the archdeacon of Oxford; by Hugh bishop of Lincoln; by Pope Celestine III and by King Richard I. When Westminster tried to challenge this alienation, in 1197, the case came before papal judges-delegate, headed by Bishop Hugh, who upheld the nuns' title, provided that the annual pension of five marks continued to be paid to the sacristy.[107] Abbot William had no choice but to concede the church on these terms, and Abbess Juliana through her chaplain, solemnly undertook to pay the pension.[108] Senior royal servants had occupied the church for so long during the middle decades of the twelfth century, presumably in response to royal wishes, that Henry II would regard Bloxham as being at his own disposal.

Westminster's churches in Rutland also presented administrative problems. King Edward had intended that the whole geographical area which came to be known as Rutland would pass to the abbey on the death of his widow, but the land was retained by King William I.[109] He granted to Westminster only the tithes of Rutland, adding certain 'mother churches' with their appurtenant lands, which had previously been held by a royal clerk. This grant was confirmed by William Rufus.[110] The royal grant included tithes on the borders of Lincolnshire, in Bulby and Elsthorpe, which Abbot Walter granted to one of his clerks.[111] Abbot William granted twenty-one marks annually from two of the Rutland churches, Oakham and Hambleton, to sustain the monastic infirmary,[112] while in 1197/8, Hugh bishop of Lincoln confirmed both churches to the abbot and convent, so that the monks received annually from the incumbent a pension of thirty marks to maintain a hospital.[113] The pension, at the lower figure of twenty-one marks, was confirmed to the convent by Abbot Ralph, who also granted to a secular tenant a hereditary lease of a two-virgate holding appurtenant to Oakham Church, at a rent of 2s.[114] Another of the Rutland churches, Uppingham, was claimed by a local landholder, but in 1210, following an assize of darrein presentment, Abbot Ralph was adjudged the lawful possessor. When the defendant surrendered the advowson, he and his heirs were admitted to confraternity.[115] Given its distance from Westminster, Uppingham church presented problems of effective oversight, but by securing the goodwill of the former litigant, a local notable, the abbey could maintain its hold over the advowson.

---

[107] *Westminister Abbey Charters*, no. 225 and note.

[108] *Ibid.*, nos. 323, 481.

[109] Harvey, *Westminster Abbey and its Estates in the Middle Ages*, p. 47.

[110] *Westminster Abbey Charters*, nos. 45-6, 55-6.

[111] *Ibid.*, no. 303.

[112] *Ibid.*, no. 321.

[113] *English Episcopal Acta IV*, no. 212.

[114] *Westminster Abbey Charters*, nos. 336-7.

[115] *Ibid.*, no. 338.

Oakham and Hambleton were the real plums among Westminster's Rutland churches, and naturally enough they were prized by royal clerks. In this instance the clerk was James le Salvage. Evidently he regarded his rights as entrenched, because in 1206 he fined three palfreys for a grant from King John that the tenants of Oakham church and its appurtenant chapels were to be quit in perpetuity of suits of shire and hundred courts, and of customary payments to sheriffs, and their officers and bailiffs.[116] James had earlier served Archbishop Hubert Walter, and it seems that he moved to the royal clerical staff shortly after the archbishop's death in 1205.[117] Probably it was royal favour which prompted his institution to these rich churches, but Westminster asserted its financial claims and James swore in chapter at Westminster that he would render thirty marks annually to Westminster from Oakham church. He would try to obtain permission from the pope, and from the diocesan bishop (of Lincoln) to make this payment, but if they refused, he would grant in lieu thirty marks from his churches of Swanscombe and Stockbury (Kent).[118] These had presumably been acquired while he was in the service of the archbishop. He was also challenged over Hambleton church, and agreed to render twenty marks annually.[119] Westminster reinforced its control over Oakham church and its dependent chapels in the course of the thirteenth century, and also retained the advowson of Uppingham. But Rutland was remote from Westminster's main areas of interests, and it proved difficult to maintain its other ecclesiastical property there. Hambleton church and a dependent chapel were lost to the bishop of Lincoln; and following separate pleas in the royal court, the Norman priory of St. Fromond's won control of St. Peter's, Stamford, which James le Salvage had held of Westminster; and the Augustinian priory of Launde (Leics.) gained control of Wardley church.[120]

Nearer home, St. Mary Newchurch in London was lost under rather different circumstances. It was initially donated to the abbey, together with its appurtenant properties, by Alward the clerk of London, and was successively confirmed to Westminster by William I, twice by William II and again by Henry I.[121] The latter confirmations were probably requested in response to the seizure of the church by a royal officer, Eudo *dapifer*. He held it in 1100, and granted it to St. John's abbey, Colchester, which supported its own claims by a series of blatant forgeries.[122] Despite subsequent confirmations of the church to Westminster by King Stephen and by Pope Adrian IV, it was not recovered.[123]

---

[116] *Ibid.,* no. 150.

[117] *Ibid.,* no. 483 note.

[118] *Ibid.,* no. 482.

[119] *Ibid.,* no. 483.

[120] Emma Mason, 'Westminster Abbey's Rutland Churches', *Rutland Record,* 5 (1985), p. 165. For St. Fromond's other churches in Stamford, see D. Matthew, *The Norman Monasteries and their English Possessions* (Oxford, 1962, reprinted Westport, CT. 1979), p. 99 and note 2.

[121] *Westminster Abbey Charters,* nos. 40, 49, 54, 90.

[122] J. Armitage Robinson, *Gilbert Crispin, abbot of Westminster* (Cambridge, 1911), pp. 158-66.

[123] *Westminster Abbey Charters,* nos. 109, 166, 244.

Royal officers might be the chief predators on Westminster's churches in the London area, but in the countryside there was an added menace from thugs. The church of Wennington, in Essex, granted by Eadser and his wife Ealvida, was confirmed both by King Edward and by William I.[124] The wording of King William's writ indicated that unnamed persons - presumably rival claimants to the church - had tried to intrude into it, to the detriment of Westminster's interests. The problem recurred, and Henry I ordered the bishop of London to render justice on the armed men who broke into Wennington church by night.[125]

The complexities of feudal inheritance affected Westminster's control over Sawbridgeworth church in Hertfordshire, which lay on estates held by the family of de Mandeville. After the death of William I de Mandeville, his wife Margaret de Ria was married to the *curialis* Otwel Fitz Count, who thereby acquired Mandeville lands. Like many other notables, he was drowned in the wreck of the White Ship in November 1120, when his estates escheated in King Henry I. In consultation with the bishop of London, the king granted Sawbridgeworth church to Westminster abbey.[126] The king also ordered that all goods and supplies which the monks' officers at Sawbridgeworth could swear to be their demesne possessions should be quit of tolls - a privilege worth fining for, to bring it into line with the abbey's other properties, since Westminster had recently acquired a general exemption from toll on its lands overall.[127] The lands of the late Otwel Fitz Count were granted at farm by the king to the notable William d'Aubigny 'the Breton.' Evidently the monks of Westminster complained to him about harassment by his officers, since William issued a writ addressed to his French and English officials and tenants in Sawbridgeworth, reminding them that he was the custodian of Sawbridgeworth church and its property, and that the monks and their possessions there were to be left in peace. Any further dispute must be heard in his presence. His men must do right to the monks and their tenants, and render their tithes.[128] It is conjectural whether the monks at Sawbridgeworth simply constituted a small cell to administer the abbey's property there, or whether they also performed pastoral duties in the earlier twelfth century.[129]

William de Mandeville II succeeded to his family lands in 1166, and evidently raised

---

[124] Harmer, *Anglo-Saxon Writs*, no. 73; *Westminster Abbey Charters*, no. 35 and note.

[125] *Westminster Abbey Charters*, no. 84. For an analogous situation concerning a church of the abbey of St. Benet of Holme in this period, see Harper-Bill, 'Bishop William Turbe and the Diocese of Norwich', pp. 151-2.

[126] *Westminster Abbey Charters*, nos. 86, 203. On Otwel Fitz Count and the Mandeville inheritance, see also C. Warren Hollister, 'The Misfortunes of the Mandevilles', *History*, 58 (1973), pp. 18-28.

[127] *Westminster Abbey Charters*, nos. 85, 87.

[128] *Ibid.*, no. 469 and note.

[129] For discussion of pastoral activities undertaken by monks at this period, see Marjorie Chibnall, 'Monks and Pastoral Work: a problem of Anglo-Norman History', *Journal of Ecclesiastical History*, 18 (1967), pp. 165-72; Kemp, 'Monastic Possession of Parish Churches in England in the Twelfth Century', pp. 144-5; Giles Constable, 'Monasteries, Rural Churches and the *Cura Animarum* in the Early Middle Ages', in his *Monks, Hermits and Crusaders in Medieval Europe* (London, 1988), pp. 349-89; see also his 'Monastic Possession of Churches and 'Spiritualia' in the Age of Reform', in *Il Monachesimo e la Riforma Ecclesiastica 1049-1122*, Universita Cattolica del Sacro Cuore (La Mendola 1968, Milan 1971), Miscellanea del Centro di Studi Medievali, No. 6, pp. 304-35; T. L. Amos, 'Monks and Pastoral Care in the Early Middle Ages', in T.F.X. Noble and J. J. Contreni, eds. *Religion, Culture and Society in the Early Middle Ages*, (Kalamazoo, 1987), pp. 165-80.

the question of Sawbridgeworth church, which had been granted to Westminster by the king without the consent of William's forebears. But this grant was of long standing, and had been ratified by the ecclesiastical authorities.[130] All that remained for William to do was to confirm the church to Westminster, for the souls of himself and his kindred, and that of King Henry II.[131] Its revenues were assigned to the sacristy,[132] and when Abbot Laurence presented his clerk Mr. Maurice as perpetual vicar, it was stipulated that Maurice must pay £15 annually to the sacristy, and render episcopalia and other dues, besides rendering accounts of the stock of the attached lands. After the death of Maurice, everything would revert to the abbey, together with all stock and improvements. But if Maurice died just after making an annual payment, then the abbot would either pay it back to Maurice's assign, or else grant him custody until the following Michaelmas.[133] Evidently Maurice could drive a bargain as well as any abbot - after all, that is what Laurence employed him to do.

While abbatial clerks could be kept in check, this was not the case with the grandest of the king's employees. Time and again, Henry II's powerful official, Richard of Ilchester, recurs in the Westminster charters. Like others of Henry's *curiales*, he gained posts on both sides of the Channel. During the abbacy of Laurence, Richard was both archdeacon of Poitiers and parson of Westminster's church of Datchworth (Herts.). Acting together with Abbot Laurence, he requested the bishop of Lincoln to present the clerk Elias to the perpetual vicarage of that church. Elias, who was apparently a clerk of the Bishop, Robert de Chesney, undertook to pay an annual pension of two besants to Richard, but if the latter relinquished that church, or died, then the pension would revert to Westminster.[134] The reversion presumably occurred when Richard of Ilchester was elected bishop of Winchester in May 1173,[135] but the advowson was claimed in the time of Abbot William by another *curialis*, Hugh of Buckland. In 1192, Westminster agreed to surrender the advowson, provided that any clerk presented to that church would solemnly swear in chapter at Westminster that he would pay a pension of £1 to the abbot and convent.[136]

Whether or not Richard of Ilchester had played a part in weakening Westminster's title to Datchworth church is conjectural, but he was certainly up to no good as regards others of its properties. Westminster held land in Staines (Mddx.) by virtue of grants of King Edward and William I.[137] Probably in the reign of Henry II, some alienation occurred,

---

[130] *Westminster Abbey Charters*, nos. 170, 203.

[131] *Ibid.*, no. 470.

[132] *Ibid.*, nos. 170, 185, 211, 283.

[133] *Ibid.*, no. 284.

[134] *Ibid.*, no. 468. On Elias, see also no. 222 and note.

[135] John Le Neve, *Fasti Ecclesiae Anglicanae 1066-1300 II. Monastic Cathedrals*, compiled by Diana E. Greenway (London, 1971), p. 85.

[136] *Westminster Abbey Charters*, no. 320.

[137] Harvey, *Westminster Abbey and its estates in the middle ages*, p. 354; *Westminster Abbey Charters*, nos. 38, 53.

because, between 1188 and 1194, Westminster obtained from Herbert le Poer, archdeacon of Canterbury, a charter by which he restored land at Staines which his (unnamed) father took from the abbey and treated as his own demesne, and which Herbert himself later held of the abbot at a rent of ten shillings per annum. Herbert was shortly to be elected to a bishopric, and naturally he chose to be discreet about the fact that he himself was the son of a bishop - the deceased Richard of Ilchester.[138]

The churches of Battersea and Wandsworth had long been held by the abbey, and their income assigned to the infirmary,[139] but they also lay on the northernmost fringe of the bishopric of Winchester. At some stage during Richard of Ilchester's episcopate he seems to have claimed them, and (probably in response to protests) effectively restored them under the guise of a grant to sustain the infirmary.[140] His donation, or restoration, was confirmed in July 1193 by his successor at Winchester, Bishop Godfrey de Lucy. Perpetual vicars were to be instituted to both churches by the bishop of Winchester, to whom they would render all proper oblations, and they would also render the monks six marks annually from Wandsworth, and two marks from Battersea.[141] Powerful men could manipulate the abbey's ecclesiastical property to a fairly late date in the twelfth century, but eventually even they had to move with the times, and make proper provision for parish churches by appointing perpetual vicarages.

The foregoing accounts represent only a selection of the problems which Westminster experienced in controlling its churches. This survey is inevitably biased in its portrayal of the management of Westminster's churches. Those which were contested, for their high income, have left a trail of documentation - one which was not generated by the poorer churches - or those less desirable for other reasons. As a result of this imbalance attention has focused on eastern England, while Mercia is barely mentioned. Royal intervention - and the intrusion of royal clerks - is a theme which runs through the surviving records - but these again probably did not affect every church. On one level we can discern acceptance on the part of Westminster of the need to compromise principles for the sake of a guaranteed income, a more relaxed attitude fostered by the awareness that an ever more pervasive canon law, and the activities of energetic archdeacons, would defend their parochial rights in far flung dioceses. Moreover - although *curiales* could be a nuisance on some occasions, on others they - or their associates - could be exceptionally well-placed to further the interests of Westminster - and might consider that their own status was enhanced by doing so. Many of the Westminster charters of John's reign are attested by the Exchequer staff - the very men who so often heard lawsuits such as those of darrein presentment.[142] But parallel with this growing recourse to the lawcourts, and to civilized compromise, Westminster reserved the right to deploy spiritual weapons whose power was still feared by transgressors - and down to the last years of John's reign, solemn grants issued by its abbots occasionally concluded by threatening transgressors

[138] *Westminster Abbey Charters*, no. 457 and note.

[139] *Ibid.*, no. 169, 177.

[140] *Ibid.*, no. 231.

[141] *Ibid.*, no. 232.

[142] *Ibid.*, pp. 18-19, and extensive references given there.

with anathema.[143]

Westminster had been a privileged and highly favoured royal church in King Edward's reign - and was to become so again during the reign of Henry III. But intervening kings showed little positive enthusiasm for the abbey - reserving their generosity for the other churches which each individually chose to patronize. Westminster needed to husband its existing resources as best it could - not least its parochial churches.

*The Leverhulme Trust, the Nuffield Foundation and the British Academy generously funded successive phases of my work on the Westminster Abbey charters. I am grateful to the late Dr. Jennifer Bray for her assistance throughout this project; to Miss Barbara Harvey, Dr. Diana Greenway, Dr. Jane Sayers and Dr. David Bates for their views on the documents discussed here, and to the staff of Westminster Abbey library for much patient help. Miss Brenda Bolton, Dr. Janet Burton, Dr. Antonia Gransden, Dr. Brian R. Kemp and the Revd. Martin Dudley contributed bibliographical references, and Dr. Christopher Harper-Bill discussed with me the conclusions which he drew from his own work on the administration of parochial churches in East Anglia during the twelfth century, but I accept sole responsibility for any omission or misinterpretation.

---

[143] *Ibid.*, nos. 329, 335-6.

THE ABBEY OF BURY ST EDMUNDS AND NATIONAL POLITICS IN THE REIGNS OF KING JOHN AND HENRY III[1]

by

Antonia Gransden

The spiritual prestige and temporal power of St Edmund's abbey give the attitudes of its abbots and monks to national politics more than antiquarian interest. The reigns of King John and Henry III are of course especially noted for their constitutional crises, preceded by civil war. Taking each reign in turn, our present purpose is twofold: first, to examine and try to explain the attitudes of the abbot and monks to those crises, an enquiry which will entail some discussion of the possibility of their active participation; secondly, to consider the abbots' and monks' attitudes to King John and Henry in respect of matters other than national politics. At the outset it should be emphasized that the king in his personal capacity was not yet clearly distinguished from him as ruler.[2] On the contrary, he personally was recognised as the fountain head of political power and the hub of the administration. With regard to the abbot and monks of Bury, they could actually see the king carrying out his monarchal duties during his visits, frequent in Henry III's case, to the abbey. A good example is Henry's visit, discussed below, from 6 to 22 February 1267.[3] Another point to bear in mind is that the abbot did not necessarily share his monks' views. As far as is known he did so under King John, but during the baronial period in Henry III's reign he apparently differed from the monks on some issues. Nor is it certain that the monks were necessarily in unison. However, although they might be divided on domestic matters, the evidence suggests that they thought alike about national politics.

It is particularly hard to discover what the abbot and monks thought about the crisis of 1215 because no contemporary, general chronicle survives from Bury for that period. Although there is a very detailed account of a crisis at that time in the abbey's domestic history, the *Cronica de Electione Hugonis Abbatis postea Episcopi Eliensis*,[4] its purpose was limited to recording the disputed election of Hugh de Northwold to the abbacy in succession to Samson. Any sidelights it throws on the monks' attitudes to national events are purely incidental. Nevertheless, sidelights there do seem to be. This is not wholly surprising since King John played a crucial part in the dispute, while at the same time he was negotiating with the barons.

[1] I am deeply indebted to Dr John Maddicott for reading a draft of this article in typescript and making many useful comments. He was especially helpful with regard to Abbot Simon de Luton's political sympathies.

[2] Kantorowicz points out that, although in thirteenth century England the king as a private person could be distinguished from the crown, the king as king could not; E.H. Kantorowicz, *The King's Two Bodies, A Study in Medieval Political Theology* (Princeton, 1957), 359-66 *passim*. We are not here concerned with the king as a private person, but with the king as king, whether he was fulfilling his role as a ruler, or as a Christian monarch giving generous gifts to the church, or whatever.

[3] See below p.77. Many more examples can be found in the Calendars of public records.

[4] Printed *The Chronicle of the Election of Hugh Abbot of Bury St. Edmunds and Later Bishop of Ely*, ed., with an English translation, R. M. Thomson (Oxford Medieval Texts, 1974), henceforth referred to as *Electio Hugonis*.

The crisis at Bury was precipitated by the monks' election in 1211 of Hugh de Northwold as abbot without giving the king a choice of candidates in the customary way. John, therefore, refused his assent. Immediately the convent divided; one party supported the abbot elect and the other a rival candidate, the sacrist Robert de Graveley. The dispute,which involved appeals to archbishop, pope and king, dragged on until early in 1215 when John at last gave his assent to Hugh's election. The final negotiations took place at Runnymede, at the same time as John was coming to terms with the barons. In fact Hugh gained his victory only five days before the grant of the Magna Carta.

It is not impossible that some of the barons in opposition to John had espoused Hugh de Northwold's cause. There are two passages in the *Cronica de Electione*[5] which could be interpreted as suggesting that Hugh was a baronial sympathiser. Hugh, it says, met the king near London in the autumn of 1214 to ask him for his assent to the election:

> "My lord king," he said, "I have laboured hard to gain your favour and obtain an answer ... but so far have got absolutely nowhere." The king replied, "What do you want me to say? I have to consider myself and my crown before you and your honour. You have incited rebellion against me from which you can expect no good!" But when Hugh had, justifiably, stoutly denied this, the king added, "I was not thinking of you in particular, but especially of certain others."[6]

The other passage purports to record what the sacrist, Robert de Graveley, said when the king visited Bury a little later. At the end of his visit Hugh offered to conduct him out of the town. Robert burst out:

> "My lord king, this man who is with you and behaves as if he were the Elect, is doing his best to deprive you of your royal crown. Unless you immediately, with royal foresight, make him abandon this wicked scheme, it is to be feared that he will soon achieve what he has begun against the royal dignity."[7]

Both these passages may, of course, have had a limited, local connotation. Perhaps the references are only to the king's right to decide abbatial appointments, and not to the wider right which John claimed of ruling as he thought fit, free from the constraints which the barons sought to impose on him. Nevertheless, the passages could have the wider meaning. If so, it would indicate that Hugh sympathised with the baronial cause. His later career (he became bishop of Ely in 1229) lends weight to this idea. He is among

---

[5] For the election dispute see *ibid.*, xxv-xlvii. For the possible relationship of the dispute with John's conflict with the barons 1213-15 see *ibid.*, xliv-xlvi; *The Customary of the Benedictine Abbey of Bury St. Edmunds in Suffolk*, ed. A. Gransden (Henry Bradshaw Society, xcix, 1973), xxv; A. Gransden, 'A democratic movement in the abbey of Bury St Edmunds in the late twelfth and early thirteenth centuries,' *Journal of Ecclesiastical History*, xxvi (1975), 38-9. Cf. below p.69 and n.11.

[6] "Domine mi rex, laboraui sustinens super adquirenda gratia uestra et audire per uos seu per Wyntoniensem responsa, cum nullum adhuc penitus recepissem." Ad quem rex: "Quid uis ut dicam tibi? Ego potius diligo me et coronam meam quam te uel honorem tuum. Excitasti enim bellum contra me, a quo nequaquam bonum consequetur effectum." Quod cum dominus Hugo instanter negasset, ut decuit, adiunxit rex: "Non utique propter te specialiter hoc dixi, set et propter alios quosdam". '*Electio Hugonis*, 116.

[7] "'Domine mi rex, iste homo qui se gerit electum uobis assistens, modis omnibus et uiribus coronam regiam nititur a uobis auferre. Et nisi regia prouidentia idem ab hoc malicioso proposito celerius choeceatur recedere, timendum est ne huius rei exordium, hucusque contra regiam dignitatem ab eodem prosecutum, in breui sortiatur effectum". *Ibid.*, 126, 128.

the witnesses to the 1225 reissue of Magna Carta;[8] he attended the 1252 parliament which demanded redress of grievances before the grant of an aid, and personally took a firm stand against the king;[9] and in 1253, the year before he died, he was among those who witnessed the bishops' sentence of excommunication against violators of Magna Carta.[10]

Roger of Wendover, writing at St Albans, states that the barons met at Bury in 1214.[11] He asserts that they came ostensibly *causa orationis* and swore on the high altar that, if King John broke the terms of Henry I's coronation charter, they would all withdraw their fealty and wage war against him until he agreed to their demands. Since there is no concrete evidence corroborating Wendover's statement, it has been treated with scepticism. However, if in fact Hugh de Northwold and his party were pro-baronial, such a meeting is not wholly improbable. Although Wendover does not date the assembly, he places it after an entry for October 1214. This, combined with the statement that the barons met *causa orationis,* suggests the possibility that the barons gathered for the feast of St Edmund, king and martyr, on 20 November. The feast would have given the barons a chance for political discussion, under cover of the crowd that the occasion always attracted.

If some of the monks were pro-baronial, the question arises whether they took an active part in the opposition. A mandate which John issued on 18 December 1215, after he had re-established his power, could be interpreted as evidence of involvement: the king orders the prior and sacrist to destroy the defensive wall which they had built around the abbey and town, and to expel his enemies (both male and female) from the latter.[12] However, this mandate seems to indicate most strongly that the insecurity of the times had caused the monks to build such a wall, and only proves that at the time of writing some of the king's enemies were inside it. The intruders' presence reveals nothing about the monks' possible political activities. They probably could not have expelled the intruders even if they had wanted to. As will be seen, the abbot's authority over the town completely broke down during the Barons' War in Henry III's reign. The same may well have been the case in 1215 and 1216. Indeed, in 1216 Savary de Mauleon and the earl of Salisbury drove from Bury many 'knights and noble ladies' who had fled there; the fugitives then hid in the Isle of Ely.[13] However, it is not unlikely that the Bury monks

---

[8] J.C. Holt, *Magna Carta* (Cambridge, 1965), 357. It should be noted, however, that there are nineteen other abbots among the witnesses.

[9] Matthew Paris, *Chronica Majora,* ed. H.R. Luard (Rolls Series, 1872-83, 7 vols., henceforth referred to as *Chron. Maj.*), v. 330-2.

[10] *Ibid.,* v. 375.

[11] Roger Wendover, *Flores Historiarum,* ed. H.G. Hewlett (Rolls Series, 1886-9, 3 vols.), ii. 111-12; also Matthew Paris, *Chron. Maj.,* ed. Luard, ii. 582-3. For this meeting see: *Electio Hugonis,* 189-91; *Bury Customary,* ed. Gransden, xxv n.i; Gransden, 'A democratic movement,' 38 and n.l Cf. above p.68 and n. 5

[12] 'Datum est nobis intelligi quod vos firmatis villam vestram Sancti Edmundi que sita est in terra pacis. Et immo vobis mandamus que opus inceptum ad villam illam firmandam penitus prosterni faciatis eicientes ab eadem inimicos et inimicas nostras qui in ea sunt et excommunicationis vinculo innodantur, quia licet de privilegio Sancti Edmundi deberant homines ipsius et tenentes de feodo suo tuti existere, excommunicati tamen ex hoc in nullo meruerunt defensionem habere vel tutamen . . .'. *Rotuli Litterarum Patentium,* ed. T.D. Hardy (Record Commission, 1835), 161.

[13] Ralph de Coggeshall, *Chronicon Anglicanum,* ed. Joseph Stevenson (Rolls Series, 1875), 177-8.

would have been reluctant to expel anyone, whether the king's enemies or not, who took refuge in the vill. The area within the four crosses, comprising Bury and its suburbs, St Edmund's *banleuca,* was a sanctuary, 'a safe asilum and refuge for the afflicted',[14] and the privilege of sanctuary was one which the monks highly prized. It must, therefore, be concluded that even if the abbot and perhaps some Bury monks were baronial sympathisers, their role in the politics of John's reign was a passive one.

There are of course a number of well known reasons for King John's unpopularity with members of the religious orders and the secular clergy.[15] There is also the vexed question whether the growth among the religious and the seculars of ideas of communal control of those in authority within their own hierarchies influenced political developments.[16] On this subject St Edmund's abbey provides a fertile field for speculation. There is a striking parallel between the monks' attempts to limit abbatial power and the barons' attempts to restrain the king. The Bury monks' struggle with their abbot probably began before Samson's election in 1182; it certainly accelerated during his rule.[17] The autocratic methods which Samson used to achieve administrative reform provoked the monks to resist his encroachment on the convent's rights and possessions. The draft of an agreement survives which represents an attempt to codify the respective rights of abbot and convent (and of the principal obedientiaries whose individual rights and duties were also in dispute under Samson).[18] It begins by exhorting the abbot to rule

[14] *Chron. Maj.,* v. 413. Paris has a number of references to St Edmund's sanctuary. Having copied Ralph Diceto's notice of the siege and surrender of Leicester in 1173, he adds: 'Dispersi sunt nobiles civitatis; et quia regem nimis in defensione suae civitatis offenderant, locum tuti refugii quaerebant, ut minas et gravamen regis evaderent. Tunc igitur ad terram Sancti Albani Anglorum prothomartyris, et Sancti Edmundi regis et martyris, quasi ad sinum protectionis confugerunt. Quia tunc temporis tanta fuit eorum reverentia, ut eorum burgi omnibus transfugis asilium et tutam protectionem ab hostibus praebuerunt'; *ibid.,* ii. 289. Roger Wendover records that Hubert de Burgh's wife, Margaret, stayed at Bury, presumably for safety, on the fall of her husband in 1232, and that Hubert himself went there briefly during his flight (Wendover, *Flores,* ed. Hewlett, iii.36); Paris copies Wendover's account but adds that Hubert went to Bury 'gloriosi regis et martyris rogaturus de tribulatione consolationem' (*Chron. Maj.,* iii.226). Paris notes that the archdeacon of Lincoln took refuge at Bury during the quarrel between Boniface, archbishop of Canterbury, and the chapter of Lincoln cathedral in 1253. He writes: "Tandem tutum credens habere refugium apud Sanctum Edmundum, quia illic et in terra Sancti Albani consueverant esse afflictorum refugia et protectiones, . . . se ad protectionem dicti Sancti Edmundi contulit et civitatem.' ; *Chron. Maj.,* v. 413. The Bury chronicle observes that the bishop of Norwich, fleeing the anger of his baronial enemies in 1263, would not have escaped 'nisi ad sancti Edmundi libertatis cicius confuggisset presidium, nusquam tutum sibi inuenisset auxilium, tunc enim in conspectu baronum ualde preciosa fuit libertas sancti Edmundi '; *The Chronicle of Bury St Edmunds 1212-1301,* ed., with an English translation, A. Gransden (Nelson's Medieval Texts, 1964, henceforth referred to as *Bury Chron.*), 27. For the respect of the Disinherited barons for St Edmund's Liberty see *ibid.,* 38-9 (s.a. 1267). Cf. below p.79

[15] See in general, with further references: A.L. Poole, *From Domesday Book to Magna Carta 1087-1216* (Oxford, 1951), 443-9; David Knowles, *The Monastic Order in England* (Cambridge, 1949), 363-70. See also C.R. Cheney, 'King John's reaction to the Interdict on England,' *Transactions of the Royal Historical Society,* 4th series, xxxi (1949), 129-50, and idem, 'A recent view of the general interdict on England, 1208-1214,' *Studies in Church History,* iii, ed. G.J. Cuming (Leiden, 1966), 159-78. (Both articles are reprinted in C.R. Cheney, *The Papacy and England 12th-14th Centuries* (London, Variorum Reprints, 1982).).

[16] For a general survey of the growth of ideas of representation and consent in the secular church and religious orders see M.V. Clarke, *Medieval Representation and Consent* (London, 1936), 293-312. On the question of the influence of clergy and regulars on the development of lay representative institutions see: ibid., 16; Antonio Marongiu, *Medieval Parliaments, A Comparative Study,* translated and adapted by S.J. Woolf (London, 1968), 37-41; and most recently, with further references, J.H. Denton, 'The Clergy and Parliament in the Thirteenth and Fourteenth Centuries, ' *The English Parliament in the Middle Ages,* ed. R.G. Davies and J. H. Denton (Manchester, 1981), 88-108, esp. 92-3 and nn. 10,11.

[17] Gransden, 'A democratic movement,' 25-36.

[18] Discussed and printed in *Bury Customary,* ed. Gransden, xix-xx, xxxix,100-7.

wisely and to respect the convent's rights.[19] A number of the clauses reiterate the monks' right in chapter to sanction by consent specific administrative acts of the abbot, for example his appointment of prior, sacrist, cellarer and chamberlain.[20] It also has clauses designed to promote just administration in the Liberty. The contents of this draft agreement closely relate to points of contention which arose towards the end of Samson's abbatiate; this suggests that it was drawn up then or shortly after his death.

Since the text of the agreement is only a draft, we do not know whether it was formulated in full, nor, if it were, whether attempts were made to implement it. However, it was probably formulated and implemented at least in part. This is suggested by two pieces of evidence. The customary, compiled c.1234, to codify the abbey's domestic usages and religious observances, has citations from the agreement.[21] Moreover, the Bury chronicle records that in 1252 and 1287 the monks elected their own prior, by way of scrutiny.[22] Certainly, during the dispute over Hugh de Northwold's election, the convent tried to extend its control over the abbey's affairs. Peter the cellarer (a supporter of the abbot elect, Hugh de Northwold) insisted that any communication with the king concerning such affairs was to be discussed openly.[23] Hugh's party also insisted that the convent should know about and sanction all letters sent in its name,[24] and have control of the conventual seal.[25] A crucial issue in the election dispute itself was the idea of consent by the majority. At one stage, when papal judges delegate were trying to settle the case, they made the parties physically divide; the contemporary election account lists the 32 monks who supported Hugh and the 30 who opposed him.[26] It does not seem improbable that Hugh acceded to the terms of an agreement, the draft of which survives, in order to win more monks to his side and so strengthen his hand in the struggle to gain royal confirmation of his election.

Thus ideas of communal control at least in relation to the abbey's affairs were well developed at Bury in the early thirteenth century. Since Hugh de Northwold's final negotiations with John about his election took place at Runnymede just when the king was negotiating with the barons over Magna Carta, it does not seem impossible that the Bury monks saw an analogy between domestic and national politics.[27] It is even possible that they regarded the agreement discussed above as a kind of local Magna Carta. The reforms which the draft agreement outlines for the administration of the Liberty were designed to safeguard the rights of the individual and are reminiscent in a very general

---

[19] For an English translation of the passage see *ibid.*, xx.

[20] *Ibid.*, 100 and n. 1

[21] *Ibid.*, xxxiv-xxxv and n.1.

[22] *Bury Chron.*, 18 and n.4, 89.

[23] *Electio Hugonis*, 68.

[24] *Ibid.*, 16, 48.

[25] *Ibid.*, 42-6

[26] *Ibid.*, 84-6.

[27] Above p.70

way to Magna Carta, Clause 39.[28] The similarity of two of these draft reforms with other clauses in Magna Carter is quite marked. The draft agreement stipulates that the abbot's bailiff should be present in court at all cases touching the crown, to ensure that justice is done in accordance with the custom of the realm; if necessary he should give evidence in the interests of justice and truth, and for this he should take no emolument.[29] This recalls two clauses in Magna Carta: Clause 36 stipulates that 'Nothing shall be given or taken for writ of inquisition of life or limb, but it shall be freely given and not refused;'[30] and in Clause 40 the king undertakes not 'to sell or deny or delay right or justice to anyone.'[31]

Finally, it should be mentioned that there is a similarity between the domestic history of Bury and that of St Albans in the early thirteenth century. Like the monks of Bury, those of St Albans tried to limit their abbot's power.[32] Their chronicler, Roger Wendover, is noted for his extreme hostility to King John, and no doubt reflected political opinions current in his community. Whether St Albans had any influence on opinions at Bury is impossible to say. However, the monks of Bury must have been in touch with those of St. Albans at about this time. The papal judges delegate appointed to try to settle the Bury election dispute held a court in the parish church of St Peter in St Albans from 26 July until sometime in August, 1214.[33] The court was attended by six delegates from Bury, three (the cellarer and two other monks) representing the party of the elect, and three (the elect's rival himself, that is the sacrist Robert, and also the precentor and infirmarer). It is more than likely that they would have lodged in St Alban's abbey. As mentioned above, Wendover has unique information, perhaps true, of a political event at Bury in 1214, which would probably have taken place in October. Wendover's successor as St Albans' chronicler, Matthew Paris, was, as will be shown below,[34] exceptionally well informed about, and sympathetic to St Edmund's abbey. Such clues suggest close contact between the two monasteries in King John's reign and in Henry III's.

Whatever the attitude of the abbot and monks of Bury to King John's rule, they do not appear to have been unduly antagonistic to him personally as king. The link between the kings of England and St Edmund's monastery had always been close, second only to the kings' link with Westminster abbey. Besides appreciating the abbey's importance in

---

[28] 'Nullus liber homo capiatur, vel imprisonetur, aut disseisiatur, aut utlagetur, aut exuletur, aut aliquo modo distruatur, nec super eum ibimus, nec super eum mittemus, nisi per legale judicium parium suorum vel per legem terre.' *Magna Carta*, c. 39.

[29] 'Ballivus tamen abbatis in omnibus agendis, quae spectant ad coronam, interesse debet et providere, ut iusticia in omnibus ubique exhibeatur et fiat secundum consuetudinem regni et patriae et, si opus fuerit, testimonium perhibeat iusticiae et veritati sed nichil ab hoc percipiet emolumenti. *'Bury Customary*, ed. Gransden, 102-3.

[30] 'Nichil detur vel capiatur de cetero pro brevi inquisicionis de vita vel membris, set gratis concedatur et non negetur.' *Magna Carta*, c.36.

[31] 'Nulli vendemus, nulli negabimus aut differemus rectum aut justiciam.' *Ibid.*, c.40.

[32] *Gesta Abbatum Monasterii Sancti Albani*, ed. H.T. Riley (Rolls Series, 1867-9, 3 vols.), i. 247-58 *passim*. For this and similar movements early in the thirteenth century at Evesham and Christ Church, Canterbury, see Gransden, 'A democratic movement,' pp. 27-8 and n.2. For such attempts to limit abbatial authority in general, with mention of the Evesham and St Albans cases, see Knowles, *Monastic Order*, 412-17.

[33] *Electio Hugonis*, 90-3, 96-9, 180.

[34] Pp.81-82, 85-86.

temporal affairs, the kings were attracted by the flourishing cult of St. Edmund. King John was drawn 'by devotion and a vow' to visit Bury after his coronation. It is true that Jocelin of Brakelond considered both John's offering at the shrine and his parting gift to the monks as inadequate recompense for the cost of the visit,[35] but otherwise John seems to have been on good terms with the abbot and monks. In December, 1203 he granted them 10 marks annually at the Exchequer for the repair of the shrine; this grant was in return for a life interest in a sapphire and ruby which he had given to St. Edmund.[36] Then, in 1208, when John took the property of all monasteries into his hands at the beginning of the Interdict, he returned St Edmund's lands, revenues and goods within three weeks. He did this out of reverence for St. Edmund. (However, the condition was attached that the abbot should answer to the king for all proceeds, save those for his own rightful necessities, 'estovers').[37] Abbot Samson himself does not seem to have regarded John with disfavour, since he bequeathed him his palfreys and jewels.[38] His successor, Hugh de Northwold, even after his long struggle with the king over his election, dined amicably with him when at last he obtained royal confirmation.[39]

There is more evidence about the attitudes of the abbot and monks of Bury St Edmunds to Henry III than there is with regard to King John. Nevertheless, it is scanty and hard to interpret. E.F. Jacob and F.M. Powicke both believed that the abbot and, by implication, the monks were pro-baronial.[40] H.W.C. Davis on the other hand described them as 'royalist.'[41] This discrepancy was partly because all three failed to understand that the abbot might hold different opinions from those of his monks. Moreover, they were perhaps also misled because the monks changed their views with remarkable frequency and rapidity, or so it would appear; at one time they seem to favour the baronial opposition, at another the king. Therefore, an historian today can pick evidence to 'prove' either that they were pro-baronial or royalist. It will be concluded below that the fluctuations in the monks' attitudes were not the result of inconsistency, but of stable principles and preoccupations reacting to different circumstances.[42]

[35] *The Chronicle of Jocelin of Brakelond*, ed., with an English translation, H.E. Butler (Nelson's Medieval Classics, 1949), 116-17. Jocelin's chronicle ends in 1202, but just possibly he wrote a few years later, in which case he could have written during the Interdict (1208-1214) which might have biased him against the king.

[36] *Rot. Litt. Pat.*, ed. Hardy, 37b. This writ was dated 18 December, at St. Edmunds. Two days later John, 'on account of reverence for the blessed martyr,' granted to the abbot and convent that they might recover all lands and tenements alienated by the keepers of their manors without the assent of the abbot and convent.

[37] See: the annals of Bury St Edmunds in *Ungedruckte Anglo-Normannische Geschichtsquellen*, ed. F. Liebermann (Strassburg, 1879), 146; *Rotuli Litterarum Clausarum*, ed. T.D. Hardy (Record Commission, 1833-44, 2 vols.), i. 110a; C.R. Cheney, 'King John's reaction to the Interdict,' 131-2.

[38] *Curia Regis Rolls*, vi. 189. Cf. W.L. Warren, *King John* (London, 1961), 172.

[39] *Electio Hugonis*, 171.

[40] E.F. Jacob, *Studies in the Period of Baronial Reform and Rebellion, 1258-1267* (Oxford Studies in Social and Legal History, ed. Paul Vinogradoff, viii, Oxford, 1925), 293-4, 303; F.M. Powicke, *King Henry III and the Lord Edward* (Oxford, 1947, 2 vols.), ii. 557.

[41] H.W.C. Davies, 'The Commune of Bury St Edmunds, 1264,' *English Historical Review*, xxiv (1909), 314.

[42] Pp.86.

The thirteenth-century chronicle of St Edmund's abbey[43] can be taken as a touchstone of the monks' political outlook - the monks' not the abbot's, since it was written for the convent.[44] Such a monastic chronicle was a corporate production and must, therefore, have reflected the views of at least the most influential part of the community. The fact that nearly all the thirteenth century monastic chronicles reveal similar attitudes, which suggests some unanimity in outlook among the religious, supports this conclusion. Unfortunately it was not until c.1264 that the Bury monks began to keep a contemporary record of current events in any detail.[45] The chronicler at that time was John Taxter whose chronicle covers the period from the Creation to 1264: two continuations, from 1265 to 1296 and from 1296 to 1301, were subsequently added.[46]

Taxter rarely comments on people or events, but he does drop an occasional hint. In his account of the Barons' War he is critical of the king and queen, and treats Simon de Montfort as a hero and martyr. He emphasises the severity of the king and his party after their victory at Evesham. Henry, the Lord Edward and the *curiales* extorted money from all prelates, taking 'nearly 800 marks from the church of St Edmund'.[47] Taxter's view of Henry was coloured by the xenophobia so typical of his age. Commenting on Henry's harsh treatment of his vanquished opponents, he asserts that he arbitrarily distributed their lands to aliens as well as to Englishmen.[48] Similarly, he remarks that had not the barons guarded the sea and coasts in 1264 against threatened invasion by the queen's forces from France, 'England would have been conquered by foreigners.'[49] Taxter's attitude to Simon de Montfort was typical of the chroniclers of the day. De Montfort was a hero - even, because of the circumstances of his death, a martyr. Like some other chroniclers, Taxter claims that de Montfort's body worked miracles.[50] It is likely that Taxter's pro-Montfortian attitude was shared by the other Bury monks. This likelihood would be the greater if, as recent research suggests, one of the two surviving motets in Simon's honour was composed in the abbey shortly after his 'martyrdom.'[51]

The question arises whether the abbots of Bury in Henry's reign were likewise pro-baronial. Henry de Rushbrook, abbot 1233-1248, did on occasion cooperate with the

---

[43] For the printed edition see abovep.70 n.14.

[44] The author of the first continuation, 1265-96, was almost certainly connected with the sacrist's office and possibly was William de Hoo, sacrist 1280-94. See A. Gransden, *Historical Writing in England, [i], c.550-c.1307* (London, 1974), 396.

[45] See *Bury Chron.*, xix-xx.

[46] Taxter's chronicle and its continuations is discussed in *ibid.*, pp. xvi-xxiv.

[47] *Ibid.*, 31-2. See below p.76 and nn. 67-69.

[48] *Ibid.*, 32.

[49] *Ibid.*, 29. See also below p.80 and nn. 100, 101.

[50] *Ibid.*, p.33. For other mentions of Simon de Montfort's posthumous miracles see: the Furness chronicle in *Chronicles of the Reigns of Stephen, Henry II, and Richard I*, ed. Richard Howlett (Rolls Series, 1884-9, 4 vols.), ii. 548; the Canterbury/Dover chronicle in *The Historical Works of Gervase of Canterbury*, ed. William Stubbs (Rolls Series, 1879-80, 2 vols.), ii. 243; *Miracula Simonis de Montfort* in *The Chronicle of William de Rishanger, of the Barons; Wars. The Miracles of Simon de Montfort*, ed. J.O. Halliwell (Camden Society, original series, xv, 1840), 67-110.

[51] See P.M. Lefferts, 'Two English motets on Simon de Montfort,' *Early Music History*, i (1981), 221.

baronial opposition. In 1240 he, together with the abbot of Battle, was the spokesman for the other abbots in their resistance to the papal subsidy, which Peter Rubeus was collecting with the king's backing.[52] And in 1244 he was one of the council of twelve chosen to examine the king's financial needs and to insist on redress of grievances as a prerequisite for the grant of a subsidy.[53] There seems to be no evidence about the political views of the next abbot, Edmund de Walpole (1248-56). However, there is information with regard to Simon de Luton whose abbacy (1257-79) covered the crucial years of the baronial administration and rebellion. And he, it seems, did not agree with his monks about national politics. He was apparently a royalist, a man on whom Henry could rely. It is true that in January 1259 he was one of the deputation of four appointed to meet Richard of Cornwall on his return from Germany, in order to discover the reason for his sudden appearance and to receive his oath to observe the Provisions of Oxford.[54] But although this deputation was appointed when the barons were in power, two other members, Peter of Savoy (one of Henry's foreign relatives) and John Mansel (the most influential of the king's clerks) were leading royalists. Perhaps the barons intended, by selecting royalists, to reassure Richard and make him more amenable. Again, Abbot Simon was summoned to Simon de Montfort's parliament in January 1265, but so were the heads of nearly all the religious houses of any consequence.[55] De Montfort was seeking as broad a base as possible to support his precarious power.

There is positive evidence that Henry trusted Abbot Simon. In May 1259, when, despite the fact that the barons were in control of the adminstration, Henry seems to have kept responsibility for procuring the ratification of the Treaty of Paris, Abbot Simon was sent with three others on an embassy to France to negotiate. Two of his companions, Giles de Bridport,[56] bishop of Salisbury, and Walter Bronescombe, bishop of Exeter,[57] were active supporters of Henry. Similarly, on 27 March, 1260, when Henry for the first time had good reason to fear the outbreak of civil war and was himself about to return from France with mercenaries, he wrote to Hugh Bigod, the justiciar, instructing him to summon various ecclesiastical and lay magnates. They were to meet him in London with their feudal service on 25 April. The baronial leaders were excluded. Only two abbots were among those summoned, the abbot of Glastonbury (Roger Forde) - and Simon de Luton.[58] Again, in October 1261, at another time of political tension, Abbot Simon was among those summoned with his feudal service. Although on this occasion the summons was much more all-inclusive than in March 1260, the leaders of the opposition were

---

[52] *Chron. Maj.*, iv. 35-6. See: W.E.Lunt, *Papal Revenues in the Middle Ages* (Columbia University Press, 1934, 2 vols., repr. New York 1965), i. 79 and nn. 181-5; idem, *Financial Relations of the Papacy with England to 1327* (Cambridge, Mass., 1939), 197-205 (esp. 202), 612.

[53] *Chron. Maj.*, iv. 362.

[54] *C Lib R, 1251-60*, 504. Cf. *Chron. Maj.*, v. 732, and N. Denholm-Young, *Richard of Cornwall* (Oxford, 1947), 98.

[55] *CCR. 1264-8*, p. 85.

[56] See R.F. Treharne, *Documents of the Baronial Movement of Reform and Rebellion 1258-1267*, ed. I.J. Sanders (Oxford Medieval Texts, 1973), 174 and n. 1, 76.

[57] See *ibid.*, 182 n. 3.

[58] *CCR. 1259-61*, 157-8. Cf. Treharne, *Documents*, 182 and n.2, and idem, *The Baronial Plan of Reform 1258-1263* (Manchester, 1932, repr. with additional material 1971), 226.

omitted.[59] Finally, in May 1267, when Henry was investing London against the earl of Gloucester, Abbot Simon and his knights were with the royal army at Stratford Langthorn (in Essex).[60]

E.F. Jacob, in the belief that Abbot Simon was pro-baronial, examined the plea rolls for 1265 to discover whether Simon used his influence to induce men within St Edmund's Liberty to actively support the barons' cause. In view of the evidence cited above, it is not surprising that he could find no evidence to support a conclusion 'that direct pressure was brought to bear by the abbot on his tenants.[61] On the other hand there were important baronial supporters within St Edmund's Liberty. The steward of Liberty, Henry de Hastings, was one of the most faithful of Simon de Montfort's supporters and one of the most obdurate of the Disinherited.[62] He finally submitted to the Lord Edward on 13 July, 1267;[63] He was pardoned on 27 July, on condition that he observed the terms of the Dictum of Kenilworth,[64] and on 27 August Abbot Simon was ordered to give him seizin of the stewardship.[65] Clearly Abbot Simon had no control over Hastings's political activities, any more than he did over those of Richard and Gilbert de Clare, successively earls of Gloucester, both of whom had holdings within St Edmund's Liberty.[66]

Nevertheless, the fact has to be explained that the king treated Abbot Simon firmly, even severely, during the period from the autumn of 1265 until the spring of 1267. On 8 September 1265 Henry imposed fined on a number of prelates. Simon suffered particularly; he had to pay 800 marks to have the king's good will.[67] Meanwhile his barony was taken into the king's hands. However, it was restored little more than a fortnight later, on 24 September; the abbot was to hold it 'until our next parliament on the feast of St Edward' (5 January).[68] On 2 January, 1266, Simon paid £266 13s. 4d. (that is 400 marks, half the fine).[69] The Bury chronicler complains that the convent was made to pay the other half, 'although only the abbot had been accused in the king's

---

[59] CCR. 1259-61, 498. Cf. Treharne, Baronial Plan, 268-9

[60] CUL MS Ff.ii.29, f.87 Cf: the Dunstable chronicle in Annales Monastici, ed. H.R. Luard (Rolls Series, 1864-9, 5 vols.), iii. 246; Flores Historiarum, ed. H.R.Luard (Rolls Series, 1890, 3 vols.), iii. 16; the chronicle of Thomas Wykes in Ann. Mon., ed. Luard, iv. 202; and Powicke, Henry III and the Lord Edward, ii. 543.

[61] Jacob, Studies in the Period of Baronial Reform and Rebellion, 303-7.

[62] See: Treharne, Documents, 284-5 and n.24, 328-9 and n. 29; idem, Baronial Plan, 273, 302, 323, 335.

[63] CPR, 1266-72, 152; CCR, 1264-8, 379.

[64] CPR, 266-72, 149.

[65] The 'Kempe' register of St. Edmund's abbey, BL MS Harleian 645, f. 78.

[66] For a list of the manors of Richard de Clare, earl of Gloucester 1243-62, in St Edmund's Liberty see ibid., f.212ᵛ. For his dispute with the abbot over the manors of Icklingham and Mildenhall see: ibid., f. 188ᵛ; CUL MS Mm. iv. 19, ff. 18ᵛ-19; BL MS Additional 14847, ff. 75ᵛ - 76ᵛ. See also: Bury Chron., p.24 (and n.3 for further references); M.D. Lobel, The Borough of Bury St. Edmunds (Oxford, 1935), 17, 132. For baronial supporters who held land in Suffolk see Jacob, op. cit., 298-9.

[67] Bury Chron., 31.

[68] CCR. 1264-8, 134.

[69] CPR. 1258-66, 525.

court. ' This was because 'the convent's men as well as the abbot's had helped guard the coast against the queen.'[70]

Henry again took strong action against Abbot Simon in the spring of 1266. He sent John de Warenne and William de Valence to Bury. They arrived on 27 May 'unexpectedly with a great band of retainers to seek out the king's enemies.'[71] The 'enemies' were Disinherited barons from the Isle of Ely who were hidden in the town and freely sold their booty there.[72] Warenne and Valence summoned the abbot and burgesses and accused them of favouring the rebels. However, at the inquest Simon cleared himself and the convent of any complicity and incriminated the townsmen, and the charge against him was dropped. The townsmen had to pay a fine of 200 marks, besides promising the abbot and convent £100 for negotiating the settlement.[73] At the same time Henry instructed Simon to appoint a new alderman for the town and also janitors for its gates 'in order to provide for its and the neighbourhood's tranquileity.' He was also to inquire who had harboured the king's enemies and their booty and under what circumstances.[74]

The visit of Warenne and Valence did not end Abbot Simon's troubles during the resettlement of the kingdom after the Barons' War. The Dictum of Kenilworth (31 October 1266) did not bring immediate peace. Some areas, including the Fenland, remained in a turbulent state for nearly a year longer. During this period Henry had to struggle to reassert his authority and to impose law and order. He stayed at Bury from 6 to 22 February 1267. While there he made a further effort to discredit the De Montforts by submitting his case against them to the arbitration of Louis of France.[75] But his main preoccupation was with the pacification of the kingdom. He issued numerous writs of protection and granted lands of rebels to loyal subjects, and pardoned rebels who had submitted.[76] He also summoned the feudal army to assemble at Bury for the siege of the Isle of Ely which was still being held by obdurate rebels, the Disinherited.[77] Unfortunately, disaffection and unrest were still rife in the town of Bury itself. On the night of 22 February the legate Ottobon, just after he had held a council at Bury to excommunicate the Disinherited, was so scared by 'certain rumours,' that he returned to London on the next day.[78] The king left on the same day, and pitched camp outside

---

[70] *Bury Chron.*, 32.

[71] *Ibid.*, 34-5.

[72] Jacob, *op. cit.*, p. 238, cites the case of an Ipswich merchant, who had helped the king besiege the Isle of Ely, and was imprisoned by the Disinherited in Bury.

[73] *CPR, 1258-66*, 604; *Bury Chron.*, 35.

[74] *CCR. 1264-8*, 197. Copies are in a number of the Bury registers: CUL MS Mm.iv. 19, f. 190ᵛ; BL MS Harleian 638, f. 36; BL MS Harleian 645, ff. 151-151ᵛ. Cf. *Bury Chron.*, 34-5, and belowp.82.

[75] *CPR, 1266-72*, 130.

[76] *Ibid.*, 32-9 passim, 129-31 passim.

[77] *Ibid.*, 33; *CCR. 1264-8*, 294, 302, 360. Cf. *Willelmi Rishanger, quondam Monachi S. Albani ... Chronica et Annales*, ed. H.T. Riley (Rolls Series, 1865), 50.

[78] *Bury Chron.*, 37. For this council and the legate's negotiations with the Disinherited see Rishanger, *Chronica*, 50-6. Cf. *Councils and Synods*, ii, 1205-1313,ed. F.M. Powicke and C.R. Cheney (Oxford, 1964, 2 pts), ii, *1265-1313*, 732-5.

Cambridge for the siege of the Isle.

At some stage Henry had taken the Liberty of St Edmund's *banleuca*[79] into his hands. He did so 'because of certain transgressions done to us and our men by certain people in the Liberty during the disturbance in the realm.'[80] On 21 February he commissioned two royal justices, Stephen de Eddeworth and John le Bretun, to hold an inquest in the abbot's presence about those charged with robberies and other trespasses 'within the town and without', and to take their moveables and extend their lands.[81] However, during his stay he apparently reached an agreement with Abbot Simon. In return for having the king's goodwill and for the restoration of the Liberty of the *banleuca*, Simon promised to pay a fine of 200 marks (in the event, his payments on 27 February,[82] 10 March[83] and 16 March,[84] 1267, amount to £200). Having restored the *banleuca*, Henry, at Simon's request, on 9 March commissioned the royal justice, John le Bretun, and 'whomever else the abbot shall depute' to inquire about trespasses in the Liberty and to do justice.[85]

However, these three occasions, in 1265, 1266 and 1267, when Henry treated Abbot Simon with a heavy hand, do not prove that Simon was ever disloyal to him. According to the Bury chronicler, in 1265, he was fined and temporarily forfeited his barony because his men and the convent's had helped guard the coasts against the queen.[86] But, since the legitimate, though baronially controlled, government issued the mandate (9 July 1264)[87] for the defence of the coasts. Simon would have had no choice but to obey. The other two cases, in 1266 and 1267, were different. Then Henry interfered with the abbot's administration of the *banleuca*, but his actions should be seen as corrective, even supportive, rather than punitive. This is so despite the fact that in 1267 he again fined Abbot Simon. His purpose in 1266 and 1267 was to ensure that St Edmund's Liberty was an orderly, loyal franchise within the kingdom; it should neither be the scene of disorder nor harbour rebels. Henry wanted the abbot to achieve the objective; if he could not, royal power would intervene to help. There is no question that Abbot Simon would not if possible have ruled the Liberty as Henry wished; the problem was that sometimes he was powerless to do so.

---

[79] The evidence that Henry had taken the *banleuca* into his hands is the fine for its restoration. See below. The writ of 16 March makes it clear that it was the Liberty of the *banleuca* which was in question, not that of the eight and a half hundreds. The relevant passage states that the fine was 'pro villa sua de Sancto Edmundo rehabenda que capta fuit in manum nostram pro quibusdam transgressionibus factis in eadem. ' Below and n. 84.

[80] See the letters patent cited in the next note.

[81] *CPR. 1266-72*, 131. Cf. Lobel, *The Borough of Bury St. Edmund's* 130.

[82] *C Lib R, 1260-7*, 263.

[83] *CCR, 1264-8*, 298.

[84] Fine Roll, 51 Henry III, PRO, C 60/64, membrane 6.

[85] *CPR, 1266-72*, 45.

[86] Above pp.76-77 and n.70.

[87] *CPR, 1258-66*, 360-1.

As has been seen, in 1266 Abbot Simon was accused, along with the burgesses, of favouring the king's enemies because the Disinherited were freely hiding and selling their loot in Bury. However, Simon certainly had no sympathy with them. Possibly the Disinherited came for safety. If so, Simon might have hesitated to expel them because of St Edmunds' privilege of sanctuary.[88] However, it is much more likely that he could not in any case have expelled them because the abbey's control over the town was tenuous at that time. Already before the battle of Lewes (4 May 1264) the abbot and convent were at loggerheads with a powerful group of townsmen. The latter had exploited the disturbed condition of the country to wrest control of the town from the abbey. They refused to obey the alderman and officials appointed by the abbot, and elected instead their own alderman and bailiffs. The ringleaders were a number of young men organized in a guild, the 'Guild of Youth.'[89] So serious was the disturbance that a baronial partizan, William le Blund, came to Bury to mediate between the parties.[90] Despite his efforts trouble with the town persisted after the battle of Lewes. At Abbot Simon's request the king issued a writ on 29 October, 1264, commissioning Gilbert de Preston and William de Boville to hold an inquest into the injuries to, and transgressions against, the abbot and his church, which were to the detriment of his Liberty, done by certain men of the vill.[91] The townsmen, fearing for their liberties, submitted[92] and came to an agreement with the abbot.[93]

There is a contemporary tract describing the activities of the 'Guild of Youth.'[94] The surviving text is incomplete owing to the loss of a folio. It was written after the battle of Evesham (4 August, 1265), which it mentions, but nothing else is known for certain about its date. However, possibly its purpose was to exonerate the abbot when in May 1266 he was accused by John de Warenne and William de Valence of 'favouring' the Disinherited.[95] Abbot Simon certainly managed to put the blame on the townsmen.[96] The tract on the 'Guild of Youth' emphasises his helplessness in face of the townsmen who committed 'innumerable enormities against the king's peace.' They had launched an armed attack on the abbey, breaking open the abbey gates. Simon was away from Bury but returned in haste when he heard of the rising. The townsmen shut him and his officials out of the abbey. This happened, the tract points out, before the beginning of the civil war. During the civil war itself, which the tract dates from the battle of Lewes to the

---

[88] Cf. above p.70 and no. 14.

[89] See Davis, 'The Commune of Bury St. Edmunds, ' 313-15. Some of Davis's conclusions are corrected in Lobel, *op. cit.*, 126-9, esp. 127 n.l. Cf. below p.82

[90] Davis, *op. cit.*, 314.

[91] *CPR, 1258-66*, 375. A copy is in the sacrist's register, CUL MS Ff. ii.33, f.32.

[92] See the contemporary account of their submission, printed Davis, *op. cit.*, 317.

[93] For the text of the agreement see *The Pinchbeck Register*, ed. F. Hervey (Brighton, 1925, 2 vols.) i. 56-7.

[94] Printed Davis, *op. cit.*, 316.

[95] Above p.77 and nn. 71-3. Davis, *op. cit.*, 315, was wrong to conclude that the tract was drawn up for legal proceedings shortly after the Dictum of Kenilworth (31 October, 1266).

[96] Above p.77 and n. 73.

battle of Evesham, 'all was peace and tranquileity within the town' except for the 'internal conflict' caused by these 'wicked young men.' Whether or not the tract was written to exonerate Abbot Simon before Warenne and Valence, he certainly convinced them of his innocence, and they convinced the king.[97]

It is now necessary to consider why the Bury monks were pro-baronial while Abbot Simon was a 'royalist.' The views of the Bury monks were typical of those held by other members of religious orders. Usually the religious agreed about politics with the secular clergy, who tended to side with the barons. In fact many bishops supported Simon de Montfort.[98] John Taxter makes it clear that the Bury monks were moved partly by patriotism. Taxter's xenophobia, mentioned above,[99] included the foreign relatives of King Henry and Queen Eleanor. They 'behaved unbearably,' like tyrants, wherever they held sway, subjecting the people to 'despotic oppressions and demands.'[100] Taxter also deplores the loss of England's continental possessions, citing a satyrical verse on Henry's cession of 'nearly all' the territory.[101]

A more practical, less emotional reason for objecting to the king was taxation. It is a truism that the growth of royal and papal taxation and other financial impositions were a cause of hostility to the government. The Bury chroniclers, John Taxter and his continuator, dwelt on them in great detail, with angry comments.[102] They blamed the king as well as the pope for papal exactions since they were imposed for the king's use, whether to enable Henry to conquer Sicily for Prince Edmund, or to settle the kingdom after the Barons' War. The chroniclers' laments about such financial oppression cannot be dismissed as mere expressions of men's perennial hatred of taxation. There is enough evidence to prove that as the thirteenth century progressed the abbey's financial position suffered serious deterioration.[103] Although, as will be seen, Taxter's continuator shows no sympathy for the Disinherited because of their depredations, on one point they did in fact espouse the cause of all monks. One of the objections which they made to Ottobon at his council at Bury in February 1267 was that: 'abbeys and other religious houses, which were built with the wealth of their predecessors, are now ruined by the extortions and taxes of the king and legate, and so have to deny their accustomed alms and hospitality.'[104]

---

[97] See Henry's two writs of 12 June 1266 cited below p.82 and n. 117, and above p.77 and n. 74.

[98] See David Carpenter, *'St Thomas Cantilupe: his political career'* in *St Thomas Cantilupe Bishop of Hereford. Essays in his Honour*, ed. Meryl Jancey (Friends of Hereford Cathedral, Publications Committee for the Dean and Chapter, Leominster, 1982), 59-62.

[99] p.74 and n. 49.

[100] *Bury Chron.*, 29.

[101] *Ibid.*, 25.

[102] *Bury Chron.*, xxv-xxvi, 20 (s.a.1255), 40-5 (s.a. 1268), 60-1 (s.a.1275), 63 (s.a.1277), 104-13 (s.a. 1292).

[103] *Ibid.*, xxxi-xxxii.

[104] 'Item, [exhaeredati] significant Legato, quod Abbatiae, et aliae domus religiosorum, aedificatae sunt de bonis praedecessorum suorum, quae nunc per extorsiones et tallagia Regis et Legati destruuntur; et ideo nequeunt fieri eleemosynae et hospitalitates, sicut solebant.' Rishanger, *Chronica*, ed. Riley, 55. Cf. above p.77 and n. 78.

It is not impossible that the Bury monks were influenced by the political views current at St Albans. In King John's reign and early in Henry III's Roger Wendover had written his chronicle with a strong pro-baronial bias. His reviser and continuator, Matthew Paris, made this bias even more marked. Indeed, his chronicles are the most virulently partizan of any composed in the thirteenth century. There was a natural affinity between St Albans and St Edmunds. Both were exempt monasteries and cult centres. They both had to defend themselves against the authority of the diocesan. In the 1160s the abbot and prior of Bury had supported the abbot of St Albans against the aggression of the bishop of Lincoln.[105] In 1253 the five exempt houses in England drafted a confederation of mutual protection against anyone who tried to destroy or diminish their privilege of exemption.[106] The fact that in 1257 the abbot of St Albans was conservator on the pope's behalf of St Edmund's spiritual privileges within the *banleuca,* when Franciscan friars tried to establish themselves there, must have had reinforced contact between the two abbeys.[107] Matthew Paris has a passage extolling equally the privilege of sanctuary possessed by St Albans that possessed by St Edmunds.[108] Moreover, Matthew perpetrated the legend that Offa, king of Mercia (757-96) discovered St Alban's relics and founded the monastery in his honour.[109] Perhaps in claiming a royal founder for St. Albans he sought to emulate St Edmunds; its (alleged)[110] founder, Cnut, was a king, as indeed was St Edmund, its patron saint.

The evidence for some interconnection between Bury and St Albans in King John's reign has already been discussed.[111] In Henry's reign Matthew Paris was very well informed about events at Bury, which suggests that news from Bury readily reached St. Albans. This could have been because monks from St Albans stayed there on the way to St Albans' priory at Wymondham in Norfolk. Moreover, it is noticeable that Henry on his Lenten pilgrimages to the East Anglian shrines[112] quite often went to St Albans shortly

---

[105] *Gesta Abbatum Sancti Albani*, Riley, i. 139. For the course of the dispute see ibid., i. 137-58, and M.D. Knowles, 'Essays in Monastic History IV. - The Growth of Exemption,' *Downside Review*, 1 (1932), 215-17. At the same time the abbot of Bury St Edmunds was engaged in a dispute with his diocesan; *Gesta Abbatum*, ed. Riley, i. 145. Knowles, *op. cit.*, 212-13, was wrong in thinking that there is no evidence to support that of the *Gesta* on this point. See A. Gransden, 'The Question of the Consecration of St Edmund's Church' in *Church and Chronicle in the Middle Ages, Essays in Honour of John Taylor*, ed. Graham Loud and Ian Wood (Hambledon Press, London, 1990).

[106] *Gesta Abbatum*, ed. Riley, i. 391-4.

[107] See the 'Kempe' register, BL MS Harleian 645, ff. 220ᵛ, 242ᵛ. For Urban IV's defence of St Edmund's spiritual privileges within the *banleuca* during the abbey's dispute with the Franciscans see *Memorials of St Edmund's Abbey*, ed. Thomas Arnold (Rolls Series, 1890-6, 3 vols.) ii. 268.

[108] Cited above p.70 n.14.

[109] For Matthew Paris's *Vita Offarum*, written c. 1250, see Richard Vaughan, *Matthew Paris* (Cambridge, 1958), 198-94. It is printed *Matthaei Paris ... Historia Majora ... duorum Offarum Merciorum Regum ... et viginti trium Abbatum S. Albani Vitae ...* (London, 1640), ed. William Wats. For the (legendary) foundation of St Alban's abbey by Offa II see *ibid.*, 26-32, and *Gesta Abbatum*, ed. Riley, i. 4-5. (The *Gesta* until c. 1255 was also written by Paris; Vaughan, *op. cit.*, 185).

[110] See A. Gransden, 'The Traditions and Legends concerning the Origins of St. Edmund's Abbey, '*English Historical Review*, c (1985), 9-24 *passim*.

[111] Above p.72.

[112] See below p.83 and n. 125.

after staying in St Edmund's abbey.[113] This would have given Matthew Paris a chance to hear news from Bury. Sometimes Henry went to Bury soon after visiting St Albans. Perhaps a St Albans' monk joined the royal entourage, and, on his return to St Albans, told Matthew about affairs at Bury. As will be seen, Matthew has a revealing comment about one of Henry's visits to Bury.[114] Such contacts between the two monasteries make the suggestion that the political outlook of the monks of St Albans influenced the Bury monks feasible.

Why, then, did Simon de Luton hold different views from those of his monks? First and foremost it must be remembered that the abbot's status was different from that of the monks. He was a tenant-in-chief of the crown, responsible for the barony of eight and a half hundreds. He was liable for feudal service and for attendance at the 'Great Council' and parliament. He was, therefore, more involved in, and better informed about, national politics than were his monks. His approach to politics was more statesmanlike and pragmatic; he must have been less swayed by emotion and idealism than were his monks. It is not unlikely that he felt less strongly about taxation than did the monks because, by the division of the abbey's property between abbot and convent, the abbot's holdings were considerably less.[115]

Abbot Simon must have been well aware of the necessity of having the king's favour. The king was the source and protector of the abbey's privileges. Simon particularly needed his support against the dissident townsmen of Bury, Good examples of how Henry supported Simon's authority over the *banleuca* are provided by the crises of 1264 and 1266. The royal writ of 29 October, 1264, instructing Gilbert de Preston and William de Boville to hold an inquiry in Bury was issued at Simon's request, and the inquest was specifically to discover transgressions against his Liberty.[116] In 1266, shortly after the royal justices, William de Valence and John de Warenne, had sat within the *banleuca*, Henry issued two writs to Simon on 12 June. The first stipulates that St Edmund's Liberty should suffer no prejudice from their session.[117] The second writ is the mandate already mentioned.[118] In fact, it gave full recognition of the abbot's privileges: he was to appoint the alderman and janitors of the town because the inquest had testified that it was his right to do so, and the instruction that he was to hold his own inquest implicitly recognized his jurisdiction over the *banleuca*.

There is, therefore, no evidence that Abbot Simon was pro-baronial in act or thought.

---

[113] See below pp.85-86 and Henry visited Bury St Edmunds/St Albans or St Albans/Bury St Edmunds in quick succession (after intervals ranging in length from a few days to a little over two weeks) in 1236, 1238, 1242, 1245, 1251, 1252, 1256 and 1258; see Theodore Craib, *Itinerary of Henry III 1215-1272* (unprinted typescript in PRO), 124, 138, 162, 177, 181-2, 218-19, 228, 251, 268.

[114] Below p.86.

[115] For example, the convent's assessment for the sexennial tenth granted by the Second Council of Lyons in 1274 was 241 marks 3s. 6d., i.e. about £160; the abbot's assessment was £100. *Bury Chron.*, 60. Cf. below p.83 and n. 119.

[116] Above p.78 and n. 91.

[117] *CPR. 1258-66*, 604. A copy is in the sacrist's register, CUL MS Ff.ii.33, f.32. Cf. *Bury Chron.*, 34-5

[118] See above p.77 and no. 74.

In so far as he incurred Henry's displeasure, it was because he failed to keep order in the Liberty. This reservation aside, he was a man whom Henry could, and did, trust. Nevertheless, the difference between Abbot Simon's viewpoint and that of his monks should not be exaggerated. It was limited in scope, only encompassing national politics. In fact, on other matters his monks were as 'royalist' as he was. They shared his concern that order should be kept in St Edmund's Liberty. They were particularly harmed by insubordination and revolt in Bury itself. The division of the abbey's property between abbot and convent allocated the town with its *banleuca* to the convent.[119] The sacrist was virtually lord of the borough.[120] He ruled it and received all dues from its markets and fairs and the like, while the cellarer held the manor of Bury. All that remained to the abbot was his position as feudal overlord; the burgesses did homage to each abbot on his succession. Therefore, both sacrist and cellarer were in full accord with Abbot Simon when with Henry's help he tried to restore order within the *banleuca*. The monks had no more sympathy for the Disinherited than did Abbot Simon. The Bury chronicler considered them little better than brigands. 'They were more dangerous to meet than she-bears robbed of their cubs, and freely seized whatever they wanted.'[121]

Abbot and monks alike must have appreciated Henry III's veneration for St Edmund. It seems to have been surpassed only by his veneration for another sainted Anglo-Saxon king, Edward the Confessor, patron saint of Westminster abbey. Henry's devotion to St Edmund is well attested. He named his second son, Edmund ('Crouchback') after him. On 18 January, 1245, two days after Edmund's birth, Henry wrote to Abbot Henry de Rushbrook ordering him to tell the monks that his son had been named after 'the glorious king and martyr,' their patron saint.[122] And in 1253 he sent 12 *oboli de musca* and 20 measures of wax worth £40 for the feast of the translation of St Edmund (29 April), as votive offerings on account of his and Prince Edmund's infirmity.[123] Henry attended personally the feast of St Edmund (20 November) in 1235 and 1248[124] and nearly always included the abbey in the tours of East Anglian shrines which he was accustomed to make in Lent during the period of his personal rule.[125] When the barons were in power he no longer went on these Lenten pilgrimages. But in the autumn of 1272, from 2 to 12 September, he again stayed in the abbey. While there he was truck by his final illness,[126] from which he died at Westminster two months later (16 November).

---

[119] See Edward I's confirmation of the division; W. Dugdale, *Monasticon Anglicanum*, ed. J. Caley, H. Ellis and B. Bandinel (London, 1817-30, 6 vols.), iii. 156, 157.

[120] See Lobel, *Borough of Bury St. Edmunds*, 16-17.

[121] *Bury Chron.*, 34 (and cf. 38-9.).

[122] *Ibid.*, 13.

[123] *CCR, 1251-3*, 465.

[124] *CCR, 1234-7*, 210; *ibid., 1247-51*, 127; Craib, *Itinerary of Henry III*, 122, 204.

[125] For Henry III's Lenten pilgrimages of the East Anglian shrines see Powicke, *Henry III and the Lord Edward* i. 80-1, 135, 190, 313; ii. 588.

[126] Rishanger, *Chronica*, ed. Riley, 74. Riley states in the marginal caption and index that Henry died in St Edmund's abbey. This is wrong and not in any case what the *Chronica* says. It reads: 'Et cum ad Abbathiam Sancti Edmundi, Regis et Martyris, declinasset, gravi languore corripitur, qui eum non deseruit usque ad vitae finem.' For Henry's death at Westminster see Powicke, *Henry III and the Lord Edward,* ii. 588.

Henry was a generous benefactor of the abbey church and St Edmund's shrine. When he did not attend St Edmund's feast, he seems regularly to have sent wax for tapers. For example, in 1240 he ordered the sheriff to supply the sacrist of Bury with 500 lbs of wax for 1000 tapers to light the shrine.[127] Henry also made rich gifts of gold in various forms, usually for St Edmund's feast day, to add to the splendour of the abbey church and the dazzling glitter of the shrine. For the feast in 1252 he sent 'a fine crown with four flowers on its rim, worth £10 in all, to be hung on the shrine', besides 12 bezants and 12 *oboli de musca*,[128] and when in France in 1262 he ordered 36 *oboli de musca* and 3 ounces of gold to be sent 'without fail,' 'for fastening to the shrine *(attachiandas feretro)*.'[129] In 1257 he sent 36 *oboli de musca* for the feast, to be paid for out of the revenues of the abbey during the vacancy[130] (31 December 1256 - 12 January 1258), and Queen Eleanor, who attended the feast personally with the royal children, gave 30 bezants on his behalf.[131]

Sometimes it is not clear from the records whether or not a gift was specifically for St Edmund's feast. For instance, on 8 February 1247 payment of £59 2s. 5d. was authorized to Henry de Frowik, goldsmith, for a golden communion cup worth 9 marks 10s, which the king had given to the abbey.[132] Similarly, on 3 February 1255 17 marks was allowed for the purchase of two gold buckles, one for St Edward and the other for St Edmund.[133] Henry's generosity was not limited to gifts of gold; he also gave other valuables. For example, on 30 June 1257 the sheriff of Norfolk and Suffolk was instructed to buy a cope of samite worth 10 marks, to be given to the prior and convent for the adornment of St Edmund's shrine.[134]

Royal visits often elicited gifts. A visit was normally preceded by a gift of wax for tapers in the church. In 1242 Henry stayed in the abbey from 17-18 March; on 25 March the sheriff was allowed on his account 75s for 100 lbs of wax for tapers to be put in St Edmund's church ready for the king's arrival.[135] During visits or shortly afterwards Henry was especially generous. In 1242, he gave, besides the wax, 9 *oboli de musca* (worth 15d each), and 3 bezants (worth 26d each) to be placed on St Edmund's shrine before he arrived.[136] While there, he gave two gold brooches of 14s 4d weight and 12 more *oboli de musca*.[137] In 1251, on 30 March, twelve days after a six day visit, Henry

---

[127] *C. Lib R, 1240-5*, 9.

[128] *CCR. 1251-3*, 152-3, 427.

[129] *CCR. 1261-4*, 162-3.

[130] *CCR. 1256-9*, 161-2.

[131] *C Lib R, 1251-60*, 428.

[132] *C Lib R, 1245-51*, 106.

[133] *C Lib R, 1251-60*, 194.

[134] *Ibd.*, 383.

[135] *C Lib R, 1240-5*, 114. For a similar grant in 1244 see *ibid.*, 244.

[136] *Ibid.*, 114.

[137] *Ibid.*, 113.

allowed 44 marks from the issue of the general eyre to pay for four silver candlesticks placed around the shrine, besides 30 marks for the completion of the new altar front, and in addition gave generously to the parish churches and hospitals in Bury.[138] During his visit from 5 to 10 March 1256 Henry gave the abbot £20 to have the picture in front of the high altar finished, under the sheriff's view.[139]

Both abbot and monks must have valued Henry's visits because of his important contribution to the abbey's spiritual prestige. In addition, visits brought temporal benefits. For example, shortly after his visit in June 1244, Henry sent the prior a cask of wine,[140] and, more important, while at Bury in March, 1251, he granted the sacrist thirty oaks from Inglewood for the repair of the belfry[141] and 40 marks for their transport.[142] Less than a week after his departure from Bury in February 1234, Henry executed business to the abbey's advantage. The abbey had been in his hands from 29 August 1233, when Abbot Richard de Insula died, until 1 February 1234, when Henry gave his assent to the election of his successor, Henry be Rushbrook, and restored the temporalities. Shortly afterwards Henry spent two days at Bury (12-14 February) and on 20 February, when at Thetford, he instructed the royal treasurer to allow £11 19s. from the abbey's revenues during the vacancy, to pay for the alms distributed to the poor of Bury at Abbot Richard's funeral.[143]

Sometimes the abbot and monks exploited a royal visit to impress on the king the nature of St Edmunds' liberties. On 21 March, 1242, at Tivetshall, three days after visiting the abbey (17-18 March), Henry made two concessions in explicit recognition of its liberties: he instructed the treasurer to allow the abbot all murder fines and common fines, amercements of vills and tithings, and forfeitures levied by the recent justices in eyre within the Liberty of the eight and a half hundreds and from the abbot's tenants outside the Liberty:[144] and he instructed the justices of assizes to commit a case of novel desseisin concerning a tenement within St Edmund's *banleuca* to the abbot's steward.[145] Besides deferring to old liberties, the king granted new ones. On 19 March, 1235, when staying in the abbey, he granted the abbot the right to hold two annual fairs in the suburbs of the town.[146] In view of Henry's generosity, it is not surprising that abbot and convent seem to have welcomed Henry's visits - provided he did not stay too long. This apparently was the case in September 1252. Matthew Paris asserts that Henry remained

---

[138] *C lib R., 1245-51*, 343-4.

[139] *C lib R., 1251-60*, 275.

[140] *CCR, 1242-7*, 202.

[141] *CCR, 1247-51*, 423. Henry had made a similar grant of 20 oaks on 7 August, 1250; *ibid.*, 311. Cf. the next note.

[142] *C lib R, 1245-51*, 343. Later, in a writ of 9 June, 1251, Henry gave the abbot and convent permission to use the 40 marks to buy more wood for the repair of the belfry; *CCR, 1247-51*, 544.

[143] *CCR, 1231-4*, 379.

[144] *CCR, 1237-42*, 404-5.

[145] *Ibid.*, 434.

[146] *CCR, 1234-7*, 61; *C CH R, 1226-57*, 196.

in the abbey for nearly three weeks, because he was ill, ' to the great inconvenience of that house.'[147] Matthew exaggerated the length of the visit - Henry was there for only about two weeks. However, he probably records the monks' reaction correctly. This was one of the times when Henry was at St Albans shortly (a week) before he went to Bury.[148] His exceptional generosity to St Edmund's shrine in this year was perhaps prompted not only by gratitude to the saint for his recovery, but also the wish to compensate the monks for his prolonged stay.[149]

The Bury monks, therefore, although politically sympathetic to the baronial oppositions to King John and Henry III, were in some other respects as 'royalist' as Abbot Simon himself. This was not because they were inconsistent but because they, like their contemporaries, were imbued with the medieval idea of kingship. In addition, they had the interests of their abbey at heart. They accepted that the king should be just, observe the laws and customs of the realm and take the advice of his native-born magnates; in so far as they considered that King John and Henry III fell short of this ideal, their sympathies were with the barons. But a medieval king should also have some merits not strictly speaking of a political nature. He should be valiant, successful in war, personally congenial to his subject, and pious. A king earned praise or blame according as to how he measured up to these standards. John gained practically no credit for military talent and little for congeniality or piety. Henry on the other hand won popularity above all for his piety. This aspect of Henry appealed to the abbot and monks of Bury. But they were also much influenced by corporate self interest. This was equally true of other monks; a recent scholar, indeed, claims that the main reason for Matthew Paris's 'constitutional' viewpoint was concern for the interests of St Albans, which were injured particularly by taxation.[150] Certainly, all monks tended to dislike the king when his rule conflicted with their interests, and to like him when it was favourable. However, their idealistic view of kingship sometimes held its own against institutional selfishness. They were not incapable of attaching paramount importance to national concerns, notably to the barons' attempts to enforce just rule.[151] Again, with regard to Henry, although his generosity to their churches and shrines benefited the monks materially, their approval of him in this respect was no doubt partly because they liked a pious king.

---

[147] Chron. Maj., v.304.

[148] See above pp.81-82 and n. 113.

[149] Above p.84 and n. 128.

[150] Vaughan, Matthew Paris, 139-40.

[151] The St Albans' Flores Historiarum praises the baronial administration from 1259 to 1260. See Flores Historiarum, ed. Luard, ii.439. Cf. Treharne, Baronial Plan of Reform, 212, and Gransden, Historical Writing, [i]. 418.

LAYFOLK WITHIN CISTERCIAN PRECINCTS

by
David H. Williams

Many Cistercian monasteries in the Middle Ages were surrounded for reasons of security by quite massive precinct walls, like that which still remains in part at Sweetheart Abbey in the south-west of Scotland. Access to the abbey was meant to be achieved only by means of a sturdily-built gate-house. This building will have been the first impression medieval travellers and visitors would have gained of any particular monastery, and when they reached it and sought admittance, they might well have echoed in spirit the words of the Psalmist, 'Open to me the gates of righteousness: and I will enter and give thanks to the Lord' *(Ps 118/19)*, for beyond it lay what was meant to be a haven of peace and holiness. The gate-house was the immediate point of contact between the enclosed monastic community and the outside world, and to it came all kinds and classes of people. The passing traveller seeking shelter, the pilgrim come to fulfil a vow, the refugee fleeing from war or persecution, the pensioner looking for an eventide home, the sick and aged and poor hoping for a measure of care, the dying seeking to end their days in a holy place, the would-be servant seeking a position, and perhaps the local miscreant incarcerated for a time in the gate-house cells. All these might well find admission within the walls of the monastery, but for practical reasons, the great mass of the deserving poor received their charity, alms or dole, at the gate; whilst outside it might hang around the local nee'r do-wells and cause trouble or fight or amuse themselves with sports,[1] for a gateway was, as in Old Testament times, a favourite meeting-place.[2]

The gate-house was the domain of a monk nominated as porter, just as Solomon appointed 'porters at every gate' of the Temple *(2 Chron. 8/14; A.V.)*. The Rule of St Benedict saw the gate-house as being continually manned: the porter 'was to have a cell near the gate, so that persons who arrive may always find someone at hand to give them a reply',[3] whilst the Cistercian Charter of Charity included the "gate-keeper's cell" amongst the regular places to be constructed before a community took up residence in a new foundation.[4] It was all as if in response to the prophecy of Isaiah: 'your gates shall be open continually, day and night they shall not be shut' *(Is 60/11)*. *The Rule of St Benedict* demanded that the porter should be 'a wise old man'; his became a very responsible position; he had to be almoner, gaoler, business-man and watch-man; and several Cistercian porters were elected directly from that office to an abbacy. Amongst his particular tasks was that of discerning who were the genuine guests and callers - whom he would eventually direct to the guest-house, and who were the deserving poor - who would be shown the way to the lay infirmary.[5] One of his major duties, which lies by

---

[1] Cf. D.H. Williams, *The Welsh Cistercians* (Caldey, 1984) I. 144.

[2] Cf. *Ruth 4/1-4, Psalm 69/12*.

[3] D. Parry, *Households of God* (London, 1980) 180.

[4] L. Lekai, *The Cistercians* (Kent State U. P., 1977) 448.

[5] S.F. Hockey, *Account Book of Beaulieu Abbey* (Camden Fourth Ser. 16: Royal Hist. Soc. 1975) 174; *Beaulieu : King John's Abbey* (Pioneer Publns., 1976), 71.

definition outside the brief of this lecture, was to arrange the distribution of such money, food and clothing, as might be possible to the poor - sometimes great crowds of them - who had to wait without the gate. This work of charity was something for which the Cistercian Order became noted; which earned it quite often the commendation of the Book of Proverbs, 'Let her works praise her in the gates' *(Prov. 31/31)*

The sheer weight of numbers meant that only a small fraction of the sick, the aged and the poor could be allowed in, and it was the porter's responsibility to determine who these should be. Numbers of occasional, permanent or semi-permanent residents of this category were perhaps never very great. Zwettl in Austria *(1218)* had accommodation for some thirty of the needy infirm,[6] Beaulieu in Hampshire *(1270)* gave food and shelter every night to some sixteen poor men,[7] at Ford in Devon[8] and Margam in Glamorgan[9] there were endowments to maintain in each case at least three paupers - but that is not say there were no others. In the fourteenth century, Sibton in Suffolk had its *stagiarii* (old-stagers) similarly cared for.[10] There is also only scanty numerical evidence at the time of the English suppression of the monasteries *(1536-9)*, but it suffices to show that this particular work of charity continued. At Furness in Lancashire at least a dozen poor men,[11] and at Whalley in the same county no less than twenty-four,[12] who had paid something towards their maintenance *('poor corrodians')*, were kept in the lay infirmary; at Garendon in Leicestershire five impotent people were sustained by alms,[13] whilst at Warden in Bedfordshire seven poor people of both sexes were maintained.[14] St Mary's, Dublin, was reported to maintain 'many poor men, scholars, and orphans'.[15] There is evidence that occasionally monks were qualified in medicine, and that sometimes expert medical help might be called in to a medieval Cistercian monastery, but it is less clear as to whether the sick and poor in the lay infirmary received much more than simple loving care,[16] as well as confession and absolution.[17] Occasionally, too, there is evidence of sick people of some distinction resorting to a Cistercian house; the classic example in Wales was that of the lord of Powys, Gruffydd ap Gwenwynwyn *(ca. 1260)* who recovered after

---

[6] Lekai (1977) 448.

[7] Hockey (1976) 71.

[8] G. Oliver, *Monasticon Exoniensis* (London, 1846) 338.

[9] Williams (1984) I, 181.

[10] P. Brown, *Sibton Abbey Cartularies and Charters* (Suffolk Record Soc. : *Suffolk Charters* VII-X, 1985-88) I, 2.

[11] D. H. Williams, 'Tudor Cistercian Life, II' in *Cîteaux* XXXIV ; 3-4 (1983) 308 (No.114).

[12] Ibid. II, 309 (No. 135).

[13] Ibid. II, 308 (No. 115).

[14] Ibid. II, 309 (No. 134).

[15] G. C. Carville, 'Economic Activities of the Cistercians in Ireland' in *Cîteaux* XXII : 3-4 (1971) 286-7.

[16] *Statuta* I, 65 (1157), 84 (1175/32); H. d'Arbois de Jubainville, *Études sur des Abbayes Cisterciennes* (Paris, 1858) 224; C. H. Talbot, 'Beaulieu Account Book' in *Cîteaux* IX : 3 (1958) 195.

[17] H. Tribout de Morembert, 'Deux Bulles pour Cîteaux' in *Cîteaux* XXI 3-4 (1970) 306.

being 'very ill in a certain monastery' ; that was, indubitably, Strata Marcella Abbey, close to his power base at Pool.[18]

The ordinary run of poor and sick people came to be housed in a purpose-built complex referred to as the 'hospice' or 'hospital of the poor' or the 'secular infirmary'. Certainly, by the close of the twelfth century or early in the thirteenth, these were present in the larger monasteries right through Europe, and in some cases replaced earlier edifices. A secular infirmary (called later, *ca. 1230*, the 'infirmary of the poor seculars') is on record at Warden by about 1180,[19] and at Furness by about 1190.[20] One was founded at Fountains in 1199 and was extended or re-built a few decades later.[21] There was a lay hospital ('the house of the sick and destitute') at Heiligenkreuz in Austria by about 1200,[22] one was on record that year at Walkenried,[23] one was noted at Michaelstein in Germany in 1208,[24] whilst a new one was built at Zwettl in Austria ten years later.[25] At Pipewell in Northamptonshire the 'great chamber' of the lay infirmary had a new roof raised about 1300.[26] At the Cistercian nunnery of Bijloke in Ghent was to be seen the second largest medieval hospital ward in Europe, next only to that at Tonnerre in Burgundy.[27] The lay infirmary at Fossanova in Italy was ten bays in length.[28] The secular infirmary stood usually within the monastic precincts; this is on record at Chorin in East Germany[29] and at Sedlec in Bohemia.[30] Usually, it was sited close to the monastery gate; this had the obvious advantage that sick and poor people were kept at some distance from the cloister and didn't have to go wandering far from the point of entry. Infirmaries proximate to the gate are on record at Fountains,[31] at

---

[18] Williams (1984) I, 182.

[19] G. H. Fowler, *Cartulary of Warden* (Publns. Bedfordshire Hist. Rec. Soc., XIII, (1931) 228-30; D. N.Bell, 'The English Cistercians and the Practice of Medicine' in *Cîteaux* XL (1989) 170 No. 18).

[20] 'Duchy of Lancaster Charters; in the *36th Report of the Deputy Keeper of the Public Records*, Appendix 1 (London 1875) 179.

[21] R Gilyard-Beer and G. Coppack, 'Excavations at Fountains Abbey' in *Archaeologia* 108 (1986) 151.

[22] J.N. Weis, *Urkunden des Cistercienser-Stiftes Heiligenkreuz* (Fontes Rerum Austriacarum XI : Pt. 1; Vienna, 1856) 27-8 (No. XX), 74 (No. LXIII); L. Grill, 'Das Armenhospital der Heiligenkreuz' in *Cist. Chronik* N.S. 55-56 (July, 1961) 22n.

[23] F. Winter, *Die Cistercienser des Nordöstlichen Deutschlands* (Gotha, 1868-71) II, 143.

[24] J. de la Croix Bouton, *Histoire de l'Ordre de Cîteaux* (Westmalle, Belgium) II (1964) 256; Winter (1868-71) II, 143; Cf. *Statuta* I, 500 (1218/75).

[25] Lekai (1977) 381.

[26] Bell (1989) 169 (No. 12).

[27] L.T. Courtney, 'The Hospital of Byloke Abbey', noted in *Cîteaux* XXXVIII : 1-2 (1987) 106; A.M. Dustin, *Belgique-Abbayes et Béguinages* (Brussels, 1973) 16-17.

[28] A.L. Fotheringham, 'Introduction of Gothic Architecture into Italy' in *American Jnl. of Archaeology* VI (1890) 44.

[29] P.W. Gercken, *Codex dipl. Brandenburgensis* (Salzwedel, 1769) II, 494.

[30] C.J. Erben, *Regesta Bohemiae et Moraviae* (Prague 1855-90) IV, 505-6 (No. 1269 of 1343 A.D.)

[31] F.A. Mullin, *A History of the Cistercians in Yorkshire* (Washington, 1932) 93.

Sibton[32] and at Zwettl;[33] postulated at Furness[34] and, here in Wales, at Margam.[35] At Foucarmont *(1233)* in France the 'domus leprosum' was next to the scriptorium but separated from it by a hedge.[36] In at least two instances, both here in Wales, the lay hospital was sited something like a mile away from the abbey; could the reception of people with infectious diseases have dictated this? The cases in point are Neath and Tintern, where the later grange names of Cwrt-y-clafdy and Secular Firmary respectively bear witness to their origins.[37] The French house of Aiguebelle had an 'hospital of the poor' one and a half leagues distant.[38]

The published accounts for Beaulieu Abbey covering the year of 1270[39] give a comprehensive picture of the varied and relaxed diet in its lay infirmary, assisted by the ample supplies sent to it from various departments of the monastery and by the fact that the rules regarding guests abstaining from butter, cheese and eggs, on fast days, did not apply to the sick. The inmates of the hospital of Beaulieu could consume broth prepared from gruel, herbs and vegetables, staple items included a daily measure of beer and a small white loaf, whilst cheese was also to be had; meat was permitted in 1270 to the sick poor,[40] and that served at Beaulieu was primarily mutton or lamb but also beef and pork accompanied by beans and peas, and there was seasoning - pepper, salt, almonds and cumin. Fish eaten included herrings, cod, hake and mackerel; a reflection perhaps of Beaulieu's maritime position and shipping interests. Bowls, dishes and pitchers were bought, canvas and straw was provided - presumably for bedding, and turf and firewood- for cooking and to keep the inmates warm. Apart from monastic staff there was a hired servant. Only a very small return came from monies left by the deceased and from the sale of their clothes.

Father-abbots on visitation might well take an interest in the conduct of these lay hospitals, and that notable abbot of Savigny, Stephen Lexington, inspecting the monastery of Jerpoint *(1228)* laid down that linen and better food and drink be provided in the hospital of the poor,[41] and visiting St André-en-Gouffern *(in 1232)* ordered that better bread be provided in its secular infirmary.[42] Indeed, at Beaulieu, it cost the

---

[32] Brown (1985-88) I, 2; IV, 11 (No. 952 of 1263 A.D.)

[33] Lekai (1977) 381.

[34] J. C. Dickinson, *Furness Abbey* (HMSO, 1965) 9.

[35] D.R.L. Jones, 'Margam in the post-dissolution era' in *Trans. Port Talbot Hist. Soc.* III: 2 (1981) 8-9.

[36] B. Griesser, 'Registrum Epistolarum Stephani de Lexington' in *Analecta S.O. Cist.* 8 (1952) 214 (No. 4 of 1233 A.D.)

[37] Williams (1984) I, 182.

[38] Bouton II (1964) 256.

[39] Hockey (1975) 34, 177-82.

[40] *Statuta* II, 80 (1270/3).

[41] B.W. O'Dwyer, *Stephen of Lexington : Letters from Ireland* (Kalamazoo, 1982) 169 (No. 87), Cf. 165 (No. 63); 'Crisis in the Cistercian Monasteries in Ireland' in *Analecta Cist.* XXXII (1976 : 1-2) 48.

[42] Griesser (1952) II, 208 (No. 5).

community over twice as much to run the lay hospital as it did to maintain the needs of the monks' own infirmary.[43] All this care could only be achieved at some expense, met in part by donations or bequests from benefactors. These included grants of lands made to Warden *(ca. 1180)*[44], to Furness *(ca. 1190)*[45] and to Holm Cultram *(ca. 1235)*,[46] amongst many other houses. There were also gifts of money - as to Santes Creus in Spain *(1229)* to assist with clothing the poor,[47] and to Poblet for the upkeep of beds and bedding *(1263-68)*.[48] Bonport in France had no less than twenty-four charters granting lands or rents towards the care of its poor and sick lay inmates.[49] Newminster and Stanley had thoughtful and practically-minded benefactors who endowed a lamp in their hospitals.[50] Nor was spiritual provision neglected; larger infirmaries of the poor came to have their own chapel. Certainly, Furness [51] and Tilty[52] in England did so; so, too, did Zwettl,[53] and by 1205, Stürzelbronn in Lorraine.[54] Arnsburg in Hesse received a grant for the upkeep of a sanctuary lamp in the chapel of its secular infirmary *(1278)*,[55] whilst at Santes Creus in Spain one donor, wishing to be buried in the portal of the infirmary of the poor, made a bequest to allow the construction of an altar dedicated to St Peter in its chapel *(1229)*,[56] The infirmary chapel at Poblet was dedicated to St Catalina,[57] at Sibton to St John the Baptist,[58] and at Valasse to St Mary and St John the Evangelist.[59]

---

[43] Ibid, II, 214 (No. 4).

[44] Fowler (1931) 38, 80-81.

[45] A. Cottam, 'Granges of Furness' in *Trans. Hist. Soc. Lancashire and Cheshire* 80 (1928-29) 83; VCH, *History of the County of Lancashire* II (1966) 127.

[46] F. Grainger and W.D. Collingwood, 'Register and Records of Holm Cultram' in *Trans. Cumberland and Westmorland Antiq. and Archaeol. Soc.* Record Ser. VII (1929) 30-31, Cf. 5.

[47] E. Fort i Cogul, 'Regesta de Sant Bernat Calvo' in *Studia Monastica* XI : 1 (1969) 48.

[48] A. Altisent, 'Dotacio de Llits' in *Studia Monastica* 12 (1970 : 1) III - (of 1260-68 A.D.); Cf. A.W. Crawley-Boevey, *Cartulary of Flaxley* (Exeter, 1887) p. V.

[49] Bouton (1964) 256.

[50] J. T. Fowler, *Chartularium de Novo Monasterio* (Surtees Soc., LXVI, 1875; publ. 1878) xv, 171; W. de Gray Birch, 'Collections towards the History of Stanley' in *Wilts. Arch. and Nat. Hist. Magazine* XV (Dec. 1875) 251.

[51] Jones (1981) 8-9.

[52] W.C. Waller, 'Records of Tiltey Abbey' in *Trans. Essex Arch. Soc.* N.S. VIII (1903) 359.

[53] Lekai (1977) 381.

[54] *Statuta* I, 310 (1205/16).

[55] L. Baur, *Urkundenbuch des Klosters Arnsburg* (Darmstadt, 1849) 107 (No. 162).

[56] Fort i Cogul (1969) 48; 'El Senyoriu de Santes Creus' (Barcelona, 1972) 76.

[57] I. Richards, *Abbeys of Europe* (Feltham, London, 1968) 108.

[58] Brown (1985-88) I, 2.

[59] F. Sommènil, *Chronicon Valassense* (Rouen, 1868) 70n.

Prince Llywelyn the Great *(1199)* noted in a charter to Aberconwy Abbey that 'it belongs to the monks to give food and lodging to travellers and guests', whilst Gerald of Wales told how the white monks 'incessantly exercise more than any others, the acts of charity and beneficence towards the poor and strangers'.[60] *The Rule of St Benedict* had dictated that 'all who arrive as guests are to be welcomed like Christ',[61] and the General Chapter of their Order had emphasised that fitting hospitality should be shown (1190-91.)[62] The great majority of these lay-visitors were accommodated in another purpose-built complex, the guest-house or hospice. As early as the mid-twelfth century, the Empress Matilda is said to have constructed two large guest-houses at Mortemer in France;[63] at Boyle in Ireland note was made in 1202 of 'the great stone house of the guests'[64] at Kingswood in England a new one was being built in 1242.[65] The guest-halls at Buckfast[66] and Kirkstall[67] were extended towards the close of the thirteenth century, and the remains of the hospice dating from the same period are still to be seen at Orval in Belgium.[68] At Basingwerk in Wales an enterprising abbot built additional guest accommodation *(about 1500),* the result was that the guests became so numerous that at meals they had to be served in two sittings.[69] Guest-houses lay within the precinct, but set a little apart from the conventual buildings - so as not to interfere with monastic calm, and often perhaps (as at Tintern) near the Great Gate, the point of entry. The guest-house would need its own kitchen - that at Duiske in Ireland was in course of construction in 1228;[70] the visitors' horses would need tethering and feeding - hence the guest stables noted in the accounts of Kingswood Abbey for 1263.[71] At the annual visitation the guest-house too might be inspected - as at Lilienfeld *(1316)* when better provision of bedding was suggested.[72] Visitors probably heard Mass in the gate-house chapel - but at least one abbey, Orval in Belgium, had its own guest-house chapel, dedicated to

---

[60] Williams (1984) I, 170.

[61] Parry (1980) 140.

[62] *Statuta* I, 118 (1190/1), 142 (1191/43).

[63] L. Musset and R. Aubreton, *Abbaye Notre-Dame de Mortemer* (Rouen, 1979) 6.

[64] R.A. Stalley, *The Cistercian Monasteries of Ireland* (Yale U.P., 1987) 44.

[65] V.R. Perkins, 'Documents relating to the Cistercian Monastery of Kingswood' in *Trans. Bristol and Glouc. Arch. Soc.* XXII (1899) 202.

[66] S. Brown, 'Medieval Buckfast Abbey' in *Devon Archaeology* 1 (1983) 9; MS Notes (Arch. Dig., Open Day, 24th Sept. 1983).

[67] Bond (1989) 96; Cf. Dickinson (1965) 12.

[68] L-E. Halkin, *Orval, Neuf Siècles d'Histoire* (Liége, 1970) 41.

[69] Williams (1984) I, 175.

[70] G.C. Carville, *Norman Splendour* (Belfast, 1979) 68.

[71] Perkins (1899) 220

[72] H. Watzl, 'Fragmente eines Heiligenkreuzer Visitations- chartenprotokolls' in *Cist. Chronik* N.F. No. 53 : 4 (Dec. 1960) 52.

St Marguerite.[73] The abbot could hear visitors' confessions.[74]

The guest-house was the responsibility of the monk designated as guest-master, and he was assisted by at least one *conversus*.[75] In the early years lay servants were discouraged in guest-houses, unless there were more guests than usual *(1152)*.[76] At Cîteaux, when a guest arrived at the gate the porter sent a message to the abbot, and on his approval the visitor was escorted to the church for prayer, and then to the guest-house where the guest-master was to receive his visitors with a deep bow or complete prostration.[77] These were the marks of humility demanded by the *Rule*.[78] He decided who ate when and where, and who slept where. He could speak with all the guests, and with his attendant *conversus*, and it was the guest - master's duty, aided by two brothers, to wash the hands and feet of the guests at the same time that the weekly maundy was taking place in the monastery.[79] At Beaulieu *(1270)* the porter and the guest-master were spared any personal embarrassment because the type of persons who could be received, the food they would eat, and the length of their stay, were all carefully laid down in writing.[80] There are several instances on record where the parents or families of monks exceeded their stay by far, and they had to be told to leave; this happened at Coëtmaloën *(1210)*,[81] Longvillers *(1231)*[82] and Vaux-de-Cernay *(1232)* in France,[83] and at Jerpoint in Ireland *(1228)*.[84]

In the earlier years, before abbots came to have their own establishments, they generally ate in the guest-house with the travellers and pilgrims, but, in England, 'if many guests came' the abbot 'can and ought' to eat with the community; in any event, he was not to dawdle over meals taken with guests *(1203)*,[85] Gervase, the first abbot of Louth Park, as he approached death confessed in his *Lamentation* how he ate 'sumptuously with the guests while his brethren were famishing with hunger in the

---

[73] Halkin (1970) 58.

[74] *Statuta* II, 1 (1225/5).

[75] D'Arbois de Jubainville (1858) 223-4; E.g: *Statuta* I, 526 (1220/46).

[76] *Statuta* I, 48 (1152/17).

[77] D'Arbois de Jubainville (1858) 202-3.

[78] Parry (1980) 140.

[79] D. Choisselet and P. Vernet, *Les 'Ecclesiastica Officia' Cisterciens du XIIème Siècle* (La Documentation Cist., 22; Oelenberg Abbey, Reiningue, 1989) 304-5, 332-3; D'Arbois de Jubainville (1858) 232-34.

[80] Talbot (1958) 194-5.

[81] *Statuta* I, 371 (1210/12), Cf. Lekai (1977) 380.

[82] Griesser (1952) 192 (No. 12).

[83] Ibid. 216 (No. 10).

[84] O'Dwyer (1982) 157 (the monastery is believed to be Jerpoint).

[85] *Statuta* I, 288 (1203/19).

refectory.[86] The monks and *conversi* serving at the tables in a Cistercian guest-house were to speak only if absolutely necessary, as when a sign for bread or water or salt was not understood *(1258).*[87] The diet was a disciplined one. No meat was served,[88] and no butter, cheese or eggs were allowed on Fridays, in Advent and Lent, on the Ember Days and on certain vigils, though in the early thirteenth-century milk products were permitted on the latter two groups of fast-days.[89] Abbot Stephen Lexington calculated *(1232)* that the guest-house of his monastery at Savigny needed each day as much bread as was consumed by twenty monks in the refectory.[90] The provision of such hospitality was again met in part by grants and benefactions. The Count of Geneva freed Tamié (which stood on a major routeway) from all tolls and taxes because of 'its custom of giving hospitality to voyagers'.[91] The General Chapter of the Order *(1190),* trying to restrict the further acquisition of lands, excepted instances where such were necessary to generate extra income not only to sustain the community but also to meet the expenses of. hospitality.[92] Sibton in Suffolk received the tithes of the parish of Rendham for this purpose *(ca. 1240),* as well as a grant for 'utensils and cloth' to assist with the reception of guests converging there.[93] A bishop of Schwerin *(1269)* granted an indulgence of forty days to donors aiding the 'heavy burden' which Doberan in East Germany experienced in maintaining its guest-house.[94]

Once again, the accounts for Beaulieu Abbey *(1270)* give a picture of its guest-house.[95] Who was entertained there? First, nobles, ecclesiastics and others of distinction. Other 'decent' travellers of lesser rank who arrived by the third hour of the day remained perhaps only to eat; those coming after lunch stayed the night. In addition, the guest-house gave shelter each night to thirteen poor people selected by the porter. There might also be the parents or close relatives of members of the community; their free stay was restricted to two nights, and they could come once or twice each year. There would be other guests sent in by the abbot, or grooms and workmen sent over by the prior or the cellarer. Hospitality was also afforded from Christmas Eve until after dinner on

---

[86] C.H. Talbot, 'The Testament of Gervase of Louth Park' in *Analecta S. O. Cist.* VII (1951) 38.

[87] *Statuta* II, 441 (1258/17).

[88] B. Lucet, *Les Codifications Cisterciennes de 1237 et 1257* (Paris, 1977) 333.

[89] B. Lucet, *La Codification Cistercienne de 1201* (Rome, 1964) 148; Lucet (1977) 334; D'Arbois de Jubainville (1858) 222-3; *Statuta* III, 157 (1276/27); Cf. I, 83 (1175/8), 141 (1191/38), 148-9 (1192/15); Cf. Brown (1985-88) IV, 106 (No. 1182).

[90] Griesser (1952) 227-8.

[91] F. Bernard, *L'Abbaye de Tamié : Ses Granges* (Grenoble, 1967) 21; B-J. Martin, *Histoire des Moines de Tamié* (Saint-Étienne, 1982) 20.

[92] *Statuta* I, 118 (1190/1); Cf. J. von Frast, 'Urkunden des Stiftes Zwettl' in Archiv. *für Kunde osterreichischer Geschichts-Quellen* II (1849, Pr. 2) 423.

[93] Brown (1985-88) II, 32 (No.29), 303 (No. 417), Cf. 97 (No. 1162).

[94] Lekai (1977) 381.

[95] Hockey (1975) 33, 269-82; Cf. Talbot (1958) 194-5.

St Stephen's Day to as many poor people as there were monks in the monastery. There was provision also for feeding women relatives, and other ladies who could not be refused without scandal, though it is not clear where they ate.

In the guest-house also the diet was a varied one, though no meat was served. There was clear class distinction in the grades of bread and beer provided to the different ranking guests, as also in the type of broth, and the frequency of pittances of fish, butter and cheese. Only guests of rank, dining with the abbot, could have wine served to them. Herring was the common fish served, but cod, eels, mackerel, ling, hake and salmon - the latter obviously kept for the more notable visitors - were also served. The Beaulieu accounts for its guest-house also mention gruel, salt, and honey, and refer to bedding - both blankets and sheets, to cloth and towels, to turf, firewood and straw. The poor guests on leaving could take any bread left over with them , but grooms were not to take drink to the stables.

The duty of hospitality could, indeed, be a heavy burden, costing Vale Royal *(1336)*, for example, nearly one-quarter of its gross annual income.[96] When times were difficult for them, a number of monasteries successfully petitioned the General Chapter for permission not to receive guests for a fixed term, usually one, two,[97] or three years,[98] but during that period of dispensation no novices could be received nor any un-necessary building works undertaken.[99] Several monasteries complained about the demands hospitality made upon their resources. Margam Abbey, on the route to Ireland, grumbled *(1336)* that 'being on the high road, and far from other places of refuge, the abbey is continually over-run by rich and poor strangers'[100] Netley, near the Solent, claimed to be impoverished *(1338)* due to giving aid and hospitality 'to the large numbers of mariners coming and going';[101] Bindon *(1348)* near the coast,[102] and Quarr *(1536)* in the Isle of Wight were also noted ports-of-call for sailors.[103] The Staffordshire abbey at Dieulacres grumbled about the demands for hospitality from 'people with grooms, horses and greyhounds' *(1351)*,[104] and, in similar vein, Lubiąż in Silesia had to receive huntsmen whom the monks said were 'as hungry as wolves' *(1280)*.[105] A mixed bag, a motley

---

[96] VCH, *History of the County of Chester* III (1980) 160.

[97] E.g: *Statuta* II, 308 (1246/35, 36).

[98] E.g: *Statuta* II, 238 (1241/41).

[99] *Statuta* II, 475 (1261/2).

[100] Williams (1984) I, 171; R. Midmer, *English Medieval Monasteries* (London, 1979) 278; Mullin (1932) 88, O'Dwyer (1982) 206.

[101] VCH. *History of Hampshire* II (1903) 147; C. G. Harper, *Abbeys of Old Romance* (London, 1930) 212.

[102] *Cal. Patent Rolls* 1348/52.

[103] VCH, *History of Hampshire* II (1903) 138-9.

[104] VCH, *History of the County of Stafford* III (1970) 232; Cf. F.H. Crossley, *The English Abbey* (London, 2nd. edn; 1939) 68.

[105] J.W. Thompson, 'The Cistercian Order and Colonisation' in *American Jnl. of Theology* XXIV (1920) 93.

crowd, could be found in Cistercian guest-houses, and it is little wonder that Gerald of Wales complained about 'the noise of the people' in the hospice at Strata Florida.[106] More serious, there could be unpleasant incidents. A young man was killed in a brawl at the guest house of Margam *(ca. 1180)*,[107] whilst visiting grooms stabbed guests to death during stable-brawls at Furness *(1246)*[108] and at Croxden *(1273)*[109] More serious still, a mob destroyed the guest-house at Zbraslav in Bohemia *(1308)*.[110]

The customary of Cîteaux ordered the guest-master to 'treat with solicitude all guests whether sick or poor or others',[111] and the guest-house at Kotbacz in Poland could be described as a place where 'many benefits are disbursed to the nobles and the common people, to rich and poor' *(1278)*.[112] There was class distinction. At Beaulieu *(1270)* the guests were graded at the gate-house, and those on horse-back were kept separate from those arriving on foot, and given hospitality according to their status *(vide supra)*.[113] Gerald of Wales once objected to being treated as an ordinary traveller, and at being placed 'in the public hall among the common guests'.[114] At Salem in Germany *(1300)* there were two guest-masters, one to look after the 'decent folk', the other to care for the 'lower guests'.[115] Savigny had more than one hospice,[116] and at Tintern there may have been two quite separate guest-wings to provide for this distinction.[117] At Sorø in Denmark *(1347)* it was said that there were 'various guests, greater and lesser'.[118] At Longpont in France wine was only served to those who were termed 'guests of privilege' *(1214)*.[119] Such might drink from goblets with silver bases.[120] (Wine was also served at

---

[106] Williams (1984) 172.

[107] Ibid. 175.

[108] T. A. Beck, *Annales Furnesienses* (London, 1844) 207.

[109] M. Lawrence, 'Notes on the Chronicle of Croxden' in *Trans. N. Staffs. Field Club*, LXXXVI (1951-2) B. 38.

[110] J. Emlera, *Petra Zitavského Kronika Zbraslavská* (Fontes Rerum Bohemicarum, IV; Prague, 1884) 166 (No. CVII).

[111] Choisselet and Vernet (1989) 332-3; Cf. J. E. Madden, 'English Cistercians in the Thirteenth Century' in *Catholic Hist. Rev.* XLIX : 3 (Washington, 1963) 357.

[112] Thompson (1920) 93.

[113] Hockey (1975) 33.

[114] Williams (1984) 175.

[115] K. Schreiner, 'Zisterziensisches Mönchtum' in K. Elm and P. Joerissen, *Die Zisterzienser, ergänzungsband* (2nd edn; Cologne, 1982) 111.

[116] Griesser (1952) 229.

[117] P. Courtney, 'Excavations in the Outer Precinct of Tintern Abbey' in *Medieval Archaeology* XXXIII (1989) 99.

[118] J. Langebek, *Scriptores Rerum Danicarum* (Copenhagen, 1776) IV, 535; F. Hall, *Bidrag till Kännedomen om Cistercienserorden i Schweden* (Cefle, 1899) 30n.

[119] L. Duval-Arnold, 'Le Vignoble de Longpont' in *Le Moyen Âge* LXXIV (1968) 224.

[120] *Statuta* III, 61 (1268/11).

Stams in Austria).[121] At Sibton, a corrodian was allowed to eat in the refectory 'with the better sort of people' *(1323)*.[122] Guests could be buried within the monastic precincts, the lesser bell sounding twice at the time of interment, but class distinction carried over even into death. A simple guest went to his last resting-place without a sung service, but if he was a priest or religious he was carried into the choir; nothing unduly at fault there. Generally, however, if the abbot thought fit, 'having regard for the person', that is, if he was important enough - perhaps having been a benefactor, then chanting at his funeral could be allowed.[123] In fairness, it must be said that this restriction was probably enjoined so that the community were not unduly taken from their normal work and routine to attend burial services.

The more important guests included royalty. Here in Wales, after the death of Prince Llywelyn the Last *(1282)* some of his chattels were found at Cymer Abbey,[124] but he being dead and Wales conquered, it was King Edward I who visited Cymer, Valle Crucis and Neath, and stayed for some time at Aberconwy in the spring of 1283.[125] He was a frequent visitor to Cistercian houses throughout his kingdom, and especially to Holm Cultram during his Scottish campaign; he was there the day before he died at nearby Burgh-by-Sands.[126] His visits are traceable by the state documents issued during his stay at one monastery or another. Other English monarchs visiting houses of the Order included John - staying with his army twice at Margam, en route to and from Ireland in 1210,[127] and Edward II who stayed briefly at Tintern, Margam and Neath in his last days of freedom in the autumn of 1326.[128] One of the most assiduous monastic visitors was Louis IX of France, St Louis *(1226-70)*, who when calling at his own foundation of Royaumont would visit the sick monks and even help serve the community in its refectory.[129] Not all royal visits to Cistercian houses were happy ones. King John died *(1216)* shortly after a stay at Swineshead, and in later years men said that he died, not of dysentery, but of a poisoned drink administered to him by its monks.[130] King Sverker of Sweden was murdered on Christmas Day, 1156, by his stable-boy whilst on a visit to Alvastra Abbey.[131]

---

[121] K. Linder, 'Grundherrschaft Stams' in N. Grass, *Beitrage zur Wirtschafts und Kulturgeschichte des Zisterzienserstiftes Stams in Tirol* (Innsbruck, 1959) 198.

[122] Brown (1985-88) IV, 106 (No. 1182.)

[123] *Statuta* I, 72 (1160/13), (1161/4); Cf. Lucet (1964) 127, Choisselet and Vernet (1989) 292-95.

[124] Williams (1984) 172.

[125] Ibid. 50.

[126] Grainger and Collingwood (1929) 139; Cf. G.E. Gilbanks, *Records of Holm Cultram* (London, 1899) 83.

[127] Williams (1984) I, 172.

[128] Ibid., I, 51.

[129] A. Dimier, *St Louis et Cîteaux* (Paris, 1954) 67, 71-4.

[130] H.E. Hallam, *The New Lands of Elloe* (Leics. U.P., 1954) 33.

[131] I. Swartling, *Alvastra Abbey* (Stockholm Studies in the History of Art, 17; 1969) 20.

Occasionally, a royal stay was facilitated by special accommodation. Edward I gave stone for a chamber to be built at Stanley Abbey for his own use *(1290)*,[132] but there is no record of it thereafter. At Santes Creus in Spain, Kings Peter III *(1276-85)* and James II *(1291 -1327)* of Aragon built a palace for themselves linked to the cloister;[133] its remains are there to this day. King Martin I *(1400)* constructed a royal residence within the monastery of Poblet.[134] Monasteries formed useful meeting-places. Here in Wales, Prince Llywelyn the Great called together all the native princes to Strata Florida Abbey in 1238, and there caused them to swear allegiance to his son, David, as his rightful successor.[135] At Poblet Abbey in Spain, James I of Castile planned the conquest of Majorca in 1228.[136] At Boulbonne in France *(1272)* Philip III of France and James I of Aragon met to discuss peace terms.[137] Such hospitality to monarchs and their retinue was, of course, a mixed blessing to many a house, but some good could result from it. Because it entertained him and his troops, King John excused Margam from a heavy tax imposed upon the other English and Welsh abbeys of the Order,[138] Henry II visiting Fountains presented it with wine,[139] and gave twenty oak trees to Croxden in similar circumstances the same year *(1244)*;[140] calling at Combermere *(1245)* he granted the community the right to hold a market and fair on their manor at Drayton.[141] Poblet, host to the conqueror of Majorca, gained a new daughter-house on that island, the monastery of Nuestra Senora de la Real *(1236)*.[142]

An important component amongst the visitors to a Cistercian house might well be pilgrims, come because of indulgences promised to those who visited such and such an abbey and gave alms towards its maintenance. No less than fifty-one British bishops made such a grant of indulgence in favour of Furness Abbey,[143] and no fewer than ten to visitors to Vyssí Brod in Bohemia on the anniversary of the dedication of its church.[144]

---

[132] P. Fergusson, *Architecture of Solitude* (Princeton U.P., 1984) 147; VCH, *History of the County of Wiltshire* III (1956) 273.

[133] J.F. Arenas, *Los Monasterios de Santes Creus y Poblet* (Madrid, 1985) 54; F. Rahlves, *Cathedrals and Monasteries of Spain* (London, 1966) 211; B. Rosenman, 'The Tomb Canopies of Santes Creus' in Cîteaux XXXIV: 3-4 (1983) 229.

[134] J. Sumption, *Pilgrimage* (London, 1975) 247.

[135] Williams (1984) I, 172.

[136] Richards (1968) 97.

[137] *DHGE* X (1938) 63.

[138] Williams (1984) I, 172.

[139] *Cal. Close Rolls* 1244/222-3.

[140] Ibid. 1244/225.

[141] VCH. *History of the County of Chester* III (1980) 152.

[142] Bouton (1964) 230.

[143] VCH, *History of the County of Lancashire* II (1966) 120.

[144] M. Pangerl, *Urkundenbuch zu Hohenfurt* (Fontes Rerum Austriacarum, 23; Vienna, 1865) 24 (No. XVIII), 48 (XLIV), 53-4 (L), 54 (LI), 61-2 (LVIII), 62 (LIX), 64 (LXII) 72 (LXXI), 87-8 (LXXXVII), ranging in date from 1270 to 1346.

Similar indulgences were granted in respect, amongst others, of Bonneweg *(1290)* in Luxemburg,[145] to Fürstenzell *(1274)*[146] and Raitenhaslach *(1275)* in Bavaria,[147] and to Walkenried in Brunswick *(1291)*,[148] Visitors were encouraged by like indulgences to make offerings at Fontguilhem in France *(1309)* to assist the construction of its new church and cloister,[149] and at Llantarnam here in Wales *(1398)* following a disastrous fire.[150] Many pilgrims might be attracted by a particular object or shrine which a monastery might have to boast, though there is some evidence that these were not always genuine but fulfilled a need for hard-pressed communities to find extra finance. Several abbeys claimed to have a relic of the Holy Cross - amongst them Dore in Herefordshire,[151] Strata Marcella in Wales,[152] and La Boissière in France;[153] Holy Cross in Ireland[154] and Santes Creus in Spain took their dedication from the same. Whilst a Cistercian monk was bishop of Lerida in Spain, the relic of the Holy Cross in his cathedral found its way to the abbey at Poblet, but after the bishop's death the monks were forced to return it.[155] Upon the dedication of the new church of Sta Maria a Fiume in Italy, a portion of the Cross was sealed in its high altar *(1196)*.[156]

Other relics connected with Our Lord included the Precious Blood at Hailes, for which a polygonal apse of five chapels was erected after its acquisition in 1270.[157] At Boxley in Kent, the weeping statue of Christ on its rood loft caused that abbey to be known as the monastery of the Holy Cross of Grace.[158] Cadouin in the south-west of France claimed to possess the Holy Shroud *(1239)*,[159] A number of houses had miraculous images of the Blessed Virgin Mary; there was one at Cambron in France - in 1322 it was profaned by a Jew who at that very moment was enlightened and became a

[145] N. van Werveke, *Urkundenbuch der Abtei Bonneweg* (Luxemburg, 1880) 35 (No. 55).

[146] J. Friedrich and others, *Codex dipl. Regni Bohemiae* (Prague, 1904-74) V : Pt. 2, 404 (No. 741).

[147] Ibid 443-4 (No. 772).

[148] J.G. Leuckfeldt, *Antiquitates Walckenredenses* (Leipzig, 1705) 85.

[149] *DHGE* XVII (1971) 981.

[150] Williams (1984) I, 177.

[151] D. H. Williams, 'Abbey Dore' in *Monmouthshire Antiq.* II : 2 (1966) 72.

[152] Williams (1984) I. 177.

[153] *DHGE* IX (1937) 584; P. Chevallier, 'L' Abbaye de la Boissière' in *Revue de l'Anjou* 14 (1855) 338-68.

[154] Stalley (1987) 115-7; D. Pochin Mould, *The Monasteries of Ireland* (London, 1976) 57.

[155] L. J. McCrank, 'The Cistercians of Poblet as Landlords' in *Citeaux* XXVI : 4 (1975).

[156] S. Volpicella, 'Cronaca di Fossa-Nova' in *Cronisti e Scrittori Sincroni Napoletani* I (Naples, 1845) 524.

[157] R. C. Finucane, *Miracles and Pilgrims* (London, 1977) 207; VCH, *History of the County of Gloucester* II (1907) 97; Cf. *Statuta* III, 149 (1275/69).

[158] VCH, *History of the County of Kent* II (1926) 154.

[159] *Statuta* II, 205 (1239/15).

Christian;[160] there was another in the gate-house chapel at Meaux *(1361)*,[161] another in the Galilee outside the west door of Tintern *(1414)*,[162] yet another at Bouro.[163] The numbers visiting these shrines could be very large indeed. The canonical visitation at Abbey Dore in 1318 revealed that crowds of people came to venerate the cross in the abbey church,[164] whilst the multitude was so great trying to observe the image of the Blessed Virgin at Meaux in 1361 that 'many were brought to death by reason of the crush'.[165] Much later, Bishop Hugh Latimer of Worcester *(1535-39)* spoke of the crowds of pilgrims passing by his home on their way to the Precious Blood of Hailes.[166]

One Cistercian shrine which attracted pilgrims from afar was that of St Edmund Rich at Pontigny Abbey in France, where there was also a chapel dedicated to St Thomas Becket.[167] Like Becket and archbishop Stephen Langton, two of his predecessors as archbishops of Canterbury, Edmund had found it necessary for political reasons to seek refuge on the Continent, and, like them also, spent some time at Pontigny. After his canonisation not only did St Louis and his family attend the translation of his remains[168] *(1247;* still enshrined there to-day) but Henry III of England also visited the monastery church *(1253),*[169] as did seemingly a stream of English pilgrims.[170] Henry III had given a chasuble and a chalice for the Mass at Pontigny on the first feast of St Edmund in 1247,[171] and a few years later granted money to allow four candles to burn at the shrine.[172] Lesser shrines included that of St Robert at Newminster.[173] Remnants of shrines can still be seen; fragments of a stone shrine exist at Abbey Dore, and a woodcased reliquary pertaining to Loccum Abbey in East Germany and dating from 1270 is still extant.[174] Yet more pilgrims might be attracted to Cistercian monasteries by the reputation of miracles wrought there. Indeed, at St Bernard's abbey of Clairvaux, as early as the 1170s was

---

[160] *DHGE* XI (1949) 586; *Statuta* III, 392 (1331/12).

[161] Midmer (1979) 218; Cf. VCH, *History of the County of York* III (1913) 147.

[162] Williams (1984) I, 177.

[163] *DHGE* X (1938) 245.

[164] C. Harper-Bill, 'Cistercian Visitation' in *Bull. Inst. Hist. Research* LIII (1980) 105.

[165] Midmer (1979) 218.

[166] Finucane (1977) 207.

[167] M. Garrigues, *Le Premier Cartulaire de Pontigny* (Coll'n. de Documents Inédits sur l'Histoire de France; 14, 1981) 233-4 (No. 184), 273-4 (No. 241); Cf. Finucane (1977) 138-9.

[168] A.A. King, *Cîteaux and her Elder Daughters* (London, 1954) 165-6.

[169] Ibid. 168; H.R. Luard, *Annales Monastici* II (Rolls Ser., London, 1865) 346.

[170] Finucane (1977) 139; E.g: *Cal. Patent Rolls* 1259/19, 1260/181, 1261/174, 1277/199.

[171] *Cal. Close Rolls* 1247/497; Cf. *Statuta* II, 315 (1247/2).

[172] Garrigues (1981) 252-3 (No. 211).

[173] Fowler (1876) xvi, 108, 225, 229-38.

[174] G. Gloede, *Das Doberan Münster* (Berlin, 1965) 72.

compiled a 'Book of Visions and Miracles'.[175] There were traditions of blind monks regaining their sight - at Dieulacres in Staffordshire[176] and Melrose in Scotland;[177] there were tombs which saw healing miracles - including those of John, a monk of Longpont in France *(1253)*,[178] and that of the lady Matilda de Bohun at Herefordshire's Abbey Dore *(1318)*.[179]

Several monasteries appear to have had specific rights of permanent sanctuary, and indeed at all religious houses refugees could hope to find a hiding-place, if only for a limited period.[180] The classic example in England was, of course, the Great Close of Beaulieu, where Perkin Warbeck, Pretender to the Crown and claiming to be Richard IV took refuge *(1497)* before surrendering,[181] and where at the time of the monastery's suppression *(1538)* thirty-two men - debtors, thieves and murderers, lived, together with their families. Many of them were aged and some very sick.[182] Mostly the right of sanctuary was respected. When *(1234)* some of the rebel forces backing Richard Marshal against Henry III fled to Flaxley Abbey - despite the Order's prohibition on receiving warriors, the armed men sent by the Sheriff of Gloucester lay in wait for them, but outside the monastery gate.[183] When an alleged murderer was arrested at Waverley *(1239)* and sanctuary was violated, its monks petitioned the king and the papal legate, its rights were upheld and the unfortunate man returned to them.[184] There are numerous other references. A robber took refuge at Bruern *(1266)*[185] and a murderer at Louth Park *(1279)*.[186] In Wales, when the travelling antiquary, John Leland, visited Margam and Tintern (*ca. 1538*) he told of their former rights of sanctuary as being long disused; at Abbey Neath parts of its 'Sanctuary Wall' were still standing in about 1700.[187]

A more permanent group of guests - certainly in British monasteries, were the corrodians; people who for past services rendered, or for financial help afforded, had

[175] B.P. McGuire, 'A Lost Clairvaux Exemplum Collection Found' in *Analecta Cist.* XXXIX (1982 : 1) 26-64.

[176] VCH, *History of the County of Stafford* III (1970) 231n.

[177] J. Stevenson, 'Chronicle of Melrose' in his *Church Histories of England* (London, 1856) 212.

[178] *Statuta* II, 394 (1253/25).

[179] Williams (1966) 72.

[180] H.M. Whitley, 'Sanctuary in Sussex' in *Sussex Arch. Coll'ns* LXI (1920) 80.

[181] VCH, *History of Hampshire* II (1903) 143; Cf. W.H. St John Hope and H. Brakspear, 'Abbey of Beaulieu' in *Arch. Jnl.* LXIII (1906) 175.

[182] G.H. Cook, *Letters to Comwell and others on the Suppression of the Monasteries* (London, 1965) 167-8.

[183] Crawley-Boevey (1887), 55-57; Cf Lucet (1964) 133; *Cal. Close Rolls* 1234/384, 393, 554; VCH, *History of the County of Gloucester* II (1907) 95.

[184] Harper (1930) 215-6, Luard (1865) II, 1239-40.

[185] *Cal. Patent Rolls* 1266/645.

[186] *Cal. Patent Rolls* 1279/346.

[187] Williams (1984) I, 176.

been granted a 'corrody' or 'exhibition' or 'livery' by a particular abbey.[188] The frequency of the practice was attested in 1222 by the Council of Oxford which forbade religious houses to sell or give corrodies to clerics or laymen, unless urgent necessity demanded it and the consent of the diocesan bishop was obtained.[189] So far as British Cistercian houses were concerned, and so far as the patchy evidence allows us to determine, not all corrodies granted in the thirteenth century were full corrodies, they do not always appear to have implied use of a chamber in the monastery concerned. A full corrody consisted of residence within the walls, regular meals and drink, heat and light, and, occasionally, other benefits such as clothing, or other services such as shaving, laundering and tailoring.[190] The provision afforded varied with the down-payment made, and with the rank and class of the recipient.

A true corrody was for life, and it was a legal entitlement - conveyed by letters patent attested by the common seal of the monastery concerned. It was a way in which long-time servants might be pensioned off, or other lay-people might find a retirement home.[191] Corrodies involving the actual residence of lay-folk appeared at Sibton Abbey in Suffolk by 1268,[192] and at Quarr in the Isle of Wight by 1300.[193] They were perhaps popularised by Edward I who from the outset of his reign vigorously continued the practice of Henry III in endeavouring to place aged or sick retainers in an abbey of royal foundation.[194] A typical demand was that of Edward II who, in sending his cook, John de Sutton, to Stratford Abbey in Essex in 1317, requested for him not only 'food and clothing, two robes yearly, and a chamber in the monastery', but also maintenance for Sutton's two attendant grooms and his two horses, and, additionally, 'candles, litter, firewood, and all other necessaries'.[195] The corrodians known in Britain were paralleled abroad by the 'prebendaries' of Montheron in Switzerland *(from 1323)*.[196] Similar institutions included the 'donados' of Poblet Abbey in Spain who had a special dormitory there,[197] the 'donats' of the Cistercian nunnery of Nonenque in France who each had a domestic servant waiting upon them *(1303)*,[198] and by the 'oblates' of Aiguebelle who could keep their wives.[199]

---

[188] D.H. Williams, 'Tudor Cistercian Life', I' in *Cîteaux* XXXIV : 1-2 (1983) 77-8.

[189] R.H. Snape, *English Monastic Finances* (New York, 1926; reprinted, 1968) 145.

[190] Williams (1983) I, 78; II, 288-94.

[191] Snape (1926) 139-45, Lawrence, ibid. in LXXXVII (1952-3) B. 52-3.

[192] Brown (1985-88) 51-2 (No. 1003).

[193] S.F. Hockey, *Quarr Abbey and its Lands* (Leicester U.P., 1970) 74.

[194] Cal. *Patent Rolls* 1271/507, 1279/305; Cf. J. Stéphan, *Buckfast Abbey* (Bristol, 1970) 106-7.

[195] VCH, *History of the County of Essex* II (1907) 131.

[196] C. Sommer-Ramer and P. Braun, *Helvetia Sacra* III/3 (I) (1982) 147, 317.

[197] Lekai (1977) 379, L.J. McCrank, 'The Frontier of the Spanish Reconquest and the Cistercians of Poblet' in *Analecta Cist.* XXIX (1973 : 1-2) 66.

[198] G. Bourgeois, 'Les granges de Nonenque' in *Cîteaux* XXIV : 2 (1973) 151.

[199] Fr. Hugues, *Annales d'Aiguebelle* I (Valence, 1863) 163.

ENGLAND: CORRODIANS' QUARTERS AT CLEEVE ABBEY, SOMERSET

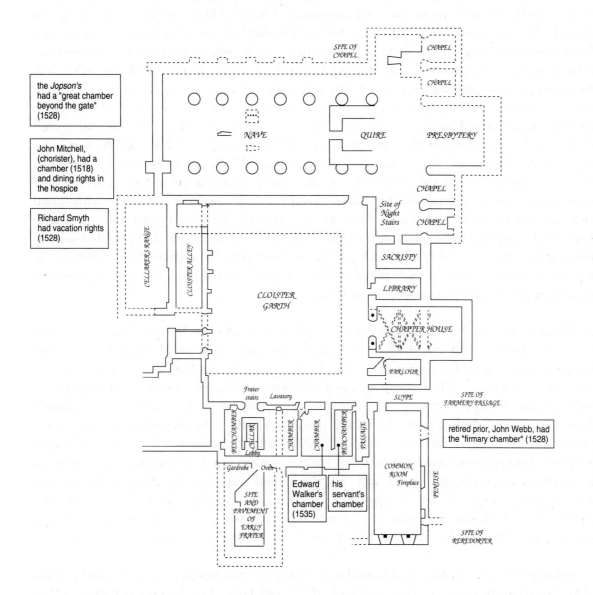

the *Jopson's* had a "great chamber beyond the gate" (1528)

John Mitchell, (chorister), had a chamber (1518) and dining rights in the hospice

Richard Smyth had vacation rights (1528)

SITE OF CHAPEL

CHAPEL

CHAPEL

NAVE

QUIRE

PRESBYTERY

CHAPEL

CHAPEL

Site of Night Stairs

SACRISTY

LIBRARY

CELLARER'S RANGE

CLOISTER ALLEY

CLOISTER GARTH

CHAPTER HOUSE

PARLOUR

Frater stairs

Lavatory

SLYPE

SITE OF FARMERY PASSAGE

retired prior, John Webb, had the "firmary chamber" (1528)

BEDCHAMBER

CELLAR

Lobby

CHAMBER

CHAMBER

BEDCHAMBER

PASSAGE

COMMON ROOM Fireplace

PENTISE

Gardrobe

Oven

SITE AND PAVEMENT OF EARLY FRATER

Edward Walker's chamber (1535)

his servant's chamber

SITE OF REREDORTER

British Cistercian houses never had more than a few corrodians, and occasionally - where, as in the case of royal nominations, it gained nothing in return, a monastery tried to resist the placing of such a pensioner.[200] Cleeve Abbey in Somerset, in its last days *(1536)* had some five people with residential entitlements of substance.[201] One was the retired prior, John Webb, who had the 'firmary chamber'; another was a chorister, John Mitchell; yet another was Richard Smyth, a vicar-choral of Wells, who 'for good and praiseworthy services' could stay at Cleeve for up to six weeks each year. Then, for 'a large and pecuniary service' to the monastery, Stephen Jopson and Margaret his wife, were granted 'the great chamber beyond the gate with other chambers adjacent'; all received residential entitlements in food and the like, as did Edward Walker, who had loaned £100 to the abbey, and had also given it £27. In return he was to receive 'a chamber situate under the east part of the fratry house with a door coming and going into the cloister and another inner chamber for his servant', together with 'good and wholesome meat and drink, daily at the table of the abbot, and also meat and drink for his servant to be taken at the table with the servants of the abbot, and also daily and nightly sufficient livery of bread and ale or beer unto his chamber'; in addition, he was to receive each year seven loads of timber for fuel, his two horses or geldings were to be catered for, and he was to receive an annuity of 18/-

Towards the close of the twelfth century, abbot Leonard of St Mary's, Dublin, angered the local clergy - who could see a loss of income, when he proclaimed the spiritual advantages that would accrue if one chose to die in Cistercian habit, and be buried in a Cistercian cemetery.[202] His statement was a reflection of current practice which extended well into the thirteenth century, whereby quite a number of lay-folk who were at death's door were indeed clothed in the habit and placed directly in the monastic infirmary. One can see the advantages that this brought to individual abbeys in terms of bequests and of property. Two reasons have been adduced for the practice; first, that death-bed donations were frowned upon by the Order, and that the formal receipt of the dying person in this way, by-passed that official disapproval;[203] second, and perhaps more to the point, the burial of lay-folk within Cistercian precincts - save for certain exceptions, was not sanctioned until 1217; but if habited, they were so entitled to interment.[204]

Amongst those so clothed and buried were the great and mighty, monarchs and princes - like Llywelyn the Great at Aberconwy *(1240)*[205] and James I of Aragon at Poblet *(1276)* - which latter house received a substantial legacy.[206] Gerald of Wales asserted that

[200] *Cal. Patent Rolls* 1271/594; VCH, *History of the Countuy of Essex* II (1907) 126; *History of the County of Kent* II (1926) 153; *History of Shropshire* III (1979) 232; G. Wrottesley, 'Chartulary of Dieulacres' in *Colln's Hist. Staffs* (William Salt Arch. Soc. N.S.) IX (1906) 295-6.

[201] Williams (1983) II, 303 (Nos.32-35), 304 (No. 60).

[202] Stalley (1987) 105.

[203] Lekai (1977) 292.

[204] Stalley (1987) 205.

[205] Williams (1984) I, 183.

[206] McCrank (1975) 262.

humbler dying folk *(ca. 1200)* were carried off by the monks of Abbey Dore from nearby villages and 'by corrupt persuasion' in wheeled vehicles to their abbey.[207] More surprisingly, even dying women were so clothed. An instance occurred at Valroy in 1196,[208] and the practice earned censure from the General Chapter in 1201,[209] but it continued - another case being reported from Fontguilhem in 1205.[210] Gerald of Wales said further of the monks of Dore that amongst its dying people so clothed were two women of some substance, and he alleged that 'with all the solemnity of psalms and prayers with which men were wont to be made monks', these two ladies were each 'made a monk with tonsure and cowl complete'.[211] (I wonder what happened if death did not come, and a monk newly professed in these circumstances regained his strength and vigour? Would he wish to continue in the religious life?). Not all dying benefactors were clothed. A sick man in the lay infirmary at Ripalta Scrivia in Italy added a codicil to his will, thus benefiting the monastery *(1261)*;[212] when a local knight was dying, the abbot of Louth Park sent a covered cart to bring him to the monastery and there, in his death-chamber, was signed and sealed his grant of a manor to the abbey *(1342)*.[213] As late as this time, however, a count of Foix *(1344)* might express a wish to be placed in Cistercian habit when at the point of death.[214]

As for the dead, the early injunctions of the Order allowed only sovereigns and prelates,[215] founders,[216] guests and hired workers dying within a monastery, to be buried in its precincts.[217] Before the close of the twelfth century several infringements of these rules were noted, raising the ire of local bishops,[218] and continued into the thirteenth century - including the alleged burial of women at Vieu Ville Abbey in Brittany *(1201)*.[219] Policy was changed in 1217 to take account of what was by then a prevalent and lucrative practice; henceforth the burial of seculars was permitted if their parish priest

---

[207] Williams (1984) I, 183.

[208] *Statuta* I, 202 (1196/27).

[209] Ibid. I, 266 (1201/15).

[210] Ibid. I, 313 (1205/28).

[211] D.H. Williams, *White Monks in Gwent and the Border* (Pontypool, 1976) 8.

[212] A. F. Trucco, *Cartario dell'Abazia di Rivalta Scrivia* II (Bibl. della Soc. Storica Subalpina, IX; Pinerolo, 1911) 75-6 (No. CCXXVIII), Cf. 244-5 (No. DCCXVI of 1258). Similar instances can of course be found elsewhere.

[213] E. Venables, *Chronicle of Louth Park Abbey* (Lincs. Rec. Soc. I, 1891) 59-61.

[214] *DHGE* X (1938) 64.

[215] *Statuta* I, 47 (1152/10).

[216] *Statuta* I, 68 (1157/63).

[217] *Statuta* I, 19 (1134/XXVII); Lekai (1977) 450 (No. XXIV).

[218] Cf. *DHGE* XIV (1960) 1030, XVI (1967) 448; *Statuta* I, 129 (1190/59). 139 (1191/26), 161 (1193/19), 410 (1213/28, 30), 421 (1214/20).

[219] *Statuia* I, 266 (1201/15).

agreed.[220] Many monasteries, Dore,[221] Furness[222] and Margam[223] amongst them received grants of land in return for promise of burial, excavations at Holm Cultram have shown a number of wounded and palsied people interred in the cemetery north of the church,[224] whilst at Rushen in the Isle of Man, there is plenty of evidence of adults and children buried throughout the choir and transepts.[225] The interments at Øm have been plotted.[226] Burials of French nobles at Ste Ange in Petra (Constantinople) constituted a problem when the site had to be abandoned. *(ca. 1222).*[227]

Where richer people were concerned, individual monasteries became associated with specific dynasties. At Rushen were buried King Olaf the Black *(1225)* and Magnus, the last Norwegian king of Man *(1265)*.[228] At Poblet were interred the kings of Aragon,[229] and at Boulbonne the counts of Foix who had a mausoleum chapel built there *(1262)*.[230] A later count, however, had all the family remains translated to tombs before the high altar *(1302)*.[231] The list of such dynastic associations is endless, and one Hungarian nobleman who was to be buried at Borsmonostor (Hungary) presented that abbey *(1237)* with a serf and his son for the specific purpose of caring for his grave.[232] Monasteries might jealously guard their traditional links, as when a dispute arose between Clairlieu and Stürzelbronn *(1214)* as to which of those abbeys should have the body of the recently deceased Duke of Lorraine.[233] The Scripture says, 'Where your treasure is, there will your heart be also' *(St Matt. 6/21)*, and so heart-burials were by no means unknown. The heart of Robert Bruce I was interred at Melrose which he had greatly endowed *(1329)*;[234] When the foundress of the New Abbey near Dumfries died in 1289, the heart of her husband, John Balliol, was buried with her, and the monastery soon gained the colloquial name of

---

[220] *Statuta* I, 465 (1217/3), 472 (1217/29); Cf. *DHGE* XIV (1960) 1030.

[221] Williams (1984) II, 203.

[222] Beck (1844) 134, *Duchy of Lancaster Charters* (1875) 181.

[223] Williams (1984) II, 202-3.

[224] H. N. Garner, *Øm Kloster Museum* (Århus, 1973) 34.

[225] L.A.S. Butler, 'Abbey of St Mary of Rushen' in *Jnl. Brit. Archaeol. Assoc.* CXLI (1988) *passim*.

[226] Garner (1973) 25.

[227] R. Clair, 'Les filles d'Hautecombe' in *Analecta* S.O. Cist. XVII (1961 : 3-4) 272.

[228] J.G. Cumming, 'Rushen Abbey' in *Antiq. Manniae* (Manx Soc., XV, 1868) 38.

[229] *DHGE* XVII 91971) 972, Arenas (1985) 63.

[230] *DHGE* X (1938) 63, Cf. 59, 61.

[231] Ibid. 64.

[232] L. Lekai, 'Medieval Cistercians and Hungary' in *Analecta Cist.* XXXII (1976 : 1-2) 257.

[233] *DHGE* XII 91953) 1044.

[234] C.H. Talbot, *Cistercian Abbeys of Scotland* (London, 1939) 25; J.C. Carrick, *Abbey of Newbottle* (Edinburgh, 1907) 29.

Sweetheart Abbey.[235]

The last major group of lay-folk in any Cistercian monastery, and in the latter days often by far the largest, were the servants. From early on, the white monks had realised that as well as *conversi* or lay-brothers paid assistance was necessary. To quote the *Exordium Parvum* (written sometime after 1134), the founders of the Order 'decided to admit also hired workers, for they realised that without their help they would be unable to observe fully the precepts of the *Rule* by day and by night'.[236] These early employees were called 'mercenaries', and it is clear from the provisions made for their diet, and, if occasion arose, for their burial, that some of them at least were resident within the walls.[237] Statute, however, was to forbid the engagement as mercenaries of blood-relatives of members of the community *(1195)*[238] Some of these mercenaries were quite young - often referred to as 'boys', though that term was frequently used in the way one might refer to stable - 'lads' in Britain to-day.[239] Boys employed to work in the skinner's , tailor's and weaver's rooms of an abbey had to be at least twelve years old *(1195)*,[240] and there were boy-servants in the guest-hall of Furness *(1264)*.[241] There was, of course, gradation amongst the mercenaries, clearly shown at Beaulieu in 1270 with its servants, grooms, and pages, in that order of importance.[242]

As the number of *conversi* dwindled in the thirteenth century, so the mercenaries came to occupy quite important positions. At Kingswood near Bristol, in 1256, paid servants included a baker, a brewer, a miller, a forester, a stableman, a skinner and a swine-herd.[243] In the later Middle Ages the gradation between different groups of 'servants' became even more pronounced, and (where residential) their entitlements varied correspondingly. The 'top servants' or 'gentlemen' or 'officers of the abbot', as they were variously called, would receive a formal, detailed indenture; the lowlier 'waiting servants' generally did not.[244] The claims for compensation made to the Court of Augmentations after the Suppression, supplemented by other sources, tell us something of the duties and of the benefits enjoyed by the 'top servants'. To take one example; Robert Dawson, appointed in 1512 to be Porter of the West Gates at Fountains, was also to act as Guestmaster, and to double up as the abbot's man-of-business and as his personal attendant on feast-days;

---

[235] *DHGE* XIV (1960) 1037; Talbot (1939) 67.

[236] Lekai (1977) 459.

[237] Lekai (1977) 448-9 (No. XIII), 450 (No. XXIV).

[238] *Statuta* I, 184 (1195/15).

[239] *Statuta* I, 183 (1195/6); Cf. Hockey (1975) 20; J.S. Donnelly, *Decline of the Medieval Cistercian Laybrotherhood* (Fordham U.P., New York, 1949) 65 nn. 5,6,7.

[240] *Statuta* I, 184 (1195/15).

[241] Beck (1844) 219.

[242] Hockey (1975) 20.

[243] Perkins (1899) 211-13.

[244] Williams (1983) II, 284.

BELGIUM: the 13th Century *Guest House* at Orval Abbey.

BELGIUM: the 13th Century *Prison* at Villers Abbey.

SCOTLAND: Portion of the *Precinct Wall* at New Abbey (Sweetheart).

FRANCE: the 13th - 14th Century *Gate House* at Longpont Abbey.

in addition his wife, Ellen, was the monastery's laundress-in-chief. They received for life: 'a house or hospice newly built without the West Gates, a water meadow by the River Skell, all intestines of animals and sheep killed for the use of the monastery (excepting those assigned at Christmas to the larderers)'; each week they were entitled to have fourteen loaves of bread and twelve flagons of beer, and each day as much fish or flesh of the day as two monks would receive. As a former guest-master myself, I like the undertaking Dawson gave 'to receive and welcome the abbot's guests diligently and courteously in word and deed, and in settlement of their expenses to treat them as gently and mildly as he could'.[245] The latter clause suggests that the guest-house had become a semi-independent undertaking; it seems to have become in part privatised.

In Tudor days, in English monasteries, an obvious regard for the daily liturgical round and for the maintenance of standards of choral worship, saw the presence of song-schools. (with usually four boy-pupils) at Boxley, Buckland, Furness and Newminster. At Cleeve the musical standard will have come under the critical ear during his periods of residence of the vicar-choral from Wells *(vide supra)*, and at Coggeshall and Stanley of corrodians who were former members of the Chapel Royal. More formal and general education was rendered necessary by the presence of boys in a monastery, and non-choristers were also taught. Lay schoolmasters and pupils were to be found in the last years at Stanley, Whalley and Woburn, whilst at Ford, a Mr Tyler, M.A., was both to teach 'letters and grammar' to the boys of the monastery, and also, in response undoubtedly to the injunctions of the Crown Visitors, to interpret in the refectory the Scriptures to the brethren.[246]

A final, and perhaps never large group of visitors were 'guests' in the same sense as those who are detained at Her Majesty's pleasure to-day; in other words, prisoners, often held in cells at the gate-house. This was certainly the case at Kingswood *(1240)* where the cellarer paid the porter 8d for the maintenance of a prisoner.[247] and at its mother-house of Tintern where John Edmund *(1536)* was appointed to the 'office of porter, and keeper of the gaol and garrett'.[248] Substantial remains exist of the medieval gate-house prison at Villers in Belgium, the dungeons of which overlooked the channel bounding the abbey. A gate-house prison has also been postulated at Bordesley.[249] It is not always possible to distinguish in the records between the prisons provided by statute for refractory monks and those built for delinquent laity, but they were undoubtedly separate - as is suggested by the mention in the plural of 'prisons' at Pforta in East Germany *(1344)*,[250] Occasional mention is found of the use of Cistercian prisons; perhaps the most revealing came from a clerk who complained *(1347)* that he had been held for five weeks at Zlatá Koruna

---

[245] G.M. Hills in *Collectanea Archaeologica* II : 1 (1863) 268; Cf. J.T. Fowler, *Memorials of Fountains Abbey* (Surtees Soc., CXXX, 1918) 235-39.

[246] Williams (1983) II, 299.

[247] Perkins (1899) 196.

[248] PRO, LR 1/228, f. 6d.

[249] P. Rahtz and S. Hirst, *Bordesley Abbey* (Brit. Arch. Report 23, 1976) 7.

[250] E. Halbband, *Urkundenbuch des Klosters Pforte* (Geschictsquellen der Provinz Sachsen, 33; Halle, 1893) 567.

Abbey in Bohemia; to quote, 'in foul prisons, kept in chains'.[251]

What about women? The earliest injunctions of the Order made it crystal clear that women were not to pass through the monastery gate, whilst monks and *conversi* were strictly forbidden at any time, or for any reason, to live under the same roof with women.[252] As the twelfth century progressed, and a series of new abbey churches were built, ladies were allowed to enter such a Cistercian church but only on the day of its dedication or within the octave;[253] quite frequently they outstayed their welcome.[254] The general prohibition remained, and especially inhibited were women who were breast-feeding.[255] The injunction against women was repeated quite often into the thirteenth century,[256] and strongly re-inforced by Abbot Stephen Lexington of Savigny *(1230)* who enjoined not only that women were not to proceed beyond the gate, nor to spend the night in the gate-house, but also that if a monk or *conversus* was caught alone with a woman, he was to be flogged weekly in chapter until the next visitation.[257]

Gregory IX *(1227-41)* forbade princes and nobles to take women into a Cistercian house,[258] but Innocent IV *(1250)* allowed noble women to enter, though they were still forbidden to eat meat, or spend the night, in an abbey,[259] a restriction broken by distinguished company at Preuilly only three years later.[260] The General Chapter re-iterating *(1262)* the rule against the entry of women took this papal concession into account.[261] When later in the thirteenth century *(1297)* the observance of the regulations appears to have weakened, the General Chapter attempted to stem any further infringements.[262] So did local visitations - as that at Dore in Herefordshire *(1318)* where women had obviously been entering the precincts. It was enjoined that henceforth women pilgrims were to be provided for at the abbey gate, and that the practice of allowing women in to pick, wash, and prepare flax, was to cease.[263]

---

[251] M. Pangerl, *Urkundenbuch des Cistercienserstiftes Goldenkron* (Fontes Rerum Austriacarum, 37; Vienna, 1872) 102-3 (No. LIIIa), 107-9 (No. LVIa).

[252] *Statuta* I, 14 (1134/VII); Lucet (1964) 126, 321; Lekai (1977) 449 (Nos. XVII, XVIII).

[253] *Statuta* I, 61 (1157/10), 138 (1191/22), 160 (1193/12); Lucet (1964) 127, (1977) 321-2.

[254] E.g: *Statuta* I, 180 (1194/55), 361 (1209/23), 427 (1214/53); *DHGE* IX (1937) 1008.

[255] *Statuta* I, 67 (1157/58); Lucet (1964) 126-7, (1977) 321.

[256] *Statuta* I, 171 (1194/70); III, 41 (1266/28), 131 (1274/18).

[257] O'Dwyer (1982) 158, 166.

[258] Lucet (1977) 247.

[259] *Statuta* II, 350 (1250/23).

[260] *Statuta* II, 396 (1253/32).

[261] *Statuta* II, 3 (1262/11).

[262] *Statuta* III, 288 (1297/3).

[263] Harper-Bill (1980) 105, Cf. 107.

The statutes of successive General Chapters down to the midst of the thirteenth century show frequent breaches of the rules against women. Ladies entered the Austrian abbey of Heiligenkreuz during the Sacred Triduum in 1193 and received Holy Communion,[264] an abbot of Foucarmont in France *(1194)* was reprimanded for familiarity with women;[265] no less than three breaches of the regulations were alleged at Egres Abbey, then in Hungary, within a dozen years *(1200-12)*;[266] and an abbot of Knockmoy in Ireland *(1240)* was censured because he had his head washed by a woman.[267] There were more prominent transgressions: the queen of France spent two nights in the infirmary at Pontigny *(1205)*, heard the sermon in chapter, and attended the procession in the cloister;[268] when the new church of Savigny was consecrated *(1220)* it was said that nuns both sang in the choir and ate in the refectory.[269] When Queen Eleanor of England spent three weeks at Beaulieu *(1246)* nursing a sickly Prince Edward, the prior and cellarer lost their jobs in consequence.[270]

It was difficult to keep women out, especially when as at Vaux-en-Ornois *(1193)*[271] and at Beaulieu-en-Bassigny *(1216)*[272] they wanted to place alms on the altar. It was more difficult still when they made a forcible entry. There were a wave of these between 1193 and 1210,[273] and at Carnoët in Brittany *(1195)* monks were forced to take refuge on one of their granges.[274] The firm refusal to admit women may have accounted for the monks of Pontigny, about 1249, cutting off St Edmund Rich's right arm, and placing it in a portable reliquary which could be carried out to the gate. One woman sang the praises of St Edmund so enthusiastically that she had to be restrained.[275] After St Edmund's right arm was severed it was said that miracles at Pontigny became rarer, and indeed the monks needn't have bothered to mutilate the saint; six years later, because of the national associations, English women were officially permitted to enter the precincts at Pontigny to visit his shrine.[276] The known Cistercian policy of exclusion of women may also have accounted for a Greek bishop of Patras *(1273)* successfully appealing to the General

---

[264] *Statuta* I, 165-6 (1193/41).

[265] *Statuta* I, 174 (1194/22.)

[266] *Statuta* I, 389 (1212/1); *DHGE* XV (1963) 28-9, Lekai (1976) 262.

[267] *Statuta* II, 223 (1240/40.)

[268] *Statuta* I, 308-9 (1205/10).

[269] *Statuta* I, 522 (1220/27).

[270] VCH. *History of Hampshire* II (1903) 141; Hockey (1976) 329-30.

[271] *Statuta* I, 161 (1193/18).

[272] *Statuta* I, 453 (1216/18).

[273] *Statuta* I, 162 (1193/28), 195 (1195/85), 224 (1198/4), 373 (1210/20).

[274] *Statuta* I, 194-5 (1195/83), 199-200 (1196/11).

[275] Finucane (1977) 29, 87.

[276] H.R. Luard, *Chronica Majora* V (London, 1880) 113-4; King (1954) 168.

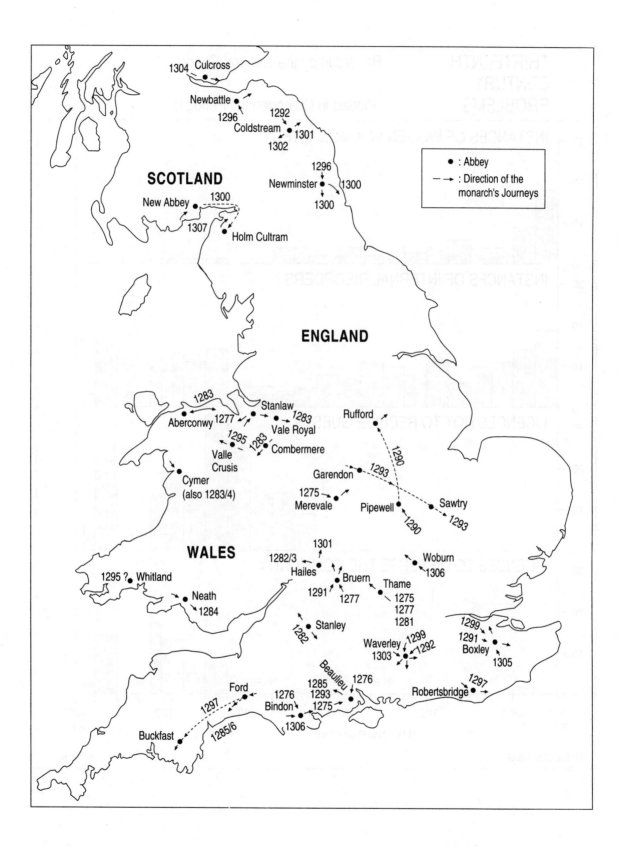

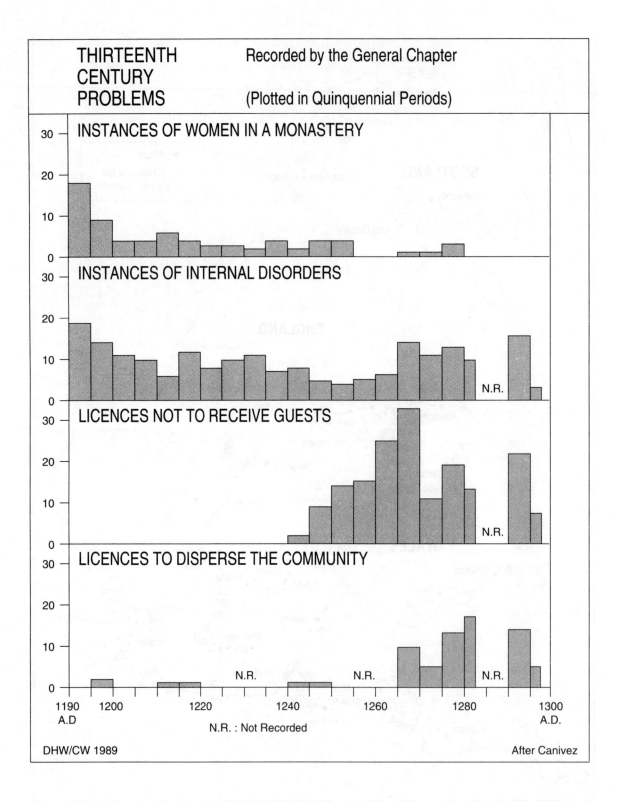

THIRTEENTH CENTURY PROBLEMS

Recorded by the General Chapter

(Plotted in Quinquennial Periods)

INSTANCES OF WOMEN IN A MONASTERY

INSTANCES OF INTERNAL DISORDERS

LICENCES NOT TO RECEIVE GUESTS

LICENCES TO DISPERSE THE COMMUNITY

N.R. : Not Recorded

DHW/CW 1989

After Canivez

Chapter to allow two Cistercian monks and two *conversi* to guard a hospice he had founded, 'so that' to quote, 'suspicious women might be kept away'.[277]

There was a tendency in the thirteenth century for women to try to live near the monastery gates through which they could not pass. An interesting example was that of three monasteries in Aquitaine (Berdoues, Gimont and Perseigne; *1246*) where Arab women lodged in houses near the gates as concubines with the Arab workers of those monasteries.[278] When, in 1278, the abbot of Wettingen in Switzerland applied to the General Chapter for permission to disperse his community, he was told to get rid first of the women living near the gate-house.[279] Many years before, in 1154, an early statute prohibited women from spending the night in buildings outside a Cistercian gate-house,[280] but special buildings for female guests without the gates did come to be built. They are on record at Staffarda in the Piedmont,[281] at La Ferté *(1231)*,[282] at Vaux-de-Cernay,[283] and at St Bernard-op-Scheldt *(1341)*;[284] Holm Cultram had its 'Womanhouse' *(1538)*, its location uncertain but possibly within the precincts.[285]

Near the time of the Suppression in England, the position varies. As noted above, married couples - servants and corrodians respectively, lived in buildings outside the gate-house of Fountains and Cleeve respectively. Other couples lived in gate-houses, as at Bindon[286] and Grace Dieu,[287] and married people certainly lived within the precincts at Combermere, Garendon, Rufford, and Tintern, and a widow, my Lady Dorset, at Tilty.[288] In the lay-infirmary at Warden there were seven women as well as seven men,[289] whilst at Biddlesden four women lived outside the precincts but came in to work in the dairy.[290]

The early fathers of the Order: Robert, Alberic, Stephen, and, above all, Bernard, would have looked more than askance at such situations. But times had changed. The

---

[277] *Statuta* III, 123 (1273/50).

[278] *Statuta* II, 308 (1235/33).

[279] *Statuta* III, 183 (1278/16).

[280] *Statuta* I, 58 (1154/24).

[281] C.E. Boyd, *A Cistercian Nunnery in Medieval Italy* (Cambridge, Mass., 1943) 73.

[282] King (1954) 121.

[283] M. Aubert, *L'Architecture Cistercienne en France* (Paris, 1947) II, 146-7.

[284] B. van Doninck, *Obituarium Monasterii Loci Sancti Bernardi* (Bornhem, 1901) 37.

[285] PRO, E 315/399, f. 51.

[286] PRO, E 315/93, f. 31.

[287] PRO, E 315/91, ff. 33d-34r.

[288] Williams (1983) II, 303-5.

[289] Ibid. 309.

[290] Ibid. 310.

large numbers of *conversi* many monasteries had enjoyed in the twelfth century generally dwindled rapidly towards the close of the thirteenth, and by the year 1400 there were hardly any left.[291] Lay servants had to take their place on an increasing scale.[292] The way things were going was hinted at by the General Chapter as early as 1237 when it ruled that if any abbey had less than nine *conversi* it could employ hired men in the kitchen, something which had been previously forbidden.[293] The way things were going in England came in the 1332 figures for Bordesley: thirty-four monks, eight *conversi* and one novice but seventeen serving men,[294] and in the 1349 roll-call at Newenham: twenty monks and three *conversi* but no less than eighty-eight layfolk, of both sexes, within its walls.[295] In the fourteenth century there was also a general decline, sometimes very marked, in vocations of choir-monks, though there was something of a revival in the fifteenth.[296] Taken together, all this meant that in a number of abbeys there was a lot of spare accommodation in which officers and servants, corrodians and pensioners, could be accommodated. Corrodians brought a certain initial return to the monastery; having servants resident with benefits mostly in kind, meant a smaller financial outlay than would otherwise have been the case.

When the Suppression came in England and Wales, Aberconwy - not many miles from here, may have had as few as five monks in 1536, but the abbot told how he had to maintain forty persons, besides poor people and strangers.[297] The work of hospitality carried on. At Quarr there appear to have been some eleven monks, but thirty-eight officers and servants. Netley had some thirty-two mostly resident officers and servants.[298] When the Earl of Sussex investigated the involvement of Whalley Abbey in the Pilgrimage of Grace *(1537)* he said he was prevented from gathering evidence by the 'large number of the abbot's fee'd men'.[299] Lay-folk - whether visitors or servants, always played a part in Cistercian history, but by the later Middle Ages they formed perhaps the greater part of the wider community within the walls. The early ideal of an abbot with at least a dozen monks setting forth into a remote area to labour with their own hands, had long since disappeared. That does not mean that there was no spiritual life left, there frequently was; the witness of the Cistercian martyrs of the Reformation shows that. But, for better or for worse, the multitude of lay folk within the precincts meant that Cistercian life had greatly changed.

---

291. Lekai (1977) 91, 343-44.

292. Mulin (1932) 76-7.

293. *Statuta* I, 115 (1189/27); II, 169 (1237/3).

294. Rahtz and Hirst (1976) 19.

295. J.A. Sparks, *In the Shadow of the Blackdowns* (Bradford-on-Avon, 1978) 99; J. Davidson, *Newenham Abbey* (London, 1843) 86.

296. Lekai (1977) 91-2.

297. Williams (1983) II, 307 (No. 105).

298. Ibid. II, 309 (Nos. 123, 125).

299. Lekai (1977) 380.

Abbreviations:

DHGE   :   A. Baudrillart and others (edit.)., *Dictionnaire d'Histoire et de Géographie Ecclésiastiques* (Paris, 1912 -)

PRO   :   Public Record Office (Chancery Lane) London.

Statuta   :   J. Canivez, *Statuta Capitulorum Generalium Ordinis Cisterciensis* (Louvain, *Revue d'Histoire Ecclésiastique,* 1933-41).

VCH   :   Victoria County Histories (London).

THE ABBEYS OF BYLAND AND JERVAULX, AND THE PROBLEMS OF THE ENGLISH SAVIGNIACS, 1134-1156

by
Janet Burton

O f the new reformed orders and congregations which emerged in the late eleventh and early twelfth century in France and Brittany, the first to reach the British Isles were Tiron (founded 1109) and Savigny; the latter under the guidance of its founder, Vitalis, developed from a hermitage into an abbey between 1112 and 1115, and became the centre of a congregation of houses in England, Wales and France. Vitalis's abbey was situated on the borders of Brittany, Normandy and Maine; and the passage of the Savigniacs across the channel was no doubt facilitated by the close tenurial links of this area with England and Wales, as well as by king Henry I's personal acquaintance with the founder. Savigny sent out its first plantation to England in 1124 when monks were invited by Stephen, count of Mortain and later king of England, to settle at Tulketh in Lancashire. Here they founded a community which became more famous at its second site at Furness (1127). Between 1127 and the union of the congregation of Savigny with Cîteaux in 1147, nine more houses had been established in England and Wales which were or came to be directly dependent on Savigny. These were Neath (1130) Basingwerk (1131), Quarr (1132), Combermere (1133), Stratford Langthorne and Buildwas (1135), Buckfast (1136), Byland (1138) and Coggeshall (1140). There were by that date also three second generation houses: Swineshead (1135) and Calder (1134, refounded 1142) dependent on Furness, and Jervaulx (1145), which came to be a daughter house of Byland.[1]

The purpose of this paper is to look again at one source which I feel is worthy of closer attention and to consider what it has to tell us of the nature of early Savigniac settlement, with particular reference to two Yorkshire houses, Byland and Jervaulx. The fifteenth-century cartulary of Byland abbey, now London BL MS Egerton 2823, once contained a *Historia Fundationis* of Byland, and one of Jervaulx. The manuscript has sustained some damage, and the folios at the beginning, which comprised the narratives, have been lost. They were, however, transcribed by the antiquarian Roger Dodsworth and others before 1649 from the cartulary then in the possession of John Rushworth of Lincolns Inn, and now survive in Oxford, Bodleian Library, MS Dodsworth 63.[2] The

---

[1] The secondary literature on the congregation of Savigny in England is thin. There is a short, general discussion in D. Knowles, *The Monastic Order in England, 940-1215* (2nd edn. Cambridge, 1963), 227-8, 249-51, and an account (unsatisfactory in many ways because of errors) in B. D. Hill, *English Cistercian Monasteries and their Patrons in the Twelfth Century* (Urbana, Illinois, 1968), 80-115. For the relationships of English Savigniac houses to one another, see Janet Burton and Roger Stalley, 'Tables of Cistercian affiliations', in *Cistercian Art and Architecture in the British Isles*, edited by Christopher Norton and David Park (Cambridge, 1986, repr. 1988), 400. On the problem of the filiation of Byland, discussed in this paper, see Knowles, *Monastic Order*, 249-51, Hill, *English Cistercian Monasteries*, 98-9, and D.Nicholl, *Thurstan, Archbishop of York, 1114-1141* (York, 1964), 201-4.

[2] Oxford, Bodleian Library MS Dodsworth 63. The history of Byland occupies fos 9-31 and that of Jervaulx, fos 42-56. The former evidently began on fo. 10v of the Byland cartulary, and the latter on fo. 15 (MS Dodsworth 63, fo. 9 and fo. 41). A note on fo. 56 states 'Examin' 23° Octobris 1649'. Following the narratives there are, from fo. 58r, transcripts of charters from the Byland cartulary: 'ex registro cartarum monasterii de Bellalanda ... penes Iohannis Ryssheworth arm(igerii) de hospitio Lincolniense 24 Marcie 1647'.

texts have been printed, though with some errors and omissions, in Dodsworth and Dugdale's *Monasticon Anglicanum*.[3]

The text of the Byland history identifies its author: it was written by Philip, third abbot, who ruled the house between 1196 and 1198, and who had formerly been head of the monastery of Lannoy in the diocese of Beauvais. Philip used the testimony of the elders of the house, but relied mostly for his information on the reminiscences of the aged second abbot, Roger, who after 54 years in that post had been allowed to resign in 1196. The Jervaulx history does not name its author, but the fact that it was copied into the Byland cartulary suggests that it was written at the mother house. Indeed, the many references to the abbot of Byland as *'abbas noster'*, point to the place of origin as Byland. It may be possible to go further than this in suggesting an identification of the Jervaulx author. First, the two histories are very similar in style and format, although this is obscured by the way the text of the Byland history was printed by Dugdale in the *Monasticon*. Both histories comprise narrative interspersed with charters, indicating that the author(s) had access to the written records of both monastic scriptoria. The charters are included in the printed Jervaulx history, but all but one of the documents in the Byland section were omitted by Dugdale. A glance through Dodsworth's transcript, in contrast, makes clear similarities in organization and style which argue for a common author. The manuscript text, indeed, contains even stronger evidence that Philip was author of both narratives. There are textual comments in the Byland section, some of them omitted by Dugdale, which refer to the Jervaulx history following (e.g., *'prout inferius patebit'*), suggesting that the two texts formed something of a sequence. Moreover, the Byland history concludes with a passage, also omitted by Dugdale,

> Nunc vero qualiter egressus est conventus a domo nostra Joreualle(nsis) tempore predicti Rogeri predecessoris nostri et de fundacione ipsius posteris nostris volumus innotescere prout idem predecessor noster nobis oretenus pluries intimavit.[4]

> (Now we wish to note for those who come after us, how the convent of Jervaulx went out from our house in the time of the said Roger our predecessor, and of its foundation, as our same predecessor told us many times.)

We have to remember here that we are dealing with a text which is at least two stages removed from the original, autograph version of abbot Philip. This passage may be a scribal or editorial addition, medieval or seventeenth-century; because we have only a late copy we have no way of assessing its status. However, when we take into account the similarity in style and format of the Byland and Jervaulx histories, and the textual

---

[3] Roger Dodsworth and William Dugdale, *Monasticon Anglicanum* I (London, 1655), 869-77 (Jervaulx) and 1027-34 (Byland). Reference in this paper is to the more readily accessible revised edition, William Dugdale, *Monasticon Anglicanum* ed. J. Caley, H. Ellis and B. Bandinel, 6 vols in 8 (London, 1817-30), V, 349-53 and 568-74. As D. C. Douglas explained (in an essay entitled 'The Grand Plagiary' in *English Scholars* (1939), 31-59), although the *Monasticon* is generally attributed to Dugdale, it was a collaborative effort, much of the original thinking for the collection coming from Dodsworth. Dodsworth was the collector, and Dugdale's major contribution was to prepare the volumes for the press. The first volume, which contains the Byland and Jervaulx narratives, was published with a joint attribution in 1655, the year after Dodsworth's death; the two names were on the second volume (1661) but the final volume (1673) carried only the name of William Dugdale.

[4] Oxford, Bodleian Library, MS Dodsworth 63, fo. 31r. Quotations from the *Historia* in this paper are taken from the Dodsworth MS; reference is made to both the manuscript and printed text.

indications of a common authorship, I think we can suggest that Philip was the author of both texts which were possibly designed to form a narrative sequence.[5] If the two histories are similar in style, they are similar too in purpose. Philip stated his aim to recount the '*causam, formam et modum sive processum fundacionis domus nostrae*', the foundation of Byland. He provided few details after the mid 1150s, beyond noting the move to the final site of the house in 1177. His unstated aim, or theme, was to record, in writing, the independence of Byland from Furness and Calder, and to establish its status as a daughter house of Savigny.[6] Similarly the theme of the Jervaulx history may be said to be the clarification of its constitutional status and its dependence on Byland as its mother house.

It would be beyond the scope of this paper to give a full review of the evidence for the reliability of the texts. We may say that generally, when put alongside other sources, they stand up well. There are no obvious literary borrowings such as characterize the *Narratio Fundationis* of Fountains.[7] The author was evidently less familiar with events at Jervaulx than at Byland, and this no doubt accounts for some confusion of dates and names - such as the mistaken identification of earl Conan of Richmond with his father, count Alan. The *Historia* demonstrates the limitations of memory of a man who was eye-witness to many of the events he dictated, but whose recollections were blurred by the passage of time. One of the most convincing features of the *Historia* as a source is the willingness of the author to admit either when his sources failed, or contradicted each other.[8] The Byland and Jervaulx histories are the earliest known Cistercian foundation histories in England,[9] and are deserving of a critical edition.

What, then, does this Byland source tell us of the nature of Savigniac settlement in the North? In 1134/5 the abbey of Furness, at the invitation of a lay patron, not here named but to be identified as Ranulf Meschin, sent out a colony of monks, the conventional number of thirteen, to occupy a site at Calder in Cumberland.[10] In 1137 the house was

[5] Why Dugdale should have omitted the passages concerned is problematic, but the most likely explanation is that he was more interested in printing the documents and charters relating to Byland, than in the integrity of the *Historia* as a narrative. Christopher Brooke has made the point that some of the doubts which have been shed on the authenticity of the Llantony chronicle stem in part from the way the text is printed in Dugdale; see C. N. L. Brooke, 'Monk and Canon: some patterns in the religious life of the twelfth century' in *Monks, Hermits and the Ascetic Tradition*, Studies in Church History 22, ed. W. J. Sheils (1985), 109-129, especially 125-6, and D. Knowles, C. N. L. Brooke and Vera London, (eds), *The Heads of Religious Houses, England and Wales, 940-1216* (Cambridge, 1972), 172.

[6] There is no indication in the text that the stimulus to write came from any source outside the abbey. Dr. Gransden suggested the possibility that Philip may have been inspired to write history by the example of Ailred of Rievaulx, or by William, Augustinian canon of Newburgh, a house which shared a common lay patron with Byland (Antonia Gransden, *Historical Writing in England, c. 550-c. 1307* (London, 1974), 290,. Certainly in late twelfth-century Yorkshire Philip was not writing in a literary vacuum.

[7] See L. G. D. Baker, 'The Genesis of English Cistercian Chronicles: the Foundation History of Fountains Abbey', I and II, *Analecta Sacri Ordinis Cisterciensis* 25 (1969), 14-41, and 31 (1975), 179-212.

[8] See the use of phrases such as '*ut a quibusdam dicebatur*', '*ceterum secundum aliorum estimationem*', '*ceterum vt quorundam relacioni*': *Historia* fos 10r, 11v; *Mon. Ang.* V, 349-50.

[9] Gransden, *English Historical Writing*, 290.

[10] Hill, *English Cistercian Monasteries*, 98, wrongly identifies the founder as Ranulf de Gernons, earl of Chester. The founder is not named in the *Historia*, but it is clear from a papal bull in favour of Calder II, that the grantor of the original site was Meschin: *Mon. Angl.* V, 250. The *Historia* gives the date of the occupation of Calder I as 35 Henry I, 1134; the Furness Coucher Book gives the date as 10 January 1134/5, although as a source it is not the most reliable: *The Coucher Book of Furness Abbey*, pt i, ed. J. C. Atkinson, Chetham Society (1886), 11.

devastated by an invading army of Scots, and the monks, whom Philip claims 'had lived in great distress and deprivation' ('*in magno labore & defectu vixissent*'), went back to Furness.[11] The return of a colony to its mother house through economic pressure was not unusual, and the records of Cistercian houses reveal other instances of temporary disbandment of a site. What was unusual was the reception which the monks received. For reasons on which Philip was not quite clear, the monks were refused entry. According to some people, he said, the problem lay with the fact that Gerald, abbot of Calder, refused to resign his abbatial office, and it would be inconvenient for there to be two abbots and two convents within one house. The sounds very much like the party line adopted at Furness. The other reason suggested was more basic; it was economic. The Furness monks berated their colleagues as 'weak and womanly' ('*quasi desides et effoeminatos*') for having abandoned their house 'for so little' ('*pro modico*') and returning to Furness to live in greater plenty. Now the dismissal of a Scottish raid as a small affair may seem rather harsh, although we have no way of assessing the severity of the attack.[12] What does ring true is the suggestion that the monks of Furness were not willing to take in more mouths to feed. The Cistercian constitution allowed houses whose numbers grew to over sixty to send out daughter houses. Whether such was enshrined in the Savigniac legislation we do not know, but it clearly made sense for convents not to outgrow their economic resources. By 1134 Furness abbey had over the ten years grown in numbers and may actively have sought a lay patron's help to set up a colony to relieve pressure on finances.

This is, one senses, often a hidden element in monastic foundations. Most monasteries and nunneries were founded by laymen, and if we are lucky their charters have survived to shed light, but only some light, on the circumstances of foundation. But what the charters do not often tell us are the influences behind the decision to found a religious house. And I suspect that monastic initiative - as a convent grew to a size which existing economic resources could not sustain - may have been a powerful factor.[13] In other words, monks actively sought lay patrons with a view to founding colonies in order to limit the number of monks in the mother house. I am inclined here to accept as plausible the second interpretation given by Philip and his sources to the actions of the Furness monks. I can certainly find no support in the text for the kind of ideological split which Donald Nichol saw in the episode. He identified the Calder monks as reformers, idealists, and saw at Furness in 1134-37 a repetition of events at Molesme, from where reformers went on to found Cîteaux, or at St Mary's, York, where a split of opinion in 1131 led to the secession to the abbey of Fountains.[14] Although the text of the *Historia* suggests that there was a great deal of bitterness between the two convents (the Furness monks are said to have spoken '*immo miserrime et spiritu vehementi acerrime*'), there is nothing here to

---

[11] *Historia*, fo. 9v; Mon. Ang. V, 349.

[12] The Byland account of the Scottish raids on Cumbria does, however, accord with those of Ailred of Rievaulx (*Relatio de Standardo*, in *Chronicles of the Reigns of Stephen, Henry II and Richard I*, ed. R. Howlett (Rolls Series, 1884-89), III, 189, 193) and Richard of Hexham (*Historia de gestis Regis Stephani et de bello Standardo*, ibid., III, 152).

[13] One might think here of the initiative taken by the Cistercian monk, Adam, in the foundation of Meaux: Janet Burton, ' The Foundation of the British Cistercian houses', in Norton and Park, *Cistercian Art and Architecture*, 33, and 35, note 51.

[14] Nicholl, *Thurstan*, 202. He speaks of this being 'another case of the conservatives who stayed at home feeling that the high-minded reformers ... should put up cheerfully with the consequences of their idealism'.

indicate that this predated the sending out of the colony in 1134, or that the foundation of Calder I was anything more than the conventional establishment of a daughter house on a site provided by a lay patron. There is no evidence that this was a case of reformers moving on to adopt a more strict way of life. If there is any feature which recurs throughout the *Historia* as an aspect of early Savigniac history, it is not reform so much as economic concerns.

Unable to re-enter Furness and with the example in mind of how Thurstan of York had provided help for the monks of St. Mary's who went on to found Fountains abbey, abbot Gerald and his monks decided to seek out the archbishop in York and ask his advice. They set off with one cart for their vestments and books, and eight oxen. I will pass over here the details of their journey as recorded in the *Historia* - how the monks acquired lay patrons in the persons of Roger de Mowbray and his mother Gundreda, and a site at Hood - and skip to 1141.[15] The events that followed indicate, I would suggest, that much of the contention in the early history of the Northern Savigniacs was caused by two factors: by economic problems, and by an ill-defined system of filiation. Roger de Mowbray proved to be a generous benefactor of the monks, and by 1141 abbot Gerald feared that the sound economic basis which the abbey was beginning to achieve under his patronage, indeed the growing wealth of the house might lead Furness to claim to be the mother house of Byland.[16] We know little of the Savigniac constitution. In the orderly Cistercian world, to be the abbot of a mother house meant a duty, an obligation to visit every daughter house once a year and see that the constitutions were being observed. Gerald's fear can only mean that the abbot of Furness would be concerned not so much with duties as with powers. It suggests a fear that Furness might claim some financial stake in the abbey, or control over the abbey property. To forestall any such claim Gerald went to the general chapter at Savigny. Here he explained the way in which the monks of Furness had refused to take in his convent when their own house was destroyed, and gained assent to a plan to make Byland a daughter house of Savigny. The date given in the *Historia* is 1142, but C. T. Clay has argued convincingly for assigning Gerald's visit to 1141, just over a year before the transfer of the convent from the site at Hood to Old Byland in September 1142.[17]

In the short term the threat to Byland came, not from Furness but from Calder. A second convent was sent to Calder after the death of Gerald which occurred shortly after his return from the general chapter, early in 1142. The *Historia* makes it clear that the timing was not accidental. It was after Gerald's death, and after the subjection of Byland to Savigny, that Furness realised that the monks did not intend to return to Calder. Hence, a second convent was dispatched under a new abbot. Evidently the re-occupation of the Calder site raised grave constitutional problems. Even abbot Philip, who could be

---

[15] For these events, see *Historia*, fos 10v-14r; *Mon. Angl.* V, 349-50. There are two versions of the sequence of events during the journey from Furness, one of them sharing details with a later narrative from Forde abbey: see *Mon. Angl.* V, 378. No mention is made in modern accounts of the foundation of Byland of the discrepancies in the *Historia*.

[16] *Historia*, fo. 14r; *Mon. Angl.* V, 350. For gifts made before 1141 by Roger de Mowbray, see D. E. Greenway, ed., *Charters of the Honour of Mowbray, 1107-1191*, British Academy, Records of Social and Economic History, new series 1 (London, 1972), nos 33, and 34-7. These latter charters are printed from transcripts in the Byland history in Dodsworth 63, and show some signs of later interpolation: see Dr Greenway's notes accompanying the printed texts.

[17] C. T. Clay, 'The Early Abbots of the Yorkshire Cistercian Houses', *Yorkshire Archaeological Journal* 38 (1952-55), 9-10.

accused of prejudice in this matter, referred to abbot Hardred 'who succeeded Gerald as abbot of Calder', *('qui . . . abbatem nostrum Geroldum apud Kaldram successit in officio pastorali').*[18] Several years later the monks of Calder II attempted to show that Hardred, as Gerald's successor, had authority over the monks of Byland, and that if the house of Byland were to continue at all, it would do so as a daughter of Calder II. This created a constitutional problem: which one was the genuine Calder convent? But there was also (if we are to believe the *Historia)* a financial aspect to the claim. Calder was a poor house, and Furness was unwilling to help out from its own resources: 'it cared little or nothing for their destruction' *('paruum aut nichil de eorum curavit destructione'),* presumably here referring to the devastation of the house back in 1137. Byland, on the other hand, had not only increased its possessions, but by this time had acquired responsibility for a daughter house, Jervaulx. The economic motive for Calder's claim is made clear: 'they (the monks of Calder) hoped that if they could reclaim our house as a daughter, then the need of the mother might in a short while be relieved by the abundance of the daughter' *('sperabant certissime quod si domum nostram possent recuperare in filiam, quod matris inopia per filie abundantiam infra breue tempus posset releuari').*[19]

The *Historia* tells us that Hardred visited Byland to lay claim to it as abbot of its mother house, and then withdrew his claim the following year in the presence of abbot Serlo of Savigny during the latter's visit to England. This took place in 1150-51, so we may place abbot Hardred's claim in 1149 or 1150. The manuscript includes at this stage two charters, not printed in the *Monasticon,* which shed significant light on the whole affair. Both are addressed to the abbot and general chapter of Cîteaux, since by this time the congregation of Savigny had merged with the White Monks. The first was issued by abbot Hardred, and remitted the claim which he had made to authority over Byland, and to property 'which we said to have been taken there *('calumniam quam habebamus adversus domum Beghlandae de subiectione eiusdem domus et de substantia quam illuc adductam diximus').* For this quitclaim the abbey of Byland had given to Calder eight oxen, six cows with their calves, five mares with their foals, one palfrey and a full set of priestly vestments. In addition, Hardred promised that if the abbey of Furness were to lay any claim to Byland, then the abbot of Calder would speak up on behalf of Byland. The second document was issued by the abbot of Savigny, and its contents are similar. He added that in the event of a claim being made by Furness, the abbot of Savigny would answer concerning the issue of subjection, and the abbot of Calder for the property of the house. This, I think, brings us to the heart of the problem. The description of the monks' journey from the gates of Furness in 1137 following the refusal of the mother house to take them in, included the detail that they had taken with them eight oxen, vestments and books. This was no mere colourful addition designed to enliven the narrative. By these charters those eight oxen are returned, with interest, from Byland to Calder. The whole affair, from Calder's point of view, had been an action for recovery of the abbey property, of which they evidently had sore need.[20]

---

[18] *Historia,* fo. 23r; *Mon. Angl.* V, 352.

[19] *Historia,* fo. 23v; *Mon. Angl.* V, 352.

[20] *Historia,* fos 24v-25v. The witnesses to both charters were Peter, abbot of Quarr (the former abbot of Furness who had opposed the merger with Cîteaux) and Walter, abbot of Rushen, Isle of Man; see Knowles, Brooke and London, *Heads of Religious Houses,* 134, 139. See appendix to this paper for the texts of these documents.

The monks of Furness, incensed by Calder's lack of spirit, took up the claim as was evidently anticipated they would. In one way, it is surprising that it took so long for Calder II and then Furness to raise the issue of Byland's subjection. The chronology of the *Historia* suggests that Hardred claimed Byland for Calder in 1149 at the earliest, possibly even in 1150. There was, therefore, evidently a delay of six or seven years between the foundation of Calder II and its claim to be the mother house of Byland. Perhaps the delay is not so difficult to understand if we see the episode against the background of the merger with Cîteaux in 1147-8, the opposition of the monks of Furness to it, and their refusal, throughout 1148, to accept it. Could it have been only *after* the merger, with Furness keen to try and go it alone, that the need for Byland's resources became more acute? We may, as well, set the episode against the growing importance of Byland. 1149 was also the year in which the status of Jervaulx was confirmed as a daughter house of Byland, so we might be seeing here a certain rivalry for the position of leading Savigniac house in the North. Whatever the reasons for the timing, the claim lingered on, and was not settled until referred to Ailred, abbot of Rievaulx. His letter describing the case and his judgement on it, survives in original form in the Archives Nationales, and a text was copied into the *Historia*.[21] Furness's claims rested on the argument that abbot Gerald had subjected Byland to Furness; that the desertion of Calder was made without the consent of Furness; and that Hardred's capitulation was invalid for similar reasons. The weakness of their argument as well as their failure to produce witnesses, led to Ailred being convinced by the case mounted by Savigny: that the place of Hood had been granted to and accepted by Savigny in the general chapter; that the monks of Furness had lost any claim they might have had by their shabby treatment of the monks of Calder I; further, in a statement revealing the wide powers of a lay patron, our author has the abbot of Savigny assert that Roger de Mowbray visited Cîteaux and in the general chapter reiterated his gift of Byland to Savigny, and Roger, as founder, 'could assign and give the monastery of Byland to the subjection of whomsoever he wished' (*'qui monasterium Bellelande assignare potuit et donare cujuscunque voluit subjectioni'*).[22] Present during the case, and witnessing Ailred's judgement, were the abbot of Garendon, acting as judge in the place of the abbot of Waverley, ten Cistercian abbots, the prior and three monks of Rievaulx and other monks. There is no date, and one of c.1155 is usually assigned. All that can be said with certainty was that it was issued after the resignation of Serlo as abbot of Savigny in 1153.

When we turn to the narrative of Jervaulx some similar themes emerge. This is how the *Historia* begins:

> Tempore regis Stephani ... fuit quidem miles generosae prosapie nomine Akarius filius Bardolfi magnus dominus terrarum et possessionum in comitatu Eboracens(is); divina gratia inspiratus hic dedit cuidam monacho serviente deo Petro de Quinciaco in arte medicine valde subtili et bene experto et quibusdam aliis monachis de Savign' quandam partem terre sue in Wandesleydale ... ubi predictus frater Petrus et socii sui prout melius

---

[21] The text of Ailred's letter is given in the *Historia*, fos 26r-29r; *Mon. Angl.* V, 352-3. It is printed in Leopold Delisle, 'Documents relative to the abbey of Furness, extracted from the archives of the abbey of Savigny', *Journal of the British Archaeological Association*, VI (1851), 423-4; calendared in *Calendar of documents preserved in France, illustrative of the history of Great Britain and Ireland, a.d. 918-1216*, ed, J. H. Round (HMSO, 1899), 297.

[22] *Historia* fo. 27v; *Mon. Angl.* V, 353.

poterant initium cuiusdam abbacie ordinare ceperunt ...[23]

> (In the time of king Stephen, there was a knight of noble family called Acaris son of
> Bardolph, a lord with great lands and properties in the county of York. Inspired by divine
> grace, this man gave to a certain monk serving God, named Peter of Quinciaco, a man very
> skilled and experienced in the art of medicine, and to other monks of Savigny, a certain
> portion of his land in Wensleydale ... where the said brother Peter and his comrades, as
> well as they were able, began to arrange for the beginning of an abbey.)

That abbey, which settled on the banks of river Ure, took the name of Fors, and was
alternatively known as Wensleydale, Charity and Jervaulx, the latter name coming to be
applied to the second and permanent site of the abbey to which the monks removed in
1156. The author admitted that he did not really know why Peter should have been in.
Richmondshire, but he recorded a tradition that he was in the household of count Alan of
Richmond and Brittany either to care for the sick, or to distribute alms to the poor. Alan
took an interest in the abbey founded by his tenant, and issued at least one charter on the
occasion of or just before the raising of the first wooden building on the site. At his own
request this was an occasion at which Alan was present, and in a scene amusingly
described, he gained for Peter the willing or grudging support of some of his own
knights.[24] The *Historia* leaves us in no doubt of the key role played by count Alan,
though not described as the founder of the house, in its development. Another benefactor
in these early days was Roger de Mowbray, who when he heard that a second Savigniac
foundation had been made in Yorkshire, gave Peter land in Masham. A later charter
testifying to the fact that the grant had been made before his first journey to Jerusalem,
dates it to 1146/7.[25]

Following the building of the wooden oratory at Fors, Alan left for his Breton estates,
and on his way there called at Savigny to inform the abbot of the new foundation, and to
grant the abbey 'then marked out rather than started' (*'tunc metatam potius quam
inceptam'*) to Savigny. It must have been shortly after this that Alan issued a charter at
Rennes, dated to 6 January, but with no year given. The original charter is in the Archives
Nationales, and a copy was entered in the cartulary of Savigny.[26] By this charter Alan
granted to the church of Holy Trinity of Savigny all his land in Ingleby into the hands of
lord Peter the monk, remitting the service of his tenant Warner, and notified named
officials of the honour of Richmond, that he had given to Peter this land, and all that he
held in the lands of the abbey. In an unusual addendum he commended Peter 'as my

---

[23] *Historia* fo. 42r; *Mon. Angl.* V, 568. For a brief account of the foundation of Jervaulx, see *Early Yorkshire Charters, (EYC)* IV, ed. C. T. Clay, Yorkshire Archaeological Society Record Series, extra series (1935), 24-6.

[24] 'Omnibus autem preparatis ad erectionem primi edificii frater Petrus quesivit comitem sicut preceperat. Qui veniens ad locum ubi domus illa deberet leuari advocavit sibi nominatim quatuor vel quinque de militibus qui secum aduenerant et dixit illis jocundo uultu quasi ludendo: "Nos omnes habemus terras magnas et possessiones. Nunc ergo propriis manibus adiuvemus et erigamus istam domum in nomine domini nostri et unusquisquam nostram terram vel redditum exhibeat in perpetuam elimosinam ad sustentacionem partis quam leuaverit". Cui suggestioni quidem eorum satis benigne consenserunt et alii consentire noluerunt nisi per conditionem': *Historia* fo. 43r; *Mon. Angl.* V, 569.

[25] Ibid.

[26] *EYC* IV, no. 27.

friend and special liege man, to whom I entrusted myself totally in my greatest danger and who proved himself to be the best guardian of my body and my life' *('Petrum ... commendo tanquam meum amicum et precipuum fidelem cui me totum et in maximo periculo commisi qui corporis uiteque mee custos optimus extitit').* This clause confirms the tradition recorded in the *Historia,* that Peter was in the household of count Alan as his physician. I considered the possibility that this charter predated the foundation in England; that Alan first encountered Peter in Brittany rather than in England, and that Peter and his two Savigniac brothers accompanied the count back to Richmondshire in order to find a site. But the wording of the charter, granting to Holy Trinity, Savigny and to Peter, land in Ingleby and all he had in the land of the abbey, suggests that the charter postdates the grants by Alan and his knights in Richmondshire, and was thus issued in 1146, in the January before Alan's death. It also indicates that Peter had accompanied Alan back to Brittany after the foundation, probably to announce to the general chapter of Savigny the establishment of a new house of the congregation.

The attitude of abbot Serlo to Alan's news about the foundation of Jervaulx shows quite clearly that it did not have official sanction and was no part of a planned programme of colonization. Although Serlo accepted Alan's gift, he did so unwillingly, refused to ratify the foundation and delayed answering Peter's request for a full complement of monks. His opposition was evidently based on English experiences:

> Sed abbas Savign', in animo suo revolvens pericula, labores et defectus quos monachi sui sustinuerant qui in Angliam diversis in locis aliis missi fuerant de Savign' ad abbatias incipiendas et construendas a quibus soepius hortabatur ut ipsos domi revocaret ... iuravit ... quod nunquam voluit ibidem conventum destinare, et gratissimum haberet, si de donatione ejusdem loci bono modo totaliter posset exui et liberari.[27]

> (But the abbot of Savigny turned over in his mind the dangers, troubles and hardships which his monks had sustained, those who had been sent from Savigny to various places in England to establish and build abbeys, and who had often urged him to recall them home. He swore that he was unwilling to dispatch a convent there, and said that he would be most grateful if he could be completely released and freed from the gift of that same place.)

Serlo then wrote to Peter, telling him that he had acted madly in beginning an abbey without the consent of Savigny.

Now this is an interesting piece of evidence. Was Serlo here referring generally to the fortunes of the Savigniacs in England or did he have one particular convent in mind? The Savigniacs fared well in securing wealthy founders who came from the royal family and from among the most powerful landowners. However, noble benefactors did not necessarily guarantee rich endowments, and keeping possession of any property in a time of disorder and civil strife such as that which accompanied the reign of king Stephen (1135-1154) could be difficult. The actual words attributed to Serlo suggest that the troubles he had in mind were encountered by monks sent directly from Normandy, and not by those daughter houses founded from English houses, that is, from Furness. Given the nature of our source, based largely on oral testimony, we should perhaps not place

---

[27] *Historia* fo. 44r; *Mon. Angl.* V. 569.

too much weight on a literal interpretation. The coincidence of the date (1145-6) makes it tempting to think that it was Furness's colony at Calder II of which Serlo was thinking, but in the absence of other evidence, we can say no more than that Serlo was aware of some dissatisfaction among the English houses.

Despite their uncertainties - the lack of a full convent of monks, for instance - Peter and his fellows were not going to give up, and sought the help of abbot Roger of Byland, who was preparing to attend the general chapter of 1147, the chapter at which the union with Cîteaux was announced. It was attended by fifteen abbots, only two British houses, Neath and Quarr, apart from Byland, being represented. Roger, no doubt the uncertainty of the constitutional status of his own house making him sympathetic to the plight of brother Peter, agreed to help. Serlo again refused to send monks from Savigny, but concurred, conditionally, with a scheme to make Peter's planned community at Fors a daughter house of Byland. The abbot of Quarr was ordered to visit Fors to inspect the site, which he did at Easter 1148, and on his assessment of its suitability was to be decided the fate of the community. He was, reluctantly, persuaded of the viability of the site, and handed over to Peter a charter of abbot Serlo granting his house to Byland.[28] This was far from being the end of the affair. Abbot Roger was worried as to the implications of the union with Cîteaux for his authority over his new daughter house, and on the advice of friends went to Savigny in 1149 to ask for a clarification of its position. It is evident that by this time, a full convent had still not been dispatched to Fors. Together Serlo and Roger journeyed on to the Cistercian general chapter, where on the advice of St. Bernard the name of Jervaulx was entered on the Cistercian rolls under the foundations for that year as a daughter house of Byland.[29] Returning to England, Roger set in motion the final stages of the foundation, and in March 1150 sent Peter and his two companions, nine Byland monks, and John of Kinstan, one of the original convent at Calder I, to set up an abbey on the site at Fors granted by Acaris son of Bardolph. The colony remained there until 1154 when poor resources forced a temporary dispersal to Byland and Furness. Interestingly, the acrimony between Furness and Byland did not prevent the Lancashire monks from taking in some of their impoverished colleagues from Jervaulx. In 1156 following the petition of the convent at Fors to Conan, Alan of Brittany's son and successor, a new site was provided at Jervaulx where the abbey ruins still stand.[30]

The Byland and Jervaulx histories illustrate several features of Savigniac history in the years up to and immediately following the union with Cîteaux. They are witness to economic difficulties encountered by some of the abbeys as well as to the success of others. They are testimony to the constitutional uncertainties of the order. B. D. Hill makes much of the unrestrained, undemocratic power of the abbot of Savigny over his

---

[28] For these events see *Historia* fos 44v-46v; *Mon. Angl.* V, 570. The charter of abbot Serlo included in the text at this point (fo. 47r) could not, as is implied, have been given to the abbot of Quarr at the general chapter of 1147 to be handed over at Easter 1148. The witnesses, Henry Murdac, archbishop of York (1147-53), Ailred, abbot of Rievaulx (1147-67), and Thorald, abbot of Fountains (1148-50), indicate that it was issued between 1148 and 1150. The most likely occasions would have been during Serlo's visit to England in 1150 or at the Cistercian general chapters of 1148, 1149 or 1150.

[29] Here, as in other parts of the text, the house is referred to as Jervaulx, although the site occupied at this date was still that of Fors.

[30] *Historia* fo. 52v; *Mon. Angl.* V, 572-3.

congregation, suggesting that it was more comparable with the powers of the abbot of Cluny than those of his counterpart of Cîteaux.[31] This argument has much to commend it. We must remember, however, that the congregation of Savigny did not legislate from an early date in the same way as the Cistercians, for an extended family. It was not until the abbacy of Geoffrey (1122-1139) that the general chapter was instituted, or that the abbot was expected to make systematic visitation of daughter houses. The power of the abbot of Savigny over his monasteries may have seemed unrestrained, but in practice it was checked by the geographical distance of many of the houses of the congregation from the centre, and even more by the inability of the machinery of the order to enforce the decisions of the abbot of Savigny.[32] The *Historia* reminds us that Furness saw its daughter houses as dependent on the mother, not the grandmother. Certainly the Lancashire monks demonstrated an unwillingness to recognise the supreme power of Savigny, even to the extent of opposing the merger,[33] while the Norman abbey, certainly under Serlo, seems to have attempted to divest itself of responsibilities, and take on no new ones - witness his reluctance to accept the fact of the foundation of Jervaulx. In more general terms, the histories reveal the role of the lay patrons, not just in the foundation but in the subsequent development of their houses - a theme which I have only been able to touch on in this paper; and the intervention of a conscientious abbot, Roger, in the affairs of his daughter house. In short, they go some way to revealing the processes of foundation which are often masked by the formal language of the charter.

We may end by asking, how do we know that Philip, as recorder of Byland tradition, can be trusted? May the Byland and Jervaulx histories be nothing more than the neurotic outpouring of an aged man, Roger of Byland, with an obsession with one question, the relationship of his house to Furness, and with bitter memories of the events of 1137? Possibly. Certainly as we have it, in one source, the tale is one-sided. But Roger is vindicated by the testimony of Ailred of Rievaulx. Ailred's letter makes it clear that the question of the filiation of Byland was a very real issue, which the Cistercian general chapter felt it necessary to refer to one of the most prominent English Cistercians of his day. Evidently it was an argument which had dragged on for at least ten years, and did not end until twenty years after Furness had first sent out its monks to the virgin site at Calder. It is small wonder, then, that when Philip came to record the '*causam, formam et modum sive processum fundationis domus nostrae*', the question of filiation should loom large in its pages, or that a similar theme should emerge in the history of Byland's own daughter house.

---

[31] Hill, *English Cistercian Monasteries*, 92.

[32] The Savigniac general chapter of 1147 was only attended by three out eleven British abbots.

[33] For documents relating to the opposition of Furness to the merger, see Delisle, 420-23, Round, 294-5.

APPENDIX

The following is a transcription from the Bodleian Library, MS Dodsworth 63 of two unpublished documents relating to the dispute about jurisdiction over Byland.

I have silently expanded abbreviated forms, except where the extension is uncertain, and in such cases parentheses are used or the word is left suspended; emendations are given in square brackets. I am most grateful to the Bodleian Library for permission to reproduce these extracts.

fo. 24v

Dominis et patribus reverendissimis A. abbati et toto capitulo Cistercii frater Hardredus' abbas de Caldra salutem. Noverit vestra sanctitas quod [nos]a cum consensu capituli [nostri]b sub presencia domini [Serlonis]c abbatis Savign' remisimus in perpetuum calumniam quam habebamus adversus domum Beghlandae de subiectione eiusdem domus et de substantia quam illuc adductam diximus. Huius remissionis gratia contulit domus Beghlande domui nostre octo boves, sex vaccas cum vitulis earum et quinque equas cum pullis earum et palfridum unum viginti solidorum et unam plenariam vestem sacerdotali. Quod si abbas Furness vel conventus voluerit aliquam calumniam mouere contra domum Beghlande de substantia quam nos calumniati sumus, domus nostra domui Furnesii se mediam opponet et pro domo Beghlande respondebit. Huius accionis testes sunt: Petrus abbas de Quarrera, Walterus abbas de Man etc.

a ego MS
b mei MS
c Johannis interlined MS; the chronology suggests that this is an error for Serlo.

(To the most reverend lords and fathers A., abbot, and the whole chapter of Cîteaux, brother Hardred, abbot of Calder, greeting. May your holiness know that we, with the consent of our chapter and in the presence of Serlo, abbot of Savigny, have remitted in perpetuity the claim which we had against the house of Byland concerning the obedience of the same house, and concerning property which we said to have been taken there. For this remission the house of Byland has given to our house eight oxen, six cows with their calves, and five mares with their foals and one palfrey of twenty shillings and one full set of priestly vestments. But if the abbot of Furness or the convent shall wish to bring any claim against the house of Byland concerning the property which we have claimed, our house shall intervene and shall answer on behalf of the house of Byland. The witnesses of this action are Peter, abbot of Quarr and Walter abbot of Man.)

Insuper [S]d abbas Savign' scripsit capitulo generali sub hac forma: / [fo. 25r]

Dominis et patribus reverendissimis A. abbati et [toto]e capitulo generali Cistercii frater [S]d. dictus abbas Savign' salutem. Noverit vestra unanimitas quo dominus Hardredus abbas de Caldra et fratres eius sub presencia nostra remiserunt in perpetuum calumniam quam habebant adversus domum Bellelande de subjectione eiusdem domus quam sui iuris esse dicebant, et de personis loci et de substantia quam de Caldra illuc adductam esse dicebant. Huius remissionis gratia contulit domus Belleland' domui de Caldra octo boves et sex vaccas cum vitulis earum et quinque equas cum pullis earum et palfridum unum viginti solidorum et unam plenariam vestem sacerdotali. Quod si abbas Furness vel conventus voluerit aliquam calumniam mouere contra domum Bellalande de subiectione eiusdem domus vel de personis loci vel de substantia quam Caldrenses calumniabantur, abbas Savign' qui tunc temporis fuerit de subieccione et personis, abbas vero de Caldra de substantia se medios opponent et pro /[fo.25v] domo Bellelande stabunt; itaqu(od) abbas de Caldra si de ipsa substantia domum tueri non possit, tantun(dem) substantiae eidem domui restituet quantum ab ea vt hic descriptum est accepit. Huius accionis testes fuerunt: Petrus abbas de Quarrara, Walterus abbas de Man etc.

Cum igitur tali attestacione capitulo generali predicte calumnie satis constabat remissio, totaliter sopita est accio paternitatis exigendae quam Caldrenses habebant in domo nostra. Predicta duo scripta missa fuerunt apud Cistercium et alia duo ejusdem tenoris remanebant penes nos ad perpetuum munimen.

^d J MS; recte S[erlo].
^e toti MS.

(In addition S[erlo], abbot of Savigny, wrote to the general chapter in these terms:

To the most reverend lords and fathers, A., abbot, and the whole chapter of Cîteaux, brother S[erlo], called abbot of Savigny, greeting. May you together know that lord Hardred, abbot of Calder and his brethren have in our presence remitted the claim which they had against the house of Byland concerning the obedience of the same house, which they said to belong to their jurisdiction, and concerning the property which they said to have been taken there from Calder. For this remission the house of Byland has given to the house of Calder eight oxen, six cows with their calves and five mares with their foals and one palfrey of twenty shillings and one full set of priestly vestments. But if the abbot of Furness or the convent shall wish to bring any claim against the house of Byland concerning the obedience of the same house, or concerning property which the monks of Calder claimed, the abbot of Savigny of the time shall intervene concerning obedience and the persons, and the abbot of Calder shall intervene concerning the property; and they shall stand by the house of Byland. There is to be this condition: that if the abbot of Calder is not able to protect his house with respect to the property, he shall restore to the same house [Byland] as much property as he received, as is here described. The witnesses of this action were Peter, abbot of Quarr, Walter, abbot of Man etc.

When the remission of the said claim, with the attestation, was thus made known to the general chapter, the action to claim paternity which the monks of Calder had against our house was completely laid to rest. The two aforesaid letters were sent to Cîteaux and two others with the same content remained in our house as a perpetual record.)

THE *VITA STEPHANI MURETENSIS* AND THE PAPAL RE-CONSTITUTION OF THE ORDER OF GRANDMONT IN 1186 AND THEREAFTER

by

Maire Wilkinson

It is argued in this paper that the *Vita Stephani Muretensis* is a paradigm, that is, a model or construct drawn from the thought forms of its author Gerald Ithier, prior of Grandmont 1188 - 1197/8, of the ideal history of the order, the history which the order ought to have had, and of which in some sense therefore he judged it to stand in need. The composition of what appears to the present writer to be a transposition myth involved suppression of what was known empirically of the order's origins in favour of an allegory, based on the actual papal reforms of the order in 1186 and thereafter, which was intended to create the belief, a double belief, as it were, that the newly canonized saint, Stephen of Muret, looked kindly on the papal reforms in question, and that the way of life he instituted for his followers drew its sanction or authorization from the papacy from its inception.

There is, however, clear and reliable evidence that the real origins of the Order of Muret-Grandmont are to be found in the Gospel itself, that is in an endeavour to live in its fulness the justificatory life of the Gospel, guided by sacred scripture, and by the comparative study of the Rules of the Fathers, probably as preserved in the versions found in rule collections related to that of the *Codex Regularum* of Benedict of Aniane.[1] As was appropriate for a religious teacher who wished his followers to live the Gospel life rather than to imitate his own, Stephen of Muret's years in the world are lost in obscurity as to personal detail in the accounts preserved in the oral tradition, the *Primitiva* tradition, of the Order of Muret-Grandmont, a tradition given written form after the founder's death. As for his years in religion, according to the *Primitiva* account, his memory was treasured by his followers as that of a model pastor of extraordinarily mortified life, who brought to them the light of truth, rather than as that of a worker of wonderful deeds surpassing the order of nature.[2]

It has long been recognized that the account of the saint's life found in the *Vita Stephani Muretensis* is at least unreliable in historical matters. One Milo of the Auvergne was not, as is alleged in the *Vita*, archbishop of Benevento between 1058 and 1070.[3] And the author of the *Vita Stephani* makes a pilgrimage to the shrine of Saint Nicholas of

---

[1] See Wilkinson, Maire: *The Vita Stephani Muretensis and the early life of Stephen of Muret* [Wilkinson - Early Life], Monastic Studies ed. Loades, Judith, Bangor, 1990, pp 102 - 126 at pp 110 - 113

[2] See *Scriptores Ordinis Grandimontensis* [SS] V, *Vita Hugonis Lacerta* [VHL] in *Corpus Christianorum Continuatio Mediaevalis* VIII, ed. Becquet, Dom Jean, Turnhout, 1968, p 167: *Stephanus pater primus et fundator totius religionis nostrae per quem divina clementia nobis et per nos ceteris lumen veritatis innotuit* .... No miracles are recorded in the *Primitiva* tradition. The *Vita* PN itself has only two, but a miracle collection was added to it.

[3] See Dunn, Marilyn: *Church and society in the eleventh and twelfth centuries: Eastern influence on Western monasticism. The case of Stephen of Muret*, unpublished Ph.D thesis, Edinburgh, 1981, for an analysis of the evidence concerning Milo's archiepiscopate which she places in the years 1074 - 1075, pp 101 - 133 at p 131.

Myra at Bari the purpose of the journey to Italy of the young Stephen of Muret and his father in 1058, although there is no reason to suppose that the saint's relics had been translated thither before1087, the date given by Orderic Vitalis.[4] 'Unreliable' is, however, in the context of the Vita Stephani an insufficient term, and it has been designated in these articles the *Vita PN*, or *pseudo-normativa*, because it has all the marks of fiction rather than of fact. It is, indeed, even more inaccurate than has generally been recognized. No Council of Chartres, legatine or otherwise, is known to have been held in 1126, as the author of the *Vita PN alleges*, the year in which he also places Stephen of Muret's death, linking the latter with the holding of the council.[5] The only legatine Council of Chartres in the 1120's for which there is evidence is that presided over by the cardinal legates Gregory and Peter Pierleone (the future Pope Innocent II and anti-pope Anacletus) in 1124.[6] These cardinals visited Muret, perhaps in 1119, but certainly not at a time when Stephen was near to death.[7] According to the account in the *Vita PN* the cardinals came to Muret eight days before the onset of Stephen's final illness, making inquiry into the origins of the order he had founded, hearing him rehearse in reply the substance of the story of his 'Italian' years found in the early chapters of the *Vita,* and predicting his entry into glory with the apostles if he persevered in his *propositum.*[8] Stephen's subsequent death, it is said, was announced to the cardinals at a Council of Chartres at which they presided soon after the latter event; and there the cardinals opined that Stephen was already in glory.[9] Not only, however, is the *PN* record of this visit greatly at variance with that preserved in the *Primitiva* tradition of the order, but it is also the case that Stephen of Muret died in 1125, not as has been generally supposed 1124.[10] Hence the substance of the *PN* version of the cardinals' visit cannot be regarded, as it has been, as tenable on account of our knowledge of an actual Council of Chartres held in 1124, for it is the assumed conjunction of the saint's death and the holding of the council which makes the only link between the *PN relatio* and verifiable history. The burden of proof thus rests with those who wish to regard the *Vita Stephani* as an essentially historical text with some unfortunate inaccuracies. And those who do not subscribe to such a view must ask why the narrative of the *Vita Stephani Muretensis,* with its mixture of apparent

---

[4] *Historiae Ecclesiasticae Libri Tredecim, Lib. VII, XII* ed. Chibnall, Marjorie, vol IV, Oxford, 1973, pp 54 - 68 and Appendix II.

[5] *Vita Venerabilis Viri Stephani Muretensis XXXVII,* in *SS, III,* p 127. Council and death are placed in Stephen's eightieth year, that is in the fiftieth year from 1076, the one date in the text. See p 112 and p 124.

[6] The best evidence for a Council of Chartres in the 1120's under the presidency of these legates is a confirmation charter of Geoffrey, archbishop of Rouen 1111-1128, to the abbey of Marmoutier, given at Chartres on 12 March and during the time of the said council (*Annales Ordinis S. Benedicti,* T. VI, ed. Martène, Dom E., Paris, 1739, App. 646 noXV.) The year date of the charter is 1123. In our view 1124 is meant, according to present reckoning, but the argument for the latter year is not germane here. For other sources pertaining to this council see Hefele, C.J., trans. and ed. Leclercq, Dom H., *Histoire des Conciles* vol V pt. I pp 647-648 and note 3 pp 648-651.

[7] See *Wilkinson - Early Life* app. A.

[8] *Vita Stephani XXXII SS* pp 121-123.

[9] Ibid. XXXVII SS p 127.

[10] See *Wilkinson - Early Life,* note 1, to which may be added Bollandus' statement that Charles Frémon (1611-1689) reformer of the Order of Grandmont, saw works of two authors, William of Dandina and one of the cognomen *a Guardia,* both members of the order, in which Stephen's death was placed in the pontificate of Honorius II, elected 15-16 December 1124. *Acta SS Febr. II, VIII Febr.,* Antwerp, 1658, 203 bc. The second author may be Pardoux de La Garde (d. 1591), but it has not been possible to consult Frémon's *La vie, la mort et les miracles de St. Etienne.* Dijon, 1647, to which Bollandus seems to refer.

carelessness and fabrication, is not set aside as valueless.

It seems to the present writer that the degree of factual inaccuracy in the text is so great, and that the teleology of the author's gloss on what happens is so cohesive, that his ignorance of or indifference to ordinary veracity cannot be supposed to have proceeded from levity. On the contrary, the text becomes intelligible if it is regarded, as was said at the beginning of this paper, as a paradigm, and a paradigm, out of the author's thought forms, which as far as the early life narrative is concerned does not re-fashion the saint. Indeed no single human act is recalled. Stephen of Muret, has, for example, no struggles with temptation, he performs no pious deeds. The author re-creates instead an *Historia Nova Ordinis Grandimontensis*, in which he gives Stephen only the identity of one who fulfils, step by step, the divine plan to establish the Order of Grandmont.[11] He fulfils the plan, moreover, as a saint who is implicitly clerical, although his clerical ordination is not referred to explicitly. That is, he is educated by a senior ecclesiastic, he mingles in the highest circles in the Roman curia, and as is well known, in the description of his death it is stated that he died *in ordine diaconatus*. But as we have it, the *Primitiva* account did not know Stephen the deacon, or even Stephen the clerk, although the saint may have been in minor orders.[12] It seems, in short, that before us in the *Vita PN* is an apparently factual text invented to illustrate the author's teleology.

The fictional qualities of this text can be shown by revealing historical inaccuracies. They can also be shown in the spiralling possibilities which result from attempts to treat it as an historical work impaired by certain errors. Mabillon, for example, seeking to resolve the apparent contradictions between what is alleged in the early life account in the *Vita Stephani,* and verifiable information about Italian history in the period in which the story is set, suggested that Milo of Benevento lived for a time (but not twelve years) in Benevento before he was elected archbishop, and that the child Stephen, like Milo also from the Auvergne, came to live with him during this time.[13] If Mabillon's suggestion be allowed, however, the chronology of the *Vita,* dependent on the one date, 1076, as it is, collapses. The real Milo died in 1075.[14] In accordance with the account in the *Vita,* Stephen must spend four years in Rome after Milo's death, and a further two years wandering in many provinces, seeking a place apt for his penance, and observing the practices of monks and canons.[15] Thus he would not have come to Muret in 1076 in his thirtieth year, but in 1081 in his thirty fifth year, and he would have died, after almost fifty years in his hermitage, in

---

[11] See esp. *Vita Stephani V: ...Egressus est enim puer de terra et de cognatione sua et de domo patris sui, ut inter gentes quas nesciebat vivendi formam disceret ad quam postmodum maxima multitudo hominum, velut de Hur Chaldaeorum et Aegyptia servitute, ad terram promissionis et virtutum montem ocius convolaret.* SS p 107, cf. *Gen.* 12, 1; and Fr. Baudouin de Gaiffier: 'Cette influence non seulement de la Bible, mais aussi de l'exégèse biblique explique le caractère souvent *peu historique,* parfois *non historique,* presque toujours *supra-historique* de l'hagiographie.' *Hagiographie et Historiographie* in *Subsidia Hagiographica* no 61, IV, Brussels, 1977 pp 139-166 at p 162. Gerald Ithier explains various modes of scriptural exegesis in his *De Confirmatione,* esp XVI SS pp 359-363.

[12] *Wilkinson - Early Life* App. B, p 125.

[13] *Annales OSB T/V LXIV, XXXVII* p 67.

[14] *Annales Beneventani M.G.H. SS. III* ed Pertz, G.H., Hanover, 1839, p 181.

[15] *Vita Stephani IX, XI,* SS p 109, p 111.

1131.[16] As may be seen, if the tale in the *Vita PN* is tampered with, reading it to obtain information about the sequence of events in the saint's early life becomes pointless, for it coheres only with itself and not with any extrinsic and demonstrable information. The author's aforesaid teleology, ceases, moreover, to be cohesive, if the narrative around which he evolves it becomes changed,for it depends on the story as it is. If we proceed to extremes, dispense with both teleology and orderly narrative, and admit the bones of the assertions in the *Vita* concerning Stephen's years in Italy as historically valid, it remains that there is no other warrant for a stay, of any length, with Milo of Benevento than the *Vita PN* and the literate (rather than oral) tradition within the order from which it came.[17] And Stephen's imitation of the practices of the Calabrian Brethren, and the authorization of his following of their rule by a certain pope repose on no other evidence than that found in the *Vita PN* itself. Against those claims there can be adduced not only the evidence of the *Primitiva* account of the origins of the Order of Muret-Grandmont, and of the life of its founder, but also later evidence of the order's practices before it was given a Rule akin in its force to the Rules of other Western monastic or religious congregations, that is evidence of practices before the time when Urban III altered the structure of government in the order in 1186.[18]

In that the *Vita Stephani Muretensis* is the official life of the saint there has been a pre-supposition that its author, even if ill-informed, will have dealt with factual matters in good faith. But the pre-supposition depends on a simple division between veracity and mendacity which overlooks the rhetorical form of optative fiction; that is, the construction of paradigms out of alleged events and circumstances whose supposed moral value transcends empirical reality. What is optative, what expresses desire, underlies the employment of *topica,* probabilities, and *topoi,* conventional themes, which appear in some measure in much medieval hagiography, by-passing, as it were, problems of verification. No other *Vita* of the eleventh or twelfth centuries, however, is known to the present writer in which moral paradigm supplants the empirical order to the same degree as it does in the *Vita Stephani Muretensis.*[19]

We cannot thus concur with the opinion which Dom Becquet formed some thirty years ago that despite apparent errors, there is a core in the tale of Stephen of Muret's early life which is trustworthy.[20] The presence in the *PN* text of yet other and significantly erroneous assertions, beyond those remarked by Dom Becquet, creates a more than ordinary need for the support of controlling evidence for anything of moment alleged there; but nothing proper to the *PN* narrative can be corroborated, either from sources external to the Order of Muret-Grandmont, or from the *Primitiva* account of the founder's early life and of the origins of the order. Indeed, as has been seen elsewhere, on

[16] *Ibid.* XII, XXXIII, SS p 112, p 124. For his alleged coming in 1076 to Muret aged 30; for his death allegedly in his eighteenth year i.e. 1126.

[17] See *Wilkinson - Early Life* pp 105-107 for these traditions.

[18] Infra pp 20-22.

[19] The primary purpose of hagiography is edification.

[20] See *Saint Etienne de Muret et l'archevêque de Bénévent Milon* in *Bulletin de la Société Archéologique et Historique du Limousin* [BSAHL] 86, 1957 pp 403-409 esp. p 404: *Malgré ces erreurs et ces obscurités, la personne de Milon fournit un repère précieux dans toute cette histoire.*

two important issues the *Primitiva* tradition contradicts what is asserted by the *PN* author.[21] There is thus on these grounds, and on those grounds yet to be discussed, abundant reason to argue that our author did not merely relate a badly transmitted story, or relate his tale carelessly, but rather that with great seriousness of purpose he invented it, concocting a tissue of pious and skilful deceptions. On his own assertion the *Vita PN* is a piece of propagandist writing. In his Prologue to the *Vita et Miracula Sancti Stephani* Gerald Ithier addresses all the Christian faithful thus:-

> ...dilectioni vestrae propolare curamus ac desideramus qualiter beatus confessor Stephanus, Grandimontensis ordinis institutor primus, ab infantiae suae rudimentis Domino Deo nostro fideliter servire proposuit ...[22]

That is, he wishes to publish to the world the way in which Stephen proposed to serve God faithfully from the early training of his childhood. And from his expectation of backbiters and those who will contradict his version of the true relation of Stephen's life and miracles, it may be supposed that what he claimed more than sixty four years after the saint's death was not well known, and that he feared some would take exception to it:-

> Resipiscant igitur insipientes falsidici, oblatrantes et contradicentes veritati ...[23]

Once our suspicion that the *Vita PN* is a work of imaginative literature has been allowed, it becomes possible to review the text as a whole rather than as a series of imperfect historical statements, and to see that its very completeness places it in the realm of fiction. As in all stories, when the author does not know what his hero is accomplishing, in this case as part of the providential plan for his founding of the Order of Grandmont, there is nothing to know. There are no periods in the *PN* account of the saint's early life uncertainly recalled or indefinite as to their consequences. Our author is indeed too much in charge of what he wished to pass off as biography; and we look in vain for indications of verisimilitude. Gerald Ithier's admission of his sources informs us of no more than his having employed them in writing. He states of his own compositions concerning Stephen of Muret's words and deeds:-

> Sub triplici etenim libello descripsimus ea que de eius dictis vel factis audire aut videre seu legere partim potuimus.[24]

His *legere partim* is a remarkable admission. Whatever has been available to him in writing about Stephen's early life, more than a century earlier, is less than he himself has written, presumably from what he has heard and seen, but without named witnesses to verify his assertions.[25] And his reference to his sources in his Prologue to the *Vita*

---

[21] See *Wilkinson - Early Life* Appendices. The *Primitiva* author is challenging the *Vita Posterior* which we believe to have been incorporated into the *Vita PN*.

[22] *Prologus SS* p 273.

[23] *Ibid.*

[24] *Tractatus de Disciplina et Correctione Morum, SS*, XIE, p 337.

[25] Gerald's *videre* is taken as referring to Stephen's miracles *post mortem*.

Stephani, ut vera quorundam veridicorum relatione comperimus, is plainly no more than a tautology.[26] These unnamed truth speakers, moreover, do not appear in the early life narrative. It is the author's voice alone which leads the reader through both story and interpretation. But without doubt a text which purports to be a history and which is arguably a paradigm of a new and improved beginning for the Order of Grandmont, the beginning which it ought to have had, deserves our careful attention in its own right. Such a text also remains worth examining on account of its resilience, despite criticism, as an historical source, although that examination will not be attempted here.

In his ninth and tenth chapters, according to the division of material in Dom Becquet's edition of the *Vita Stephani,* Gerald Ithier comes to what seems to the present writer the heart of his purpose in writing that work.[27] It will be simpler to consider first what he says there, and elsewhere what his purpose is. He relates that in 1074, a calculation from his one date, 1076, the year is not given in the passage, Stephen of Muret was moved to put into practice his desire of serving God after the manner of the Brethren of Calabria, and he besought the then pope, to whom he was well-known, to concede that he might observe somewhere in remission of his sins the order, that is ordering in religion, which he had learnt to be observed in Calabria.[28] And at length, Christ's vicar, having experienced and proved Stephen's constancy, granted what he sought, and by his authority and power by which he excels all mortals, he imposed on him all the good he would do in penance and as the reward of virtues.[29] Then he, rejoicing at the command of the supreme pontiff which he had greatly desired, departed from the curia which his blessing.

Thus, with the pope's authorization having been given, Stephen was entitled to live in a religious state *(conversio),* according to the practices of the Brethren of Calabria and to impose their rule, we are not told whether he showed the pope a written account of this, on any followers he might find. Papal authority also gave him publicly accredited reason to suppose that his proposed way of life would be one of religious conversion, of sanctification in very deed, since the good thing he undertook *(omne bonum quod ageret),* became akin to the "penance" of undertaking the crusade to gain a plenary indulgence.[30] And we may notice that in this case papal authorization made Stephen's way of life in religion not merely permissible because it had been sanctioned and

---

[26] *SS* p 273.

[27] Dom Becquet believes Stephen of Liciac, fourth pastor of Grandmont (1140-1164) author of the version of the *Vita Stephani* he has edited in *SS.* In the view of the present writer the *Vita Posterior* was drawn up under his patronage and Gerald Ithier composed the *Vita PN.* See *Wilkinson - Early Life* p 106. The argument for the latter's authorship must be dealt with elsewhere, in so far as it exceeds what is implicit in these pages.

[28] *Vita Stephani* IX *SS* p 110.

[29] *Ibid.* X *ibid.* For the papal title *vicarius Christi* in the twelfth century see Maccarrone, Michele: *Vicarius Christi. Storia del Titolo Papale, Lateranum, Nova Series,* An. XVIII N. 1-4 Rome, 1952, pp 85-107. The appearance of the title in a literary source of the late twelfth century does not merit special attention.

[30] That is, observance of the Calabrian Rule would be regarded, here and hereafter, as due satisfaction before God on the juridical authority of the supreme key-bearer. Dom Becquet sees an indulgence of some sort at issue here. See *La première crise de l'Ordre de Grandmont, BSAHL* 87, 1960, p 294 n.1 Undertaking the crusade was a substitute for canonical penance, without which, ordinarily speaking, sacramental absolution was not thought, in the period, to have been wholly operative in heaven, on account of the satisfaction still to be made for grave sins, and made according to their gravity. See Poschmann, Bernhard: *Der Ablass im Licht der Bussgeschichte (Theophaneia 4)* Bonn, 1948 p 55, p 45.

encouraged as in accordance with the canons, but also obligatory by the exercize of apostolic power in its plenitude. *Iniungo* is the verb used for the imposition of Stephen's penance, *iussio,* a magistrate's command, the substantive for the papal action which rejoiced Stephen's heart. And whatever there was of virtue in Stephen's future actions as a religious would include the virtue of acting in obedience to papal authority.[31]

As is plain, according to the view of our author, it was the pope himself who recognized that Stephen was prompted by the Holy Spirit in his resolve to live in accordance with the *propositum* he had expressed, the time having come when his soul urged him to put into practice the desire of serving God which he had conceived:-

> Cumque ... conceptum desiderium serviendi Deo ad exsecutionem operis animum perurgeret ...[32]

That is, he had reached a point when he was obliged to act or to resist the Holy Spirit unworthily. He had moved to a condition where the *lex privata* of the church pertained, the law relating to individuals called by God to a salutary course of action which, if fulfilled, becomes law for that person, and which is higher in value than the public law of the church *(lex publica). Lex privata* has no written form, although there are written references to it, on account of its divine source, for it is, as Urban II (1088-1099) put it, the law which is written in the heart by the prompting of the Holy Spirit.[33] And the just man, the man who is indeed led by the Spirit, cannot be under the law, that is impeded by the requirements of the positive law from dwelling in the freedom to which he has been brought.[34] The only authority which can determine when the sacred canons, the most weighty emanation of *lex publica,* must be set aside, is that of the supreme key-bearer, the successor of Peter.[35] In contrast to *lex privata, lex publica* has a written form, as is true of the law of the canons itself, which has been handed down on account of sins.[36] While the latter is the lower in value of the two laws, it also is the law of God and in ordinary circumstances it is sacrosanct.[37]

Why then was it necessary for the Stephen of Muret of the *Vita PN* to have recourse to the apostolic plenitude of power in order to imitate the practices of the Calabrian Brethren, and to instruct others, in time, so to do? As is well known, any diocesan bishop

---

[31] In *Vita Stephani* XXXII, Stephen himself, telling this story to the visiting cardinals says: ... *cum ipsius (papae sc.) praecepto et oboedientia in remissionem peccatorum nostrorum huius paupertatis et abiectionis viam sequi proposuimus. SS* p 122.

[32] *Ibid.* IX *SS* p 109.

[33] Urban II's statement, perhaps made in the chapter or Saint-Ruf, on the relationship between the two laws is followed here. See *Decreti Gratiani C.XIX q.IIc.II.* in *Corpus Iuris Canonici I* ed. Friedberg, E., Leipzig, 1879, 839. (See *Rom.* 2, 15. which Urban cites).

[34] *Ibid.* 840.

[35] Our gloss on Urban's judgement in the case under discussion here in which the canons are to be set aside by his authority. He has simply *nostra auctoritate,* but see *Dictatus Papae (Gregorii VII) VII: Quod illi (papae sc.) soli licet pro temporis necessitate novas leges condere ... Registrum, II,* 55a ed. Jaffé, Philip, *Monumenta Gregoriana in Bibliotheca Rerum Germanicarum T. II,* Berlin, 1865, p 174.

[36] *Decretum Gratiani ut cit. supra* Friedberg, 839.

[37] The ordinary inviolability of the canons was a fundamental principle in the period. See, for example, *Decreti Gratiani C. XXV q. I c.XIII.* Friedberg, 1010. The principle is implicit in Urban II's judgement.

might institute a new community of men, or women, proposing to follow a recognized monastic rule, if he judged that they were indeed led by the Holy Spirit to do so; and willingness to live in a recognized way was, in its turn, a proof that the Holy Spirit inspired the work under consideration. The positive or public law of the church in the eleventh and twelfth centuries required that a monk, or nun, be professed to a written rule, and that that rule be the work of a saint, an expert, as it were, in the *ascetica* he taught.[38] (Monastic profession involved the making of a written promise of stability, of conversion of life, and of obedience to the abbot of the community in which profession was made.)[39] And publicly vowed to observe the Rule of his community, the monk was to obey his abbot as *vices Christi in monasterio,* that is as one exercising an authority of the same descending and absolute variety as that exercized by a bishop.[40] The author of the *Vita Stephani* tells us that the holy Milo of Benevento, even the most holy Milo, had led Stephen of Muret to admire the ways of the Calabrian Brethren.[41] But even the imputation of sanctity to Milo could not convey sanction in the public law of the church to a Rule which he had not written. The Calabrian Rule is otherwise unknown, that is than in Milo's supposed approbation of it, and it was the pope's authorization which made its observances valid in public law.[42] As has been indicated, these observances would be salutary for Stephen because the vicar of Christ imposed them as penance and virtue's reward.[43] They would also be salutary for Stephen's future disciples. But as far as the present writer is aware no other instance is known, than that in the *Vita Stephani Muretensis,* of a pope's authorizing a religious rule, known or unknown to the church's public law, to a future religious community.[44]

With the assertions of the *relatio PN* in mind, one may also ask whether in reality any pope would have given his authorization to a religious rule, for a future religious order, which ignored the ordinary Christian obligation to prudence, in sustaining its adherents in temporal necessities, to such a degree that in order to live at all they must put God repeatedly to the test. The Calabrian Brethren had neither animals *(pecudes)* nor estates *(possessiones),* that is neither crop nor rent bearing lands nor pastures. Neither, being enclosed *(in claustro viventes)* did they exchange their labour for sustenance, or beg. They had cast their care very literally, as the *PN* author tells us, upon God:-

Corporalis autem subsidii sollicitudinem solummodo in Deum proiecerant . ...[45]

---

[38] See the decretal letter of Alexander II (1061-1073) *Praesentium lator (Cosaldus presbyter)* in *Decr. Grat. C. XVII q. II c.l.* Friedberg 813 and c. 26 of the Second Lateran Council, 1139 in *Decr. Grat. C. XVIII q. II c. XXV.* Friedberg, 836.

[39] See *Praesentium lator* and *Benedicti Regula LVIII 17-20* ed. Hanslik, Rudolph, Vienna, 1960, p136.

[40] *Benedicti Regula* II2; LXIII 13, Hanslik, p 19, p 147.

[41] *Vita Stephani* IX, VIII, *SS* p 109 for these epithets. Marilyn Dunn has argued that later belief in the sanctity of Milo of Benevento arose on account of its imputation in the *Vita Stephani,* upublished thesis cited above, n. 3p.

[42] Above at n. 29.

[43] *Ibid.*

[44] ...*ut ordinem quem in Calabria observari didicerat ...sibi alicubi observare concederet.* (*Vita* IX *SS* p 110) concerns the establishment of a community, not the solitary life; see above at n. 28.

[45] *Vita Stephani* VI *SS* p 108. Here the author also sets out the other practices we have cited.

When Stephen of Muret repeats the story of the Italian origins of the Rule of his order to the cardinals during their visit to Muret he refers to imitation of the Calabrian Brethren, who had neither animals nor estates, as reason to hope for Christ's mercy at the Last Day, on the grounds that he and his brethren have turned aside somewhat from the authorized way of proceeding in religion, that is, have gone beyond it in virtue:-

> ...quia a via publica aliquantulum declinavimus ..[46]

But the imprudence of the Calabrian Brethren, and in reality that of the brethren of Grandmont, was of a kind viewed in the period with suspicion as likely to produce unmanageable poverty and consequent public disrepute.[47] In the papal injunction, of his tenth chapter, to Stephen of Muret *omne bonum quod ageret ei in paenitentiam et virtutum praemium iniunxit* our author is providing an answer to the charge of recklessness which could easily be brought against the Calabrian Rule, and the Order of Grandmont. That is, whatever shortcomings the Rule might have would be made good by Stephen's following it in obedience to a papal command, and a command which made its observance salvific, since it would not only replace whatever penance was needful, but also, as has been seen, bring virtue's reward.[48] The only good work, however, to which papal dispensing power was applied in its fulness in the eleventh or twelfth centuries, with a grant of plenary indulgence, was the crusade.[49] Gregory VII might have applied the *discrimen iudiciale* on which his dispensing power was based to the institution of a new form of religious life. In his *Dictatus Papae* he states that the pope may create new laws *pro temporis necessitate*.[50] Urban II certainly granted licences for religious as opposed to monastic communities, and the PN author calls the Calabrian Brethren, whom Stephen wished to imitate, a religious congregation in his sixth chapter.[51] Urban's predecessor might then have instituted a new form of religious life placing a reliance upon Divine Providence which was heroic, or reckless, according to opinion, and he might have granted a privilege akin to a plenary indulgence to the founder of that religion, although the latter is even less probable than the former.[52] Urban II stated what was to remain the basis for the crusading indulgence. namely the hazarding even unto death of one's person and property for the love of God and neighbour.[53] The only

---

[46] *Ibid.* XXXII 45-46 *SS* p 122.

[47] John of Salisbury, a sympathetic commentator, allowed that the practices of the Order of Grandmont seemed frequently to involve putting God to the test against all the teaching of the Fathers of the Church. *Policraticus* 698d 20-26 ed. Webb, C.C.I. Oxford, 1909.

[48] cf. *Vita Stephani* XXXII 40-41. Here Stephen himself speaks of his life in religion as having been undertaken *cum ipsius (papae sc.) praecepto et oboedientia in remissionem peccatorum* ....

[49] *Dictionnaire de Théologie Catholique* VII *Indulgences*, 1608. See Paulus, Nikolaus; *Geschichte des Ablasses im Mittelalter*, 2 vols, Paderborn, 1922; chapter five vol. 1 for the crusading indulgence in the eleventh and twelfth centuries.

[50] See above n. 35.

[51] *SS* p 108. For Urban II approval of laymen undertaking a common life conjoined to that of a monastic community see *J.L.* 5456; see *J.L.* 5603 for his approval of the *specialis religio* of the sometime married women of Marcigny.

[52] The author of the *Vita Stephani* may imply in his tenth chapter that the perilous existence of the Calabrian Brethren was a form of martyrdom and that its exceptional penitential value derived from this. Of the *propositum* which provoked the privilege he has: ...*pater apostolicus, aetatem iuvenis et severitatem ordinis considerans, primo quidem obstupuit* .... *SS* p110.

[53] For his letter to the clergy of Bologna concerning the meaning of the favour granted at the Council of Clermont in 1095 see *J.L.* 5670.

evidence, however, to corroborate the claim of the *PN* author that Gregory VII acted in the way he describes is the bull *Quoniam religiosam,* which is a forgery.[54] On balance what is alleged is not likely to have happened, although it is just possible that it did. If we suppose that it did happen, we do so on the basis of the *Vita Stephani* alone which is a manifestly unhistorical source.

Further, the putative establishment by Gregory VII of the future Order of Muret-Grandmont as it is described in the *PN relatio,* is not only unique in the history of papal dealings with religious orders from the eleventh to the early thirteenth century, apart that is to say, from those established from 1186 with the Order of Grandmont itself, for all authority in the order derived from the papal grant to Stephen of Muret, it also stands as an isolated papal act in the recorded history of the order until 1159.[55] In that year Adrian IV confirmed the Way of Life of the brethren of Grandmont with his apostolic, entreaty, counsel and exhortation in his letter *Venerabiles fratres,* which conveyed the grant of his approval only in general terms, and which was therefore couched in the form of an ordinary letter.[56] Adrian IV makes no reference to the order's supposed institution by Gregory VII, and for the period of eighty years which had elapsed since Stephen of Muret entered his hermitage there are no other grants by the papacy to founder or order, that is neither confirmations of goods nor concessions of privileges, nor confirmations of others' grants, such as were commonly found in the archives of religious and monastic orders. Indeed the only known contact between the Order of Muret-Grandmont and the papacy before 1159 is the visit of the cardinals Gregory and Peter Pierleone as related according to the *Primitiva* tradition, which may have taken place, as we have suggested, in 1119.[57] If there were episcopal correspondence of any sort, that is from the bishop of Limoges, or from other bishops, to the order, it has not survived. Bernard of Clairvaux does not include the brethren of Grandmont in his list of religious and monastic congregations loyal to Innocent II during the Anacletian schism, although Ernald of Bonnevalle, his biographer, includes them in his.[58] Thus if the date of composition of Ernald's work now generally accepted be correct, that is 1155/6, his is the earliest extant reference, in a text external to the order known to the present writer, to the order's existence.[59] In this long

---

[54] The *PN* account and the narratio of the bull do not wholly concur, although the latter presumably depends on the former. Delisle repudiated the bull in *Treize chartes de l'Ordre de Grammont* in *Mémoires de la Société des Antiquaires de Normandie* 2 ser., vol 10, no 20, Paris, 1853, pp 171-221.

[55] For changes introduced in the government and structure of the Order of Grandmont in 1186 see below pp. 20-22

[56] J. Ramackers, reversing Delisle's judgement in *Treize chartes de l'Ordre de Grammont* p 174 that *Venerabiles fratres* was a forgery, assigned it to the years 1157-1159: *Papsturkunden in Frankreich,* Neue Folge, 5 Band, Touraine, Anjou, Maine und Bretagne, in *Abhandlungen der Akademie der Wissenschaften in Göttingen.* Philologisch - historische Klasse, Dritte Folge Nr. 35, Göttingen, 1956, p 25 n. 3. There is no reasonable doubt that Adrian IV confirmed the way of life of the brethren of Grandmont. Subsequent and clearly authentic papal bulls repeat the fact, and Ms. Paris BN. 10-.891, s. XII ex. - s. XIII in, provenance of Grandmont itself, f. 77r has: *Adrianus quartus . papa romanus . confirmavit vitam et instituciones . fratrum de Grandimonte. Hac confirmationem attulerunt nobis. Geraldus Lemovicensis episcopus . et eius nepos Caturcensis episcopus . Geraldus similiter dictus;* For Dom Becquet's views on the letter see *Le bullaire de l'Ordre de Grandmont* in *Revue Mabillon* [RM] 53 (1963) p 112 Addenda 4 and 5. According to Geoffrey of Vigeois, the two bishops Gerald made what appears to have been an *ad limina* visit to Rome in 1159: *Chronicle* in Labbe, Philippe, *Novae Bibliothecae Manuscriptorum* T. II, Paris, 1657, p 310. We have in consequence followed Ramacker's second *terminus.* J.L. 10163†, 25 March, The Lateran. Text in Becquet, *Bullaire.*

[57] See *Wilkinson - Early Life App.* A.

[58] *Bernardi Ep.* 126, *P.L. Bernardi Op.* 1, 278 (His letter was written in 1131-2.) *Vita Bernardi, Lib. II* no 45 *Bern. Op.* 4.

[59] Christopher Holdsworth supposes that 1155/6 may be too early. See: *Saint Bernard : What kind of saint?* in *Monastic Studies* ed. Loades, J., Bangor, 1990, n. 22.

period of obscurity, we appear to be confronted by a papally instituted religious order, according to the *PN relatio,* which in practice underwent none of the consequences normally attendant upon actual papal authorization or approval of new religious congregations.[60]

Plainly, the founder's early life, and the origins of the Order of Muret-Grandmont depicted in the *Vita PN* are set at a great remove from those found in the *Primitiva* account outlined at the beginning of this paper. As the texts preserving that first account were themselves preserved in the mother house of the order it is natural to ask why an alternative version was judged necessary.[61] Certainly the beginnings of a new explanation had been made in the *Vita Stephani* which I have called *Posterior,* and which in some form Vincent of Beauvais apparently abridged in his *Speculum Historiale.*[62] Here Milo of Benevento is said to have taught Stephen a rule of living well *(regulam bene vivendi),* during a stay of twelve years, but there is no infancy account, no imputation of a divine plan in the saint's activities, no stay in Rome, no licensing of his *propositum* in religion by the pope. The cardinals ask no more than from whom he had learnt his way of living, and why he stayed in so sterile a place.[63] We are left to infer the reply that his teacher was Milo of Benevento. Neither do the Brethren of Calabria nor the Council of Chartres form part of the story which Vincent placed in his compendium.[64] If then, despite the oddity that the volume of information concerning the saint apparently increases in ratio to the number of years which elapse after his death, for the *Posterior* and *PN* accounts are separated by at least thirty years, we continue to regard the *PN* account as reliable, we ought to find in support of our view that when their way of life was challenged, the brethren of Grandmont referred their critics to the practices of the Calabrian Brethren and their authorization by the pope, albeit his name was unknown.[65] But the evidence of authors writing in the 1180's or late 1170's, or that for example of John of Salisbury in his *Policraticus,* completed in 1159, does not give weight to this supposition.

Stephen, abbot of the canons regular of Saint-Geneviève of Paris, distinguished canonist and later bishop of Tournai, found the evangelical way of life of the Order of Grandmont, which he praises after a fashion, open to serious criticism on three counts. He is writing to Robert of Gallardon, prior of the Cistercian House of Pontigny during the years 1178-1180.[66] His subject is the obligation imposed by the vow which certain brethren had taken at Grandmont before making what appears to have been a wilful

---

[60] The order shunned written records and the business which made records necessary.

[61] For the texts in question see *Wilkinson - Early Life* pp 107-112.

[62] ibid. pp 106-107.

[63] If, as seems the case, Vincent's account is based on the *Vita Posterior,* then it was that narrative which apparently produced Milo of Benevento as the patron of Stephen of Muret.

[64] See above p 128 for the Council of Chartres.

[65] In our view the *Vita Posterior* was composed before the death of Stephen's disciple, Hugh Lacerta, in 1157.

[66] See Desilve, Jules (M. l'abbé): *Lettres d'Etienne de Tournai [Desilve],* Valenciennes - Paris, 1893, Ep. I. He dates the letter by Ep. LXXXV to Peter of Pavia, bishop of Tusculum, 1178 - 1180 and apostolic legate, who had requested he correspond with Robert of Gallardon.

transitus to Pontigny.[67] His letter is undoubtedly a piece of rhetoric in favour of the Cistercian Order, but texts of the *Primitiva* tradition of the Order of Grandmont bear out the substance of his criticisms. He alleges that the discipline of Grandmont is inordinate:-

> ...si disciplinam, que est morum ordinata correptio, apprehenderint, profecto nec
> irascetur eis Dominus, nec peribunt de via iusta.[68]

That is, if they will embrace a discipline which is a well-ordered censuring of conduct, undoubtedly God will not be wroth with them, neither will they perish, away from the path of the just. And that which in their discipline dissatisfies Stephen is this. When they themselves have seen what they do within their own walls, they publish to Him to whom all hearts are open and from whom no secret is hidden, the evidence of the secret things within their deeds, that is the evidence of accusers and defenders among themselves.

> Viderint ipsi quid intra domesticos parietes agant, et testimonia secretorum intus
> operum suorum invicem accusantium aut defendentium ei publicent, cui omne cor patet et
> quem nullum latet secretum ...[69]

They concern themselves, as Stephen complains, not with faults against a written rule, as was usual in the capitular discipline of Western monks, but with the substance of a brother's sin. Stephen of Tournai has little difficulty in finding the root of this inordinate behaviour. Those who are many in number in the order, and the great ones in government, are not clerics but laymen, not lettered men but those who exist without letters:-

> ...quorum et plures numero et praelatione maiores non clerici, sed laici, non litterati,
> sed sine litteris existunt ...[70]

Then they profess as their master not Augustine, that is as they would do were they canons regular, but, as they say, a certain good man Stephen of Muret:-

> Ipsi autem non Augustinum, sed quendam, ut dicunt, bonum hominem Stephanum de
> Mureto magistrum suum profitentur.[71]

Stephen is writing at the time of the first Albigensian Crusade and *bonus* may be a barbed reference to the contemporary increase of sects of *boni homines*.[72] In the same

---

[67] It is virtually certain that one of these was William of Donjon, later abbot of Chaalis, then archbishop of Bourges. See *Desilve* n. I p 8.

[68] *ibid.* p 4.

[69] *ibid.*

[70] *ibid.* p 13. *sine litteris* was often predicated of those without latin letters, that is ability to write in latin. Whether Stephen of Tournai also implies complete illiteracy is not clear. But see n. 116 below.

[71] *ibid.* p 14.

[72] Peter of Pavia, to whom a copy of this letter was sent (see Ep. LXXXV) took part in the First Albigensian Crusade, and Stephen of Tournai himself was to accompany the legate Henry of Albano to Toulouse in 1183. But if this is sour comment, it is not an accusation of heresy, from the context of the rest of the letter.

passage he says of the brethren of Grandmont themselves that if one inquires of them whose order they are, they reply: "We are sinners." If one asks others, they say that they are Good Men. Further in the province of their origin and mother house, that is, the Limousin, their cells are called *Bonummie*.

The institutes of these 'Good Men' also aroused Stephen's suspicions. They did not call the little book containing these the Rule, but the Life, *Vita:-*

> Libellus eciam qui eorum institutiones continet, non regula appellatur ab eis
> sed vita ...[73]

He glosses this unsatisfactory state of affairs as follows. We think, he says, that either the rule of these men was not handed down by Dom Stephen of Muret, or if it was, it was a rule unknown to the Roman Church. And how indeed, he continues, could the supreme pontiff give a privilege to those who neither were in nor had come into his cognizance?

> Credimus quia necdum tradita erat a domino Stephano de Mureto regula istorum, aut,
> si tradita erat, sancte Romane ecclesie incognita erat. Et quomodo poterat summus pontifex
> privilegium dare his qui necdum erant vel in noticiam suam nondum venerant.[74]

Earlier in his letter to Robert of Gallardon Stephen had called the brethren of Grandmont *viri evangelici,* men of the Gospel, men not careful for what they ate or drank or put on.[75] He was, however, referring to their poverty, and to their dependance upon Providence to survive, and not to observance of the Gospel as a rule which they believed they observed in its fulness, and which would thus be justificatory, yielding eternal life.[76] Neither was he referring to their observance of the rule of the Gospel as the observance of things written in the heart, and not in the letters which kill (II. Cor.3: 4-6.), an observance which gave a structure of authority and obedience in their order which was radically different from the structure of authority which provided the basis of the public law of the Western church in the twelfth century.[77] Neither was he referring to their observance of the rule of the Gospel as a living rule of the Spirit, which prohibited a vowed obedience like that of the contemporary Western monk to the written rule and to

---

[73] *Desilve*, Ep. I p 14.

[74] *ibid.* p 15: Adrian IV merely heard a verbal relation, predicts fratribus *nostris referentibus* as he says, of the *Vita fratrum Grandimontensium*, and confirmed or strengthened it with his apostolic encouragement; text in Dom Becquet's *Le bullaire de l'Ordre de Grandmont*; above, n. 56. He did not make a substantial grant, establishing the practices of the order in the church's public law on the basis of his authority, of the kind which Stephen of Tournai had in mind. Alexander III's solemn privilege to the order, *Quanto amplius tenemur*, 8 March, Tusculum, is placed by Dom Becquet in 1171/2 (*Bullaire RM* 46 (1956) p 87 no 6.), J.L. 14.271 has 1171-1181. In part on the basis of Stephen of Tournai's ignorance of it, and in part on the basis of other evidence not directly germane here, we would place it in the last years of Alexander's pontificate, that is, contemporaneously with Stephen's letter, or a little later.

[75] *ibid.* p 4.

[76] See below at n. 93.

[77] That is, a structure in which authority descends from God to appointed individuals.

the abbot of his community, because its own command was absolute. As Stephen of Muret taught: *Non est alia regula nisi evangelium Christi.*[78] Stephen of Tournai does not indeed appear to have known what institutes were written in the little book called *Vita*, nor in what way the brethren of Grandmont were held to observing these institutes. He appears only to have known what he states, namely that they did not call their practices a rule, and that these had not been formally sanctioned by the papacy.[79]

John of Salisbury, however, in the same passage of his *Policraticus* noted above, alleged:- Some have Basil, others Benedict, and yet others Augustine, but these men, the Grandmontines, have a unique master, the Lord Jesus Christ:-

> Alii Basilium, alii Benedictum, hi Augustinum at isti singularem magistrum habent Dominum Jesum Christum.[80]

John is asserting here that the Gospel itself was the way of life of the Order of Grandmont. He does not specify that in consequence of their evangelical observance they were not professed to any written rule, but he certainly knew that they were not professed to a rule in the manner of Benedictine monks.[81] This is in part implicit in the contrast made between Christ the 'unique master', that is teacher, and the authors of other rules. It is also plainly expressed in an earlier passage of commendation of the brethren of Grandmont among whom:-

> ...solus Christus ingreditur, cuius innituntur gratiae, iactantes cogitatum suum in eum qui parvulos enutrit ...lilia vestit agri et omnibus sperantibus in se aut constitutionis suae obtemperantibus legi necessaria praestat ut nichil desit his qui se eius non subtraxerint voluntati.[82]

They rely on Christ's grace, casting their care on Him who rears little ones, clothes the lilies of the field and supplies what is necessary to all hoping in Him and obeying the law of His making, so that nothing is wanting to those who have not withdrawn themselves from His will. John is writing here of a reliance on divine providence which does not even admit the dictates of necessity (above he has *omnia necessitatis imperia excluserunt*). On a daily basis what the brethren eat or wear is at God's disposal, precluding the fixed provision of a rule. Law for them is to live in obedience to the actual providences of God

---

[78] *Liber Sententiarum Stephani (Sent) SS* I p 5.

[79] The terms of *Venerabiles fratres* indicate that Adrian IV understood a confirmation of something other than a monastic rule, in the usual sense, to have been granted; above n. 56.

[80] Above n. 47. Here 699c. John of Salisbury visited Apulia before February 1154 and again in 1155-6 spending some three months with Adrian IV at Benevento (*Policr.* 623b). He may have gained direct knowledge of Basilian monastic communities there. In these, Basilian and Benedictine practices were often conjoined for the sake of greater stability of government.

[81] See above at notes 38- 39, and *Ben. Reg. LVIII 16 ... nec collum excutere de sub iugo regulae ...* Hanslik p 135. See also *Beiträge zur Geschichte des alten Mönchtums und des Benediktinerordens,* ed. Herwegen, Dom Ildefons, Heft 3, *Studien zur benediktinischen Profess I Zur Aufnahmeordung der Regula S. Benedicti,* Rothenhäusler, Dom Matthaus: II *Geschichte der benediktinischen Professformel,* Herwegen, Dom Ildefons, Münster (Westf.) 1912.

[82] *Policraticus* 698b15-20 cf. PsLIV, 23: *Matth.* VI, 28, 30.

and all the dispositions of His will.[83] These things thus excluded the promise of future fulfilment of written regulations, and total obedience to an authority inferior to that of God Himself which a vow of the Benedictine variety involved.[84] Such a Way of Life (*Vita* - it was the direct obedience to God which was held to be vivifying) did not preclude the observance of precepts, spoken or written explaining how it was to be accomplished. But much in this *Vita fratrum* transcended the Church's positive law, and the problems of how a religious might be professed to a written rule, and follow the Rule of the Gospel awaited the solutions attempted by the Franciscans in the early thirteenth century.[85]

In different ways John of Salisbury and Stephen of Tournai record the continuance in the later history of the Order of Muret-Grandmont of the form of religious life which texts of the *Primitiva* tradition show to have been that upon which Stephen of Muret himself insisted, on the authority which he claimed to be that of the Gospel. In the sense in which, in the twelfth century, a vow to observe the written rules of the monastic or regular canonical life was understood, in Stephen's opinion its observance put a man in the debt of fulfilment before God. His chief objection to this was not simply that what was promised must be done, but also that when all had been done it could not justify, being less than the Gospel of Christ. The written rules of the holy fathers Basil, Augustine and Benedict were, he said, only the offshoots of religion and not its source.[86] He expressed the indebted state of those who undertook to observe written rules enshrining the counsels of evangelical perfection thus:-

...ante votum libertas, et arbitrium, post votum vero in legem transeunt et in debitum.[87]

No extant text explains his view of *lex* here, but from the context of the passage in question, he apparently means any written rule which, as in the case of the Benedictine Rule, was composed as law, the latter providing law in several senses. It gives detailed regulation for the daily routine of the monastery.[88] It provides norms of conduct for the community and the abbot to observe.[89] Most important, it is itself the law of the monastery, the written code which all have agreed at profession to accept; a written code with penal provisions, the well know *disciplina regularis*.[90] Stephen's *debitum* presumably refers to the obligatory observance of a written text under the authority of an abbot.[91] The brethren of Grandmont by contrast were to fear most greatly that having put their

---

[83] John confirms the continuance of Stephen of Muret's teaching that his followers must be poor, not merely expropriated singly.

[84] No abbot might command what was contrary to God's law.

[85] For example, Francis', *Regula Bullata* begins: *Regula et vita Minorum Fratrum haec est* ....See *Die Opuscula des hl. Franziskus von Assisi*, ed. Esser, Kajetan, O.F.M. in *Spicilegium Bonaventurianum* XIII, Grottaferrata, 1976 p 366.

[86] *Prologus, Dum in heremi*, SS p 66 40-42. See above at n. 61.

[87] *ibid.* pp 66- 67. Without a vow to a written rule he supposed these counsels to mean liberty.

[88] See XLI *Quibus horis oportet reficere*. Hanslik pp 102-104.

[89] See VII *De humilitate*. Hanslik pp 39-52.

[90] *ibid.* atl. 55 Hanslik p 49. *Octabus humilitatis gradus est, si nihil agat monachus nisi quod communis monasterii regula vel maiorum cohortantur exempla*. For the disciplina regularis see XXIII- XXX; XLIII- XLVI.

[91] cf. II *Cor.* 3, 4-6; *Gal.* III, 22. concerning the 'letter which kills'.

hands freely to the plough they look back, and Lot's wife perhaps come to reproach them:-

> Cavendum itaque summopere vobis est, fratres mei, ne postquam ad aratrum gratuito
> misistis manum, retro respiciatis, ne forte veniat vobis in opprobrium uxor Loth ...[92]

That is, Stephen's followers, entering freely upon their *propositum* were not vowed to a written rule. As he explains earlier in the Prologue cited here there is one faith, and of salvation there is a first and chief Rule of rules, the holy Gospel:-

> ...una est enim fides et salutis prima ac principalis Regularum Regula ... sanctum
> videlicet evangelium ...[93]

The *Liber Sententiarum,* the book of the spiritual teaching of Stephen of Muret· preserves *formulae* for the reception of a novice into the Order of Grandmont which also show that the brethren were not bound to a written rule. They made instead a present, spontaneous and unlimited offering of themselves to God in the service of the brethren, and under the authority of the pastor.[94] When Stephen received a novice into the fraternity, he summarized again the life of poverty which must be pursued, in imitation of Christ in the service of the brethren, as the novice had heard it before his probation.[95] And the novice replied:-

> Propter hoc totum sustinendum huc venire desidero, nec crescendi causa,
> sed minuendi.[96]

He confessed, or avowed, that he had been granted the desire to live the life of the Gospel in its fulness as the pastor outlined it to him, without having particularized what that life of grace would be, or what powers would emanate from his, the pastor's authority; that is without acceptance on the novice's part of a written code governing his future conduct. The novice was nonetheless absolutely obliged to perseverance in the life of religious conversion which, in the exterior expression of his desire for it, he acknowledged to his community to be a work of grace.[97] As the pastor told him, in summarizing the *Vita fratrum,* if he fell away from that life he would be lower than all other lost souls:-

> ...et si hinc in infernum caderes, omnibus aliis perditis inferior esses.[98]

---

[92] *Prologus, Dum in heremi, SS p 67.*

[93] *ibid.* p 66, 43-46.

[94] For the complex subject of vows see *D. Th. Cath. Voeu,* Séjourné, Dom Paris, 1950. Chastity is implicit in the formulae of the *Liber Sententiarum,* but is not mentioned, as is so in the rite of profession in *Benedicti Regula.*

[95] The duration of the probation is not given.

[96] *Ad novitios. Sent. SS* pp 6-7.

[97] We read the avowal thus: his desire to accept the cross (the formula's first injunction is *"Aspice crucem"*) is the fruit of grace; his intention *nec crescendi causa sed minuendi* signals the surrender of *dominatio* which he has been told must follow from remaining fixed on the cross itself (in spirit). Only grace can sustain him in such a state, and Stephen's direct teaching, after *Ad novitios,* begins *Religio est gratia, iustitia atque custodia.*

[98] *Ad noritios SS.* p5

Thus the Grandmontine brother did not become a monk as that term was understood in the law of the Western Church in the twelfth century. He did not make a written account of his promise to observe a written rule under the authority of an abbot in the monastery of his profession.[99] Neither did he live under a superior whose authority was greater than that of the rule he undertook to observe.[100] The only absolute authority in the Order of Grandmont was that of the Gospel itself, written, as Stephen of Muret put it, in the scriptures of the heart.[101] The *Vita fratrum* thus imposed an obligation on all to limitless justice, or right order, because it was alleged to be the fulness of Gospel life. Before the Rule of the Gospel even the pastor of the order was himself a subject.[102] He had the authority of teacher of his disciples in so far as his words and life conformed to the word of God which he preached; and by that authority, of being acknowledged to teach the truth of the Gospel, he was the shield of souls.[103] He exercised great powers, but powers doubly circumscribed, by the inherent authenticity of the Gospel message, and by the ability of each brother, in greater or lesser degree, to perceive the truth of the Gospel taught to him for himself, on account of the Spirit received in baptism, and in the 'second' baptism of conversion.[104] There is no intrinsic reason for making the ruler of a community of monks or religious *vices-Christi,* although it has frequently been assumed that a monastic ruler must occupy a position analogous to that of a bishop in his diocese, presumably to supply the sort of institutional strength which was certainly absent in the order of Muret-Grandmont as originally constructed.[105] But the monastic or religious leader who takes the *Regula Evangelii* as the rule of the institution he creates cannot be *vices-Christi* unless he is made so by a competent ecclesiastical authority , or has already been made so, and as has been seen elsewhere, Stephen of Muret, while perhaps in minor orders, was effectively a layman.[106]

As has been seen, Stephen of Tournai was not only doubtful about the general validity of the *Vita fratrum Grandimontensium,* he also believed specifically that the mode of correction on which it depended was badly or wrongly ordered.[107] And the charge may indeed be allowed to stand, when construed in his terms of reference, on the basis of yet

---

[99] See above at n. 38, 39.

[100] Above n. 40. A measure of abbatial dispensing power is implicit within the Benedictine Rule.

[101] *Scriptura cordis quam tibi Deus immisit tibi semper ostendit quid relinquere debeas vel agere. Sent. LXVII* [I] *SS* p 34.

[102] See *VHL20 SS* p 179. Here Hugh Lacerta criticizes the decision of conventus and pastor, is formally rebuked, but ultimately commended for leading his master, Stephen, back to God by means of greater light. The so called Rule of Stephen of Muret (below pp 21-22) concedes to the brethren in its last chapter (SS pp 98-99) the right to eject a pastor from the order who persists in trying to divert them from their way of truth. It may be supposed that here an ancient practice was preserved.

[103] *Sent.* VI [5] *SS* pp 9-10. The disciple, to the Devil: *Ego sum post eius clypeum, et verba Dei quae mihi loquitur ab universis tuis me protegent iaculis ....*

[104] It is that authentic quality of the Gospel to which Saint Paul refers in *Gal.* I: 8, 9.

[105] Saint Benedict's abbot, originally a lay abbot, is *vices-Christi* because Benedict created that model of authority for his monks.

[106] See above n. 12.

[107] Above at n. 68.

other evidence from the *Primitiva* tradition. He alleged, as we have also seen, that what was reviewed in the order's disciplinary procedures, based as they were upon the exercize of fraternal correction, was not the faults committed against a written monastic code, as was the case among Benedictine monks, but the substance of sin, the guilty interior dispositions of a brother towards God and man which were by this period matters normally reserved for sacramental confession. From the *Liber Sententiarum* in particular, it is possible to exemplify a penitential system dependent upon the authority of both pastor and brethren *ex Evangelio,* and upon the frequent use of dialogue between pastor and brethren for spiritual instruction and so to sustain Stephen of Tournai's charge.[108] Chapter XI in Dom Becquet's edition, is a *sermo de correctione* exhibiting a practice of fraternal correction apparently employing the procedure found in Matthew 18: 15-17.[109] According to the principles implicit in that procedure each brother of Grandmont was allowed a right of accusation and a right of self defence in the order's corrective discipline. (Stephen of Tournai's *invicem* in the passage of his letter which has been cited is read, as already said, as *inter se.*[110]) This mode of discipline was intended to establish a brother steadfastly as a penitent, one who knew himself to be a sinner and who was prepared in consequence to change his ways.[111] The regular discipline of the Benedictine chapter imposed punishment for infractions of a written rule, but reasoned and charitable exposition of the Rule of the Gospel, replacing the regular silence, the penal code, and the rods of Benedictine practice were intended to be the core of the penitential discipline of the Order of Grandmont.[112] As may be seen, in so far as amendment of life was concerned, the binding and loosing authority granted by Christ to all his disciples was viewed by Stephen of Muret as vested in the pastor and brethren of the order he established as a body.[113] Stephen of Tournai, by contrast held the common clerical opinion of his day that penitential discipline was a sacerdotal matter only on account of both ministry and learning.[114] Not surprizingly, he found the involvement of all the brethren of the Order of Grandmont in its penitential system inordinate.

Lay prelacy which constituted the order's government, and which Stephen of Tournai found also contrary to all that he believed fitting, was likewise based on the corrective powers of the order as a whole.[115] As he says, the numerical majority consisted of

---

[108] For the use of dialogue *VHL, Sent, passim: Wilkinson - Early Life* pp 110-111.

[109] This procedure plays a prominent part in the penitential discipline established by Saint Basil in his *Shorter Rules* from which we believe Stephen of Muret drew much inspiration.

[110] 'Mutually' is possible. In that case Stephen's imputation would be different.

[111] *Sent XI.* [I] *SS.* p.15. Here an uncharitable accuser must understand his own offence when he has failed to correct in a becoming way.

[112] *ibid.* IX [7] *SS.* p 13 ... *in quantum homo novitius suam defendit saecularitatem, tantumdem alius qui diu stetit in iustitia defendat ratiocinando suam religionem.*

[113] *Sent. LXXII* [3] *SS* p 36, for priestly absolution from sin as a culmination of this penitential discipline.

[114] He says of the Cistercian order: ... *nec idiota docet clericum, nec laicus imperat sacerdoti ... qui potestatem habet corripiendi, habet et scienciam corrigendi.* Desilve Ep I. pp 6-7.

[115] See above at n.70.

laymen.[116] Although this had not been Stephen of Muret's intention, the relatively few priests of the order had become restricted to a life of contemplation and administering the sacraments, ceasing to participate in manual work.[117] *Praelatio* thus passed in the cells to the lay members of the order who dealt with its temporal affairs, and with temporal and spiritual government of all aspects of the order's life, except things pertaining to the celebration of the divine office and sacramental matters. In all other respects clerics were thus subject to the spiritual discipline of a layman in each cell, and to the same corrective process as any other brother.[118] Hence no brother exercised *dominatio* or lordship in a cell, neither did the pastor at Grandmont claim lordship.[119] He was the focus of unity among the members of the order, but as has been seen, absolute authority was predicated only of the Gospel, and lordship belonged only to Christ.[120]

The structure of authority and obedience under which the brethren of Muret-Grandmont were governed, probably until the 1180's, when fundamental modifications were attempted, was thus radically different from that found in monasteries of the Benedictine type, or in regular canonical foundations such as Stephen of Tournai's own house of Sainte-Geneviève of Paris.[121] And the practices of the order were in so profound a way part of the *lex privata* of the church, that private law which proceeding from the Holy Spirit, placed a man above positive law, that the only authority competent to regulate them was that of the papacy, with which, as has been seen, the order appears to have had almost no contact before 1159.[122] In view of all these things, and especially in view of the primacy of the Rule of the Gospel which Stephen of Muret taught his followers, it is pertinent to ask once more why the author of the *Vita Stephani* wished his readers to believe that the founder of the order had observed as salutary, in remission of his sins, the Rule of the Brethren of Calabria to which he was obliged by papal command, drawing his own authority as a religious superior from the papal plenitude of power?[123]

The sixth prior of the order, William of Treignac (1171-1188) requested and received from Alexander III confirmation of a series of institutes intended to introduce restraints, that is exterior restraints or sanctions, in the lives of the brethren of Grandmont. As the wording of the privilege runs:-

---

[116] *idiota* (above n. 114) is probably his private gloss on *illiteratus* and thus conveys more of his attitude towards the lay order of Grandmont.

[117] Walter Map writing apparently at the time when disputes within the order had been appealed to Rome, that is 1185-86, has:- ... *clericis interius cum Maria sine sollicitudine seculi sedentibus. De Nugis Curialium in Anecdota Oxoniensia* ed. James, M.R. Oxford, 1914, pp 26-27.

[118] See, for example, *VHL* 31 830-832 *SS* p 187, where the layman Hugh Lacerta's cure of his cell of Plagne is specified.

[119] Attempts were made, as we think in the 1180's, to elevate the authority of the pastor. See below for the customary with chapters to this effect. In it lay 'presidents' of cells are called *dispensatores*.

[120] Above at notes 100, 101.

[121] In both cases a stgructure of descending authority prevailed, authority being, as it were, distilled in set channels. It was diffused within the order of Grandmont.

[122] Above p 10

[123] Above pp 6-7

>...institutionem quoque, quam ad castigationem vestram, post confirmationem felicis
> recordationis Adriani papae, praedecessoris nostri, regulae vestrae salubriter addidistis,
> authoritate apostolica confirmamus ...[124]

That is, he confirms the Institution which has been added to their rule, or way of life, for reproof or correction, after the confirmation of Adrian IV, for their spiritual advantage.[125] It thus appears that Alexander saw a text in accordance with which the brethren could be disciplined in a way that the *Vita fratrum* itself did not allow. A text of a customary, preserved in a seventeenth century copy, and known in the order as the *Institutio and castigationem* is apparently that to which the pope referred.[126] It is a customary exhibiting certain of the characteristics of a monastic penal code. There are, for example, rods in chapter with which the brethren can impose corporal punishment on each other when necessary.[127] There is to be silence at set times and in specified places, and the great silence must be observed from the end of Compline until the end of the ensuing daily chapter.[128] It is well-known that disputes erupted between the lay and clerical members of the order (Gerald Ithier states from 1185), and it seems most probable that in those disputes this document played an important part.[129]

On 15 July 1186, Urban III, having listened to representatives of the contending parties, gave what was intended as a definitive sentence concerning the problems at issue in his bull *Quanto per infusionem*.[130] Although divisions within the order deepened after the publication of the sentence, and the prior, William of Treignac, was expelled by a majority of the general chapter in 1187 and a new prior elected, the sentence was put into effect from 1188, and was to be the means of controlling the order's structure and government during the ensuing twenty years.[131] And having listened, Urban says, he decided, with the counsel of his brethren, that the hand of apostolic correction must be placed upon those things which had seemed to engender the matter of the disputes:-

> ... in his quae generare videbantur materiam iurgiorum, manum correctionis apostolicae
> de fratrum nostrorum consilio duximus apponendam.[132]

---

[124] *Quanto amplius tenemur.* See above n. 74, text in *De Antiquis Ecclesiae Ritibus IV* ed. Martène, Dom E., Antwerp, 1738, 913. (The general remission of sins also granted in the bull does not concern us here.)

[125] See above at n. 56 for Adrian IV's confirmation of the *Vita Fratrum*.

[126] See SS, XIV, and Becquet, Dom J; *L'Institution premier coutumier de l'Ordre de Grandmont*, RM, 46, 1956, pp 15-32.

[127] *Institutio* 62, SS p 524.

[128] *ibid.* 23, SS p 518.

[129] For the time given, see *De Revelatione B. Stephani*, SS, XI [B], p 277.

[130] At Verona. J.L. 15.650. Text in *Thesaurus Novus Anecdotorum I (TNA)* ed. Martène, Dom E., Paris, 1717, 627-630.

[131] Clement III deposed both priors, admitting that the election of the second might have been canonical. *Ne in questionis.* 25 June, 1188, the Lateran, J.L. 16.294. Text in *Gallia Chr.* II, Instr. 192. Renewal of Urban III's judgement in *Quanto per infusionem* began with Clement's bull, *Inter cetera que* 25 June, 1188, the Lateran. J.L. –. Partial text in Becquet *Bullaire RM* 46, 1956 no 22 p 156.

[132] *TNA* I 628b. Urban's having taken counsel of the curial cardinals is an indication of the gravity and complexity of the matters at issue.

From the *capitula correctionis* which follow two concern us here. All who entered the order were to promise obedience and reverence to the prior absolutely:-

> In primis siquidem statuentes ut qui, relicto saeculo, ad ordinem vestrum confugiunt, priori ...obedientiam, et reverentiam promittant absolute.[133]

The prior himself was granted full power in spiritual and temporal matters out of the apostolic plenitude itself:-

> ...Priori autem, tam in spiritualibus, quam in temporalibus, plenam concedimus auctoritate apostolica potestatem ...[134]

Thus out of that plenitude the pastor-prior of Grandmont was made an abbot without name. Within a short space of time he was granted the quasi-episcopal privilege of tonsuring novices and blessing sacred linens of the order.[135] At the same time the order became papally exempt, that is wholly independent of every other jurisdiction.[136] Finally, by means of the imposition of the very *capitula correctionis* mentioned above, the way of life of the Order of Grandmont, that is all its practices and prescriptive texts became dependent upon papal authority, and when not modified in accordance with Urban III's corrections they became invalid. The former might be freely observed by the members of the order with the proviso, *salva in omnibus apostolicae sedis auctoritate;* they were made subordinate to the pope's corrections with the phrase *supra positis nostrae correctionis capitulis.*[137]

Writing after the *Revelatio* of Stephen of Muret in 1189, that is after his papal canonization and public raising to the altars of the order he had founded, Gerald Ithier made these admissions concerning the *Rule of the Brethren of Grandmont,* the rule which he copied into his *Speculum Grandimontis* with the title *Regula venerabilis viri Stephani confessoris primi patris ordinis Grandimontensis.*[138] Without any doubt at all of old the Rule used to be called *Vita* by the brethren because it yields eternal life, and because it seemed to foster their habits and acts so that they might live well.[139] We however, continues Gerald, supported by a greater authority and dignity, call it a Rule, from the example of other saints who are said to have composed rules, the blessed Augustine, the

---

[133] *ibid.*

[134] *ibid.* at d.

[135] Probably 25 or 26 June, 1188, by Clement III. *Religiosam vitam,* the Lateran, J.L. –. Text *DAE IV* 985. See Becquet, *Bullaire,* nos 23b and 27.

[136] *ibid.* Two ounces of gold were to be paid annually for this liberty. They are entered in the first manuscript of the *Liber Censuum* but after 1192. See *Le Liber Censuum de l'Eglise Romaine* ed. Fabre, P. Duchesne, L. *(Bibliotheque des Ecoles Francaises d'Athenès et de Rome,* Second Series) vol I, Paris, 1910, p 203.

[137] *TNA* I, 628f, 629a.

[138] Ms. Archives Departementales de la Haute Vienne 112, Grand Seminaire 10, p XXXVI, transcription of the abbe Nadaud s.XVIII. *Regula Fratrum Grandimontensium* is the title used by the papal chancery.

[139] *De Confirmatione XXXVII, SS* p 375.

blessed Benedict, the blessed Basil, because in our day, God granting, it has been confirmed and privileged by ecclesiastical authority, and because the *revelatio* of blessed Stephen has been celebrated, by whom it was instituted, put in good order and composed.[140]

Urban III's corrections of the way of life, or rule in the wider sense, of the brethren of Grandmont, and these are not corrections *de verbo ad verbum* of a text, but principles of modification for all the texts and practices of the order, are relatively few in number, but they are of profound importance. From those cited here it is evident that they were intended to alter the structure of authority and obedience in the order fundamentally. Thus in so far as any text of the order called a rule incorporates these corrections, as does the so called Rule of the Venerable Stephen, that rule was not, as Gerald Ithier asserts, instituted, ordered and composed by Stephen of Muret. He had taught that absolute obedience, surrendered in chapter one of the rule text in question to the prior of the order, was owed only to the Rule of the Gospel.[141] Neither did he ordain that his followers be professed to observe a rule text. He asserted instead the law of the Spirit which frees from merely legal observances, and required his followers to make a total offering of themselves to God in the service of the brethren.[142] Gerald Ithier, however, writes of the Rule of Stephen that it is that which the brethren have professed and put upon their necks.[143] It is in the licence with veracity which Gerald allows himself in calling the rule which incorporates Urban III's corrections the Rule of the Venerable Stephen that we see the variety of thinking which led to the creation of the *Vita PN*.

There seems little doubt that as Dom Becquet stated the *Vita Stephani Muretensis* was intended to illustrate the *Regula Stephani*.[144] He places both texts, however, in the years 1140-1163, a time in the view of the present writer some thirty years too early.[145] In chapter thirty two of his edition of the Vita, the dying saint speaks of the continuance of God's providence in the order after his death. The security of that providence will remain for his followers, he says:-

> Si ... in hac regula de evangelio sumpta perseveraveritis.[146]

As may be seen, the rule of which he speaks is taken out of the Gospel. It is not the *Regula Evangelii* itself with its absolute authority, the authority on which the *Vita fratrum* had been established. We may compare the words of Stephen's dying homily as

---

[140] *ibid.*

[141] Dom Becquet's edition of the Rule, II in *SS*, follows via Migne, that of the Dijon editors of 1645 which omits *absolute*. But Gerald Ithier's text in *Speculum* has: *Quisquis hanc religionem ... ingredietur primo promittat obedientiam deo et pastori qui eum recipiet, suisque successoribus absolute*. The same reading is given in Ms. Clermont-Ferrand, Bibliothèque Municipale 151, in a transcription s.XVII of the Rule from *Speculum*.

[142] See above, p 16

[143] *De Confirmatione*, LXXXVIII *SS* p418. See also Ms. Limoges, Séminaire 10, *Regula, cl ... polliceatur etiam presentem regulam, et cetera huius religionis instituta usque in finem se fideliter observaturum. p XXXVII.*

[144] *SS, III, Monitum.*

[145] *ibid.*, and *RM*, 43, 1953, *Les premiers écrivains de l/Ordre de Grandmont* pp 125-130.

[146] *SS* p 124.

recorded in the *Primitiva* tradition:-

> ...Deus aget curam de vobis sicut bonus Dominus ... tali quidem vobis dico pacto, si in
> vita ista remanetis; si autem de vita recesseritis, ego ei iniuriam facerem, si vobis sua
> promitterem ... quin bene totum esset necessarium quod Deus praestitit mihi; similiterque
> faciet vobis, si in vita hac remanseritis.[147]

Here he is taking his last opportunity to drive home the core of his teaching
concerning the *Vita fratrum*, and perseverance in a rule taken out of the Gospel rather
than in the life of the Gospel itself, as has been seen, is precisely what he had prohibited.
The text of the *Vita Stephani PN* in all extant versions, and all have the phrase cited
above, must in consequence be posterior to the granting of absolute authority by Urban
III to the pastor of Grandmont in 1186, and so also to the creation of a rule text
subordinate to the authority of the pastor, and to that of the pope.[148] As for that new
rule, it appears to have been put together out of the written *Vita fratrum*, and other texts,
to incorporate the corrections of Urban III and the ideas of its compiler. Its ascription
implies the blessing and approval of the newly canonized Stephen of Muret.

As has been seen, the Stephen of Muret of the *PN* account will teach his disciples the
alleged practices of the Calabrian Brethren, actually those of the Order of Muret-
Grandmont itself, on the authority of an unnamed pope. There is no word in this account
of the Rule of the Gospel or of the *Vita fratrum*. The account seems to the present writer,
as was said at the outset, a paradigm, and a paradigm of the real papal re-constitution of
the order's practices, their rule in the widest sense, by Urban III in 1186. The clerical
minority of the order received most advantage from the reforms of 1186 and thereafter,
and we may suppose that a story of the impeccably clerical origins of the order founded
by Stephen of Muret, published on the word of their prior, provided a history which they
found congenial. But whatever their reaction, the *PN* text appears quickly to have
become part of the regular mensal and liturgical reading of the order, thereby establishing
story and interpretation in the perceptions of those who heard them.[149]

---

[147] *VHL 27, SS* p 183.

[148] The reforms of 1186 diminished the authority of the Gospel Rule or *Vita fratrum* and elevated that of the pastor.

[149] See marginal comment in a contemporary hand in Ms. A. D. de la Haute Vienne, 449, Grand Séminaire 68, a rearranged
version of the *Vita Stephani s.XII ex. - s.XIII in.*.

'WHO HATH CHOSEN THE BETTER PART? (LUKE 10,42)' POPE INNOCENT III AND JOACHIM OF FIORE ON THE DIVERSE FORMS OF RELIGIOUS LIFE

by

Fiona Robb

On 11 January 1199 Pope Innocent III (1198-1216) wrote to Joachim, abbot of Fiore (d.1202), on the nature of the religious life, a theme dear to them both.[1] Joachim had asked that the pope grant a dispensation to a certain canon of the church of Acerenza who wished to put on the monastic habit in the belief that this would cure him of his grave illness. Innocent's response was direct and to the point. 'It is less', he writes, 'his habit than the willingness and stability of his regular profession, which makes the monk'.[2] The Pope here disregards the juridical and exterior distinction of religious habit and custom[3] in favour of the interior orientation of will which, he implies, is the determining factor in the progress towards virtue. At the same time, Innocent is over-riding the traditional superiority of contemplation over action in the economy of salvation. His assumption appears to be that the predominantly active canon,[4] in so far as he is suitably guided in spirit, is as worthy a candidate for salvation as the monk, who is more inclined to be contemplative.

This letter is a rare glimpse into the relationship between these two important spiritual leaders who, far from being juxtaposed in this way, are usually seen as representing divergent and opposing trends - Innocent, characterised by his reformist zeal in religion[5] and politics;[6] Joachim[7], for his part, seldom given much attention save in a rare footnote

---

[1] O.Hageneder and A. Haidacher (eds.), *Die Register Innocenz' III*, Bd.I, *Pontifikatsjahr 1198-1199* (Graz-Koln, 1964), (hereafter *Register* I), p757; J.P. Migne (ed.), *Patrologia Latina* (Paris, 1855-1864), *Innocentii III Opera Omina*. 4 vols. (hereafter *PL*), 214,480; A. Potthast (ed.), *Regesta Pontificium Romanorum*, 2 vols. (Berlin, 1874), (hereafter *Potthast*), 1,572.

[2] *Register* I, p757 'monachum faciat non habitus, sed professio regularis, ex quo a convertendo emittitur et recipitur ab abbate'

[3] M.Maccarrone, *Studi su Innocenzo III, Italia Sacra*, Studi e documenti di Storia Ecclesiastica, 17 (Padua, 1972), (hereafter Maccarrone, *Studi*), p364.

[4] G. Constable and B. Smith (eds.), *Libellus De Diversis Ordinibus Et Professionibus Qui sunt In Aecclesia* (Oxford, 1972), (hereafter Constable, *Libellus De Diversis*) p57 on canons: 'Their task is to teach the people, take tithes, collect offerings in church, remonstrate with delinquents, reconcile the converted and the penitent to the church'; C.N.L. Brooke, 'Monk and Canon: Some Patterns in the Religious Life of the Twelfth Century', *Studies in Church History* 22 (Blackwell, 1985) pp109-129.

[5] Maccarrone, *Studi*; H. Tillmann, *Pope Innocent III* (1954, trans. Walter Sax, North-Holland, 1980); U. Berlière 'Innocent III et la réorganisation des monastères bénédictines', *Revue Bénédictine* 20 (1920) pp22-42; A. Fliche 'Innocent III et la réforme de l'église', *Revue Historique Ecclésiastique* 44 (1949) pp87-152; B.M. Bolton, *The Medieval Reformation* (London,1983), (hereafter Bolton, *Medieval Reformation*) pp55-79, 97-111; B.M. Bolton, 'Via Ascetica: A Papal Quandary', *Studies in Church History* 22 (Blackwell, 1985), (hereafter Bolton, 'Via Ascetica') pp161-191.

[6] D.T. Waley, *The Papal State in the Thirteenth Century* (London, 1961); E. Kennan, 'Innocent III and the first political crusade: a comment on the limitations of papal power', *Traditio* 27 (1971) pp231-249.

[7] M. Reeves, *The Influence of Prophecy in the Later Middle Ages* (Oxford, 1969), (hereafter Reeves, *Influence*); M. Reeves and B. Hirsch-Reich, *The Figurae of Joachim of Fiore* (Oxford, 1972), (hereafter Reeves and Hirsch-Reich, *Figurae*); H. de Lubac, *Exégèse Médiévale: Les Quatres Senses de L'Ecriture* (Paris, 1961) II, 1; A. Williams (ed.), *Prophecy and Millenarianism: Essays in Honour of Marjorie Reeves* (London, 1980), (hereafter Williams, *Prophecy*); B. McGinn, *The Calabrian Abbot: Joachim of Fiore in the History of Western Thought* (New York-London, 1985), (hereafter McGinn, *Calabrian Abbot*).

on fringe or heretical movements[8]. This position is perhaps understandable, however, given what would appear to be the condemnation of Joachim's doctrine of the Trinity at the Fourth Lateran Council of 1215, organised and presided over by Innocent.[9] In this context, the letter of January 1199 assumes a precious importance as the only known instance of correspondence between the pope and the abbot of Fiore.

Despite this lack of correspondence, however, there is evidence that Innocent's religious thought was influenced by Joachim's in several significant areas. The pope's use of Joachim's symbolic representation of the Trinity in his sermons and letters and his identification of the Tetragrammaton in accordance with Joachim's are somewhat surprising examples of Joachim's influence upon the pope.[10] More pertinent to the history of religious orders are the parallels between the ideas of Innocent and Joachim on action and contemplation, on monastic and preaching orders, and on the place of married men and women in the religious life. This similarity of approach is most notably discernable in Innocent's policy of attempting to unite different groups into one religious profession.,[11] which would have had the effect of combining the traditionally distinct roles of Martha and Mary in a single structure. One manifestation of this desire to achieve unity from diversity came about in December 1200 in a suggestion of quite extraordinary boldness and vision made by the pope to the leaders of the Humiliati of Lombardy.[12] Faced by this heterogeneous group containing three elements, canons, monks, and married laity, Innocent proposed that all should come together in one canonical *regulare propositum,* living together under one rule.[13] As he said, the Church is composed of a diverse multitude of offices and orders, arranged in battle camps like so many different military orders.[14] Or, translated into the language of monastic spirituality, one might say that Martha and Mary were no longer competing rivals in the attainment of grace. Instead, each could assist the other in the pursuit of that long desired intimacy with Christ in heaven, and so exist together in a state of charity and love. Innocent is stressing, therefore, the interdependence of all Christian vocations, as opposed to the hierarchical placing of one Christian way of life on a scale above the other.[15] Chenu, attempting to analyze this shift away from a purely monastic theology of salvation, suggests that 'the

---

[8] R.W. Southern, *Western Society and the Church in the Middle Ages* (Harmondsworth, 1970), p269 where Joachim is described as a 'violent and apocalyptic' character; F. Oakley, *The Western Church in the Later Middle Ages* (London, 1979), pp185-188, 205-206 deals with Joachim's influence on subsequent heresies.

[9] J. Alberigo et al (eds.), *Conciliorum Oecumenicorum Decreta* (Bologna, 1973) pp240-241. See also S. Kuttner and A. Garcia y Garcia, A New Eyewitness Account of the Fourth Lateran Council', *Traditio* 20 (1964), pp115-178, especially pp156-163.

[10] Much work remains to be done on this complex subject.

[11] Maccarrone, *Studi,* pp262-306.

[12] *PL* 214,921-922; *Potthast* I, 1192; for the Humiliati see B.M.Bolton, 'Innocent III's Treatment of the Humiliati', *Studies in Church History* (Blackwell, 1971) pp73-82; G. Tiraboschi, *Vetera Humiliatorum Monumenta* 3 vols. (Milan, 1766-1768), (hereafter Tiraboschi, *VHM*); J.Hinnebusch, *The Historia Occidentalis of Jacques de Vitry* (Fribourg. 1972) pp144-146.

[13] *PL* 214,922; *Potthast* I, 1192.

[14] *PL* 214,921 'Ecclesia tamen non solum propter varietatem virtutum et operum, sed etiam propter diversitatem officiorum et ordinum, dicitur ut castrorum acies ordinata, an qua videlicet diversi ordines militant ordinati'

[15] For the emergence of this tradition in the twelfth century see Constable, *Libellus De Diversis* pp xxv, 15-16; C.Bynum, 'Did the Twelfth Century Discover the Individual', *Journal of Ecclesiastical History* 31 (1980) pp5-8

monastery could no longer be considered the "city of God" to which one would lead society. Society existed and Christians lived in it: to do so was their calling. Secular callings or states of life were matter for grace and salvation'.[16]

Innocent was the first to see the implication for the new forms of religious life resulting from these social changes. His religious reforms only become comprehensible when his broad grasp of the changing religious aspirations of ordinary Christians is truly appreciated. Innocent's proposal to the Humiliati in December 1200 reveals something of his incisive understanding of the contemporary religious scene. This imaginative and audacious suggestion, anticipating, as it does, thirteenth century developments, might even lead us to consider Innocent as something of a prophet. The problem which the Church faced was how it might reach those bands of faithful who were demanding its ministry in the towns.[17] Most of the new religious orders of the twelfth century, such as the Cistercians and Carthusians, ignored the towns and were generally firmly rooted in 'desert' isolation. By encouraging such groups as the Humiliati of the Lombard cities, Innocent hoped that this vacuum would be filled so that true religion could flourish in an urban as well as a rural setting.

Considerable debate, dating to the beginnings of Christian ascetic communities in the East, centred on the respective roles of Martha and Mary, and their precursors in the Old Testament, Leah and Rachel.[18] In his *Conferences,* based on his conversations with holy men in the Egyptian desert, John Cassian appeared to place the part of contemplative Mary above that of active Martha.[19] His account of the commentary of Abba Moses on *Luke* 10,38-42, where the Martha-Mary story is told, seemed to leave no doubt. 'The Lord, you see, placed the chief good in divine contemplation. All the other virtues, however necessary and good and useful we deem them, must be placed on a lower plane because they are sought for the sake of this one thing'.[20] Gregory the Great (590-604) showed a similar concern with the conflicting demands of action and contemplation, a conflict upon which, as the first monk-pope, he was well qualified to speak. Gregory's solution was to acknowledge the intrinsic superiority of contemplation over action, whilst maintaining that the office of ministering to the faithful was not only indispensable to the Church, but also demonstrated a subjugation of self-will which was necessarily part of the path to humility.[21] It was not until the advent of the Cistercians in the twelfth century that a more integrated view of the Martha-Mary dichotomy emerged, a view which saw the roles of active service and silent contemplation as equally important.[22] Bernard of Clairvaux in his famous treatise to his disciple and former monk, Pope

---

[16] M-D.Chenu, *Nature, Man and Society in the Twelfth Century* (Chicago, 1968), (hereafter Chenu, *Nature*) p222

[17] L.K.Little, *Religious Poverty and the Profit Economy in Medieval Europe* (London 1978)

[18] *Luke* 10,38-42; *Genesis* 29-30

[19] O.Chadwick, *John Cassian* (Cambridge, 1950); for a reinterpretation of this view see P.Rousseau, 'Cassian, Contemplation and the Coenobitic Life', *Journal of Ecclesiastical History* 26 (1975) pp113-126.

[20] O.Chadwick, *Western Asceticism* (Philadelphia, 1958), pp199-200

[21] J.Richards, *Consul of God* (London, 1980) p57

[22] C.J.Holdsworth, 'The Blessings of Work: The Cistercian View', *Studies in Church History* 10 (Blackwell, 1973) pp59-76, esp. pp64-66

Eugenius III (1145-1153), lamented the absence of his former spiritual son from the embrace of Rachel, whose consolation Eugenius still desired in vain.[23] Bernard did not counsel total withdrawal, but simply advised that all actions be based on thoughtful consideration of what is most necessary, and suggested that action became senseless and ineffective unless preceded by some form of contemplative thought, the only guard against a hard heart.[24] For the Cistercians, action and contemplation were no longer utterly separate, but formed a balanced and integrated whole.

By the time of Innocent's pontificate, perceptions of the roles of Martha and Mary were once again changing, this time in response to a growing awareness of the validity of every Christian vocation and the interdependence of all the faithful in one body in Christ.[25] The traditional sense of hierarchy amongst the various Christian callings was giving way to a philosophy of mutual respect and toleration, with the evangelical awakening amongst the laity adding a further dimension to this phenomenon.[26] Innocent's role in this process was crucial. As Maccarrone has observed, Innocent's response to the Humiliati is characteristic of his imaginative and flexible approach to religious movements.[27] But in this particular case the role of Innocent's advisors in the early years of the pontificate must also be taken into account. They were men who had been tried and tested in the monastic life, and who had themselves experienced many vicissitudes. Foremost amongst them was Rainier of Ponza (d.1207-1209).[28] Rainier was Innocent's confessor, but he was significantly also the *intimus*, disciple, and confidant of the abbot Joachim.

Both Rainier and Joachim had begun their monastic careers as Cistercians. The anonymous *vita* of Joachim, known to have been written by a close companion of Joachim, describes Joachim's apparent withdrawal from the Order and Rainier's visit to him at the solitary retreat of Petralata in the Sila mountains in the autumn of 1188 - 'First to join him was Rainier, a saintly man, who from that time was inflamed with a zeal for the truth, and who was greatly learned and of eloquent speech. He came from the ends of the kingdom, from the islands of Ponza, to hear the wisdom of the new Solomon'.[29] We know from the *vita* of Joachim written by his former scribe, Luke, archbishop of Cosenza, that Joachim spent some time at the Cistercian house of

---

[23] J.Anderson and E.T.Kennan (eds.), *De consideratione ad Eugenium papum tertium libri quinque*, Cistercian Studies 37 (Kalamazoo, 1976) I:1

[24] *Ibid.*, I,6

[25] Constable, *Libellus De Diversis*, p15, 'Love in others what you yourself do not have, so that another shall love in you what he does not have, so that what either does shall be good for the other and those shall be joined in love who came separate in works'

[26] Chenu, *Nature*, pp202-208

[27] Maccarrone, *Studi*, p286

[28] H.Grundmann, 'Zur Biographie Joachim von Fiore and Rainers von Ponza', *Deutsches Archiv* 16 (1960), (hereafter Grundmann, 'Zur Biographie') pp437-546; B.Griesser, 'Rainier von Ponza und seiner Brief an Abt Arnald von Cîteaux (1203)', *Cistercienser Chronik* 60 (1953), (hereafter Griesser, 'Rainier von Fossanova') pp151-167; B.M.Bolton, 'For the See of Simon Peter: the Cistercians at Innocent's nearest frontier', *Monastic Studies* (Headstart, 1990), I, pp 146-157

[29] Grundmann, 'Zur Biographie', p534 'Ibique primus accessit ad eum frater Rainerius, modo ut confidimus sanctus vir, ex tunc veritatis zelo succensus, liberalibus eruditus, sermone disertus, qui venit a finibus regni de insula Pontiana audire novi sapientiam Salomonis'

Casamari in 1183-84.[30] The last time that Joachim and Rainier are mentioned together is in the Statutes of the Cistercian General Chapter of September 1192, when both were declared *fugitivi*[31] Further indication of the close friendship between Rainier and Joachim is provided by evidence of the concurrent development of a pseudo-Rainier and a pseudo-Joachim literature in the mid-thirteenth century.[32] In the years before his death in 1202, Joachim finally withdrew to Fiore to found his own Order, approved by Celestine III in 1196.[33] Rainier meanwhile, took a different path, returning to the Cistercian Order. By 1198 he had ascended to a position of authority and respect in the Church which was in stark contrast to his previous notoriety as *fugitivus*.

Joachim had not always been so aloof from the Order of which he had first been a member. It was, after all, under his abbacy that the Benedictine monastery of Corazzo adopted Cistercian customs, probably in 1173, when it became affiliated to the abbey of Fossanova.[34] In 1186 Joachim, having abandoned his brethren at Corazzo, went in search of a more demanding way of life, eventually withdrawing to his retreat at Petralata.[35] It is to this period that his *De vita Sancti Benedicti* can be dated, a work in which he severely criticises the Cistercians' failure faithfully to observe the Rule of St Benedict.[36] The *De vita* reflects Joachim's own unreserved insistence upon the absolute observance of full monastic poverty, and in it he rebukes the Cistercian Order for its involvement in the distracting business of the secular world and its desire for material gain.[37] Joachim also demonstrates his conviction that the Cistercians cannot at the same time satisfactorily pursue both the active and contemplative lives. Any attempt to do so would be detrimental to the full observance of the Rule, and moreover would result in the water of action extinguishing the fire of contemplation.[38]

Joachim's belief that the parts of Martha and Mary could not be sufficiently

---

[30] *Ibid.*, pp539-541

[31] J.M.Canivez, *Statuta Capitulorum Ordinis Cisterciensis ab anno 1116 ad annum 1786* 8 vols.(Louvain, 1933-1941), I, *Ab anno 1116 ad annum 1220* (hereafter Canivez I), p154

[32] Reeves, *Influence*, pp38-39, 52-58

[33] *PL* 206,1183

[34] B.McGinn, 'Joachim and the Sibyl: An early work of Joachim of Fiore from MS 322 of the Biblioteca Antoniana in Padua', *Cîteaux* 24 (1973) p103

[35] Grundmann, 'Zur Biographie', p533; for an illuminating analysis of these events see S.Wessley, '*Bonum est Benedicto mutare locum:* The role of the 'Life of Benedict' in Joachim of Fiore's Monastic Reform', *Revue Bénédictine* 90 (1980) pp314-338, (hereafter Wessley, '*Bonum est Benedicto*')

[36] C.Baraut, 'Un tratado inedito de Joaquin de Fiore: *De vita Sancti Benedicti et de officio divino secundum eius doctrinam',* *Analecta Sacra Tarraconensia* 24 (1951) pp33-122, (hereafter *De vita Sancti Benedicti*)

[37] *Ibid.*, pp68-69; Wessley, '*Bonum est Benedicto*', pp324-325; S.Zimdars-Swartz, 'Joachim of Fiore and the Cistercian Order: a Study of *De vita Sancti Benedicti*', *Simplicity and Ordinariness*, Cistercian Studies 61 (Kalamazoo, 1980), (hereafter Zimdars-Swartz, 'Joachim of Fiore') p299

[38] *De vita Sancti Benedicti*, p68 'Sicut enim qui librare quereret aquam et ignem, ut nec aqua ignem extingueret, nec ignis aque copiam desiccaret, sed et ignis arderet iugiter et aqua semper in sua quantitate persisteret, sic qui querit temporalibus affluere et spiritualia non minuere, verbo predicationis insistere et silentio vacare, actionibus servire et contemplationi quiescere, frustra laborat'

performed by one and the same order leads him to the conclusion that separate orders are required to fulfil the active and contemplative roles. He distinguishes between an order for contemplative monks whose task it would be to reflect upon theological complexities, pronouncing upon the correctness of particular doctrines, and an order for preaching monks, who armed with the knowledge supplied by their fellow theologian-monks, would proceed to exhort the faithful to follow these moral precepts.[39] According to this paradigm, Leah is equated with the holy bishop Germanus, whose soul appeared to Benedict during its ascent to heaven,[40] as well as with the life of action and preaching. Rachel, on the other hand is linked to Benedict and to the life of silence and contemplation.[41] In the *Liber de Concordia,* written between 1184 and 1200, and certainly post-dating the *De vita,* Joachim elaborates this idea.[42] These two ways of life, of preaching and of contemplation, are placed alongside the other Christian vocations in the broader context of the society of all Christian believers.[43] The choice of a religious life should no longer be centred solely upon the alternative ways of Martha and Mary, but must also take into account other forms of religious life, all of which are equally worthy.[44]

Joachim was a trenchant and outspoken critic of the blatant shortcomings of the order to which he had once belonged. Nevertheless, he still attributed a crucial role in his theology of history to the Cistercian Order as mediator between the second and third *status.*[45] He identifies the beginning of the third age, that is, the gestation of new orders and groups, with the departure of abbot Robert from Molesme in 1098 and the resultant foundation of the New Monastery at Cîteaux.[46] Joachim's symbolic interpretation of the concordances between the Old and New Testaments attributes to each *status* a movement from the number 5 signifying gestation, to the number 7 signifying perfection. This is a prophetic motif which seems unique to Joachim at this time.[47] Thus in the third *status,* that of the *ordo monachorum,* Joachim links these first five monasteries to the first five

---

[39] *Ibid.,* p63 'Igitur in beata Scholastica cisterciensium unanimitas designatur, que licet sancta et innocens, ut imbecillis tamen femina, ardua montis scandere et tam arta nequivit. Non solum autem, sed et vir domini Benedictus ad eam descendere caritate compulsus est, quia hi qui possent in ordine in alto stare, et iam stare incipient, compellentur propter infirmos fratres aliquantulum a rigore suo flecti et ad eos qui infra sunt condescendere, et vincente caritate humilium etiam pernectare cum illis compellentur inviti. Sit istud, si sic oportet, sed utinam sic oporteat, ut reficientes nos ad invicem spiritualibus epulis, totam noctem futurarum calignum ducere contingat insompnem'

[40] *PL* 66 ch35

[41] *De vita Sancti Benedicti,* pp67-68 'Eodem modo secundus populus, quem Germanus designat, in ea vita principaliter electus est quam designat Lya, tertius, quem significat Benedictus, in ea vita quam designat Rachel, alter, videlicet, in predicatione et actione, alter in silentio et quiete'

[42] E.R.Daniel, 'Abbot Joachim of Fiore: *Liber de Concordia Novi ac Veteris Testamenti',* Transactions of the American Philosophical Society 73 part 8 (1983), (hereafter *Liber de Concordia)*

[43] Reeves and Hirsch-Reich, *Figurae* pp238-240

[44] *Ibid.;* compare with Constable, *Libellus De Diversis,* pp15-16, and Chenu, *Nature,* pp217-223

[45] *Liber de Concordia,* pp408-422; E.Pasztor, 'Gioachino da Fiore, S.Bernardo e il monachesimo cisterciense', *Clio* 20 (1984) pp547-561

[46] *Liber de Concordia,* p415; *De vita Sancti Benedicti,* p60

[47] Reeves and Hirsch-Reich, *Figurae,* pp14-19

Cistercian foundations, but seems not to include the houses of the Order in the final and perfect seven.[48] Instead, he sees the Cistercians leading the movement from Egypt into Israel, that fertile land in which the teachings of Christ were destined to flourish.[49] At the head of this Cistercian expedition is none other than Bernard of Clairvaux, the Order's first saint, and in truth another Moses. But like Moses, Bernard was not to live to see the fruits of the Promised Land.[50]

In the *De vita* Joachim sees the Cistercian Order symbolised not by the strength of St Benedict who had ascended all 1700 feet to the very summit of Monte Cassino, but by his weaker sister, Scholastica, who remained down below.[51] The Cistercians, therefore, do not represent for Joachim the long awaited *viri spirituales*[52] of the third *status* and it is clear that he does not expect the Order to maintain its dominant position in monasticism for much longer. On the contrary, he suggests in the *Liber de Concordia* that the religious life to come will take several forms. 'The order of monks', he ways, 'will be an order of many diverse kinds because many divisions are pleasing to God'.[53] Here he refers to *Ephesians* 4, where St Paul exhorts the faithful to unity 'that you walk worthy of the vocation in which you are called, with all humility and mildness, with patience, supporting one another in charity', and where the various Christian vocations - apostle, prophet, evangelist, pastor, and doctor - are all accorded equal status within the overall framework of mutual support and unity of faith in Christ. Indeed, Joachim is writing in that spirit of toleration which motivates many authors of several twelfth century treatises on the proliferation of religious orders and, like them, he tends to see virtue in every sort of religious devotion.[54] Whether or not Joachim is the self-appointed *novus Benedictus*[55] of the new age,it is implied that his Order of Fiore, established and approved by 1196, is to be the true vehicle for the *viri spirituales*. Such has been the conclusion of recent research by Stephen Wessley, which has directed us towards this view of Joachim as a monastic reformer in addition to the more conventional view, seeing him as an esoteric prophet.[56]

---

[48] *Liber de Concordia*, pp411, 415, 419

[49] *Ibid.*, p413 'Hoc si ita est, non absurde videtur mihi completum esse secundum concordiam similitudinem quinque tribuum et quinque ecclesiarum in ordine Cisterciensi, quippe cum in nostris temporibus compleri oporteat per similitudinem mysterii transitum Iordanis et transitum Iudaismi ad gratiam'

[50] *Ibid.*, p417 'Bernardus Cisterciensis monachus...dux omnium et magister, eo quod esset ductus a spirtu et manus domini esset cum eo, factus est etiam quasi alter Moyses, qui non tam filios suos quam fratres et filios suorum educeret de Egypto; for Bernard as Moses, see also *De vita Sancti Benedicti*, p86 'Missus est sanctus Bernardus in spiritu Moysi'

[51] *De vita Sancti Benedicti*, pp63,68

[52] Reeves, *Influence*, pp135-144; McGinn, *Calabrian Abbot*, p113

[53] *Liber de Concordia*, p409 'In tertio simile aliquid futurum est in ordine monachorum, qui, videlicet, ordo in multis speciebus divisus est, quia multe sunt divisiones gratiarum'

[54] Compare with Constable, *Libellus De Diversis*; Chenu, *Nature*, pp217-223

[55] Wessley, 'Bonum est Benedicto', p317

[56] *Ibid.* pp314-328; Wessley, 'Female Imagery: A Clue to the Role of Joachim's Order of Fiore', J.Kirshner and S.Wemple (eds.), *Women in the Middle Ages* (Oxford, 1985) pp161-178

In one of his drawings in the *Liber Figurarum,* the *Dispositio Novi Ordinis Pertinens Ad Tercium Statum,* Joachim extends these ideas of diversity within unity amongst religious groups.[57] This ground plan for the Church that was to come encapsulates all the forms of religious life which he considered indispensable to the Church: not only the aforementioned pastors and doctors, but also martyrs, contemplatives, preachers, secular clergy, and last but not least the *conjugati.*[58] This last group was one which most twelfth century discussions on the many forms of religious life had hitherto neglected to mention.[59] The *conjugati* comprised married men and women following religious precepts in their own homes, eating, drinking and dressing ascetically, working with their hands, and giving any surplus goods to the poor. Joachim stresses that although the diverse functions within the Church must be separately fulfilled, these groups, particularly the married lay people, do indeed form one single structure, one 'order' within the Church.

That Joachim's prophetic and practical ideas were well known in contemporary Italy cannot be disputed. The abbot of Fiore was a well respected figure in his own lifetime and was acquainted with a whole succession of popes. Not only did he receive permission to write his three major works, the *Liber de Concordia,* the *Expositio in Apocalypsium,* and the *Psalterium decem chordarum,* from Lucius III in 1184, but this permission was subsequently re-confirmed by Urban III in 1186, by Clement III in 1188, and also by Celestine III, to whom Joachim probably presented the *Liber de Concordia.*[60] Copies of Joachim's other major works could also be found at the Curia for, in his testamentary letter of 1200, Joachim had ordered that these should be submitted to Rome for papal approval.[61] Nor was this approbation merely papal. In 1191, King Richard I of England summoned the abbot to meet him at Messina.[62] whilst the Emperor Henry VI, in what was left of his brief reign, became one of the greatest patrons of the Florensian Order.[63]

What then did Innocent III know of Joachim? His confirmation of the privileges of the Florensian Order in 1204 came two years after the death of the abbot.[64] Did Innocent himself ever read Joachim's work? A recent author has suggested that Innocent May have been influenced in his interpretation of the Melchisedich figure by the *Liber De Concordia*[65] and indeed, it is worth noting that Joachim himself had a highly exalted

---

[57] Reeves and Hirsch-Reich, *Figurae,* pp232-248; L. Tondelli, *Il Libro Delle Figure* II (Torino, 1940), (hereafter Tondelli, *Il Libro*) tavola XII

[58] Reeves and Hirsch-Reich, *Figurae,* pp238-240; Tondelli, *Il Libro,* tavol XII

[59] Constable, *Libellus De Diversis;* Chenu, *Nature,* pp202-238

[60] McGinn, *Calabrian Abbot,* pp22, 24, 28

[61] Reeves, *Influence,* pp28-30

[62] McGinn, *Calabrian Abbot,* p26

[63] *Ibid.,* pp27-28; Grundmann, 'Zur Biographie', p543

[64] *Potthast* I, 2092

[65] R.E. Lerner, 'Joachim of Fiore as a link between St Bernard and Innocent III on the Figural Significance of Melchisedich', *Medieval Studies* 42 (1980) pp471-476; for the passages in Joachim see *Liber De Concordia,* pp253, 323, 329

view of the papal office.[66] It is certain that, as a young cardinal in the Curia much involved in business there, Innocent would have known of the activities of this highly individualistic prophet.[67] However we can indicate a far more direct connection by which Innocent came into almost daily contact with Joachite ideas during the first few years of the pontificate. It is to Rainier of Ponza, the *intimus* of both men, that we must now turn in this comparison between Innocent's and Joachim's ideas on the religious orders.

Rainier's reinstatement, after his apparent lapse in 1192, was marked by his appointment as papal legate in Leon, Castille and Portugal in 1198.[68] Almost immediately he was diverted to undertake the crucial mission to Languedoc and it is this mission which seems to have secured his reputation with the pope.[69] In October 1198 Innocent wrote to Rainier in fulsome terms: 'The odour of your name is pleasing and follows the sweetness of your fame, by which the honesty and dignity of your religion are exalted everywhere.'[70]

Forced by ill-health to withdraw from Languedoc in July 1199,[71] Rainier seems to have become Innocent's confessor for at least the next few years.[72] His significance in this role cannot be overestimated for, while at the forefront of the new religious developments of the period, he was also well informed on Joachim's views on these and other related issues. Rainier, however, remained a Cistercian after his friend and mentor Joachim had left the Order, although he was also actively involved in the official papal examination of the *proposita* of new religious groups during the years 1199-1202. He was a member of a three-man commission which examined and corrected the formula and way of life of the First and Second Orders of the Humiliati in June 1201.[73] Equally significant was Rainier's summons by Innocent to interpret an extremely vivid papal dream at a crucial moment during the consideration of the canonization process of Gilbert of Sempringham at Anagni in December 1201 and January 1202.[74] Such contemporary sources as Innocent's letters to the Humiliati and the *Book of St Gilbert*, bear testimony to the intimacy between the pope and his confessor. This close relationship is further

---

[66] *Liber De Concordia*, p402 'In ecclesia incipit generatio quadragesima secunda anno vel hora qua deus melius novit. In qua, videlicet, generatione peraca prius tribulatione génerali et purgato dilegenter tritico ab universis zizaniis, ascendet quasi novus dux de Babilone, universalis scilicet ponifex nove Ierusalem, hoc est sancte matris ecclesie'

[67] J.C.Moore, 'Innocent III's *De Miseria Conditionis Humanae*: a *speculum curiae*', *Catholic Historical Review* 68 (1981), p554 on the extent of Innocent's involvement in curial affairs whilst a cardinal

[68] *Register* I, pp132-134, 134-135, 135-138, 145-147, 190, 234-235, 338-339, 352, 594, 672-673, 722-723; Griesser, 'Rainier von Fossanova', pp153-154

[69] *Register* I, p136; *PL* 214,82; *Potthast* I,95 'virum probatae vitae et conversationis honestae potentem divino munere in opere et sermone'; Griesser, 'Rainier von Fossanova', p154

[70] *Register* I, p594; *PL* 214,373; *Potthast* I,402 'Gratus tui nominis odor, et suavis tuae famae dulcedo, per quam tuae religionis dignis undique laudum praeconis exaltatur'; Griesser, 'Rainier von Fossanova', pp154-155

[71] *PL* 214,1053

[72] Caesarius of Heisterbach, *Dialogus miraculorum* 7,6 'Renerio iam dicti Innocentii confessori'; the Cistercian General Chapter of 1199 also regarded Rainier as being in the pope's favour, Canivez I, pp245-246

[73] Tiraboschi, *VHM* II,p140, 16 June 1201 and p136, 12 June 1201

[74] R. Foreville and G.Keir, *The Book of St Gilbert* (Oxford, 1987), pplxxx, 175-177

demonstrated by the extraordinarily explicit letter from Hugolino, then Cardinal-Bishop of Ostia and papal legate in Germany, to the abbots of Fossanova, Casamari and Salem.[75] In 1207-1209 Hugolino, in a moving letter reminiscent of the evocative language of twelfth century monastic authors,[76] wrote to console the Cistercians on news of Rainier's death. Hugolino's tremendous outpouring of grief is surely a reflection of Rainier's spiritual presence in the papal Curia. Not only does Hugolino refer to himself as Rainier's spiritual son,[77] but he also alludes several times to the holy man's considerable learning.[78] Significantly, Hugolino described the leading pressure on Rainier's life as an on-going conflict between the life of action and the life of contemplation: 'And although out of obedience he was sometimes buffeted by the anxiety of a Martha, he used to flee straight to the feet of Jesus with Mary, and compensate for the struggle of brief labour with the lasting sweetness of the Word of God'.[79] Yet, according to Hugolino, Rainier was able to resolve this dilemma by combining action and contemplation in equal proportion.[80] Hugolino's testimony clarifies Rainier's role as papal confessor to Innocent 'whose innocence he used to commend to the Lord with prayers and tears'.[81]

In spite of Rainier's practical involvement with a variety of new orders, he remained devoutly Cistercian, on occasion acting as mediator in disputes between the pope and the Order. Such discord had become a regular feature of the Order in recent years, threatening to split it irreparably.[82] Innocent was loathe to stand by and see the Cistercian Order disintegrate through internal wrangling and external scandal.[83] In 1202 he wrote to the first four daughter houses of Cîteaux - La Ferté, Pontigny, Clairvaux, and Morimond - admonishing them severely amongst other things for their damaging quarrel with the mother house of Cîteaux and their usurpation of episcopal privileges. The Pope even went so far as threatening quite openly to abolish the Order unless it instituted

---

[75] E.Winkelman (ed.), 'Analecta Heidelbergensia' Varietà, Archivio della Società di Storia Patria 1 (Rome, 1879), (hereafter Winkelman, 'Analecta') pp363-367

[76] B.P.McGuire, Friendship and Community. The Monastic Experience 350-1250 Cistercian Studies 95 (Kalamazoo, 1988) pp231-295; C.Morris, The Discovery of the Individual 1050-1200 (London, 1972) pp97-107; C.H.Haskins, The Renaissance of the Twelfth Century (Harvard, 1927) pp29-44

[77] Winkelman, 'Analecta', p364 'Dic ergo, mi pater, utquid me filium tuum in mundi huius utero reliquisti, antequam me produceres ad spiritualis nativitatis et lucis, ut prius meus desineres esse pater, quam patris possem filius appellari'

[78] Ibid., p365 'in facunditate sermonum, in elegantia et urbanitate verborum Origenem sequebatur et Didimum'; Hugolino also refers to Rainier's spiritual writings, Ibid., p366

[79] Ibid., p364 'Et quamquam aliquando ex obedientia in Marthe sollicitudine turbaretur, cum Maria ad pedes Ihesu continuo fugiebat et momentanei laboris agonem longa verbi dei dulcedine redimebat'

[80] Ibid., pp364-365 'Plangat Martha, lamentetur Maria, quia sol de celo visus est cecidisse, quandilo pater tantus rebus cessit humanis, qui contemplativus pariter et activus fulgoris sui gratiam iugiter infundebat'

[81] Ibid., p366 'Novit hec plenius summus pontifex papa Innocentius, cuius innocentiam domino orationibus et lacrimis commendabat'

[82] J.B.Mahn, L'Ordre Cistercien et Son Gouvernement (Paris, 1951) pp187-189

[83] J.Leclercq, 'Les Epitres d'Alexandre III sur les Cisterciens', Revue Bénédictine 64 (1954) pp68-82; G.Constable, Monastic Tithes from their Origins to the Twelfth Century (Cambridge, 1964) pp188, 194-195, 280-281, 292-293; A.H. Bredero, 'The Canonisation of St Bernard and the Rewriting of his Life' J.R.Sommerfeldt (ed.), Cistercians Ideal and Reality Cistercian Studies 60 (Kalamazoo, 1978) p92 on the scandal of Geoffrey of Auxerre's forced resignation from the abbacy of Clairvaux in 1165

internal reforms.[84]

The dispute over primacy was clearly still raging in 1203 when Rainier himself intervened in the form of a highly significant letter addressed to the recently elected Arnald-Amaury, abbot of Cîteaux (1202-1212).[85] In this letter, Rainier reveals his awareness of the problems of the Cistercian Order, and his language clearly echoes that of Joachim.[86] Rainier rebukes Cîteaux and her daughters for their contentious behaviour and loud complaints, and, above all, for those spurious ordinations on account of which, 'the Cistercians were reckoned not so much an order as a horror'.[87] Rainier goes on to stress how fully aware Innocent is of these disputes and urges the order to receive the letters of the pope with all meekness and maturity, so that stability may be established.[88] Rainier's harsh and intemperate language reflects the fear that his order is about to enter into an irreversible decline, that it will be weakened and finally swept away. In an emotional statement, he says, 'already our order has completed that third stage of spirituality and already the seeds of dissension appear. Christ lived, it is said, for thirty three and a half years in the flesh, which if you multiply into three such spiritual states, you will find that the order has already passed this time. And since I have tried to promote your name always with much sincerity before God and men, I am bound to exhort you in writing, hoping and praying that you shall believe all spiritual matters lest under your hand this ruinous calamity shall occur'.[89] Rainier here uses Joachim's apocalyptic vision to evoke the idea that the Cistercians, although the initiators of the third status, will not be the new *viri spirituales*. Nor, following Joachim's 5-7 symbolism,[90] will the order now provide the final seven monasteries of the *ordo monachorum* to come.[91] Rainier concludes by reminding Arnald-Amaury that the pope himself has no intention of neglecting this matter, even to the point of scrutinizing the whole Order very closely 'under a lamp', for the Cistercians have already blotted the papal register with their scandalous behaviour.[92]

---

[84] *PL* 214, 1106-1107

[85] Griesser, 'Rainier von Fossanova', pp163-166.

[86] Rainier exactly reproduces Joachim's division of history into three *status* as a succession from the lay order, through the clerical order, to the monastic order: compare Griesser 'Rainier von Fossanova', p163 with Reeves, *Influence*, pp135-136. Rainier also gives a long exposition on the historical symbolism of the number 4: compare with Reeves and Hirsch-Reich, *Figurae*, pp224-231

[87] Griesser, 'Rainier von Fossanova', p165 'ita ut propter hec et his similia iam non ordo sed horror a plurimis estimetur'

[88] *Ibid.*, p166

[89] *Ibid.*, pp165-166 'Et nos de similibus similia formidemus, quia iam ordo quandam spiritalem etatem terciam consummavit et iam apparent semina iurgiorum. Christus triginta tribus annis et medio creditur in carne vixisse; quos si multiplicaveritis in tres tales spirtales etates, invenietis ordinem hec tempora paululum pertransisse. Et quia nomen vestrum coram deo et hominibus in multa semper sinceritate studui promovere, eo securius incitor ad scribendum, quo profundius non ociosa carita persuadet optans et supplicans, ne omni spiritui credere debeatis et ne sub manu vestra fiat hec calamitas ruinosa'

[90] Reeves and Hirsch-Reich, *Figurae*, pp14-19

[91] Griesser, 'Rainier von Fossanova', pp163-166

[92] *Ibid.*, p166 'Non est negociorum obliviosus summus pontifex executor, qui iam in registro iussit litteras memorie commendari, et talem forsitan mittet, qui scrutabitur Jherusalem nostram diligenter nimium in lucernis, hisi scandali materia cicius succidatur'

However, Innocent could not, for the moment at least, dispense with the Cistercian Order, which had established a reputation as the staunchest of papal allies.[93] Like Joachim, who saw the Cistercians as being symbolised by the weak Scholastica and those preaching monks who remain below the heights of contemplation, Innocent considered that the principal function of the Cistercian was to proselytise, and not merely to contemplate. He perceived the role of Martha as of more immediate importance than the role of Mary, hardly surprising in view of his reforming aims. Indeed, in July 1199 he had written to Rainier in Languedoc, stressing to him the need to sacrifice the pleasures of Mary for the cares of Martha. Through the fecundity of preaching, Leah would compensate for Rachel's sterility.[94] The Cistercians were one of the groups to whom Innocent turned in his search for men to undertake the task of preaching. He particularly encouraged the order's mission in Languedoc, first through Rainier, and then in 1204 by dedicating to Arnald Amaury his sermon collection in which he expounded upon the excellence of preaching.[95] The virtue of preaching, he wrote, is that it is the means by which the soul is recalled from error to truth and from vice to virtue, by which those who have gone astray are set on the right path, having been thoroughly converted and instructed in the faith, encouraged to hope, and strengthened in charity.[96] Later that year Innocent again wrote to Arnald-Amaury, explaining why the Cistercians were so well suited to the task of preaching. The simplicity and humility of these monks, he asserted, meant that they were exceptionally well qualified to refute the fabricators of perverse dogmas such as the Cathars in Languedoc.[97]

The Cistercians' initial response to the pope's call was short-lived and after the failure of a brief preaching expedition on foot by word and example, it became abundantly clear to both parties that the Order would not adapt to the model so energetically proposed by the pope.[98] Unwilling to devote itself so exclusively to the active life of Martha, the Cistercian Order deeply resented Innocent's attempt to impose upon it this unwanted burden.

Innocent's encouragement of the Cistercian mission in Languedoc represents only one of several avenues of approach taken by the pope in his task of combatting heresy and evangelising the faithful. One feature which recurs in his numerous initiatives with religious movements is his desire to unify diverse groups of religions by bringing them together under one all-embracing *regulare propositum*.[99] In the case of the mission to

---

[93] M.Stroll, *The Jewish Pope: Ideology and Politics in the Papal Schism of 1130*, Brill Studies in Intellectual History, 1987; C. Thouzellier, *Catharisme et Valdèisme en Languedoc à la fin du XII siècle et au debt du XIII siècle* (Paris, 1969), (hereafter Thouzellier, *Catharisme*)

[94] *Register* II, p238; *PL* 214,675-676; *Potthast* I,785

[95] *PL* 217,309-312

[96] *PL* 217,311-312 'Tantae numque virtutis est praedicatio, quod animam revocet ab errore ad veritatem, et a vitiis ad virtutes; prava mutat in recta, aspera convertit in plana; instruit fidem, erigit spem, et roborat charitatem'

[97] *PL* 215,359; *Potthast* I,2229 'in quibus etiam vigere credimus charitatem, ut animas suas pro fratribus suis ponant, si necessitas Ecclesiae postulavit, qui tanto sunt ad confutandos fabricatores perversorum dogmatum aptiores, quanto muias in eis quid reprehendere valeat, valebit aemulus invenire'

[98] Thouzellier, *Catharisme*, pp199, 205

[99] Maccarrone, *Studi*, pp268-289

Livonia, Innocent exhorted the Augustinians, the black canons regular and the white Cistercian monks to overcome their differences of habit and custom. The different coloured habits and the diversity of rules served only to hinder the Christianisation of the pagan Balts.[100] As with the Humiliati in 1200 and the nuns of Rome in 1204,[101] Innocent wanted to impose a uniformity of rule, dress, and discipline, to counter a senseless diversity in forms of religious life. This idea of a *regulare propositum,* although commonplace in papal documents, was developed and given a fuller meaning by Innocent, in line with those strands of Joachite thought on functional diversity, which the pope may well have learnt through his discussions with his confessor Rainier.[102]

In the Humiliati were to be found three of Joachim's orders of the Church[103]: monks, canons, and *conjugati,* who were also granted the privilege of preaching every Sunday on matters which did not impinge on Christian doctrine.[104] Once again, in an attempt to avoid scandal through excessive diversity, Innocent had quite seriously considered bringing the three separate branches of the Humiliati into one *propositum.*[105] Did the Humiliati perhaps represent to Innocent a microcosm of the whole Church, a society of men and women, monastic, clerical and lay, ranging over some of the most basic aspects of religious life? Here indeed were the pastors, contemplatives, preachers and *conjugati* of Joachim's vision of the diverse orders within the Church, so vividly portrayed in his drawing in the *Liber Figurarum.*[106] The expert called in to examine the monastic and clerical elements of these groups was none other than Innocent's confessor and Joachim's disciple, Rainier of Ponza.[107]

That this scheme of Innocent's came to nothing does not detract from its originality. The Humiliati were approved with Rainier's blessing in June 1201 in their three distinct orders.[108] It had proved quite impossible to unite these different elements under one rule as Innocent had originally proposed.[109] Innocent may have been inspired by Rainier's example and Joachim's vision in his initial proposals to the Humilaiti. Equally, it is possible that the final structure of the Humiliati was influenced by the realisation, expressed so forthrightly by Joachim in his criticisms of the Cistercians, that different functions must take different forms, and that the roles of monk, canon and laity ought to

---

[100] *Ibid.,* p270

[101] *Ibid.,* pp272-278; B.M.Bolton, 'Daughters of Rome; All one in Christ Jesus', *Studies in Church History* 27 (Blackwell, 1990) pp101-115

[102] Maccarrone, *Studi,* pp268-269

[103] Reeves and Hirsch-Reich, *Figurae,* pp232-248

[104] Tiraboschi, *VHM* II, pp133-134

[105] *PL* 214, 922 'in unum honestam et regulare propositum confometis'

[106] Reeves and Hirsch-Reich, *Figurae,* pp232-248

[107] Tiraboschi, *VHM* II, pp136, 140

[108] *Ibid.,* II. pp128-148

[109] Maccarrone, *Studi,* p286

remain distinct. Paradoxically, it was Rainier, equally accomplished in both theology and sermonising, who exemplified the ideal to which Innocent aspired. Perhaps it was also Rainier who convinced Innocent of the impossibility of realising this ideal in any practicable form, whilst directing the pope at the same time towards Joachim's vision of religious orders. Whether or not this proves to be the case, there is a striking similarity between the ideas of Innocent and Joachim on the function of religious orders and their relation to one another. Given this similarity, it is by no means surprising to find that a direct link existed between the two men in the person of Rainier.

It was Majorie Reeves who first posed the question of how it was that Joachim came to be considered a prophet by later generations without being one in a literal sense.[110] One tentative answer might lead us to Innocent. It was he, after all, who approved Francis and Dominic[111] and both their orders later claimed Joachim as the prophet who had foreseen their arrival.[112] In considering the careers of Innocent and Joachim therefore, the distinction between prophet and reformer, mystic and pragmatist, becomes blurred. Who then was really the prophet and who the pragmatist? Such questions may yield no hard and fast answers, but surely serve as useful routes of inquiry.

---

[110] Reeves, *Influence*, p135

[111] Bolton *'Via Ascetica'*, pp; Bolton, *Medieval Reformation*, pp67-79

[112] Reeves, *Influence*, pp161-228

THE SPIRITUALITY OF ST PETER DAMIAN
by
Gordon Mursell

he appearance in recent years of critical editions of most of the major works of
Peter Damian[1] allows for much more secure study of this prominent eleventh-
century hermit-monk and church reformer. Damian's writings cover a wide range of
subjects, but his primary focus of interest remains the life of the church and the
contemporary issues addressing it, which during the thirty-two years covered by his
writings (1040-72) included simony (and in particular the validity of simoniac
ordinations), monastic reform, clerical morals and celibacy, papal authority, and
ecclesiastical schism. Damian's own involvement in the church reform movement, centred
in and around Ravenna, has recently been fully documented and studied[2]; and the extent
of his activities in the wider church, in particular as papal legate and cardinal-bishop, has
also been thoroughly explored[3]. The purpose of this article is to examine, with reference
to the sermons of Peter Damian (which have themselves recently been made the subject of
an excellent critical edition)[4], the spirituality that underlies and informs his work and
concerns.

The sermon-collection comprises 56 extant sermons, assembled and revised by Damian
himself: they were originally preached at a wide variety of places, most (though not all)
for general (i.e. not exclusively clerical or monastic) audiences. Most were written in
honour of saints (twenty-one of them honouring martyrs), though there are also sermons
for Maundy Thursday, feasts of the Holy Cross, and the dedication of a church. The fact
that most of them are concerned with the Christian life in general, and in particular with
the veneration and imitation of the saints, rather than with specific issues of church
reform, makes them an excellent source for an exploration of what might be called
Damian's spirituality. First, however, we need to clarify what we mean by that
fashionable but ill-defined term.[5]

---

[1] Dr Kurt Reindel's edition of the letters, one hundred and eighty in total, which comprise the major part of Damian's output, is
appearing in *Monumenta Germaniae historica* (Die Briefe des Petrus Damiani, 4 vols., Munich 1983-): three volumes have so
far been published. Damian's poetry has been edited by Margaret Lokrantz, *L'opera poetica di S.Pier Damiani* (Stockholm:
Studia Latina Stockholmensia 12 (1964)). An English translation of the letters is being undertaken by Fr Owen J. Blum OFM in
'The Fathers of the Church' (Mediaeval Continuation) series (*The Letters of Peter Damian*, Washington DC: Catholic University of
America Press, 1989-).

[2] See Hans Peter Laqua, 'Traditionen und Leitbilder bei dem Ravennater Reformer Petrus Damiani (1042-1052)' (*Munsterische
Mittelalter-Schriften* 30, Munich: Wilhelm Fink (1976)).

[3] See, inter alia, J.Leclercq, 'Saint Pierre Damien, ermite et homme d'eglise' (*Uomini e dottrine* 8, Rome, 1960); G. Lucchesi,
'Per una vita di San Pier Damiani. Componenti cronologiche e topografiche', in *San Pier Damiano nel IX centenario della morte*
(1072-1972) vol.1 (1972) pp13-179 and vol.2 (1972 pp13-160; H.E.J. Cowdrey, *The Age of Abbot Desiderius* (Oxford:
Clarendon Press, 1983); Giuseppe Fornasari, Pier Damiani e Gregorio VII: dall 'ecclesiologia "monastica" all 'ecclesiologia
"politica"?, in *Fonte Avellana nel suo millenario*, vol.1 *(le origini)* (Atti del V Convegno del Centro di Studi Avellaniti, 1982),
pp151-244.

[4] *Sancti Petri Damiani sermones*, ed.G. Lucchesi, CCCM 57 (1983).

[5] For the sermons, see G. Lucchesi, 'Il sermonario di S. Pier Damiani come monumento storico, agiografico e liturgico', in *Studi
Gregoriani* X (1975), pp9-67.

The Swiss theologian Hans Urs von Balthasar has recently drawn attention, in his study *The Glory of the Lord*[6], to the importance of beauty in the western spiritual tradition, understanding beauty not simply as an aesthetic category but as in essential attribute of God - that which makes God desirable, or attractive. At the risk of an appalling *reductio ad absurdum*, von Balthasar's thesis could be summarized thus: Christian theology maintains that God is the ultimate ground of all that is, and thus of what came to be called, in scholastic theology, the four transcendentals: that is, God is ultimate unity, truth, goodness, and beauty. Without the fourth transcendental the other three are both incomplete and, quite precisely, boring; in other words, without beauty, oneness, truth and goodness have no power to draw or attract us. God may be one, and true, and good; but if he is not also beautiful - that is, the goal of all our deepest desires and longings - then he has no power to draw or attract us. Now if the first two transcendentals (oneness and truth) may be said to be the object of Christian theology, and the third the object of Christian ethics, then beauty is the object of Christian spirituality; and its primary subject matter is not patterns of prayer, or static structures of spiritual states and disciplines, but the nature and dynamic of desire, and above all of the desire for God.

This emphasis on the desirability of God is central to the theology of St Augustine, and thus to the whole western spiritual tradition that followed after him. Many western spiritual writers in the monastic tradition, following the example of St Gregory the Great, took up the theme with enthusiasm and made it central to their theology of the monastic life. But if Gregory was their exemplar, especially in the extensive allegorizing of the Song of Songs and its application to the spiritual journey, it was Augustine whose spirituality implicitly informs almost all they wrote. And of these writers, no one - not even St Bernard - explored this theme more energetically than St Peter Damian.

The theme of the desire for God appears so frequently in the sermons of Peter Damian as to be virtually a commonplace; and the reason why it is rarely adverted to may well be because it is precisely as a commonplace, a literary convention or even rhetorical device, characteristic of most medieval sermons, that it is normally viewed. Yet it may be the case that these (to modern ears) often florid effusions about a longing for God, for heaven, and so on, are more than merely empty rhetoric or monastic propaganda. The concern of the remainder of this article is to examine the theme, to consider its context and principal sources, and to draw some tentative conclusions about its implications.

We may begin with Sermon 28, for the feast of St Alexis who, according to the hagiographical tradition familiar to Damian, was born of wealthy fourth-century Roman parents, married at his parents' bidding but immediately afterwards responded to what he believed to be God's call to leave home and live in solitude and poverty, eventually returning home but in disguise, never revealing his true identity. The appeal of this sobering story to a monastic ascetic and strenuous opponent of clerical marriage like Damian is obvious[7]; and it seems likely that the sermon is designed to encourage the pursuit of monastic virtues by those hearing or reading it, even though Damian stops

---

[6] *Herrlichkeit: Eine theologische Ästhetik* (1962, second edition 1969), English translation *The Glory of the Lord: a theological aesthetics* (ed. J.Riches & J. Fessio, 7 vols., Edinburgh: T. & T.Clark, 1983-).

[7] Damian's attitude to marriage in general is scarcely more positive than that of his patristic forebear St Jerome.

short of exhorting married people literally to copy St Alexis, telling them instead to concentrate on bringing forth godly offspring. Yet Damian does not simply use the occasion to produce a traditional monastic celebration of *contemptus mundi*. Instead he offers what is in effect a miniature treatise of mystical theology whose dynamic is the desire for God.

Perfection, Damian tells us, is a process: it does not happen all at once. He writes: "As the mind, seized by the fire of divine love, is lifted up on high through heavenly desire (caeleste desiderium), it is raised to the summit of interior perfection as though by means of certain ascending grades"[8] He goes on to make it clear that this process is likely to be a slow and often erratic one: indeed we shall not be able to progress at all in responding to this heavenly desire until we have successfully disposed of its opposite, the *desiderium carnale*.

Damian then analyses the stages of our growth into perfection by relating them both to the four key stages in the life of St Alexis, and to two different scriptural texts: Jesus' image, in St Mark's Gospel (4:26-29) of the kingdom of heaven being like a seed that bears fruit during the night; and the vision of the prophet Ezekiel concerning a flowing river outside the Temple (Ezek.47:3-5). This kind of schematizing is of course characteristic of medieval writers on the spiritual life, as it is of St Gregory the Great, whose influence on Damian was unquestionable and whose own homilies on Ezekiel contain many similar expositions.[9] Yet the spirituality that underlies it is important. *Desiderium caeleste* and *desiderium carnale* conflict with each other; but, in using the same substantive to denote both, Damian leads us to consider the possibility that they differ only in virtue of seeking very different ends. Furthermore the story of St Alexis enables him to underline the fact that the longings of the flesh do not wane as the person travels towards heaven: on the contrary, they increase. What enables the person to overcome them (or rather, to *redirect* them) is pure grace (or, as Damian sometimes implies, the action of the Holy Spirit): hence, perhaps, Damian's choice of the Biblical texts in Mark and Ezekiel in each of which what happens is something *done to* the person, rather than something the person actively chooses or sets in motion. Damian writes, in typically colourful prose:

> the Holy Spirit boiling up within him (exaestuans in eo) drenched the furnace of youth
> and the illicit movements of alluring passions with the hidden moisture of its dew, and thus
> consumed all the kindled lust which could have burned naturally in his innermost heart.[10]

Alexis' desire for heaven causes him to renounce worldly goods, status and even marriage (Damian nowhere speaks of what his wife had to say on the matter) and endure solitude and poverty. He passes this test (Damian significantly describes it as the beginning of his novitiate), because though still weak he was growing stronger "through the hope of heaven which his desire had conceived in his mind".[11] But then he voluntarily submits himself to a far greater test by returning home and living incognito: he has to

---

[8] Serm.28:3, CCCM 57 p163.

[9] See (among many other examples) his *Hom.in Ezech.* II:8, PL 77:1027-41, esp. 1027-30.

[10] Serm.28:6, CCCM 57 p168.

[11] Serm.28:4, CCCM 57 p165.

struggle to choose between the two alternative and (to Damian) antithetical objects of his desire - between, in effect, earthly or heavenly marriage; and by the outpouring of the Holy Spirit he succeeds in holding fast to his longing for heaven. But the crucial point for Damian is the overwhelming difference between the two alternatives: his description of the "torrent of eternal contemplation: which, by the time Alexis reaches the fourth and last stage of his mystical journey is "not sought through faith but already grasped through vision (species)"[12], makes it abundantly clear that the heavenly reward is out of all proportion to the cost involved in reaching it (and thus the heavenly object of desire disproportionately greater than the earthly one).

Something of what underlies this uncompromising spirituality is to be found in Sermon 45, for the feast of the Nativity of the Virgin Mary. Exhorting his hearers to "mortify (mortificare - literally, to make dead), for love of Christ, every pleasure of. earthly lust"[13], he goes on:

> Let us now taste, beloved, with Christ the transient bitterness of temporary death, so
> that afterwards we may deserve to attain to the eternal sweetness of his resurrection. What
> he did for us, he also asks us to do ourselves...It is fitting that whoever offers himself to his
> Redeemer hastens to attain to his company. The one who follows in his footsteps on the
> way is the one who longs (anhelat) to rejoice with him in heaven. The one who makes him
> his leader on the journey is the one who desires (desiderat) to share in its destination...Let
> no one foolishly seduce you, brothers, or deceive you with the security of an empty hope.
> For we cannot rejoice here is this world and then reign there with Christ (Non enim
> possumus hic gaudere de saeculo et illic regnare cum Christo).[14]

The unequivocal antithesis between the two worlds is doubtless derived from the spirituality of St Paul.[15] Damian, like St Gregory before him, pursues it to its logical conclusion. To desire God is to desire heaven; and the joys that await those who persevere incomparably outweigh anything even imaginable, let along attainable, here below.

The reason why this is so may be best explained by reference to one of many sermons in which Damian draws on the rich imagery of the Song of Songs, a sermon celebrating the holy virgins Flora and Lucilla. The text from the Song of Songs which Damian expounds in this sermon describes the beloved 'dwelling between my breasts', which Damian interprets as meaning that he dwells within the hearts of the two holy virgins. He goes on

> The beloved therefore dwells between the breasts of each virgin, because unfailing love
> and desire (amor ac desiderium) for him is never erased from their memory.[16]

---

[12] Serm.28:7, CCCM 57 p168.

[13] Serm.45:9, CCCM 57 p271.

[14] Serm.45:10, CCCM 57 p271.

[15] See, e.g., Romans 5:14-17.

[16] Serm.35:3, CCCM 57 p212.

This text is important, for it makes clear a central aspect of the Augustinian spirituality to which Peter Damian is heir, and which informs everything he writes on this subject. For Augustine it is the fact of God's presence in our memory that causes us to desire him, and more negatively that causes us to be dimly aware of how nothing else can every satisfy that desire.[17] This desire is always, and literally, an *ecstatic* one, leading us out of ourselves; and - and this is crucial - it is profoundly affected by its object. Augustine says that the more you seek God the more you are enlarged - the perfection of the object sought gradually transforms the subject[18], thereby increasing our capacity for God.[19]

It is this, of course, which explains Damian's uncompromising antithesis between God and anything (or anyone) else as the object of our desire; for where the desire for other ends at best leaves us dissatisfied and at worst enslaves us, the desire for God transforms us in the very act of desiring him. In turn, Damian tells his brethren at Fonte Avellana that they are to make themselves as desirable as possible for their spouse, as the bride did in the Song of Songs: except that they are to strive to be fragrant with the cassia of prayer, the myrrh of holy reading, the cinnamom of psalmody, and so on.[20] He proceeds to described the essence of this mystical marriage in language that is at once sensual and sternly ascetic:

> Let Christ be all she (the soul) speaks, all she delights in, all she tastes, all she lives. Let her breath Christ, long for (flagitet) Christ, be on fire for (aestuet) Christ, name Christ with her mouth, reflect on Christ in the constant meditation of her heart. Let her love no one else, and let her burn (inardescat) for him alone with all her being. Let her call to him with the utmost cry of desire (summis desiderlii vocibus), let her rouse him to come to her with sighs and constant weeping. Let her be adorned with many virtues so that she may by her own beauty invite him to come in to her. For insofar as she feels deeply that he for whom she burns (aestuat), for whom she is anxious, and for whom she longs (inhiat) should come to her, she is already crying out with joy: 'The voice of my beloved is knocking: "Open to me, my sister, my dearest, my perfect one" (Song of Songs 5:2)'.[21]

Language at once sensual and sternly ascetic: it is important to underline this point. Damian uses a wide range of words to denote desire and, as has already been pointed out, the same words are used for both rightly and wrongly directed desire. Thus he speaks of St Eleuchadius longing for heavenly riches, using the verb *concupisco* that is normally associated with longing of a very different king.[22] Like St Gregory before him,

---

[17] For this, see St Augustine, *De Trinitate*, esp.XIV; Isabelle Bochet, *Saint Augustin et le desir de Dieu* (Etudes Augustiniennes, Paris 1982), p157; A. Solignac, 'La memoire selon saint Augustin' (note complementaire 14 in the Bibliotheque Augustinienne edition of the *Confessions* (BA 14)), pp 557-67, esp. pp564-6).

[18] "melior meliorque fit quaerens tam magnum bonum", de Trin.XV:2, 2, BA 16 p422.

[19] "Satiat enim quarentem in quantum capit: et invenientem capaciorem facit, ut rursus quaerat impleri, ubi plus capere coeperit", *Tract. in Ioh. Evang.* 63:1; see Isabelle Bochet, op. cit., p173 n5.

[20] Serm.73:9, CCCM 57 p439.

[21] Serm 73:9, CCCM 57 pp439.

[22] Serm. 6:11, CCCM 57 p41. See also Serm. 18:6, where Damian describes the Church filling the noses of human minds with the "scent of heavenly desire" (odorem caelestis concupis-centiae); CCCM 57 p114.

he constantly makes use of imagery of fire or heat to express this desire: words like aestuo, inardesco, ardor, accendo, inflammo, incendium, incaleso recur throughout his sermons.[23] But this language can also be used of the fires of hell[24], or of lust.[25] In itself, then, the desire that exists within each of us is morally neutral: indeed, insofar as it is a response to the presence of God within each of us, it is a divine gift: what matters is its goal. If we allow what Damian calls the *inquietudo caritatis,* the restlessness of love[26], to be directed towards an earthly end, it will both enslave and diminish us; if it is directed towards God by means of what Damian, following St Augustine, calls a *caritas ordinata,* a rightly-ordered love[27], it will transfigure us.

It is important to emphasize that, in the spirituality of St Peter Damian, this desire for God is far from being a narrowly individual affair. In Sermon 35, the second of two for the feast of the holy virgins Flora and Lucilla, he describes them as spouses of Christ; but despite having one husband between them they know no jealousy: indeed "they fuse their two souls into one as through the glue of love" (per caritatis glutinum, a favourite expression of his).[28] There is a strongly corporate dimension to Damian's spirituality, a recognition that the desire for God in no way diminishes our love or responsibility for our neighbour. This theme finds its fullest exposition in his famous letter to the hermit Leo of Sitria, usually known as the "Liber qui dicitur 'Dominus vobiscum'"[29], but recurs regularly throughout his sermons. In the second of two sermons on the feast of St Vitalis, Damian tells his hearers to desire the company of him and of other martyrs and asks SS Vitalis and Ursicinus to "teach us to keep the bond of love (vinculum caritatis)": he describes St Vitalis as being "kindled by a twofold love (geminae caritatis successus) both to liberate his neighbour who was facing death, and to restore to God the purity of his image".[30] This is a striking summary of another central theme in Augustinian spirituality: the restoration, through grace, of the purity of the image of God within us is impossible without an active love of neighbour. In another sermon, to his monks at Fonte Avellana, Damian writes:

If...we do not want to wither away like barren trees,...let the root of our hope always hold fast through the glue of love (glutinum caritatis) to the humanity of our Redeemer.

---

[23] For this theme in Gregory, see Patrick Catry, Desir et amour de Dieu (chez saint Gregoire le Grand) (Recherches Augustiniennes X, Paris: 1975, pp271-303, repr. in Parole de Dieu, amour et Esprit-Saint chez saint Gregoire le Grand, Vie Monastique 17, Bellefontaine: 1984, pp85-120), esp. chap.5.

[24] See, e.g., Serm, 37:6-7, CCCM 57 pp227-8.

[25] See, e.g., Serm. 8:4, CCCM 57 pp47-8.

[26] Serm. 6:13, CCCM 57 p43.

[27] See Serm.19:4, CCCM 57 pp124-5; Serm.33:11, CCCM 57 pp282-3. For its use in Augustine, see Serm.100:2, PL 38:603-4; Serm.21:3, PL 38:143; De civ. Dei 15:22, CCSL 48 pp487-8.

[28] Serm.35:2, CCCM 57 p212.

[29] ed. Reindel, Die Briefe des Petrus Damiani (Monumenta Germaniae Historica), vol.1, no. 28, (Munich, 1983, pp248-78; English translations by P. McNulty, St Peter Damian: Selected Writings on the Spiritual Life: (London: Faber & Faber, 1959, pp53-81); and Owen J. Blum, The Letters of Peter Damian (The Fathers of the Church: Mediaeval Continuation), vol.1, no.28, (Washington DC: Catholic University of America Press, 1989, pp255-89).

[30] Serm. 17/2:9, CCCM 57 p104.

Only thus, he goes on, can we bear good fruit. But this can only happen if our souls are rendered fruitful by the Holy Spirit, who "pours forth light into our minds, arouses desire (desiderium excitat), and infuses strength. From that fruitfulness comes our tears, compunction within our minds, and confession of our sins"[31]

This corporate dimension of Damian's spirituality - the inseparability of our desire for God from our desire to love and save our neighbour - is of great importance, not least because (as the "Dominus vobiscum" letter shows) it strongly influences his ecclesiology. The theme of the essential unity and interdependence of Christians through Christ recurs regularly in his sermons[32], notably (and appropriately enough) in his sermon for the dedication of a church. Damian describes a basilica as consisting of stones and cement; and, since the temple of God is the people of God, the stones represent human beings and the cement is the "adhesive glue of love" (tenax coagulum caritatis). It is this cement alone that prevents the structure from collapsing; and the only true members of the church are those who are bound together by love.[33]

Despite this, it will by now be apparent that this spirituality is unequivocally and unapologetically otherworldly, and that it gives rise to the thoroughgoing asceticism. But it also gives that asceticism an inner dynamism which must have formed the essence of its attractiveness for people like Damian: it is not unreasonable to suppose that God, for Damian as for Augustine before him, had to be very desirable indeed if he were to be worth seeking; for only a God like that could lure him, body and soul, from the manifold objects of desire that this world offered. It remains to consider some of the implication of this spirituality for the rest of Damian's thought.

It is, first of all, in this context that Damian's emphasis on virginity needs to be seen. In the first of his two sermons on the holy virgins Flora and Lucilla Damian uses the Song of Songs to make some important points: the virgins, like the bride in the Canticle, sleep, but their hearts are awake - they are asleep to the lusts of this world and yet awake and on fire with their love for God. And when their beloved knocks on their door, they are summoned to give up the delights of contemplation for "labour and struggle" in the world.[34] In a sermon for the Nativity of the Virgin Mary, Damian goes further: physical virginity is of no value unless it is accompanied by an interior purity; indeed, as Damian writes, "it often happens that a life burning with love after committing sin is more pleasing to God than an innocence that has become sluggish through the security of virginity".[35] A virginity that is merely avoidance of carnal entanglements is sterile; but a willed embracing of chastity in response to the desire for God can be unimaginably fruitful: in the first of two sermons on St John the Evangelist that are classics of ascetic spirituality, Damian describes how he, forsaking the wedding chamber of nuptial intimacy, "transmuted every passion for carnal allurements into the pleasure of heavenly

---

[31] Serm.21:3, CCCM 57 pp136-7.

[32] See, e.g., Serm. 19:2, CCCM 57 pp122-3; Serm.41:2, CCCM 57 p252; Serm. 50:4, CCCM 57 pp317-8.

[33] Serm .72:9, CCCM 57 pp426-7.

[34] Serm. 34:3-6, CCCM 57 pp206-8.

[35] Serm.46:18, CCCM 57 p288.

delights", as a result of which his heart became "a kind of furnace of divine love (caminus quidam divini incendii)" for his brothers with a love that, like that of Agus, embraced the whole world.[36]

True virginity, then, involves not so much a *suppression* of worldly desires and lusts as their *redirection* towards a higher object; and an immediate consequence of that redirection is a willingness to give up even the delights of contemplation for the spiritual combat against evil, and the loving service of one's fellow human beings. This involves an accurate self-knowledge, a willingness not only to praise but to imitate the saints, and a costly battle against both internal and external enemies. Responding to the desire for God is no easy option but relentlessly hard work, a lifelong struggle whose ultimate goal transforms us through grace even while we are still struggling. This is what Damian says in a sermon on the feast of St Apollinaris:

> As you consider these things, beloved, return into yourselves (ad vosmetipsos redite), analyse your actions with the utmost care, and then those who freely hear the praises of the martyrs must take care to make their own a praiseworthy life...For those who worthily proclaim the praises of the saints are the ones who live praiseworthily themselves; and the ones who listen profitably to the virtues of the brave are those who burn with a love for imitating the heralds they have heard. Otherwise, what good does it do you to see others established in the heights while you yourself descend headlong into the depths?...Do you lack external enemies? Turn your hand within yourself, and you will find many rebellious citizens. Overcome pride, strangle anger, extinguish lust (libido), suppress greed, destroy envy...It will do you no good to be defended against enemies outside while you are overwhelmed by vices from within.[37]

Elsewhere Damian tells his hearers to submit themselves to the divine scrutiny, for "each one of our desires (desiderium), whether of good or of evil, that is found in our mind is discerned by God".[38]

The desire for God, then, far from isolating people from this world, is more likely to precipitate them into it, but with their sights firmly set on the next one. Damian tells the people of Ravenna that the more their patron St Apollinaris suffered persecution, "the more ardently he was inflamed with love of God":[39] indeed God keeps him alive despite his sufferings precisely in order to kindle yet more his longing for heaven.[40] This extract from his second sermon on St Apollinaris gives some indication of the importance of the desire for God in the Christian life:

> We, however, beloved brothers,...who have so many signs of virtue set before our eyes
> for us to imitate, must take care to strive with every desire towards that beatitude in which

---

[36] Serm. 63:9-10, CCCM 57 pp369-70.

[37] Serm. 30:6, CCCM 57 p177. On self-knowledge, see also Serm. 74:4, CCCM 57 p445.

[38] Serm. 72:12, CCCM 57 p430.

[39] Serm. 31:2, CCCM 57 p181.

[40] Serm. 32:3, CCCM 57 pp186-7.

we know that those who triumph over the world already rejoice in the reward for their labours. Let us hold fast to their footsteps on the way, and let us desire their company in heaven, Certainly we shall be there what they are, if we would be here what they were[41]... Let us not, then, be separated on our journey, if we want to be united at its goal. Let us not refuse to drink the cup of temporary bitterness, who desire to attain to the sweetness of everlasting safety...For it is a 'feeble soldier who wants to conquer before he has begun to fight, who wants a victory without a battle, or hungers after (anhelat) the palm without a victory.[42]

The key themes in Damian's spirituality are all adumbrated here: the importance of a rightly directed desire, the essentially corporate dimension of our journey towards its goal, and the unrelenting struggle that journey will require, all of which is as nothing in comparison with the transfiguring glory of its destination. If, in other words, you desire heaven enough, you can endure anything. And that desire ennobles us,[43] enabling us not only to overcome vices and evil but even to turn them to creative account:[44] it sets the traditional monastic virtues of patience,[45] humility[46] and obedience[47] in a dynamic, vividly eschatological perspective. More important still, it reverses worldly wisdom and power: in his sermon on St Matthew, Damian shows how Christ summons Matthew to redirect, so to speak, his desire for temporal wealth into a desire for heavenly treasure;[48] and he concludes

> Furthermore, and so as to give sinners a firm hope, Christ chose for the chief place among his apostles not people regarded by human beings as just, or who seemed outstanding by their holiness, but those who were unacquainted with justice, and even sinners: not people like Zechariah, who "observed all the commandments of the Lord...(Lk 1:6), or Nathaniel, "in whom there was no guile (Jn 1"47)"..., or Simeon, in whom the Holy Spirit dwelt...;but simple and sinful people...,so that each of them could sincerely say "By the grace of God I am what I am (1 Cor.15:10)".[49]

The desire for God is accessible to all: it imparts an interior integrity, a life that shines with "the clarity of divine wisdom"[50] a purity on fire with the twofold love for God and

---

[41] Compare St Jerome's "Esse incipe, quod futura es" (Begin to be now what you will be hereafter), Epist.22:41, CSEL 54 p210.

[42] Serm. 32:5, CCCM 57 p188.

[43] See, e.g., Serm. 67:3, CCCM 57 p409.

[44] Serm. 17/2:5, 6, CCCM 57 pp100-2.

[45] For which see, e.g., Serm.37:10, CCCM 57 pp229-30; Serm.3:9, CCCM 57 p14; Serm.24:6, CCCM 57 p152.

[46] See, e.g., Serm.4:1, CCCM 57 pp16-17; Serm. 4:6, CCCM 57 pp21-2; Serm. 45:9, CCCM 57 p271.

[47] See, e.g., Serm.32:7-11, CCCM 57 pp189-93; Serm. 37:11, CCCM 57 pp230-1.

[48] Serm. 51:6, CCCM 57 p325.

[49] Serm. 51:15, CCCM 57 pp329-30.

[50] Serm. 42:6, CCCM 57 p261.

neighbour,[51] a beauty untouched by worldly persecution.[52] Damian tells his hearers to "long for the foolishness which enlightens its students" and which is the antithesis of worldly wisdom.[53]

It is time to draw some conclusions. The theme of the desire for God in the writings of St Peter Damian is deeply indebted to earlier writers, above all to St Augustine and St Gregory. Lucchesi has pointed out that Damian cites Gregory more often than any other patristic writer, and that he was the only confessor in honour of whom he built both a church and a monastery.[54] Furthermore most of the aspects of Damian's understanding of desire are to be found in Gregory: the antithesizing of worldly and heavenly objects of desire, the emphasis on interior holiness and combat, the rigorous relationship of *contemptus mundi* and *desiderium Dei,* and the primacy of love. Damian, like Gregory, was, in Jean Leclercq's phrase, "a contemplative condemned to action":[55] like him, he. strove to make the traditional monastic virtues accessible to everyone; and, like him, he understood that desire is also hard work, a daily effort, a constant struggle against laziness, temptation, vice, as well as against that kind of easy self-preoccupation which is no substitute for genuine love.[56]

Yet if St Gregory gave Damian his style and context, it was St Augustine who both gave him his theme and showed him its power. Like Damian, Augustine had to find a good that was almost irresistibly desirable if it was to triumph over the perils of *cupiditas* and *concupiscentia,* in other words over wrongly ordered desire. The idea that the greatness of the object desired enlarges the subject desiring it; the image of God as a lover or heavenly spouse; the belief that we are, in virtue of our creation in the image and likeness of God, inbued with an infinite desire which no finite end can satisfy; and the overwhelming need for grace to assist us in directing that desire towards its only true end[57] - all these are fundamental themes in the spirituality of Augustine; and their influence on Damian was immense.

There is, however, one important (one might almost say ominous) respect in which Damian goes much further than Augustine had done. Unlike Augustine, he appears to give no value at all to the beauty of this world, not even (as with Augustine) as a signpost whose beauty points beyond itself to its Creator.[58] The result is an even more unequivocal

---

[51] Serm. 46:10, CCCM 57 p282.

[52] Serm. 68:8-9, CCCM 57 p417-8.

[53] Serm. 57:11, CCCM 57 p355.

[54] G. Lucchesi, 'Il sermonario di S. Pier Damiani come monumento storico agiografico e liturgico', in *Studi Gregoriani* X (1975), p18.

[55] *The Love of Learning and the Desire for God* (London: SPCK, 1978), p36.

[56] See Patrick Catry OSB, 'Amour du monde et amour de Dieu' (*Studia Monastica* 15 (1973), pp253-75, reprinted in *Parole de Dieu, amour et Esprit-Saint chez saint Grégoire le Grand*, Vie Monastique 17, Bellefontaine 1984, pp61-84).

[57] though Damian attributes that assistance more directly to the work of the Holy Spirit. See, e.g., Serm.21:3-4, CCCM 57 pp136-8.

[58] See, e.g., *Confessions* X:6.

antithesis, perhaps closer to St Jerome than to St Augustine, between this world and the next; and in view of Damian's impact on the life of the church both locally and internationally, it is hard to escape the conclusion that his spirituality exercised a profound and destructive influence on the Christian understanding of marriage and sexuality.

Nonetheless, and whatever its consequences, this spirituality is central to an understanding of all that Damian wrote. Without a recognition of the overwhelming importance he attached to the desire for God, his passionate concern for monastic reform or clerical morals appears only shrill or fanatical. And by constantly relating this theme to the imperative of the twofold love (of God and neighbour), Damian prevents it from becoming a narrowly individual search for perfection, allowing it instead to offer the monastic life an inner dynamism which must have made it intensely attractive. Moreover, Damian makes it into something much more than merely the preserve of a sinless elite: indeed, as we have seen, he comes close to suggesting that the sinner, like St Matthew, is more likely to respond to it because such a person knows what it is to desire - the problem is only that he was desiring the wrong thing. There can be little doubt that Damian passionately believed in what he wrote, if only because he lived it without compromise or apology. There can be even less doubt about the fact that in St Peter Damian the eremitic and monastic reform movement of the eleventh century found an apologist of exceptional power.

THE MONASTIC PRIEST
by
Martin Dudley

The questions of whether or not monks should be priests, of how many priests there should be in a monastic community, if any, and of the work that such monk-priests should be permitted to do, are not merely academic or historical. They are questions faced today by individual monasteries, congregations, and orders of monks. There is also the wider question of the relation between monastic and secular priesthood and the influence of the former, and its distinctive lifestyle, on the shape and spirituality of the latter.[1] The Dominican theologian Edward Schillebeeckx has characterised the

---

[1] The Literature is extensive. The following have been consulted in preparing this paper:

Amos, Thomas L.
'Monks and Pastoral Care in the Early Middle Ages,' in *Religion, Culture, and Society in the Early Middle Ages: Studies in Honor of Richard E. Sullivan*, Kalamazoo, Michigan 1987, pp. 165-80.

Congar, Yves
'Modèle monastique et modèle sacerdotal en Occident de Grégoire VII (1073-1085) à Innocent III (1198), in *Études de Civilisation Médiévale [Mélanges offerts à E.-R. Labande]*, Poitiers, 1974, pp. 153-160.

Constable, Giles
'Monasteries, Rural Churches and the *Cura Animarum* in the Early Middle Ages,' in *Settimane di studio del Centro italiano di studi sull'alto medioevo*, XXVIII, Spoleto 1982, pp. 349-89 [reprinted in *Monks, Hermits and Crusaders in Medieval Europe*, London 1988].

de Vogüé, Adalbert
'Less chapitres de Benoît et du Maître sur le sacerdoce,' *Benedictina* 20 (1973).

....
'Le prêtre et la communauté' monastique.' in *La Maison-Dieu*, 115 (1973).

....
The Rule of Saint Benedict: A Doctrinal and Spiritual Commentary, Cistercian Publications, Kalamazoo 1983.

Dubois, Jacques
'Office des heures et messe dans la tradition monastique,' in *La Maison-Dieu*, 135, Paris 1978, pp. 61-82 [reprinted in *Histoire monastique en France au XIIe siècle*, London 1982].

Havener, Ivan
'Monastic Priesthood: Some Thoughts on Its Future in America.' in *Worship*, vol. 56, no. 5 (September 1982), pp. 431-41.

Leclerq, Jean
'Monachisme, Sacerdoce et Missions au Moyen Age: Travaux et Résultats Récents,' in *Studia Monastica*, volume 23, 1981, pp. 307-23.

....
'On Monastic Priesthood According to the Ancient Medieval Tradition,' in *Studia Monastica*, volume 3, 1961, pp. 137-55.

Nussbaum, Otto
Kloster, Priestermönch und Privatmesse, Bonn 1961.

Rousseau, Oliver
'Priesthood Monasticism,' in *The Sacrament of Orders*, London 1962, pp. 168-80.

Seasoltz, R. Kevin
'Monastery and Eucharist: Some American Observations,' in William Skudlarek, editor, *The Continuing Quest for God: Monastic Spirituality in Tradition and Transition*, Collegeville, 1982.

Vogel, Cyrille
'La multiplication des messes solitaires au moyen âge. Essai de statistique,' in *Revue des Sciences Religieuses*, 55 (1981) pp. 206-213.

....
'La Règle de S. Benoit et le culte chrétien. Prêtremoine et moine-prêtre', in *Atti del 7 Congresso internazionale di studi sull' alto medioevo II*, 1980, Spoleto 1982, pp. 409-27.

....
'La vie quotidienne de moine en occident à l'époque de la floraison des messes privées' [I regret that I only have a photocopy of this article without publishing details. It cites 'La Règle de S. Benoit ...' and so appeared after 1982 but does not appear in the bibliography in *Medieval Liturgy*.]

....
Medieval Liturgy: An Introduction to the Sources, translated and revised by William Storey and Niels Rasmussen, Washington D.C., 1986.

....
Une mutation cultuelle inexpliquée: le passage de l'Eucharistie communautaire a la Messe Privée,' in *Revue des Sciences Religieuses*, 54 (1980 pp. 231-50.

period from the end of the tenth to the end of the eleventh century as that of the monastic priest, in which monasticism was offered as an ideal to clergy and laity alike and in which a threefold profile of the priesthood was put forward such that even secular priests were expected to live in community, were obliged to engage in choral prayer and had to live in complete abstinence without the benefit of wife or concubine.[2] Given that cenobitic monasticism from Pachomius to Benedict was predominantly a lay movement, we must enquire how it came about that monasticism was thought to offer a model for all clergy and how some 75% of monks were priests or deacons by the tenth century.[3]

In very broad terms, we may speak of three periods, each associated with a particular development. The first, from the beginning of monasticism until the eighth century. The second from the eighth century to the eleventh, in which we see the Carolingian reform of the Church and the rise to dominance of Benedictine monasticism. The third period, the eleventh and twelfth centuries, that of monastic crisis. By the time that monasticism began to develop, at the beginning of the fourth century, the bi-polar structure of the Church had already established itself. The people of God were divided into clergy and laity. The clergy themselves were further divided by a hierarchy of rank and function recognised and codified by the law of the Roman state. That law gave clergy a preferential position in society, that is, in civil society, at the same time that they consolidated their status with ecclesiastical society by virtue of the *potestas ordinis*. The organisation of worship emphasised the set-apartness of the clergy. The area around the altar where they sat was marked off from the rest of the church. When the Emperor Theodosius tried to occupy a seat near the altar, Ambrose sent him back to the nave with the faithful. But there was also a division within the body of the faithful between those who lived in the world and tried, to the best of their ability, to observe the rules of faith and morals and who formed the majority and the lay elite - monks, virgins, widows - a minority who yet remained lay and were not clericalised. The imperial Church was frequently triumphalist and many of the clergy, perhaps most of them, enjoyed their special status and clung to power and privilege. Monks, together with consecrated virgins and widows, in their flight from the world witnessed to a certain incompatability between the Kingdom of God and the empire, even a Christian empire. Ordination, involving as it did both status and temptation, imperilled that witness and was not desired by the earliest monks. It is likely that some of the hermits were priests, but, as a general rule, priests who had chosen the eremitical life rather than hermits who had been ordained.

There is early evidence, however, of monastic communities and individual monks being involved in various kinds of pastoral work and in liturgical activities in public churches, in Rome, Constantinople and other cities. This was not an entirely uncontroversial development, as we know from Gregory the Great's letter to Abbot Maurus in which he speaks of the care of churches being inherent in the priestly office and, having entrusted the church of St Pancratius to monks, requires that a *peregrinum presbyterum* be appointed to live in the monastery and celebrate the Mass in the church without being a monk.[4] It is unclear how long he held to his position for there is clearly a difference

---

[2] E. Schillebeeckx, *The Church with a Human Face*, London 1985, p. 165.

[3] Y. Congar, op. cit., p. 154.

[4] Epistle XVIII, *A Select Library of the Nicene and Post-Nicene Fathers of the Christian Church*, Second Series. Vol. XII, Grand Rapids, Michigan 1976, 2nd part, p. 150.

between principle and practice in that he frequently used monks to promote the mission of the Church, as, for example, in sending Augustine to England, and for pastoral work. Only a small number were ordained. The increasing involvement of monks in missionary and pastoral work together with the influence of a different monastic ethos, that of the Irish monks, led to a significant growth in that number. A further factor seems to have been the adoption by numerous monasteries of the Rule of St Benedict, and we must now ask whether it contained something that encouraged and facilitated this development.

THE RULE OF ST BENEDICT

There are two chapters in the Rule concerned with priests: chapter 60 'Priests who may wish to live in the monastery' and chapter 62 'The priests of the monastery'[5] The former states that the requests of those in priests's orders who ask to be admitted to the monastery are not to be granted too readily. If they persist, it must be made clear that they will have to observe the whole discipline of the Rule, without mitigation. Such a priest 'may be allowed to stand next in order to the Abbot, and to give the blessings and to say mass, but only at the Abbot's biddings.' They will be given a position of respect because of their priesthood and it is therefore all the more important that they should give a good example of humility. That chapter 62 is separated from 60 by a chapter on the reception of pilgrim monks suggests that it belongs to the group of chapters, 58-61 inclusive that are concerned with admissions to the monastery. Chapter 62 itself belongs to those chapters concerned with order, mutual respect, and the offices of abbot, prior and porter. The monk-priest is another one who, like the cellarar, deans and provosts, occupies an office within the community and must be seen to be worthy of it. 'If the abbot wants to have someone ordained priest or deacon for him,' writes Benedict, 'let him choose from his own monks one who is worthy to exercise the priesthood. The one ordained must be on his guard against elation and pride, and not presume to do anything but what is commanded him by the Abbot, realising that he is now all the more bound to submit to regular discipline. And let him not by reason of his priesthood forget the obedience and discipline of the Rule, but advance more and more into union with God [*magis ac magis in Deum proficiat*]'.

De Vogüé holds that the Benedictine Rule, in its treatment of priesthood, introduces a new aspect as compared to earlier rules. First, the Rule allows priests to be admitted to the community. This was not allowed by Augustine, by the Rule of the Four Fathers, or by the Master. In the Augustinian Rule, the priest is an external figure with responsibility for the community but no part in it. It has been argued that this twofold arrangement of a community superior and an external priestly authority reflects the situation of St Augustine's earliest community, which was of lay-people, and not of the later community of clerics at Hippo.[6] In the Rule of the Master, chapter 83, we read: 'Priests are to be considered outsiders in the monastery, especially those who retain and exercise their presidency and preferment in churches. If their choice is to live in monasteries for the love of God and for the sake of discipline and the pattern of a holy life, even so it is only in

---

[5] I have used the translation of the Rule by Dom Bernard Basil Bolton OSB, Ealing Abbey, London 1970.

[6] de Vogüé, *The Rule*, p. 81.

name that they are called fathers of the monastery, and nothing is to be permitted them in monasteries other than praying the collects, saying the conclusion, and giving the blessing.' The abbot himself is identified as a layman and nothing is said about allowing any of the monks to be ordained. There was provision for daily communion, but this was not a celebration of the Eucharist, and in De Vogüé's view the monks went to the Sunday celebration in the parish church presided over by one of the diocesan clergy, but there is no specific mention of this. A diocesan priest did come into the monastery for the Eucharist on the occasion of the abbot's election and on the patronal feast day of the oratory. Benedict reveals a changing relationship between cenobitism and the clergy. The monastery was thereafter strong enough, and its hierarchy sure enough of itself, to receive without risk persons belonging to the hierarchy of the Church.'[7] Second, Benedict envisages the promotion of monks to holy orders. This was already a widespread custom but had not received ratification in a rule. Though Pachomius would not have solitaries· accept priesthood at any price, holding the clerical state to be opposed to the monastic state, Benedict does not follow him in this.[8] Shortly after Pachomius we find monks regularly ordained to provide the sacraments for their communities. This is the motive, the one and only motive, says de Vogüé, for the provisions in chapter 62, that there might be monks who can celebrate the Eucharist at home and among themselves, without needing to to out or to call in an outside priest. That chapter mentions just one priestly function, *officium altaris,* service of the altar. This is the only activity offered to the monk-priest, when the care of souls and the government of the community was in other, perhaps lay, hands. Dom Rousseau goes so far as to speak of an opposition between monasticism and priesthood within Benedictine monasticism.[9] Some of the caution displayed in the Rule might be explained by the pride and vanity of some priests, a recurrent problem within a hierarchically ordered church and one that was amplified by the sort of sacralization of office that took place from the fourth century onwards.

Benedict's monks heard the mass in their own oratory. The monastery thus paralleled the Church, was an adjunct to its life as a largely autonomous ecclesiastical entity. The monks did not go out to services in the parish, diocesan priests did not need to come in to celebrate in the monastery, and by imparting a hiddeness to its liturgy, by the use of screens and by other measures, the monastic community became truly enclosed. As De Vogüé says, it became both more integrated with and more separate from ecclesiastical society.[10] A further factor in the movement towards the ordination of monks can only be given a cursory mention here. It is the development of the *missa privata,* the private Mass, most frequently a votive or requiem Mass said by the priest for the intention of a benefactor who paid a stipend for it.[11]

In the second period, the eighth to eleventh centuries, the number of monk-priests rose

---

[7] de Vogüé, ibid., p. 292

[8] *Vita Pachomii,* ch. 24; P.L. 73, 245; cited by de Vogüé, ibid., pp. 292 & 297 n.19.

[9] Rousseau, op. cit., p. 170.

[10] de Vogüé, op. cit., p. 293.

[11] see my contribution 'Monks and Liturgies: the Influence of the Monasteries on the Development of the Medieval Liturgy, in J. Loades [ed], *Monastic Studies: The Continuity of Tradition,* Bangor 1990, pp. 21-33.

substantially to the point where all the monks in some houses were ordained. Perhaps 80% were not ordained in the eighth century, 40% in the ninth, and 25% in the tenth Constable cites the interesting example of 300 monks listed in the great foundation charter of Fruttuaria in 1022/5.[12] 38%, including the superiors, were priests, 14% deacons, 18% sub-deacons, making 70% ordained. There is some evidence to suggest that many of the ordained monks had entered the monastery as children, had had the benefit of a monastic education and so could read, write, and participate fully in the liturgy, and that the *conversi,* who had entered as adults, were often illiterate and were not ordained unless they subsequently learned to read and write. The increased number of priests was needed both for the celebration of private Masses and for the pastoral care of the large number of parishes owned by the monasteries.

THE MONASTIC IDEAL

As monasticism entered the eleventh century it was heavily clericalised. It was also considered, because of its ascetic and penitential nature, the highest Christian calling and that in which salvation was most sure. In 1049 when Pope Leo IX was elected, the reform party gained power in the Roman Church. A particular feature of the party was its monastic root. Associated closely or loosely with the reform were the monks Hildebrand, later Gregory VII, Frederick of Lorraine, Abbot of Monte Cassino, later Stephen IX, Humbert of Silva Candida, a monk of Moyenmoutier, Anselm of Lucca, former pupil of Anselm of Bec, and the hermit of Fonte Avella, Peter Damian, as well as Abbot Hugh of Cluny. United in opposition, the party was divided in the execution of its reforming policies. This was partly because of a contradiction at the heart of its position. Monasticism was the ideal to which they were all committed, but there were still the complex realities of earthly life to be dealt with. The reformers rejected the Carolingian programme for the conversion of the world by a divinely-instituted monarchy to which the clergy also would be subordinate. Some of them, including Gregory himself, believed instead in sacerdotalism, in the conversion of the world by a priestly hierarchy to which all other temporal powers were subordinate. Gregory saw the need to reform the clergy. He was concerned about simony and clergy marriage because the claim of the Church to govern mankind required a high moral stance and that entailed a programme of reform. But his real intention was the establishment of right order in the world and that meant sacerdotal supremacy. The ascetical-monastic hierarchy was replaced by a clerical-sacerdotal hierarchy.

This was ultimately a different objective from that of the monastic reform pioneered by Cluny. Under St Hugh, Cluny had continued in the tradition of spirituality established by Odo. Its prevailing characteristic, despite the splendour of Cluny, was contempt for the world, that 'vast and treacherous ocean' which daily threatened shipwreck to those who voyaged upon it.[13] Cluny therefore fostered withdrawal from the world and doubted the possibility of its conversion or conquest. Cluniac spirituality was eschatological. Overshadowing its life was the great and terrible day. Gregory believed in judgment and believed that the best means of crossing life's ocean safely was the barque of Peter. The

---

[12] Constable, op. cit., p. 364.

[13] H.E.J. Cowdrey, *The Cluniacs and the Gregorian reform,* Oxford 1970, p. 130.

best, perhaps, but at Cluny they doubted that even the best was safe. For a time the two approaches went forward together, but the tension remained. It was not really possible to affirm the world at the same time as calling upon the clergy to deny worldliness. When the latter principle was rigorously applied, as it was through the post-Tridentine seminary, the clergy found themselves in opposition to the world. The reaffirmation of the world after Vatican II had led to a questioning of the necessity for the celibate, siminary-trained priest and his clerical spirituality. As the monastic vocation has again come to be seen as a vocation that is separate from priesthood, so a similar pattern of questioning has occupied the monks. Gregory replaced the distinction between monks, other lay people and clerics with one between monks and clerics on the one hand and the laity on the other.

Some evidence for the medieval understanding of the relationship between the monastic and clerical vocations comes from the relation of both to the canons regular. *Vita apostolica,* a term which used to apply to monks living in poverty in their *vita communis,* came to be applied to canons regular, who were much encouraged by Hildebrand in their semi-monastic life, as well as to clerics and priests involved in pastoral and apostolic work.Hugh of Saint-Victor, writing about 1134 in the *De Sacramentis,* devotes a chapter to orders among the monks. He claims that orders are granted to monks by way of indulgence, as a favour, that they may live more quietly, that is, that they should be able to celebrate the Eucharist.[14] The Cistercian in Idung's *Dialogue Between Two Monks* written about 1155, thought that Master Hugh nodded at that point in his writings, like Homer of old.[15] He and his Cluniac interlocutor were arguing about the Norbertines or Premonstratensians, who did not want to be monks and who, I quote the Cistercian, 'deny that they are monks because they want to be called preachers and parish priests'[16], offices not permitted to monks, for Jerome says that the role of a monk is not to teach but to lament.[17] The Norbertines, it seems, said they were not monks but canons regular, a name dismissed by the Cistercian as tautological, and they further claimed that because they were clerics they had the duty of preaching by the very fact of their clerical status. When the Cistercians say in reply that monks who also hold Holy Orders, because they are clerics, have the duty of preaching by the very fact of their clerical status, the Norbertines cite Master Hugh, and say that the clerical status of monks is a favour not a right.[18] Bishops and priests in their churches and abbots in their monasteries have the cure of souls and so have an obligation to preach, but monks do not and should not claim such a right.[19] The Cistercian goes on to argue, first, that the clerical status belongs to monks on the basis of the Rule, chapters 60 and 62, which he quotes, and second that the Augustinian Rule of the Norbertines makes no mention of

---

[14] Hugh of Saint Victor, *On the Sacraments of the Christian Faith,* trans. by R.J. Deferrari, Cambridge, Mass. 1951, pp. 260-61.

[15] *Cistercians and Cluniacs: The Case for Cîteaux,* Kalamazoo 1977 [cited as Dial., with section and paragraph numbers] Dial. II, 46.

[16] Dial II, 39.

[17] Dial II, 40.

[18] Dial II, 45.

[19] Dial II, 49.

priesthood, because it was written for nuns. And third, he repeats a most interesting argument from Isidore of Seville, that there are two kinds of monks, hermits and cenobites; the former imitating Elijah and John the Baptist, the latter imitating the Apostles. And ordination cannot be a mere indulgence to those who are imitators of the Apostles.[20] The Cluniac observes that by the Cistercians reasoning the tables have been turned: monks hold clerical status because it is their due and the Norbertines hold it by way of favour. The respect for the priest, which we have already noted in Augustine's Rule, arises, says the Cistercian, from the fact that it is the parish priest who cares for a community of nuns in his parish, says mass, gives them communion, and hears their confessions, and so they are to respect him. The Cluniac does not demur on this point, but he asks what this clerical status is and the Cistercian answers in the way that we would from our reading of the Rule expect: it is to officiate at the altar.[21]

This office had come to be seen increasingly as one of both privilege and danger. Among the many private prayers included in the Sacramentaries were a substantial collection of *apologiae,* in which the priest bewails his sinfulness and asks to be allowed to make the sacrifice despite his unworthiness Immediately before the Secret in the Mass, the *oration super oblata,* the priest asks for the prayers of those who are gathered around the altar in the words *Orate fratres.*[22] The presentation and arrangement of the gifts has been completed and the priest, set apart from the people to serve the altar, stands alone before God as the people's mediator. Throughout the Middle ages that petition for prayer has a personal note expressing the need of the unworthy priest for prayer: *Orate pro me* or *pro me peccatore,* or again *pro me misero peccatore* and *pro me miserrimo peccatore.* The unworthy priest was in considerable danger in celebrating the mysteries. Peter Lombard wrote in the *Sentences* that the men chosen as clergy for spiritual ministration are to be those who can worthily handle the Lords sacraments. 'For it is better,' he says, quoting Gratian, 'for the priesthood of the Lord to have few ministers, than to have many useless ones, who bring a grave burden on their ordainers.' 'The men who ought to be ministers of Christ are those who are adorned by the sevenfold grace of the Holy Spirit and whose doctrine and spirituality are transfused by grace into others, lest sordid lives crush with their feet the heavenly pearls of spiritual words and divine offices.'[23] Our Cistercian also stresses this need for a holy life. So great is the dignity, so lofty the service of the altar, that even those who are holier than other human beings - that is, good monks - are scarcely worthy of exercising that office. And he repeats the frequently cited examples of holy monks who fled and indulged in all sorts of subterfuges in order to avoid ordination. The mediatorial role was not something that they, so conscious of their sins, were willing to accept and which they would certainly never seek. Here, at last, Cluniac and Cistercian are of one mind. Their dialogue goes like this:

> Cluniac: What is the rationale, then, that yearnings for priesthood so tickle modern monks that they all want to be ordained to the priesthood whether they are worthy of it or not?

---

[20] Dial II, 55.

[21] Dial II, 57.

[22] J.A. Jungmann, *The Mass of the Roman Rite,* New York 1955, vol. 2, pp. 82-90.

[23] IV, 24, chap. 3.

> Cistercian: Perhaps it lies in the fact that they take pleasure in the honour attached to the higher status, never giving a thought to its burdens and dangers. The higher status, even if it is held with propriety, is sought after with impropriety. The monk who is worthy of ordination becomes a priest only when coerced, but the unworthy one does not have to be coerced.[24]

The Cluniac concludes that clerical status is not bestowed on a monk as a favour, rather the favour is to deny it to him. Following the same path a little later, the Cistercian again picks up Isidore's analysis, the Apostles were the first clerics, to whom the Lord said, 'You have left all and followed me,' and the monks are their imitators. It would be absurd to deny the service of the altar to the imitators of the Apostles, so it is rather the case that the monks, in their excessive humility denied themselves holy orders, judging themselves unworthy of the most holy service of the altar.[25] And the Cluniac again describes the mental outlook of the modern monks as altogether different because all of them, worthy and unworthy, want to be ordained.[26]

We might also consider the much cited example of St Jerome, the father of monks. We have seen already his objections to monks being ordained and he was himself ordained only after stiff resistance. He made it clear that his ordination would not interfere with his life as a monk. He honoured the clergy as those who 'succeeding to the Apostles, consecrate Christ's body and make us Christians' and who feed and judge Christ's sheep, but he was also concerned about the temptations to which they were exposed. And he shrank from the exercise of pastoral responsibility and sacerdotal function. One letter reports that, even though there was a shortage of priests in his monastery at Bethlehem, Jerome refused 'for reasons of bashfulness and humility' from exercising his ministry as a priest.[27] What sort of priest was he then? Well not one that medieval theology understood very well. When Aquinas defines the priest's office in terms of the consecration of the Eucharist, together with baptism and the administration of the other sacraments, he separated the Eucharist from the others. The latter a priest was only bound to administer when he had the cure of souls for they are only accomplished when used by the faithful. The Eucharist is accomplished in the consecration of the bread and wine in which a sacrifice is offered to God. The priest is obliged to consecrate the Eucharist on account of the Orders he has received. He argues that everyone is bound to use the grace given to them when opportunity serves. That the ability to offer sacrifice is such a grace which is to be valued with reference not only to the faithful, but also and chiefly to God. 'Accordingly it is not lawful,' he writes, in opposition to views expressed by Alexander of Hales and St Bonaventure,'for a priest, even if he does not have the cure of souls, to cease altogether celebrating.'[28]

We see, therefore, a double strand in the development of the monastic priest. The more primitive thread is that which affirms the possibility of monks being priests but

---

[24] Dial III, 57.

[25] Dial III, 43.

[26] Dial III, 44.

[27] J.N.D. Kelly, *Jerome*, London 1975, p. 58.

[28] St Thomas Quinas, *Summa Theologiae* 3a, 82, 10.

approaches the idea with caution. The sole function of the priest will be service of God and his community by saying mass. He must therefore be a holy person. The fear of approaching the altar unworthily leads to the refusal to seek orders and a mistrust of anyone who does aspire to ordination. The other strand affirms both the normality and the desirability of ordination. Behind this is a eucharistic theology that encourages multiple celebrations of the eucharist because of the efficaciousness of the sacrifice offered to God, together with the economic factors involved in monasteries owning churches and providing pastoral care. There has to be some special pleading here, justifying the pastoral ministry and preaching of monks. On the negative side there is the seeking after honours which is so alien to the monastic vocation.

MONASTIC PRIESTHOOD TODAY

So, what is the relationship of monasticism and priesthood today? The post-war crisis in the catholic priesthood, a crisis both of theology and practice, has had its affect in the monasteries. The understanding of priesthood, its biblical roots, its relation to eucharistic presidency, have all been critically examined. So have questions about the meaning of the contemporary monastic life for those whose priestly ministry takes them outside the community and away from the common observance of the rule. After a review of the historical material in a lecture given in 1960, Jean Leclerq ventured to draw some conclusions that were relevant to the prevailing situation, and which echo and expand the views of Dom Oliver Rousseau, who, in 1955, pointed to the difficulty many people have in realising that 'the true character of monasticism in no way presumes access to sacred Orders.'[29] The main conclusion was that there is a fundamental difference between being a monk and being a priest, between monachism and priesthood, but that a combination was possible provided that, in normal circumstances, the principles of the monastic life were not sacrificed but enforced. A fundamental principle is that of being a foreigner to the world. In Benedictine monasticism, this is achieved by the cenobitical life, itself characterized by asceticism and prayer. The monastic life is orientated towards God. The priesthood, as an office and function, is orientated towards the world. The role of the priest is ministerial, preaching the word and administering the sacraments to and for his people. This is not so for the monk-priest. First, his priesthood is not an essential part of the monastic vocation. It is exceptional and does not belong to the institution as such. And, second, that priesthood is not ministerial. It is not normally a pastoral priesthood. It is ascetical, contemplative, ordered to the offering of sacrifice. This interpretation was confirmed by the Lateran Council of 1123 when it recognized the lawfulness of the priesthood for monks, whilst restricting their activity. They were forbidden to impose public penances, to visit the sick, to administer extreme unction, and to celebrate public masses. What was left to them, ask Leclerq? And answers, their private mass.[30]

Leclerq delivered his paper at an interesting moment in the life of the Church, in the month in which the preparatory commissions for the Second Vatican Council were set up. He stressed that the chapter of history of 'the monastic priesthood' must find its place in the broader history of the theology of priesthood. That broader history was about to take

---

[29] Rousseau, op. cit., pp. 170, 177-80; J. Leclerq, 'On Monastic Priesthood', pp. 137-55.

[30] Leclerq, ibid., p. 151.

a significant turn. One consequence of this was that the link between admission to solemn vows, necessary for choir monks, with full rights of active and passive voice in the community, and acceptance of holy orders was dropped. Previously a dispensation had been required and was rarely given. Now there was a possibility of choice for the monk, the abbot and the community.

In consequence, the percentage of monks who are priests is, it seems, gradually declining. Not all modern monks want to be ordained or expect to be ordained. In 1985, there were 8886 Benedictine monks worldwide; 3156, that is 35.5%, were not priests. Five years before, in 1980, of 9158 monks, 3109, that is 33.09%, were not priests.[31] The proportions vary in different congregations and the variety can be explained by historical rather than theological factors. Houses of the English Benedictine Congregation, for example, serve a large number of parishes. The largest EBC house, Ampleforth, has 98. professed monks, of whom only 13 are not priests. By contrast, in houses of the Congregation of Subiaco, Ramsgate, Prinknash, Pluscarden, and Farnborough, a much larger proportion are not priests. At Pluscarden, there are 12 priests to 17 non-priests. We might be tempted to think that Subiaco, formerly the Cassinese Congregation of the Primitive Observance, follows a more primitive pattern. In fact the Congregation as such as no policy and it is left to the individual monastery to decide its own policy. This will, of course, depend upon the aptitude of individual monks, the needs of the community and the kind of work in which the community is involved. Monasteries with little or no parish involvement will not need priests for pastoral work. Dom Gilbert Jones, Abbot President of the Congregation of Subiaco, summed up the prevailing mood when he wrote

'I think it would be true to say that for some time - and certainly since Vatican II - there has been a movement towards the lay monastic state and the wishes of the individual are always taken into account by the Abbot. The overriding principle, however, in admitting a man to the monastery is that he wishes to be a monk, according to the Holy Rule.'[32]

---

[31] Figures taken from the *Benedictine Yearbook 1990*.

[32] In a personal letter, 9 July 1990.

FRIARS AND CANONS:
THE EARLIEST DOMINICANS
by
Simon Tugwell OP

In this paper I want to have another gnaw at what is, I fear, a rather old bone, which is still something of a bone of contention between Dominican historians and indeed between Dominicans in general. I want to look again at the process in 1215 which resulted in St Dominic and his fellow preachers adopting the Rule of St Augustine and becoming, for a time, canons regular.

The essential outline of the story is clear.[1] By the end of 1201 Dominic was subprior of the cathedral chapter of Osma and the former prior, Diego, who had recruited Dominic for the chapter, had become bishop. A chance encounter in the early spring of 1206 with the papal legates entrusted by Innocent III with the mission against heresy in the south of France led to Diego and Dominic, and probably some other clerics from Diego's retinue,[2] becoming involved in this mission, which indeed took on a new nature thanks to Diego's advice. He saw that the great advantage possessed by the heretics was that they looked like real apostles, in the eyes of the populace, so he suggested that the Catholics must beat them at their own game, imitating in everything the manner of the apostles, travelling round on foot, begging their bread from door to door. To show he meant business, he gave a lead himself. Both the recruitment of new preachers and the change of strategy were quickly approved by Innocent III. Diego himself took a prominent part in the mission until his death at the end of 1207, commuting between Osma and

---

[1] The standard life of Dominic is that by M.H. Vicaire, *Histoire de St Dominique*, 2nd ed., Paris 1982; since this work provides abundant references to primary sources, I shall not cite such evidence here for straightforward and well-known aspects of the story. In the text and in the following notes some regular abbreviations are used:

AFP = *Archivum Fratrum Praedicatorum*.

K = V.J. Koudelka, ed., *Monumenta Diplomatica S. Dominici* (MOPH XXV), Rome 1966, cited by document number.

Lib. = Jordan of Saxony, *Libellus*, using the paragraph numbers in the edition in MOPH XVI.

MOPH = *Monumenta Ordinis Fratrum Praedicatorum Historica*.

[2] Jordan of Saxony (Lib. 20) says that Diego retained 'a few clerics' with him, but Pierre des Vaux de Cernai, *Historia Albigensis* 21 (ed. P. Guébin and E. Lyon, vol. I, Paris 1926, p.23) states that he contented himself with a single companion. It is undoubtedly true that, in general, Cernai is much better informed than Jordan about the events of 1206; nevertheless there are signs of a Dominican tradition that cannot simply be discounted, deriving, in however garbled a form, from people whose association with Dominic went back to his time in Osma (Bologna Canonization Process 14, 29, 35; MOPH XVI pp. 135, 147, 153-154), including a confused story of people being associated with Dominic's preaching even before he left Spain (ibid. 35). It is likely that the 'canons of Osma' mentioned in these accounts were in fact canons who had become Dominicans; it is not clear that any of the people citing their evidence would otherwise have known them. And there is some tantalisingly mysterious evidence of an Osma tradition, quite independent of the Dominicans, identifying as canons of Osma two people known to us from Dominican sources as Dominicans who were certainly attached to St Dominic in 1216 and may have been with him much longer (cf. V.D. Carro, *Domingo de Guzman*, Madrid 1973, pp. 357-364). Jordan names one Spaniard, also called Dominic, who was with St Dominic in 1207 (Lib. 31), and altogether six Spaniards (not counting John of 'Spain', or Navarre, who is actually said to have been born in France) are listed by Bernard Gui among those who chose the Rule of St Augustine with Dominic in 1216 (MOPH XXII pp.149-157). It is difficult to believe that all of these were present independently of Diego. It is, of course, quite possible that at first Diego only kept Dominic with him and then, as he realised the extent of the task facing the preachers, brought more men from his diocese to reinforce the mission.

Languedoc,[3] and he left Dominic, and probably some others, to work full-time in the papal mission. He also founded a house at Prouille for women rescued or converted from the heretics, which soon became a monastery of nuns.

In 1213 a new legate was appointed for the region, Peter of Benevento, and it was presumably on his authority that the preaching mission was revamped and Dominic put in charge of it in 1214 and 1215, with his headquarters in Toulouse.[4] In the early months of 1215 Dominic acquired a house in Toulouse and some people began to put themselves formally at his disposal as his subjects. In the early summer Bishop Fulk of Toulouse gave them official standing in his diocese as a kind of preaching institute. In October he and Dominic asked the pope to confirm its identity and name as *ordo praedicatorum*. Instead of doing this, the pope advised Dominic to get his brethren to choose an approved religious rule, and. he urged the bishop to give them a church. In July 1216 they were indeed given the church of St Romanus in Toulouse. On 22 December 1216 Honorius III formally took the community of St Romanus under his protection, as being a house of canons regular. Successive papal bulls between then and 1220 progressively brought out into the open the fact that Dominic and his companions were not just another group of canons, they were *ordo praedicatorum*. From 11 February 1218 onwards they are explicitly called *fratres ordinis praedicatorum* (K 86). In 1220 Dominic summoned a General Chapter at Bologna, which produced the first Constitutions to govern the life and work of the brethren explicitly as an Order of Preachers. Dominic died in 1221, after the second General Chapter, but the task of completing and updating the Constitutions has gone on up to this day.

The question which has not yet been entirely answered concerns the significance of the pope's intervention and its outcome. What exactly is meant by saying that Fulk and Dominic wanted the pope to confirm an *ordo* which would be and be called *praedicatorum*? To what extent did the adoption of the Rule of St Augustine in 1216 represent a break with what Dominic had previously been trying to establish? Was the point of Innocent's advice that the preachers ought to become a religious community, or that, being already a religious community, they ought to adopt an approved Rule in line

---

[3] See Jarl Gallén, 'Les Voyages de S. Dominique au Danemark. Essai de datation', in R. Creytens and P. Künzle, edd., *Xenia Medii Aevi Historiam Illustrantia oblata Thomae Kaeppeli OP*, Rome 1978, vol. I pp. 73-84, especially pp. 79-84.

[4] In *Dominique et ses Prêcheurs*, Fribourg and Paris 1977, p.45, Vicaire recants his earlier belief that Dominic was operating in Toulouse in 1215 on the authority of the papal legate, and argues instead that he had his mandate from the bishop. An official letter from Dominic in this period (K 61) gives permission for an ex-heretic to be given lodging in Toulouse like anyone else 'quousque super hoc nobis vel sibi (the landlord, that is) expressius mandatum faciat dominus cardinalis'. Vicaire is no doubt right to say that this clause does not of itself prove that Dominic was acting on the authority of the legate. In fact the letter makes it clear that he was acting on his own authority as 'predicationis minister'. But it seems that the seal he used to authenticate the letter was exactly the same as the one he had used in 1208, when he reconciled a converted heretic to the church 'auctoritate domini abbatis Cisterciensis, apostolice sedis legati' (K 8) (on the seal, cf. Koudelka's notes on K 8 and K 61). This must mean that the Predicatio, whose 'minister' Dominic was in 1215, was seen as being essentially the same as that of 1208, i.e. it is still the papal mission, falling therefore directly under the authority of the legate. In 1208 Dominic had no authority of his own; in 1215 he does, so of course his language is different. But it is striking that he does not anywhere in K 61 suggest that the local bishop has any say in the matter. The legate may deal directly with the landlord or he may deal with the 'minister' of the Preaching. All of this surely suggests that Vicaire's earlier view was correct, that the renewed Predicatio of 1215, like the earlier one, rested on the authority of the papal legate, not the local bishop. This did not exclude the possibility of preachers on the papal mission also being given local responsibilities by the bishops, as Dominic was for a time 'vicar general' of Carcassonne and, later, parish priest of Fanjeaux.

with the policy which would shortly find official expression in Constitution 13 of the fourth Lateran Council?[5]

To understand the nature of the *ordo praedicatorum* whose confirmation was sought in vain in 1215, we must return briefly to 1206. The motives which led Diego to propose and the preachers to adopt a policy of radical austerity, of mendicancy, were apostolic.[5a] There is no hint that the adoption of poverty was the solution for anyone to the kind of inner struggle which is so evident in the life of Francis of Assisi. Poverty was adopted because it was the most promising missionary strategy in the circumstances. Later on we find Dominic engaged quite frankly in a sort of competition in austerity with the heretics, to lure their followers away from them by showing that he was even more adept at their kind of holiness than they were.[6] But this does not mean that Dominic was personally indifferent to poverty. Unlike Francis, he did not start with a personal quest and shape his life accordingly; his life was shaped by the needs of others. But the life so shaped was one into which he threw himself whole-heartedly. Poverty became a deeply cherished ideal, no doubt because Dominic realised for himself the underlying evangelical link between poverty and preaching. The missionary situation did not just suggest a strategy, it also revealed an aspect of the gospel.

From this time forth, as Jordan of Saxony tells us (Lib. 21), 'he began to be called, not subprior, but *frater Dominicus*'. *Frater* does not have the sort of semi-technical sense it has in some slightly later Franciscan sources;[7] it was a normal designation for all kinds of religious. Jordan is not saying that Dominic began to be called 'friar Dominic' rather than 'canon Dominic', he is saying that he was no longer called 'subprior'[8] - presumably because be resigned his subpriorship at this time. But he went on being a canon of Osma and as such was addressed indifferently as 'frater Dominicus', 'dominus Dominicus' and 'dominus frater Dominicus'. It is particularly striking that one of the first people to join the preaching as a subject of Dominic, Peter Seilhan, to the end of his life referred to

---

[5] It has often just been assumed that Dominic was asking for papal confirmation of a new religious order: e.g. W.A. Hinnebusch, *History of the Dominican Order*, vol. I, Staten Island 1965, p.41; L.K. Little, *Religious Poverty and the Profit Economy in Medieval Europe*, Ithaca 1978, p. 157; Guy Bedouelle, *Dominique*, Paris 1982, p. 75; V.J. Koudelka, *Dominikus*, Olten and Freiburg im Breisgau 1983, pp. 17-18. In his suggestive article, 'L'Ordre de Saint Dominique en 1215', AFP 54 (1984) pp.5-38, Vicaire is more cautious. He takes it for granted that it was not Dominic's intention, in 1215, to turn his preachers into a religious order based on the Rule of St Augustine (p.31), but he leaves it open whether they were to be regarded as a religious community of some other kind.

[5a] If we may believe a story reported by Stephen of Bourbon, on the authority of brethren who were with Dominic in Languedoc, Diego must already have made an attempt to preach against heresy before reaching Montpellier, only to find himself discredited in the eyes of the populace by the wealth and splendour of his appearance, which contrasted noticeably with the poverty and lowliness of the heretical preachers (A. Lecoy de la Marche, *Anecdotes Historiques ... tirés du recueil inédit d'Étienne de Bourbon*, Paris 1877, p. 79).

[6] Ferrandus 22-23 (MOPH XVI pp. 225-228). Something of the impact of Dominic's competitive austerities can be seen in the Languedoc Canonization Process 15-17 (MOPH XVI pp. 181-182).

[7] E.g. Legenda Trium Sociorum, ed. Théophile Desbonnets, Grottaferrata 1974, 28:13 and 35:3, referring to people 'becoming *fratres*'. 'Fraternitas' may well have been Francis' own word for the group of his initial followers (I Celano 38, in *Analecta Franciscana* 10, Quaracchi 1926-1941, p. 30); it was certainly a term he used later (e.g. *Regula non Bullata* 5:4; *Testamentum* 27).

[8] There is nothing improbable in 'subprior' as a mode of address. Cf. the story in Gerald de Frachet, where prior Albert of St Catherine's, Bologna, says to the Dominican prior, 'Boni rumores, prior' (MOPH I p.84). On Albert, see V.J. Koudelka, AFP 43 (1973) pp.14-20. Cf. also Constantine of Orvieto 58 (MOPH XVI p. 326).

Dominic as 'domnus Dominicus',[9] which he would surely not have done if Dominic insisted on being 'frater' rather than 'dominus'.

There is no suggestion, then, that Dominic saw himself or was seen as becoming a different kind of religious. Until at least April 1216 (K 71) he was addressed as a canon of Osma, and so he was, even if he had been deputed to work outside his diocese. He was in the same position as most of the other preachers, who were largely Cistercians working outside their monastery.

This was, of course, the essential weakness of the mission. It depended on the preachers who belonged elsewhere. And Diego was aware of the problem. At the time of his death, according to Jordan of Saxony (Lib. 28), he was proposing, with the pope's consent, to 'ordinare' suitable people to be preachers in the south of France, whose job it. would be to combat heresy and support the faith. 'Ordinare' here probably does not mean 'ordain', it retains its more general sense of 'appoint'.[10] Diego's plan was not to produce new priests, but to produce full-time preachers, priests whose insertion into the *ordo* of the church would be precisely that they were preachers, members of the *ordo praedicatorum,* with no other responsibilities. Whether or not Diego himself used the phrase 'ordo praedicatorum' in connection with his project, there was surely a genuine continuity between his plan and the *ordo praedicatorum* set up by Fulk and Dominic in 1215. Puylaurens may be oversimplifying the story, but he does not really falsify it, when he says, 'Ne cepta predicatio remaneret (i.e. come to a standstill), de ordinandis perpetuis predicatoribus contra hereticos est provisum, Domino inspirante, et hac de causa sub beato episcopo domino Fulcone ordo predicatorum principaliter est exorsus.'[11]

It is even possible that Diego had taken some steps towards the realisation of his dream. After the debate with the Waldensians at Pamiers in 1207 a secular cleric, Arnaud de Crampagna, placed himself at Diego's disposal *(obtulit se),* and at the same time Durandus of Huesca and a party of his followers returned to the Catholic church and, in due course, won recognition from Innocent III as Poor Catholics, one of whose main concerns was to combat Albigensianism. It is quite likely that, had he lived, Diego would have put Arnaud to work as a preacher, and we cannot rule out the possibility that Durandus too would have become part of his preaching team.[12] We know that Fulk was present at Pamiers, as well as Dominic,[13] and he was presumably aware of Diego's intentions.

---

[9] In the document formalising the division of the Seilhan property, Dominic is always referred to as 'dominus Dominicus' or 'dominus frater Dominicus' (K 62); and Bernard Gui informs us that, to the end of his life, Peter Seilhan used to invoke 'domnus Dominicus' whenever life got him down (MOPH XXIV p.59).

[10] The ambiguities of 'ordinare' can be seen in the Decretals, X 1.14. 4-5, where the word is used (1) for making arrangements for the staffing of churches *(in ordinandis ecclesiis),* (2) of appointing people to a cure of souls *(ne ullus in eis contra decreta … ordinetur; personas quae in ecclesiis tui episcopatus ad curam animam fuerint ordinandae),* and (3) of ordination to the priesthood *(in presbyteros ordinari).*

[11] Cuillaume de Puylaurens, *Chronica,* ed. J. Duvernoy, Paris 1976, p. 54. The Dominicans definitely believed that the order was founded to carry on the type of mission that Diego pioneered (Étienne de Bourbon, ed. cit. p. 79).

[12] Cernai, ed. cit. I pp. 43-44; Puylaurens, ed. cit. p. 48. On the possible link with Diego's project, see Vicaire in *Cahiers de Fanjeaux* 2 (1967) p. 172.

[13] Cernai, ed. cit. I p.43.

Whatever the precise nature of the link many be, it is surely the case that the *ordo praedicatorum* of 1215 was the institutional embodiment of Diego's vision.

What then was Innocent III being asked to confirm? We have no strictly contemporary account, only that of Jordan, written about 1232. He says that Fulk and Dominic went to the pope to beg him 'confirmari fratri Dominico et sociis eius ordinem qui predicatorum diceretur et esset' (Lib. 40). How far this echoes the actual language used in 1215 is something we must assess in due course.

The main problem in interpreting Jordan's text is to know how to take *ordo*. The word could already mean what we mean by a religious Order.[14] But it also had a more general meaning. Edmund of Abingdon sums up all conceivable categories of christian in the phrase 'omnes sanctorum ordines in terra'.[15] And even if the older, rather simple, use of the word 'ordo' to divide up society into such classes as 'coniugati, continentes, praedicatores' or 'oratores, bellatores, laboratores' was making way for the more elaborate schemes found in the sermones and status of the 13th century, the older categories were still available.[16] Jacques de Vitry, for instance, can still use the classic triad 'coniugati, viduae, virgines'.[17]

What is interesting in this passage of Jacques de Vitry, though, is that he exploits 'ordo' to mean both social or professional category and a pattern of religious observance. He argues that all christians are 'regulares', not just those who 'transeunt ad religionem', in that they all live by the rule of the gospel and by the observances proper to their 'ordo'. He instances secular clergy, married men, widows, virgins, soldiers, merchants,[18] farmers and artisans, but says that the same principle applies to everyone. Everyone, then, whether religious or not, belongs to an 'ordo', not just in the sense of belonging to a category, but in the sense of belonging to a category of people with a particular way of life which is proper to it.

The Franciscans took a further step, as we can see from Celano's first life of Francis and from Julian of Speyer, both of them more or less contemporary with Jordan of Saxony. According to them, Francis rebuilt three churches as a symbol of his provision of a rule of life for the three orders in the church. These three orders (friars, nuns and lay penitents) derive from earlier analyses of the church into various lists of three orders, but they are now taken over as three orders given a specific shape by Francis. As Julian puts

---

[14] For instance, in Constitution 12 of Lateran IV it is difficult to see any way in which 'Cisterciensis ordinis abbates' differs in meaning from our modern 'abbots of the Cistercian order'.

[15] *Speculum Religiosorum* 82, ed. Helen P. Forshaw, London 1973, p.78.

[16] On 'ordines' see G.G. Meersseman, *Ordo Fraternitatis*, Rome 1977, pp. 222-228; Y. Congar, 'Les laïcs et l'ecclésiologie des "ordines" chez les théologiens des XIe et XIIe siècles', reprinted in *Études d'Ecclésiologie Médiévale*, London 1983; Maria Conti, 'Structures idéologiques et structures sémiotiques dans les *sermones ad status* du XIIIe siècle', in *Archéologie du Signe*, Toronto 1982, pp. 145-163.

[17] *Historia Occidentalis*, ed. J.F. Hinnebusch, Fribourg 1972, pp. 165-166.

[18] Merchants have by now clearly won their place in christian society; contrast the earlier attitude documented by Little, op. cit. pp. 38-39.

it, 'tres ordines ordinavit', the first being the 'ordo fratrum minorum', the second that of the Poor Ladies, the third being called the 'ordo penitentium'.[19] It is only a short step from there to the claim made by the compiler of the Legenda Trium Sociorum that 'by blessed Francis, perfect worshipper of the Holy Trinity, the church of God was renewed in three orders ... each of which was confirmed by the pope in its own time'.[20] The point is not quite that Francis founded three orders, but he - paradoxically - gave them a proper *ordo*. And at least two of them, in his own lifetime, became distinctively Franciscan 'orders'. To what extent anything like the Franciscan Third Order was organised quite so early is far from clear. What we can see here is a process whereby an 'ordo' in the sense of a category of people in the church becomes an 'ordo' in the sense of a distinct organisation in the church.

This brings us to the most difficult Franciscan use of 'ordo'. In the Anonymus Perusinus (perhaps dating from the middle of the 13th century)[21] we are told that when Francis and his first companions were asked what their 'ordo' was, they replied that they were penitents from Assisi. 'For', the author goes on, 'their *religio* was not yet called an ordo'. This rather puzzling pronouncement[22] is reversed in the probably derivative Legenda Trium Sociorum, which says, 'their *ordo* was not yet called a *religio*', but if anything the Legenda makes it even clearer than the Anonymus Perusinus that whereas *religio* applies to the way of life espoused by Francis from the time of his conversion, it was only later that the word *ordo* became applicable, probably in connection with the visit of Francis and his companions to Innocent III, when Francis made his promise of obedience to the pope, and his companions promised obedience to him.[23]

---

[19] Julian of Speyer, *Vita S. Francisci* 14 and 23 (*Analecta Franciscana* 10, pp. 342, 346), and, more allusively, I Celano 37 (ibid. p. 30). Cf. the comments of Meersseman, op. cit. pp.359-363. Something very similar had happened earlier on in connection with the Humiliati. In about 1200 they approached Innocent III with the worry that the variety of their 'proposita' might cause scandal and difficulty, and he agreed that they should work out a single 'propositum', covering all their members, including those who were married. But the beginning of his letter is full of references to the legitimate diversity of 'ordines' within the church, which is for this reason called 'castrorum acies ordinata, in qua videlicet diversi ordines militant ordinati' (PL 214: 921-922). In the outcome, however, Innocent ended up approving a different scheme, whereby the different kinds of Humiliati were organised into three 'ordines': the clerics, who were to live as canons regular; the 'Second Order', of communities of lay celibates; and the 'Third Order' consisting of married lay men and women. This terminology is clearly present in Innocent's letter of 16 June 1201 (H. Tiraboschi, *Vetera Humiliatorum Monumenta*, Milan 1766-1768, vol. II pp. 143-144) Thus 'ordines' in the church have become 'ordines', in a more institutionalised sense, within the organisation of the Humiliati. It is interesting to wonder whether there is any influence from Joachim of Fiore, who depicts, in his *Figurae*, the 'ordo novus' of the third age as a 'body' containing both the various kinds of monks and (at a suitable distance from their 'monastery') the 'ordo clericorum' and the 'ordo coniugatorum', each of them understood as adopting, in this final age, a suitable form of common life (Leone Tondelli, *Il Libro delle Figure dell' abate Gioachino da Fiore*, 2nd ed., Turin 1953, vol. II, tavola XII; for a commentary, see Marjorie Reeves and Beatrice Hirsch-Reich, *The Figurae of Joachim of Fiore*, Oxford 1972, pp. 232-248). On Innocent III and the Humiliati, see Michele Maccarrone, *Studi su Innocenzo III*, Padua 1972, pp 284-289.

[20] Legenda Trium Sociorum, ed. cit. 60.

[21] Cf. Desbonnets' edition of the Legenda, p. 87; but the dating of both the Legenda and the Anonymus Perusinus remains uncertain.

[22] Kajetan Esser found it totally unintelligible (*Anfänge und ursprüngliche Zielsetzungen des Ordens der Minderbrüder*, Leiden 1966, p. 18 note 3).

[23] Anon. Perus., ed. Lorenzo di Fonzo, *Miscellanea Francescana* 72 (1972) 19c (p.445); Legenda Trium Sociorum 37. The Anonymus is consistent in using *religio* with reference to everything from 1206 onwards (see especially 44a, where 'eleven years *ab inceptione religionis*' must refer to 1206). The Legenda is less consistent, but 31 shows clearly that *religio* comes before *ordo*, referring to the *religio* which Francis had already started and looking ahead to a time when the *ordo* would be started. The connection between the *ordo* and the visit to the pope is not explicit, but it is hard to see when else the *ordo* began. The story of Francis promising obedience to the pope, and his companions to him, which is implicit in *Regula non Bullata* Prol. 3-4, is narrated in Anon. Perus. 36c and Legenda 52.

Here 'ordo' clearly does not mean way of life; that is covered by 'religio'.[24] 'Ordo' must mean something more like 'organisation', including hierarchical structure. And even though our sources for this distinction are relatively late, it is possible that they echo earlier terminology going back to Francis himself. Francis seems to have been keen that his friars should be called '*ordo* fratrum minorum', though in his own earlier terminology he refers to his fraternity as a 'religio'.[25]

Let us now return to the *ordo praedicatorum*. The phrase had a well-established contemporary use: it could be disputed who did or did not belong to the *ordo praedicatorum*, but no one doubted that what it meant was the class of people who were official preachers in the church.[26] If Dominic and his associates put in a bid for the term, that means that they were wanting to be recognised as preachers; and in as much as they were appropriating the term to their own organisation, they were making a move not unlike that made by the Franciscans when they took over the notion of the 'three orders'.

[24] Both *religio* and *ordo* are tricky words, and either can serve to give greater precision to the other. *Religio* by this time had a well-established, more or less technical, sense, so that people had a reasonably clear notion of what they meant by such phrases as *transire ad religionem*, which was used, in conjunction with *regulares*, in each of the five Compilationes which preceded Gregory IX's Decretals (E. Friedberg, ed., *Quinque Compilationes Antiquae*, Leipzig 1882, pp. 38-39, 89, 123-124, 143, 175-176). Canonists might worry about the exact boundaries of *religio* (cf. the excerpt from Hostiensis in G.G. Meersseman, *Dossier de l'Ordre de la Pénitence au XIIIᵉ siècle*, Fribourg 1961, pp. 308-309), but by and large people knew clearly enough where to draw the line. Thus, in his *ad status* sermon material, Humbert of Romans has a series on different kinds of religious, ending with the Humiliati, who are religious; this is followed by the 'fratres de penitentia', who are explicitly not religious (Hagenau 1508, Book I nos. 38, 39). And indeed they were not religious, since they could leave the 'fraternity' to 'enter religion' (*Memoriale* 31, in Meersseman, *Dossier* … p.109). But, since religious in the narrow sense could obviously not be allowed a total monopoly of the word 'religion', which was also the name of an essential christian virtue, it is not surprising to find that the way of life of the penitents (who were not 'religious') can be referred to as their 'religio' (examples in Meersseman, op. cit. pp. 44-45, 51). In the broader or in the narrower sense, *religio* can be tightened up by *ordo* (as, for that matter, can *ordo* itself). Religious life in general (or the *ordo monasticus* in general) is given a more specific focus by the *ordo* of Cluny or Cîteaux, and in the latter case in particular it made no difference whether *ordo* was taken to refer primarily to a particular set of customs or whether it was felt to mean essentially a particular monastic organisation. Similarly a 'religious' way of life, which was not 'religious' in the technical sense, could be tightened up by being organized into an *ordo*, both in the sense of a more formally regulated way of life and in the sense of a more clearly organised fraternity; both processes were going on in the 'Order of Penance' in the early thirteenth century. But conversely *ordo* could refer to any class of people; if some particular class undertakes religious life (in the strict sense), it will then become an *ordo religionis* (a phrase found, for instance, in Honorius III's letter to the Franciscans, *Cum secundum*, cited in *Enchiridion de Statibus Perfectionis*, Rome 1949, p 27). In the texts we have just been looking at from the Anonymus Perusinus and the Legenda Trium Sociorum, it makes sense for Francis and his companions to answer the question put to them either by saying that they are penitents (that is their *ordo*, their category or status), but not religious, or by saying that their *religio* is that of penitents, but they are not yet organised into an *ordo*, because they have no formal rule of life and no institutional structures.

[25] I Celano 38 (ed. cit. p.30): at the time when Francis gave his brethren their first Rule, he commented on the phrase 'ut sint minores' (cf. *Regula non Bullata* 7:2), 'I want this fraternity to be called *ordo fratrum minorum*', which suggests that it was not so called at the moment. And in the prologue to the *Regula non Bullata* (which at least antedates the death of Innocent III and is probably several years older) the order is still without a name (*quicumque erit caput istius religionis*, Prol. 3). This implies that, in Francis' own mind, his fraternity was a *religio* before it was an *ordo*. By contrast the *Regula Bullata* takes the word *ordo* for granted (7:2). On the early date of the prologue to the *Regula non Bullata* see Esser, op. cit. p. 25.

[26] Cf. the detailed account of current usage by R. Ladner, in Vicaire's expanded edition of P. Mandonnet, *Saint Dominique*, Paris 1938, vol. II pp. 49-68. Of particular interest, in view of later claims that he had predicted the rise of the Order of Preachers, is Joachim's use of the phrase, well documented by Ladner. It seems clear that he does not see any significant difference between 'ordo praedicatorum', 'ordo clericorum' and 'ordo doctorum'. In his *Expositio in Apocalipsim*, Venice 1527, f.5ᵛᵃ, he says that the 'ordo praedicatorum' is characteristic of the second age, which is exactly what he says of the 'ordo clericorum' elsewhere (e.g. *Liber de Concordia Noui ac Veteris Testamenti*, ed. E. Randolph Daniel, Transactions of the American Philosophical Society vol. 73 part 8, 1983, p. 68); and he explicitly identifies the 'ordo clericorum' and the 'ordo doctorum' (*Lib. de Conc.*, ed. cit. p. 93). The 'ordo clericorum' is one of the orders in the church, not any kind of religious order; it belongs with the 'ordo monachorum' and the 'ordo coniugatorum' with which it makes up the single people of God (*Lib. de Conc.*, ed. cit. p. 68).

But whereas what Francis was doing was turning an unregulated pattern of religious behaviour into an 'ordo', and this is no doubt what he wanted the pope to confirm, what Dominic was doing, if we may believe Jordan, was turning an ecclesiastical function, preaching, into an 'ordo'. No doubt this connoted a particular way of life - Diego had seen to that. But it did not necessarily mean and would not naturally have suggested that the preachers were to be regarded as religious.

Jordan's picture of how things evolved is clear and convincing. Before 1215 there were people associated with Dominic, but they were not bound to him by any bond of obedience (Lib. 31). The turning point, which made possible the development of a proper institution, came when Peter Seilhan and Thomas put themselves under obedience to Dominic *(obtulerunt se fratri Dominico)* (Lib. 38). This is similar to the Franciscans' first promise of obedience, which appears to be linked to the transformation of their 'religio' into an 'ordo'.

Something at least very similar to what Jordan reports must have happened in fact. The pope was not being asked to confirm the status of Dominic and his companions as preachers; their *praedicatio* already had papal authority.[27] Nor was the pope being asked to approve their way of life, which he had supported from its inception.[27a] What he was being asked to confirm was precisely the new organisation of the *praedicatio* as a self-perpetuating institute. I do not see why this should not have been presented in 1215 in terms of its being an *ordo praedicatorum*.

There is nothing in the earliest sources or in the historical situation to warrant the suggestion that the *ordo praedicatorum* in 1215 was envisaged as a religious community.[28] People who were well placed to know what the position was continued to refer to Dominic as a canon of Osma until April 1216,[29] which would surely not be correct if he had been head of a new religious community. It is only after the adoption of the Rule of St Augustine that we find Dominic called 'prior of

---

[27] Cf. above, note 4.

[27a] In his article, 'Le Modèle Évangélique des Apôtres à l'Origine de l'Ordre de Saint Dominique' (*Heresis* 1989 pp. 323-350), Vicaire takes Jordan to mean that Dominic and Fulk asked Innocent for the 'confirmation d'un "propos" religieux qui serait et s'appellerait des Prêcheurs' (p.328), which brings out a nuance which is certainly present, but is nevertheless overtranslated. Being a preacher, as understood by Diego, entailed the adoption of a particular way of life, but it was not this, as such, that Innocent was being asked to confirm.

[28] According to Humbert of Romans (*Opera de Vita Regulari*, ed. J.J. Berthier, vol. II, Rome 1889, p.3), Dominic wanted 'to obtain from the pope ... a new, strict Rule'; since they failed to obtain such a Rule, the brethren adopted from the constitutions of various canons 'quod arduum, quod decorum, quod discretum invenerunt in illis' and added more on their own account. It is difficult to know what credence to give to this tale. Jordan is surely right to imply that, in 1216, they only took over existing legislation and did not create any of their own. On the other hand, it is likely that Fulk and Dominic made it clear to the pope what the preachers' propositum was, i.e. that they intended to live by the *regula apostolica*, i.e. in mendicancy. That this would be regarded as an exceptionally strict rule is shown by the story of Innocent's reaction to Francis (II Celano 16, ed. cit. p. 140; fuller in Anon. Perus. 34a). If this is the truth of what Humbert is saying, it does not, of itself, imply that Dominic and his preachers were presenting themselves as religious.

[29] K 71, one of whose signatories is the prior of Prouille, Natalis. It is perhaps significant that on 13 December 1217 Simon de Montfort refers to Dominic simply as 'canonicus' (K 84), whereas before he called him 'canon of Osma' (K 50). After the adoption of the Rule and the gift of St. Romanus, Dominic was a canon of St Romanus, not Osma.

St Romanus'.[30] But there were no doubt certain similarities between Dominic's preachers and a religious community. As Jordan says, they began at this time 'to conform themselves to the manners of religious' (Lib. 38) (which would be an odd thing to say if they were actually religious). They evidently wore some sort of habit,[31] and new members of the community made profession in the hand of Dominic, repeating the gesture of self-oblation no doubt used by Peter Seilhan and Thomas.[32] But they were not religious, properly speaking. They had no rule except the *regula apostolica* inherited from Diego, and no formal customary.

On the other hand, they were clearly an institution, not an ad hoc group of individuals. On 25 April 1215 Peter Seilhan and his brother divided up their property, and Peter's share passed to Dominic, who received it 'pro eodem Petro Seilano et pro se et pro omnibus suis successoribus et habitatoribus domus quam idem dominus Dominicus constituerat' (K 62). The 'domus' had clearly already been established.[33] Early in the summer Fulk gave it its official charter (K 63), in which mention is made of people who may join it in the future. It looks as if the community had the right to recruit its own

[30] In fact Bertrand of Garrigues was prior of St Romanus (K 74 etc.), but in December 1216 the pope presumably did not know what else to call Dominic. It was perhaps with a view to resolving the resulting ambiguity that Dominic had the Bull reissued with slightly different wording shortly afterwards (K 81), making it clear that it was he, Dominic, not prior Bertrand, who would have to approve anyone's leaving St Romanus. Bernard Gui claimed to have documentary evidence that Dominic was called 'prior of Prouille' in 1207, but the document in question was certainly a forgery (cf. Koudelka, AFP 28 (1958) pp. 100-111). Koudelka himself is wrong to identify the unnamed prior of Prouille alluded to in K 65 and 66 as Dominic; the prior at the time was Natalis (MOPH XXIV p. 24).

[31] John of Spain received the habit from Dominic and made profession in his hand on St Augustine's day 1215, as we learn from his own account (MOPH XVI. 142). But all sorts of people wore a distinctive habit, including the Albigensians (cf. K 61) and the Poor Catholics (Meersseman, *Dossier* ... p. 283). And there may have been a particularly apostolic reason for the preachers to wear a common habit. In 1201 Innocent III decreed a special provision for the mission in Livonia, under which all the missionaries, whatever their religious profession, were to wear the same habit and practise the same observances. Although Innocent made no attempt to repeat this experiment elsewhere, it was clearly regarded as having more general application, since his decree was included in the official Compilatio Tertia in 1210. On all this, see Michele Maccarrone, *Studi su Innocenzo III*, Padua 1972, pp. 262-272. It is worth remarking that the compiler of Innocent's decretals was no other than Peter of Benevento, the legate who was Dominic's superior in the south of France in 1215.

[32] Cf. the previous note. 'Profiteri' did not necessarily mean religious profession; it could be used with reference to any public protestation that one was going to live in accordance with some formally defined way of life. The 1235 Rule of the Militia of Jesus Christ, for instance, specifies that its new recruits make profession (Meersseman, *Dossier* ... pp. 294-295). Cf. also the ruling in the 1228 Dominican constitutions: 'prohibemus ne aliquis de cetero aliquam tondeat vel induat vel ad professionem recipiat' (text in A.H. Thomas, *De oudste Constituties van de Dominicanen*, Louvain 1965, p. 360; for the date, ibid. p. 283). From Jordan's commentary on this (Letter 48, MOPH XXIII p.54) it is clear that it is not religious profession that is meant, but a profession of chastity in the world. Meersseman (op. cit. p. 118) is right to apply the whole prohibition to 'la réception d'une femme dans l'état pénitentiel'. John of Spain's own profession 'in manu' is closer to the self-oblation of Peter Seilhan and Thomas than it is to the profession of a monk or canon.

[33] It is generally assumed that Peter and Thomas made their self-oblation before this, but Jordan (Lib. 38) implies a date rather later in the year, so possibly we should not include them in the community at this stage, though K 62 makes it clear that Peter is putting himself in a position where he can no longer use his property independently of Dominic. Who else was there? If we were right to maintain that Diego contributed more people than just Dominic to the mission in Languedoc (cf. above, note 2), we may presume that there were some Spaniards in the community, including presumably the other Dominic, who was already with St Dominic in 1207 (Lib. 31). Stephen of Metz was with Dominic in Carcassonne in 1213 (MOPH XVI pp. 324-325) and is listed as one of those present when the Rule was chosen in 1216 (MOPH XXII pp. 155-156), so he was probably there in 1215. If we date Humbert's story of Dominic and six companions attending Alexander of Stavensby's lectures in Toulouse to this early period, as it is tempting to do, that would indicate a community of at least seven in Toulouse, including Dominic (MOPH XVI pp. 400-401; cf. M.H. Vicaire, *Dominique et ses Prêcheurs* pp. 60-65). William Claret had long been associated with Dominic (Lib. 29) and is listed as being present in 1216 (MOPH XXII p. 156), and may have been part of the community in 1215, though on the whole he is associated with Prouille more than with Toulouse (he seems to be representing Prouille in K 70, 2 March 1216, and in K 82, 31 March 1217).

members and to impart to them its mandate to preach.[34] Nothing is said about its being a religious community, but there is a reference to the preachers' *propositum*, to travel on foot in evangelical poverty, preaching the word of gospel truth. They propose to travel *religiose*, which does not of course mean that they will travel 'as religious'. The phrase is echoed, perhaps deliberately, in the 1220 Constitutions, which provide an admirable commentary on what it means: preachers are to comport themselves '*honeste et religiose*, like men of the gospel, following in the steps of their Saviour, speaking with God or about God with each other and with their neighbours'.[35]

When Fulk and Dominic presented themselves to the pope in October 1215, they asked him to confirm both their *ordo praedicatorum* and its revenues (Lib. 40). I have suggested that there is no reason why they should not have used the phrase 'ordo praedicatorum', though if they had used a language with a choice of articles, I presume. that they would have asked for the community in Toulouse to be recognised as an order of preachers, not as *The* Order of Preachers. Within the general category of the order of preachers (all official preachers in the church), they wanted the pope to confirm their right to be and to be called an *ordo* of preachers, that is, a structured group of preachers with a way of life appropriate to preachers.

Innocent could be expected to be sympathetic. He had supported Diego's initiative, and his approval of Durandus' Poor Catholics showed that he was prepared to support such associations of clerics living in poverty and devoting themselves to the campaign against heresy, without fitting neatly into any currently available category, either religious or clerical.[36] And Dominic's position was stronger than that of Durandus, since he was already the official head of the papal mission in Languedoc. Nevertheless, the pope refused to give him what he wanted. All he did was issue a letter confirming the properties of Prouille (K 65), and it is interesting that he did not use the standard letter which had long been available for taking religious communities under papal protection, *Religiosam vitam eligentibus*.[37] The religious status of Prouille is thus left unclear, even though it had for years been accepted locally as a monastery. With regard to Toulouse, Innocent advised Dominic to discuss with his brethren the choice of a religious Rule.

What Innocent was suggesting was surely that the *ordo praedicatorum* in Toulouse

---

[34] This could no doubt be seen as an extension of the powers granted by Innocent III to the original Predicatio (K 4).

[35] Thomas, op. cit. p. 363. One point which is left totally unclear is what provision was made for the training and ordination of recruits who were not already priests. Diego probably intended to recruit people who were already clerics, preferably already priests, but it is not clear that Peter Seilhan or Thomas were clerics, and it is unlikely that all Dominic's first recruits were already priests. But it is typical of the documents of the period that ordination seems not to interest anyone at all. It was presumably taken for granted that young Dominicans would be ordained, probably as soon as they reached the required age.

[36] Dominic, and perhaps some of his companions, were already religious, and as such technically belonged elsewhere, though there was no doubt about their good standing: they had been deputed by their bishop and accepted into the Languedoc mission on the authority of the pope. They were not at all in the same position as the freelance preachers the Council of Paris tried to curb, who were keen to take on responsibility for the preaching in a particular territory on a commercial basis (Mansi XXII 821, 901). Dominic and his preachers were given an official position in the diocese of Toulouse, but not as ordinary secular clergy; this is shown by the provision that is made for their financial support, which is quite different from that made for the support of poor diocesan clergy. Cf. Simon Tugwell, 'Dominic the Founder', *Dominican Ashram* 4 (1985) p.85.

[37] There are many instances of this formula being used, not least in the reign of Innocent III; cf. the index in C.R. and M.G. Cheney, *The Letters of Pope Innocent III*, Oxford 1967.

should become a religious community. If they agreed to this suggestion, the in line with Innocent's own policy, shortly to be formally promulgated by the Council, they ought to choose an already approved Rule. Should they prefer not to become religious, they would naturally be entirely unaffected by anything the Council might say about religious.[38]

It is not difficult to surmise what was in Innocent's mind. He had seen how difficult it was for less formal groups, like the Poor Catholics, to win acceptance in the church, in spite of papal support, and he did not want the same thing to happen to Dominic's preachers. Dominic was therefore faced with a situation curiously similar to that of 1206. Then they needed to adopt an apostolic identity to win the confidence of their audience; now, as Koudelka has suggested, they needed a respectable identity which would win them the confidence of the church.[39]

Dominic and his brethren accepted the pope's advice and, some time between April and July 1216,[40] they decided to adopt the Rule of St Augustine and some 'strict customs *(arctiores consuetudines)* about food fasting, bedding and the use of wool' (Lib. 42).[41] On this basis the new pope, Honorius III, on 22 December 1216, issued *Religiosam vitam eligentibus* in their favour (K 77). In the eyes of the church they were canons regular, under papal protection. Not a word was said of their being an *ordo praedicatorum*.

Was this a major setback for Dominic's plans? Did it make any real difference to the preachers? What did Dominic think of it all?

As usual, we do not know what Dominic thought, we only know what he did. And he did all he could to ensure that his brethren were good canons, faithful to their regular life and its observances. As in 1206, he threw himself whole-heartedly into the way of life his ecclesiastical superiors had let him in for. Otherwise his personal reaction is unknown to us, and was probably unimportant to him.

Since 1206 his position as a canon regular had meant little in practice, but now he had to explore, with his brethren, what was involved in being both an apostolic preacher and a canon regular. And it was not plain sailing. It is no doubt true that many of the observances and austerities which were formally adopted in 1216 were already familiar to him and his associates.[42] The austerities in particular had been part of the missionary programme since 1206. But the story is more complicated than that. The customs adopted in 1216 were not just a formalisation of what the preachers were already doing,

---

[38] This would still have been true even if the *ordo praedicatorum* in Toulouse had been founded after the council, as Constitution 13 applied only to religious in the strict sense. For an excellent commentary on the Constitution, see Maccarrone, op. cit. pp. 307-327.

[39] AFP 33 (1963) pp. 93-94; *Dominikus* pp. 46-47.

[40] On 21 April Dominic is still called a canon of Osma (K 71); in July he and his companions are given the church of St Romanus (K 73), which implies that they have already made their decision to become a religious community, as otherwise they would not have needed a church of their own.

[41] I have examined the development of the earliest Dominican legislation in 'Dominic the Founder', *Dominican Ashram* 4 (1985) pp. 80-96, 122-145.

[42] This is suggested by Vicaire, AFP 54 (1984) pp. 31-36.

and there is evidence that some of them proved difficult to reconcile with the apostolic labours of the brethren. It is a curious fact that on all four points mentioned by Jordan, the Order later had to rewrite its customary, and in three of the four cases the reason was that the original customary was ill-adapted to the needs of itinerant preachers.[43] The fasting laws which they adopted proved unworkable almost at once, so that Dominic habitually dispensed his companions from them when they were travelling.[44] It also seems that they took from somewhere a principle of observing the monastic great silence even on the road,[45] which cannot have made much sense and nothing more is heard of it in the later customary, which had an entirely new chapter on silence, probably substituted in 1220.[46] Just to make sure that nothing had been overlooked, a few words were added to the prologue of the customary, probably in 1220, specifying that the whole first distinction - essentially the customs adopted in 1216 - applied to the brethren only 'in their monastery'.[47]

Since the 1216 customary proved unsatisfactory for the *ordo praedicatorum,* we may wonder why they adopted it in the first place. It is difficult to see what answer we can give, except that it seemed important in 1216 to make the brethren's new identity as respectable canons as visible and public as possible. The points needing to be changed later almost all concerned the life of the brethren outside the monastery. This tends to confirm Koudelka's interpretation, that the 1216 customs were meant to give the preachers an uncontroversial identity to facilitate their acceptance by the church. By 1220, thanks to a remarkable succession of papal bulls, in which it is not hard to see the growing influence of Dominic himself, the value of the *ordo praedicatorum* as such was much more publicly recognised, so it no longer needed to veil its novelty behind the *ordo canonicus.*[48]

There were other problems too. Canons regular were committed to the service of particular churches, which was contrary to the itinerant preaching for which the *ordo praedicatorum* had been established. And canons, when they did travel, were expected to travel on horseback, with money in their purses - there was even a law to this effect in the north of France.[49] All of this went completely against the mendicancy which was central to Diego's vision of the apostolic life. In his testimony in the canonization process of St Dominic, John of Spain harks back to a time when 'the Order of Preachers carried money

---

[43] See Primitive Constitutions I 6, I 8 and I 10 (edited in Thomas, op. cit.). The brethren can be dispensed from the long fast from 14 September until Easter because of their work, and travellers are routinely allowed two meals a day throughout most of the year. The usual ban on eating meat is mitigated for travellers. And they are allowed to use whatever bedding is provided. Even the chapter on woollen clothes was changed (I 18), but this was due to the demands of mendicancy, not travelling: the brethren must use cheap material, but not necessarily wool, if it is hard to come by. Although the dating of these alterations is not certain, it is likely they all go back to 1220.

[44] Cf. Tugwell, art. cit. pp. 134-135.

[45] Ibid. p. 134.

[46] I 17. Again the dating is uncertain, but 1220 is as likely as any later date.

[47] Thomas, op. cit. p. 312.

[48] The succession of Bulls has been excellently studied by V.J. Koudelka, 'Notes sur le Cartulaire de S. Dominique', II and III, AFP 33 (1963) pp. 89-120, and 34 (1964) pp. 5-44.

[49] Council of Paris (1212) II 11 (Mansi XXII 828).

with them when they travelled and rode on horseback and wore surplices'.[50] Even if, as is often supposed, this was true only of the brethren in Paris, it was a serious abandonment of the original idea of the *ordo praedicatorum,* but what else could they do? In Paris, at any rate, Fulk's statute for the preachers had no authority, so the Dominicans had no legal existence except as canons regular and as such they were bound by the church's laws concerning canons, in which mendicancy was considered a disgrace.[51]

The *ordo canonicus* could easily have swallowed up the *ordo praedicatorum.* If it did not do so, this is largely due to Dominic, who toiled on all fronts to save Diego's vision. As John of Spain reports, Dominic worked hard to persuade the brethren to accept mendicancy.[52] He also worked hard at the papal court. But it was not until 1220 that he thought the time was ripe for an attempt to resume and complete the constitutional clarification of how the Order of Preachers was to operate.[53]

Meanwhile what of Prouille? In 1216 Prouille was listed among the possessions of St Romanus (K 77), but its religious status was once again left unclear. In 1218 the prior of Prouille sought and obtained a new issue of *Religiosam vitam eligentibus* in its favour (K 90), which makes it appear that the developments in Toulouse in 1216 had left Prouille unaffected. It is perhaps significant in this connection that Bernard Gui does not list the prior of Prouille, Natalis, among those who chose the Rule of St Augustine with Dominic in 1216. The discussion in 1216 concerned only the community in Toulouse.[53a]

Vicaire is right to indicate that our sources do not give the impression that there was a major upheaval in 1216,[54] but this was not because it made little or no difference to the preachers to become canons, it was because Dominic was essentially a pragmatist, in no undue hurry to tie up all the loose ends in some great scheme. Where an idealist like

---

[50] MOPH XVI p. 144. The Council of Montpellier in 1215 insisted on canons wearing surplices (Mansi XXII 945).

[51] Council of Paris, loc. cit. (cf. above, note 49). It is an interesting indication of how people perceived the Dominicans in the north of France that the Annales Normannici regards 'ordo Iacobitarum' as their original name, and comments that 'sibi postmodum nomen imposuerunt predicatorum' (MGH SS XXVI p. 514).

[52] MOPH XVI p.144. Dominic even got Honorius III to address a letter on the subject to the brethren (K 111). Vicaire, AFP 54 (1984) p.21, makes the good point that K 111 implies that the Dominicans had already committed themselves to mendicancy and suggests that such a commitment could only have been made at the 'General Chapter' of 1216. But in that case the brethren described by John of Spain were being flagrantly untrue to their own undertaking, and it is odd that he should speak so casually about it. And Dominic would surely have urged their own previous commitment, whereas it sounds as if he is arguing for a new decision to be made. It seems much more likely that the earlier commitment to mendicancy was enshrined only in Fulk's charter of 1215, which of course had no validity outside his own diocese.

[53] Dominic seems to have been quite deliberate in allowing himself this long to sort things out; in 1217 he seems to reckon on another two years (MOPH XVI p. 133).

[53a] Locally there was never any doubt that St Romanus and Prouille belonged together, as we can see from K 82: on 31 March 1217 a contested gift to Prouille was finally accepted as belonging to Prouille, but the document recording the settlement presents it as being made with the community of St Romanus, though when it comes to the turn of the Dominicans to sign it they make it clear that they are speaking for both St Romanus and Prouille. But the link that everyone knew about locally had still not been enshrined in any universally recognised, precise formula. If Bernard Gui is right to include William Claret among those who chose the Rule with Dominic in 1216 (MOPH XXII p. 156), he was presumably representing Prouille. But the pope had, quite properly, called for a unanimous decision made by all the parties concerned (Lib. 41), in accordance with the well-known principle of *quod omnes tangit,* so if Prouille as an institution had been regarded as directly involved in the discussion about the Rule, all its members should have been present.

[54] AFP 54 (1984) pp. 7-8.

Francis was perturbed by official attempts to turn his brethren into a more conventional religious order,[55] Dominic was always prepared to adapt his practice and his ideas to the demands of a new situation. If it was desirable to turn his preachers into canons, let them be turned into canons. It was a new adventure, not a threat, and its implications must be given time to emerge and be dealt with (or left to sort themselves out).

For Scheeben, Innocent's intervention marks a tragic failure to support what should have been a radically new venture in the church.[56] But this presupposes that there was a far clearer and narrower apostolic project than we have any right to ascribe to Diego or to Dominic. Thanks to Dominic's capacity to adapt himself to all kinds of new demands, without losing sight of the essentials of what he was doing already, the *ordo praedicatorum* emerged in 1220 enriched by the *ordo canonicus*, not engulfed by it, and endowed with a stable conventual basis which it would probably otherwise have lacked.[57]. And it was the *ordo praedicatorum* that prevailed. The preachers did not make a new beginning in 1216, when they became canons. There is no evidence that they made any new religious profession to solemnise their new status, and indeed they never did adopt a rite or formula of profession similar to those of the canons.[58] And when they came to revise and complete their legislation precisely as an Order of Preachers in 1220 they assured the priority of the *ordo praedicatorum* by inserting into the Constitutions the sweeping principle that any canonical observance could be dispensed by any superior, if it was likely to interfere with the apostolic work for which the order was founded.[59] Regular observance, and indeed a fairly strict observance, at least in theory, remained an integral part of Dominican life, but henceforth it was always to be the observance of the Order of Preachers, not the observance of canons regular. After 1220 the Dominicans progressively dropped from their Constitutions all terminology proper to canons regular.[60]

Ironically, the pope who tried to tidy up the religious map by insisting on the use of

---

[55] Cf. *Scripta Leonis*, ed. Rosalind B. Brooke, Oxford 1970, pp. 286-288.

[56] 'Dominikaner oder Innozentianer', AFP 9 (1939), especially pp. 296-297.

[57] In 1216 the *ordo canonicus* was adopted for strategic reasons, maybe, just as in 1206 mendicancy was adopted for strategic reasons, but in neither case would it be right to imagine that Dominic (or Diego) was thinking of a merely temporary expedient. Just as Dominic plainly realised an intrinsic value in the poverty of the preacher, so he surely realised the intrinsic value of religious observance; otherwise, why did he not set about eliminating it or at least cutting it down in 1220 or 1221? Unfortunately one of the most important pieces of evidence for Dominic's attitude to regular observance is ambiguous. According to Ferrandus 46 (MOPH XVI p. 245), on his deathbed he summoned twelve of the brethren in Bologna to him and exhorted them 'ad canonice religionis observantiam'; but Ferrandus is probably drawing only on Jordan, who says that Dominic urged the twelve brethren 'ad fervorem et promotionem ordinis' (Lib. 92). Almost all modern translators of Jordan take him to mean that Dominic was urging the brethren to 'promote the Order', in which case Ferrandus' account is tendentious. But is it not more likely that Ferrandus took *ordo* in Jordan's text to mean 'observance', in which case he was paraphrasing it quite accurately? The few eye-witness accounts we have of Dominic's deathbed (MOPH XVI pp. 126, 128-130, 151-152) do not help us to decide, but it is at least possible that Ferrandus' interpretation of Jordan is correct.

[58] Cf. Simon Tugwell, 'Dominican Profession in the Thirteenth Century', AFP 53 (1983) pp. 5-52.

[59] Thomas, op. cit. p. 311.

[60] Raymund of Pennafort's edition of the Constitutions in 1241 eliminates *monasterium* from the Prologue and *canonici* from the chapter on laybrothers (ed. R. Creytens, AFP 18 (1948) pp. 30, 67-68). The one remaining instance of *canonicus* was suppressed by the General Chapters of 1249-1251, which also eliminated the description of the Constitutions as a 'customary' (MOPH III pp. 43-44, 48-49, 55).

already approved rules, succeeded in the outcome in acting as midwife to an order whose novelty was so manifest that in 1255 there was a curial plan, supported by Alexander IV, to reshape Dominican legislation in its entirety and produce a new Dominican Rule. It was the order, not the papacy, that objected.[61]

So the Dominicans turned out not to be canons after all. But their dual inheritance, from the apostolic vision of Diego and the regular life of the canons, undoubtedly gave the order its characteristic stamp, and the two disparate ingredients in its make-up have lived ever after in a tension that has been, on the whole, fruitful, though it has also provided a never-failing topic for argument among the friars and their historians.

---

[61] The details of the story are not entirely clear, but the initiative for a new Dominican Rule seems to have come from the Dominican cardinal, Hugh of St Cher; it looks as if there was also some dissatisfaction among the brethren with the Rule of St Augustine. Cf. P. Mandonnet and M.H. Vicaire, *Saint Dominique*, vol. II pp. 265-272; R. Creytens, AFP 33 (1963) pp. 135-139.

SOME ASPECTS OF THE LONDON MENDICANTS

by

Jens Roehrkasten

Two trends can be noticed in the recent historiography on the mendicant orders: On the one hand there is a tendency to set the studies in a larger regional context[1], either to study the friars' impact on a larger area or - as Le Goff attempted - to use the analysis of mendicant development for some other purpose, e.g. as an indicator for the growth of towns. In a different approach the focus was shifted towards the study of the friars' activities and functions in individual towns[2]. In these texts several aspects recurred with some regularity so that a pattern of questions was formed dealing with what may be regarded as the typical problems of mendicant life in an urban environment. What were the friars' relations with the civic administration, were they involved in local politics in any way? Suspicion for such an involvement could already be justified if personal connections between individual convents and leading families can be proved. Did members of the urban patriciate join the friars and did the mendicants retain their attractiveness for these classes throughout the middle ages? Other questions of this sort concern the friars' relations with the individual groups of the populations. Were they in any way involved in the various organisations founded by merchants and artisans? Who were their supporters? Equally the friars' functions in the towns' religious and cultural life have to be defined. In this respect the role of their schools and libraries is of importance as well as their preaching activity. Especially the latter frequently led to conflict with the parish clergy and the other religious institutions in the towns. Consequently the mendicants relations with other ecclesiastical organisations, regular as well as secular, offer another field for enquiry. The problem of the life in the convents themselves has to be added to this ambitious list. Often very little is known about the friars' economic management, sometimes even the legal status of their properties. How much of their original idealism survived the realities of urban life? There could be significant differences in the adherence to mendicant principles and at times the term "mendicants", subsuming the four great orders as well as a number of smaller or less successful ones most of which did not survive the second council of Lyons of 1274, may be misleading. There could well be tensions among different mendicant convents within a town and it has also to be kept in mind that each convent was bound into the regional as well as an international organisation of its order. Although it is not complete, this list forms a good starting point for an investigation.

London is well suited to be the object of such a study. By the time of the friars' arrival the city had been the kingdom's centre of population and commerce for centuries. It importance as a place of production and trade was equalled by its significance in the ecclesiastical organisation, as the centre of one of the kingdom's most important

---

[1] B.E.J. Stüdeli, *Minoritenniederlassungen und mittelalterliche Stadt*, 1969. E. Fügedi, 'La formation des villes et les ordres mendiants en Hongrie,' *Annales ESC* 25 (1970) 966-987. J. Le Goff, 'Ordres mendiants et urbanisation dans la France médiévale,' ibid. 924-946. H. Martin, *Les ordres mendiants en Bretagne*, 1975.

[2] M. Wehrli-Johns, *Geschichte des Züricher Predigerkonvents*, 1980. F. Rapp, 'Die Mendikanten und die Strassburger Gesellschaft am Ende des Mittelalters,' in: *Stellung und Wirksamkeit der Bettelorden in der städtischen Gesellschaft*, ed. K. Elm, 1981. B. Neidiger, *Mendikanten zwischen Ordensideal und städtischer Realität. Untersuchungen zum wirtschaftlichen Verhalten der Bettelorden in Basel*, 1981. H.-J. Schmidt, *Bettelorden in Trier*, 1986.

bishoprics. By the 13th century at least eight religious houses had been established within the walls or in the vicinity. There were six hospitals, and five further religious institutions were to follow in the 13th century[3], three in the 14th century[4], adding to the diversity offered by 103 parish churches. The city's urban administration developed into a sophisticated organisation and its political leaders more than once took an active part in national politics. London also became the seat of government, important departments of the royal administration established their permanent basis there.

Another reason for choosing London is the uneven distribution of attention its mendicant convents have received. Antiquarian interest began in the first half of the 16th century and found its first culmination with John Stow. This is not the place to give a detailed account of the historiography but it is important to note that the information collected by Stow, later gradually supplemented by material from the Public Records and city archives formed the basis even of M. Reddan's survey[5]. Apart from her articles the most recent publications are based on research conducted in the 1950s and 1960s, on the Austin Friars by Roth[6] and the Carmelites by Egan and Du Boulay[7], whereas studies of the other London mendicant convents are all of an earlier date.[8] There is sufficient justification to attempt a comprehensive study of the London friaries.

Such a complete survey is, of course, not intended in this short paper. Instead I should like to sketch out one aspect which sets London apart from most other medieval towns and makes the London friaries exceptional - their connection with the kings and the royal family, which began already in the 13th century, shortly after the first convents, those of the Dominicans and Franciscans, had been established in the city. The intention is not so much to communicate new results as to discuss the potential of future work.

Once the mendicant concept of a new religious life had proved to be successful Henry III included the friars among the ecclesiastical institutions who benefited from his alms and other contributions. The London houses figure prominently among them. Royal involvement and assistance can be noticed in three areas: the foundation of new convents, the construction of conventual buildings and a general support of the friaries. An example for the latter is a royal order of 1233, when 100 pairs of shoes were to be given to the London Dominicans and 700 yards of cloth were deemed necessary to provide for both the Black and the Grey Friars[9]. According to Thomas of Eccleston's graphic account

[3] They were S. Helen's Bishopsgate (before 1216), the Domus Conversorum (1232), the hospital of S. Thomas of Acon (c.1235), the hospital of S. Mary of Bethlehem (1247) and the hospital of S. Anthony (c.1254).

[4] The hospital of S. Mary Cripplegate (1331), S. Mary Graces (1350), the Charterhouse (1370/71).

[5] VCH *London*, 1909, 498 - 519.

[6] F. Roth, *The English Austin Friars*, 1249 - 1538, 2 vols, 1961 - 1966, I, 286-296.

[7] K.J. Egan, The Establishment and Early Development of the Carmelite order in England, PhD Cambridge 1965. F.R.H. DuBoulay, 'The Quarrel Between the Carmelite Friars and the Secular Clergy of London 1464 - 68', *JEH* 6 (1955) 156 - 174.

[8] C.L. Kingsford, *The Grey Friars of London*, 1915. A.F.C. Bourdillon, *The order of Minoresses in England*, 1926. H.F. Chettle, 'The Friars of the Sack in England,' *Downside Review* 63 (1945) 239 - 245, cf. 245. W.A. Hinnebusch, *The Early English Friars Preachers*, 1951, 20seq.

[9] Cal. Liberate Rolls 1226 - 40, 233/4, cf. Hinnebusch, *Early English Friars Preachers*, 29.

the friars were still faced with severe living conditions in these early years[10]. In the following decades the Dominicans and Franciscans in particular profited from royal donations consisting of building material, cash or clothing. The building of their convents coincided with Henry III's building projects in Westminster and the two houses profited sometimes by receiving stone and timber from there[11]. Occasionally the overseers of the royal works seem to have borrowed from the friars' building sites but this is only known because the material was returned[12]. After the Carmelites had come to London in 1247[13] they were given equal assistance when their convent was built[14], while the Austin Friars, founded by Humphrey de Bohun, earl of Hereford and Essex in 1253, received donations[15].

The orders mentioned so far had found their initial support either among the citizens or the aristocracy. While the Grey Friars had received help from John Travers and other London citizens, the Dominicans had found their first patron in Peter de Roches then in Hubert de Burgh. The Carmelite house was possibly founded by Sir Richard de Grey, one of the knights who had accompanied Richard of Cornwall on his crusade. The only true royal foundation of a mendicant house in London seems to have been that of the Friars of the Penitence of Jesus Christ, better known as the Friars of the Sack, who were given 100 marks for the purchase of a site in London by Henry III[16] but this is the only indication of exceptional royal interest in this house.

Edward I continued the policy of support. When decades of royal assistance for the fabric of the Black Friars' convent at Holborn seemed to have been in vain - the Dominicans sold this property and moved to a site at Baynard's Castle in 1278 - he maintained his help for the new building project. The Franciscans could begin a complete rebuilding of their church in 1302 with the help of queen Margaret and this support was kept up by Isabella and Philippa so that by the mid-14th century the Grey Friars' church was known for its architectural splendour and the friars were even criticized for their deviation from original mendicant principles.[17]

It was a usual practice of Edward I, his son and grandson, to pay alms and pittances to the friars and sometimes other regular clergy upon their arrival in a town. These payments were recorded in the household accounts. Unfortunately this valuable information survives only for very short periods. In 1278 the London mendicants received royal alms amounting to £26 - 12 - 8, most of it going to the Dominicans and

---

[10] Thomas of Eccleston, *Tractatus de Adventu Fratrum Minorum in Angliam*, ed. A.G. Little, 1951, 8, 9.

[11] E.g. *Cal. Close Rolls 1261-64*, 169.

[12] *Cal. Close Rolls 1237 - 42*, 80.

[13] Egan, *Establishment*, 51.

[14] *Cal. Close Rolls 1272 -79*, 261

[15] Roth, *English Austin Friars*, I, 286.

[16] PRO; E 403 15A m 1.

[17] Kingsford, *Grey Friars*, 36 - 38.

Franciscans who received £9 - 15 - 6 and £9 -10 - 0 respectively, while the Austin Friars obtained £2 - 9 - 11 and the Carmelites £2. The rest was given to the Friars of the Cross, the Friars of the Sack and the Friars de Areno[18]. Royal pittances to the London friars in 1285 totalled £83 -13- 1[19]. Similar calculations can be made for 1289/90, 1296/97, 1300/1301, when Edward I paid more than £36 towards the construction of a chapel of S. Louis at the Grey Friars[20], and for 15 years in the first quarter of the 14th century, but these entries become much less common under Edward III and from Richard II's reign onwards no such payments are recorded. It has yet to be decided whether this is due to a change in the way the accounts were kept or to a gradual loss of royal interest in the friars.

During Edward II's reign the amounts paid reflect the convents' size but this does not mean that the payments were always standardised. A gift of money was obviously a sign of royal favour, on the other hand, royal favour could also be expressed in a different form. Edward I, for example, is known to have taken meals together with the London Dominicans at their house[21], just one of many indications of the close links between several English kings and this order from whose ranks the royal confessors were chosen between 1256 and 1400. Even during the king's absence payments were sometimes handed over by the royal confessor[22]. A first glance at the royal household accounts indicates that the royal attention shown to the London friars exceeds that shown to other English mendicant houses[23].

---

[18] PRO C 47/4/1 fol. 4v, 8v, 17v, 19r, 20r, v, 23v, 24r, v, 44v, 45v, 50r, v.

[19] PRO C 47/4/2.

[20] Kingsford, *Grey Friars*, 202/3; BL MS Add 7966A fol. 40v.

[21] PRO C 47/4/4 fol. 39r.

[22] PRO E 101/376/7 fol. 5r.

[23] It has to be pointed out, however, that the London friars did not receive regular royal stipends, like the Dominicans of Chester, PRO C 62 51 m 3, and the Franciscans and Dominicans of Oxford and Cambridge, e.g. PRO E 404/4/23 Nr. 69.

BENEDICTINE MONK SCHOLARS AS TEACHERS AND PREACHERS IN THE LATER MIDDLE AGES : EVIDENCE FROM WORCESTER CATHEDRAL PRIORY

by

Joan Greatrex

The earliest extant manuscript of the Benedictine Rule was written about 700 A.D. in England, probably at Worcester.[1] It is perhaps surprising that more than two centuries were to elapse before Benedictine monks were established in the cathedral chapter there by the monastic reformer and bishop, St. Oswald, who, along with other young Englishmen of the day, had received his monastic training at the French abbey of Fleury on the Loire.[2] Seeing in the Rule the embodiment of the religious ideal appropriate to the needs of their time, he and his episcopal colleagues promoted it both as a source of inspiration for all men and also as a practical guide for those who sought to enter upon the way of perfection in the cloister.

The revival and reorganisation of monastic life in the tenth century resulted in the establishment of many new monasteries as well as the reform of earlier foundations. Those who remained in the world during the unsettled years both before and after the Norman Conquest viewed these communities in their midst as beacons of light shining through the darkness of man's earthly pilgrimage, or as symbols of the heavenly Jerusalem in a world of flux. Inside the cloister the monks followed the daily routine of prayer and worship, study and manual labour laid down by St. Benedict. The monastic vocation, it should be noted, was and is to serve God and the Church by a life lived in accordance with the Gospel, in which no particular function may be considered as more than a temporary assignment under obedience. In other words, the Rule claims no more than to provide the rudiments of a fully Christian life within the monastic enclosure, with no specific obligations to those outside the gates beyond the corporal works of mercy such as hospitality and almsgiving.[3]

There is abundant evidence that the administrative competence acquired by the black monks in the management of the estates, which came to them largely through grants and bequests, was accompanied by an increasing dependence on the labour services of the local tenantry with the monks' activities confined to a supervisory role. In the same period monastic libraries were increasing their holdings, most of the manuscripts being home produced within the scriptoria which were probably modelled on the one

---

[1] It is now Ms. Hatton 48 in the Bodleian Library, Oxford. For its Worcester provenance see N.R. Ker ed., *Medieval Libraries of Great Britain*, 2nd ed., Royal Historical Society (1964) 209. D.H. Turner has attributed it to Canterbury in the handbook accompanying the Benedictine fifteenth centenary exhibition, *The Benedictines in Britain*, British Library Series no.3 (1980) 14, although Ker has rejected the Canterbury provenance (*Ibid.*,40). This manuscript has been reproduced in facsimile in *Early English Manuscripts in facsimile*, xv (Copenhagen, 1968) with an introduction by D.H. Farmer who suggests (on p.25) that it may have been given by St. Wilfrid to one of the monastic communities he founded in Mercia; but the first reference to it is in the late eleventh century in the possession of Worcester cathedral.

[2] For Oswald's career see M.D. Knowles, *The Monastic Order in England*, 2nd. ed., (Cambridge 1966) 40ff.

[3] This is in contrast with many of the religious orders founded in later times, e.g., the Dominicans, who were committed to serve as preachers and teachers after their initial period of training and theological study.

introduced by Lanfranc at Canterbury in the late eleventh century.[4] By 1202 the library at Rochester cathedral priory comprised some 280 volumes according to a list drawn up by the precentor. Worcester has no medieval book catalogues but there remain over 240 bound volumes containing manuscripts which can be dated as prior to 1300[5] The shift away from manual work as prescribed in the Rule would have been gradual; but it must have been a *fait accompli* by 1277 when the General Chapter of the black monks meeting at Reading decreed that thenceforth, in place of manual work, monks were to be assigned to other occupations such as study, writing (i.e. copying and correcting manuscripts) illuminating and book-binding according to their abilities.[6]

Long before this date the Church hierarchy had approved two measures which were intended to raise the standard of education of the secular clergy by providing for lectures in every diocese. The earlier predominance of the monasteries as the chief if not the only centres of learning had been challenged: first, by the third Lateran Council in 1179 which ordered that every cathedral church should appoint a master to teach clerks and poor scholars and, secondly, by the fourth Lateran Council in 1215 which required all cathedral churches to support a master of arts and metropolitan churches a lecturer in theology. Dr. Kathleen Edwards has concluded that these educational decrees cannot be seen as innovative within the setting of the English secular cathedral close, since many of the chapters maintained flourishing schools during the course of the twelfth century.[7]

How and if this was applied to English monastic cathedrals, in which the chapter was required to act *qua* custodian of the mother church of the diocese as well as to fulfil its obligations *qua* religious community, remains unclear until the early fourteenth century.[8] About 1305 the president of the General Chapter, Abbot Wenlok of Westminster, despatched two letters to Prior John de Wyke of Worcester requesting him to restore the lectureship in the cathedral, which had been allowed to lapse, but to delay doing so if necessary rather than recall a monk from university before the completion of his studies. The abbot states that the laudable practice at Worcester of appointing a Scripture scholar as lecturer originated in a decree of the Roman pontiffs and holy fathers addressed to every cathedral church and almost everywhere observed. Moreover, he makes it clear that the teaching of both secular and regular clergy was involved, and that the lecturer's appointment included preaching.[9]

---

[4] Rachel Stockdale in *The Benedictines in Britain* (n.1 above) 62.

[5] For Rochester the manuscript reference is BL Royal Ms.5 Bxii fo2 as quoted in Stockdale, *Op.cit.,*69. For Worcester see the list in Ker (n.1 above).

[6] The statutes are printed in W.A.Pantin ed., *Documents Illustrating the Activities of the General and Provincial Chapters of the English Black Monks 1215-1540*, Camden Society, Third Series, I (1931) 64-92; for the article referred to, entitled 'De Occupacione', see p.74.

[7] K. Edwards, *The English Secular Cathedrals in the Middle Ages*, 2nd ed., (Manchester, 1967) 185-193; the two Lateran decrees, which she discusses, are in J.D. Mansi ed., *Sacrorum Conciliorum Nova et Amplissima Collectio* (Florence and Venice, 1759-98) XXII, 227-8, c.18, and *Ibid.*, 999.

[8] The monastic cathedral was primarily an English anomaly, with very few continental parallels apart from Monreale, Sicily.

[9] These two letters have been transcribed by A.F. Leach in *Documents Illustrating Early Education in Worcester, 685 to 1700*, Worcestershire Historial Society, 31(1913)29-33. The abbot was almost certainly referring to the two Lateran decrees.

About fifteen years earlier the Worcester chapter had nominated its first two monk students to be sent to Gloucester Hall, the newly founded Benedictine house of study at Oxford.[10] Behind this decision at the community level lay a collective decision with far reaching consequences for the entire Benedictine community in England. In their forward-looking resolution of 1277 the delegates at the General Chapter had announced their intention to support a programme of monastic study outside the cloister, that is, in the university setting; and they had agreed that every house should contribute toward the building of suitable accommodation at Oxford for this purpose[11] At a time when a combination of political, social and economic pressures was affecting late thirteenth century society as a whole and was also challenging the foundations of monastic life and tradition, the monks' reaction manifested itself in a number of proposals for reform and change.[12] Slow to respond they undoubtedly were in entering the mainstream of university life, where the friars had preceded them by some forty years. But by this decision the Benedictines freed themselves from the entrenchments of their recent past and introduced a new policy which allowed them to adapt to changing circumstances and still remain faithful to the spirit of the Rule[13]

As to the numbers of monks to be selected for university training and their programme of study, there appears to have been no legislation before the statutes published by the Benedictine Chapter c. 1363. These imposed Benedict XII's decree requiring one monk in twenty to be sent to university, issued regulations covering all aspects of the monk students' life and declared that the purpose of monastic studies was not to attain the peak of academic distinction but to preach and teach: *proponere verbum Dei, in disputando et predicando habiliores ... ac eciam prompciores.*[14] However, if we may judge from the information available about the first few generations of Worcester monk students, there can be little doubt that this numerical ratio together with the *ratio studiorum* had been agreed upon and implemented at an earlier date though probably not universally enforced. A close examination of the Worcester cathedral archives furnishes sufficient data to enable us to glean insights into what must have been a policy of continuing concern to maintain these educational priorities through the next two centuries, that is until the eve of the dissolution.

Although St. Wulstan's community probably contained fifty monks or possibly more, the average number between 1290 and 1540 was forty with slight fluctuations up and

---

[10] The first recorded names occur on the cellarer's account for 1291/2 and they were John de Arundel and William de Grymeley. This account has been printed in J.M. Wilson and C. Gordon, *Early Compotus Rolls of the Priory of Worcester*. Worcestershire Historial Society, 23 (1908) 13.Both names are also in A.B. Emden, *A Biographical Register of the University of Oxford to A.D.1500, [BRUO]*, 3 vols., (Oxford, 1957-9).

[11] Pantin, *Ibid., 75*, 'De Studio'.

[12] *Ibid.,* 109-119.

[13] Dom Jean Laclercq has drawn attention to the ambivalent relationship between monastic studies and the Benedictine Rule in *The Love of Learning and the Desire for God* (New York, 1961)31-32. The absence of any *ratio studiorum* prescribed by the founder and written into the Rule means that every generation of Benedictines must face the problem afresh and, when required, devise new solutions appropriate to the needs of their day.

[14] Pantin, *Op. cit.,* II, 75.

down.[15] About 530 monks have been identified to date and included in my biographical register for these 250 years, and this is probably close to the total number; of these sixty-five are known to have spent some time at Oxford and about twenty, *i.e.*, just under one third of this group, obtained a degree. Although the inevitable gaps in existing records confine the evidence to about half of this period, the lacunae are conveniently spaced and rarely exceed three or four years at any one time. With an average of forty monks at Worcester we should expect to find that there were regularly two being maintained at university, and indeed this appears to be most frequently the case whenever numbers are stated. However, I suggest that the actual ratio was closer to one in nine on the basis of calculations from the above figures.[16]

Although we are not here concerned with claustral lecturers or lectors, there was no doubt a close connection between those who taught the young monks in the cloister and those who were assigned to give courses of lectures to the public; in some instances one person assumed both of these charges. Professor William Courtenay's recent scholarly work on this subject implies that cathedral priories in the fourteenth century were competing with the mendicant orders in providing 'instruction in grammar, philosophy, and theology both to monks and to future diocesan clergy'; he cites Norwich as an example but without any supporting reference.[17] The letters of Abbot Wenlok quoted above prove that seculars had had the opportunity to attend lectures at Worcester cathedral before 1305, and a letter noted by W.A. Pantin in a Worcester manuscript lends further support to these activities. Ms. Q.20 is a commentary on the Sentences of Peter Lombard which, together with the Bible, were the text books of theology at this time.[18] It dates from the early fourteenth century; and the letter, written on the back of the last quire, indicates that both writer and recipient were monks of Worcester and lecturers in theology and that the latter was staying at St. Augustine's Canterbury and probably lecturing to the monks there. Brother John of St. Germans is known to have been teaching at St. Augustine's in 1308, and he went on to study and lecture at Paris between 1310 and 1315. Pantin has therefore suggested that Q.20 was composed by Saint Germans in preparation for his lectures. Given the existence of cathedral lectures for the clergy at large, it is highly unlikely that on his return from Paris St. Germans' lectures would have been confined to the cloister and not allowed to benefit a wider public. If this inference is permitted, then we may surely add some of his talented confrètes like Richard de Bromwych and Ranulph de Calthrop to this lecture list.[19]

[15] D. Knowles and R.N. Hadcock, *Medieval Religious Houses, England and Wales* (London, 1971) 81 give the number as fifty which is based on T.Hearne ed., *Hemingi Chartularium Ecclesiae Wigorniensis* (Oxford, 1723)418. But the *Liber Vitae Ecclesiae Dunelmensis* edited by A.H. Thompson, Surtees Society, 136 (1923) 22 lists sixty-two Worcester monks c.1104.

[16] Norwich cathedral priory's more plentiful records permit more accurate calculations, and they reveal that about one monk in seven attended university, a third of whom also obtained degrees; see my forthcoming article "Monk Students from Norwich Cathedral Priory at Oxford and Cambridge: their Attendance Record and their Impact on their Community, c.1300 to 1500' in the *English Historical Review*.

[17] W.J. Courtenay, *Schools and Scholars in Fourteenth-Century England* (Princeton, 1987) 107.

[18] A.G. Little and F. Pelster, *Oxford Theology and Theologians, c.A.D. 1282-1302*, Oxford Historical Society 96(1934)25.

[19] The letter is on fo 34ᵛ and has been printed in J.K. Floyer and S.G. Hamilton eds., *Catalogue of Manuscripts Preserved in the Chapter Library of Worcester Cathedral*, Worcestershire Historical Society, 20(1906)119, and Pantin's notes are on a typescript insertion in the interleaved copy of this catalogue in Worcester Cathedral Library. The Oxford achievements and associations of St. Germans and of the other contemporary Worcester monk theologians are discussed in Little and Pelster, *Op.cit.*, 236-46. Also see Emden, *BRUO* under Richard de Bromwych, Ranulph de Calthrop and John de Dumbleton.

We are on indisputably solid ground when we move on to the 1340's. On the 24 November in a year that must have been soon after John Evesham's election as prior, Brother John de Preston junior presented himself in the monastery before the prior and convent and many others who were seculars *(aliorum quamplurium secularium)* and began to lecture on the Sentences *(ad legendum librum Sententiarum)*. Preston was at Oxford with Evesham in 1336/7 but his length of stay there is unknown.[20] The contents of the medieval library afford only a glimpse into Preston's possible major scholarly interests: in 1348 he procured two volumes for his use, one of them contained two treatises of Augustine on the Trinity and on the Book of Genesis, and the other was Thomas Bradwardine's work written against the Pelagian heresy.[21]

About a century later, on 6 October 1445, Brother John Lawerne, bachelor of theology, began his lecturing on the Sentences in the presence of the bishop of Worcester, John Carpenter, and of the convent and of many seculars. His surviving notebook contains, among other things, lectures on the Sentences and on the Bible, some of which were given at Oxford between 1445 and 1448, and some as suggested above at Worcester. While Preston had received his appointment from the prior *(deputatus)*, Lawerne's appointment *(deputatus* again here) came from the bishop, perhaps in the absence of the recently elected prior, John Hertilbury.[22]

Many volumes in the monastic library at Worcester were at one time or another in the hands of Lawerne. Ms.Q.27, for example, contains a list of thirty books written in his hand, presumably because he needed to use them and had removed them from the library.[23] Apart from this list only three volumes bear his name, all of which we would probably classify as works of general reference or manuals.[24]

There remain also some thirty volumes which contain copies of Lombard's Sentences

---

[20] Preston was also known as John de Preston de Somerset. His lecturing activities are known by the fact that a later monk, John Lawerne, copied his predecessor;s formal *Protestacio* into his notebook which is now in Oxford, (Bodley Ms.692, fo 99ᵛ). The *protestacio* was an abjuration in advance of any truths contrary to papal teaching which the lecturer might unwittingly propose. Preston's year at Oxford is recorded in Worcester Cathedral Muniments [WCM] C.57. Some of the lecture notes in this manuscript may also have been Preston's copied by Lawerne for his own use.

[21] These manuscripts are Worcester Cathedral F.11 and Cambridge, Corpus Christi College 24.

[22] The notebook, referred to in n.20, contains Lawerne's *Protestacio* (fo 119); it is almost identical in form to that of John Preston's except that the bishop replaces the prior. Stephen Forte's thesis 'A Study of Some Oxford Schoolmen of the Middle Fourteenth Century, with Special Reference to Worcester Cathedral Ms. F.65' (Oxford, Ms. B.Litt., c.10-11, 1947) 24, states that these lectures were given at Oxford in Gloucester College, but the wording casts some doubt on this conclusion. Preston began his lectures *in monasterio*, which I have taken to mean the chapterhouse. Although this phrase has been omitted from Lawerne's *Protestacio* he began to lecture ... *per venerabilem patrem meum et dominum, dominum Johannem Carpenter eiusdem ecclesie [Wygornie] patrem et pastorem ... deputatus ... in presencia venerabilis patris mei et domini predicti et eiusdem loci conventus ac aliorum quamplurium secularium.* Possibly Lawerne returned to Worcester to lecture at intervals while continuing to reside at Oxford and to lecture there in preparation for his doctorate, which he obtained in 1448 (according to the same notebook, fo 36).

[23] These include Old and New Testament commentaries, a volume of sermons for Sundays, a commentary on the Sentences by Peter de Tarantasia', Boethius' treatise on music and Plato's Timaeus.

[24] They are Mss. F.13, Brito vocabularis iuxta alphabeticum; F.19, Tractatus de vitus et virtutibus; Q.22, Speculum sacerdotum.

and/or commentaries on them, all but one still in their original home at Worcester.[25] Most were probably written between the late twelfth and early to mid-fourteenth centuries, many of them are glossed, some by later hands, and most show signs of constant use; no doubt they passed from one generation of scholars to the next and some would have been carried back and forth by the Oxford student monks. There is a *cautio,* for example in Ms. F.8 to which John of St. Germans' name is attached, and F.139 is a commentary composed and written at Oxford by Richard de Bromwych who bequeathed it to a grateful confrère, Henry Fouke, one of his younger contemporaries.[26] Useful sources of reference both for theological lectures and for sermons were the *distinctiones,* or dictionaries of theological terms of which Worcester possessed at least eight.[27] Finally, there appears to have been no lack of biblical commentaries available for consultation by those preparing lectures and sermons.[28]

Regrettably, there is no further evidence of the activities of monk lecturers at Worcester between John Lawerne's death in c.1482 and the eve of the dissolution.[29] It is unlikely, however, that the tradition established probably in the late twelfth century, alive in the early and mid-fourteenth and again in the mid-fifteenth centuries, lay dormant between these dates or, indeed, after Lawerne's day. There may have been disruptions as there were prior to 1305, but these were probably of short duration and caused by a similar temporary lack of qualified monks; the constant flow of Worcester monks to Gloucester College should have proved adequate under normal circumstances. The bishops surely had a continuing vested interest in improving the level of education among their parish clergy who had neither the means, nor perhaps the necessary prerequisities to seek a licence for university study. The friars' educational programme must have had some effect in larger centres like Worcester, but their academic impact and influence declined in the later fourteenth century after the Black Death, with a gradual shift of interest and emphasis in the direction of piety and preaching.[30]

---

[25] Although medieval manuscripts frequently contained several titles bound together, N.R. Ker (n.1 above) has of necessity confined himself to one title only and Floyer's *Catalogue* (n.19 above) is inadequate and long overdue for revision. Fortunately, however, manuscript commentaries on the Sentences have been noted and described by F. Stegmüller (ed.) in *Repertorium Commentariorum in Sententias Petri Lombardi,* 2 vols., Wurzburg, 1947. The Worcester list is as follows: Mss. F.2, F,3, F.31, F.39, F.43, F.44, F.50, F.54, F.56, F.60, F.69, F.107, F.108, (F.109, which Stegmüller appears to have missed), F.112, F.139, F.164, F.167, Q.20, Q.31, Q.33, Q.35, Q.46, Q.47, Q69, Q.71, Q.99; many of these, alas, are not complete and some remain only as fragments. Copies of Lombard himself exist, in part or in whole, in Mss. F.8, F.46, F.47, F.53, F.64, F.88, F.98, F.134, F.176, Q.47, Q.88; in addition, Cambridge, Peterhouse Ms.71 is a former Worcester manuscript containing Lombard's Sentences. John Lawerne's notebook (Oxford, Ms. Bodley 692) could also be added to the list of commentaries as could the copy of Peter de Tarantasia's commentary used by Lawerne (n.23 above) but now lost. Among other well known commentators are Duns Scotus (Mss. F.39, F.60, F.69), Robert Kilwardby (Ms. F.43), Richard Fitzralph (Ms.Q.71), Bonaventure (Mss.F.167, Q.69), James of Viterbo (Ms.Q.20) and Thomas Aquinas (Mss. F.107-109).

[26] Fouke does not appear to have been among those sent to Oxford but he pursued scholarly exercises within the cloister. He procured two works on canon law for the monastic library: Oxford, Bodley, Ms. Rawlinson C.428 and Worcester Ms.F.131, the latter at the cost of fifty shillings.

[27] For example, Worcester Mss. F2, F.22, F.117, F.128, F.130, Q.15, Q.25 and Q.42.

[28] The titles in Ker's list (n.1 above) identify many of the commentaries; others are Worcester Mss. F.25-28, F.81-83, Q.59, Q.66.

[29] Lawerne was living in retirement in the monastery in 1481/2 (WCM C.205), the last reference to his presence. For evidence of a sixteenth century monk lecturing see below.

[30] Courtenay, *Op. cit.,* 368-74.

The fact that good teachers were, and are, often accomplished preachers provides a connecting link between the two central themes of this paper. Thus, an endeavour to reconstruct the recorded details of the monastic preacher in action should provide the necessary base on which to evaluate the contribution of the Worcester monks in both of these important areas. Finally, it should furish sufficient evidence to afford new insights into the practical applications of monastic learning in the later middle ages.

It is not explicitly clear why the Worcester chapter obtained a preaching licence from the pope in 1289/90. However, the actual phrasing employed suggests that it was given because many of the monks were 'learned in theology'; and so it appears to have been recognised as a prudent and beneficial move to authorise them 'to preach in public before the people in Worcester and in other churches belonging to them or of their patronage'.[31] They were no doubt already fulfilling this function when occasion required, but the background to the necessity for this formal approval lay, I think, in the fitful and frequently hostile relations between convent and bishop. A series of concurrent disputes : over the prebends in the collegiate church of Westbury, over the monastic precentor's right to present candidates to the bishop during the ordination ceremony and over the number of clerks allowed to accompany the bishop on his visitations of the cathedral priory; two of these, perhaps all three, had led to litigation in the 1280's.[32] At the same time a controversy between the monks and the Worcester Franciscan community over their respective burial rights vis-à-vis the laity revealed a further source of friction between chapter and bishop because the latter was well known as a patron of the mendicant orders.[33] While it is doubtful that Giffard ever became a Franciscan himself, despite the suggestion or perhaps invitation of the minister general, in 1282 the latter gave him a share in all the spiritual benefits enjoyed by the order; in addition, by 1279 the pope was addressing Giffard as guardian of the papal privileges granted to the Friars Preachers in England.[34] With the rapid growth in papal legislation in favour of these two orders in the second half of the thirteenth century, especially Martin IV's *Ad fructus uberes* of 1281 which allowed the friars to exercise all priestly functions without the prior consent of diocesan or of the local parish clergy, it is hardly surprising to find both black monks and secular clergy concerned to defend their traditional rights. Moreover, the Worcester chapter must have felt like the psalmist who saw the enemy camped all around, since the primatial see was occupied by a Franciscan and the episcopal see by a staunch supporter of both orders.[35] In 1289/90 the cathedral priory had achieved only a

[31] W.H. Bliss, C. Johnson, J.A. Twemlow ed., *Calendar of Entries in the Papal Registers Relating to Great Britain and Ireland. Papal Letters* (H.M.S.O.) I, 510; see also Clement Price ed., *Liber Pensionum Prioratus Wigorn.*, Worcestershire Historical Society, 38 (1925) item no. 146.

[32] There is a helpful survey of these and other disputes by J.W. Willis Bund in his edition of *Episcopal Registers Diocese of Worcester. Register of Godfrey Giffard, 1268-1301*, Worcestershire Historical Society, 15(1902) 1-1v.

[33] Willis Bund, *Op. cit.*, 371, 372, 388, and also H.R. Luard ed., *Annales Monastici*, Vol.4, *Annales Prioratus de Wigornia*, Rolls Series (1869), 501-4.

[34] See Willis Bund, *Op.cit.*, 94, 156 and 116 respectively.

[35] E.g., Psalms 78 (79) and 79 (80). This legislation and these privileges are discussed in M.D. Knowles, *The Religious Orders in England*, 1 (Cambridge, 1948) 186-188. Pope Nicholas IV (1288-92) was also a Franciscan as was John Pecham, archbishop of Canterbury from 1279 to 1292.

limited objective, and they had to wait until 1300 before *Super cathedram* restricted the friars to preaching in their own churches.[36] This went some way to restore the balance and relieve the beleagured monks and parish priests.

Who were the learned theologians referred to in the papal licence? Alas, although we have the names of many of the monks in the late thirteenth century community, biographical details are scant. They would have been the last generation to have followed their courses of study entirely within the monastic enclosure and must have been the instructors of the juniors, some of whom were later selected to join the first group of monk students at Oxford.[37] One of them, perhaps, was Thomas de Seggesbarewe who died in 1299 at Rome, where he had been sent on negotiations, leaving a collection of books considered to be of sufficient value to warrant the despatch of another monk to retrieve them.[38] Others may have been among the eleven who contributed to the purchase of Worcester Ms. Q.42, which is a copy of the Distinctiones compiled by the Franciscan Brother Maurice; one other of this last group was John de Wyke who, as prior from 1301 to 1317, supported his monks at Oxford and at Paris and appears to have been concerned about the public lectures in the cathedral.[39]

Licences for preaching are, on the whole, uncommon entries in episcopal and monastic registers of all the monastic cathedrals. The Liber Albus of Worcester cathedral priory furnishes only one example which is dated in March 1318 when both the bishop, Thomas Cobham, and the prior, Wulstan de Bransford, had recently taken up their respective charges. This licence authorised the prior to assign certain monks, *i.e.,* those whom he considered most qualified for the position by reason of their reputation and learning, to the office of preaching and of absolving. The inference to be drawn from the phrasing of the document is that the chapter was responsible for a regular preaching appointment for the purpose of delivering sermons both inside the cathedral and elsewhere.[40] Some years later, as diocesan Wulstan appointed John de Lemenstre, recently returned from Oxford, to serve as penitentiary and to preach publicly within the diocese.[41] In these two instances the preaching and absolving functions are explicitly linked together, but in the fairly frequent episcopal commissions to monks to serve in cathedral, city and diocese as confessors or penitentiaries preaching is rarely mentioned.[42] Is the latter to be understood

---

[36] See note 35 above. They continued to be free to preach in public but not in cathedral or parish pulpits without invitation.

[37] Two are mentioned in n.10 above and four more in n.19.

[38] *Annales Prioratusde Wigornia* (as in n.33 above), 543. He procured at least two volumes for the library, Worcester Ms.F.37 and F.102, the latter being part of Aquinas' Summa Theologica.

[39] For example, John of St. Germans studied at Paris as well as Oxford; see Emden, *BRUO*.

[40] WCM A5, i.e. Liber Albus, fo 87ᵛ; the wording is ... *illos quos de ipsius ad predicationis officium et confessionis, vos [priorem], vel ille cui de consuetudine in ecclesia nostra Cathedrale et extra sermones competit providere videritis ydoneos et honestos ad id presentibus licenciamus;* the construction is awkward but the meaning seems clear enough.

[41] R.M. Haines ed., *A Calendar of the Register of Wolstan de Bransford, Bishop of Worcester, 1339-49,* Worcestershire Historical Society, New Series, No.4 (1966), item no. 1333.

[42] Examples of episcopal appointments of monk penitentiaries in the fourteenth century are in Reg. Maidstone, (Hereford and Worcester Record Office [HWRO] b 716.093-BA.2648/1(iv)) p.30 (AD1314) and W.P. Marett e., *A Calendar of the Register of Henry Wakefield, Bishop of Worcester 1375-95,* Worcestershire Historical Society New Series 7 (1971) item no.834 (AD1379) (The Worcester episcopal manuscript registers have been paginated).

as included in the assignment? It would seem that sometimes this may have been the case, to judge by several references to monks preaching in connection with indulgences in the early fourteenth century both at Durham and at Worcester. Bishop Walter Reynolds, for example, in 1309 offered an indulgence to all the penitent laity in Worcester who, after confession, listened to sermons by the prior or by monks chosen by him for this task; the bishop also stated that these preaching occasions could take place at any location in the diocese which the prior or monk preachers deemed appropriate.[43] There is also an interesting and unusual entry on a flyleaf of Ms. Q.4 which must have been written a few years earlier; it states that those who listen to a sermon by Brother Philip Aubyn (prior 1287 to 1296) are entitled to 295 days' indulgence.

From the mid-1340's on our chief source of information about public sermons by Worcester monks is the monastic official known as the precentor. Although his chief concerns were with the liturgical chant and the library, he was also responsible for the travelling expenses of the monk students to and from Oxford and for the entertainment of visiting preachers; thus, the details of these two items were regularly entered on his account. These *fratres predicantes,* regularly appeared at the beginning of Advent and of Lent, in Rogationtide and also on other occasions during the year, and they were usually refreshed by food and drink in the *hostillaria* or guest hall.[44] While it is unlikely that the phrase applied to Worcester monks alone, an analysis of all the extant precentor's accounts indicates that the term often included them, along with others who had received invitations to come to preach. Until the 1390's the precentor fails to include names, but at last in 1393/4 he records that he hired a horse for Brother John Dudley to return from Oxford to preach. Dudley is one of about eight Worcester monks who obtained a doctorate in theology; he had incepted the previous year but seems to have stayed on for a time.[45] From this entry, which supplies both the name of the student and the reason for his recall from Oxford, we may assume that among others whose return was required for brief periods some had been given a similar preaching assignment although the precentor may have omitted to note the purpose of the visit, an unnecessary detail if it was regular practice. Thus, for example, John Grene came back from Oxford for Easter in 1380 and John Fordham for the same feast in 1391.[46]

There are more glimpses of these activities at intervals throughout most of the fifteenth century. An unnamed monk scholar came to give the Good Friday sermon in 1412; Richard Barnesley made two journeys in 1419/20, one being for the feast of the Assumption, and he travelled back and forth from Oxford three years later for the same

---

[43] R.A. Wilson ed. *The Register of Walter Reynolds Bishop of Worcester, 1308-1313,* Worcestershire Historical Society 39 (1927) 5-6. At Durham Bishop Kellaw granted an indulgence in 1312 to those who heard the monks preach in the cathedral (Thomas Duffus Hardy ed., *The Register of Richard de Kellawe, Lord Palatine and Bishop of Durham, 1314-1316,* Rolls Series no.62 Vol.1 (1873) 250; and Durham Dean and Chapter Muniments 1.13. Pont. 1-14 include similar charters of indulgence issued by various bishops.

[44] For example, on the precentor's accounts for 1346/7, 1348/9 and 1354/5 etc. WCM C351, 352 and 355 etc.

[45] WCM C.368 and C.76 and 76a. In 1401/2 the chamberlain records a payment of 4s. 6d. to Dudley *et aliis pro uno sermone dicendo* (C.26); the reason for this entry is not given.

[46] WCM C.362 and C.367. There were at least two monk students at Oxford during these years and, since only one was sent for it is reasonable to assume that it was for a specific purpose: namely, I suggest, preaching. Both Grene and Fordham acquired doctorates in theology and later became priors, Grene in 1388 and Fordham in 1409 (WCM C.81).

purpose; William Hertilbury's preaching skills were demonstrated to the cathedral congregation in 1425/6; John Lawerne, who as a young deacon had gone up to Oxford in 1432/3, was recalled in order to preach four years later and no doubt on other occasions during his lengthy period of study; Isaac Ledbury and other confraters were assigned to preach in Advent and Rogationtide in 1449./50.[47] By 1476/7 the precentor or his clerk accountant had devised a succinct phrase to summarise the preaching expenses and replace the earlier informative entries : *in expensis diversorum venerabilium virorum predicantium*.[48] It is possible that some of these monk-scholar preachers were brought home to give homilies in the presence of their brethren only and not before the large congregations which would have flocked to the cathedral on solemn feasts and holy days. But it is more likely that they were being summoned from university on these occasions to give them experience in translating theory into practice before a public assembly. It should also be remembered that when they were recalled for the purpose of preaching at an election or visitation the proceedings on these occasions opened with a high mass and sermon at which the public were present.[49]

By including among the suitable locations for preaching the churches belonging to the priory, the papal licence or privilege of 1289/90 described above seems to suggest that this function and probably that of absolving pentitents was regarded as one of the monks' responsibilities, a reminder perhaps that spiritual as well as administrative duties were incumbent upon them as holders of lands and churches. Monks are found making frequent rounds of their manors for supervisory purposes as the bailiffs, sergeants and reeves note on their expense accounts; but only in one instance does the record enlarge our perspective by stating that the monk preached. On the first Sunday in Lent in 1335 Richard de Bromwych D.Th., already mentioned as the writer of a commentary on the Sentences, preached in the chapel of King's Norton.[50] The rural congregation that morning had the unverifiable privilege of listening to a highly intelligent and seasoned teacher, both in the halls of Oxford and within the cloister, a member of the Worcester community for over thirty years and, it seems, a fairly frequent visitor to King's Norton in the 1320's and 1330's.[51] Did he stir the parishioners to repentance with simple Gospel preaching or was he too steeped in scholastic learning to come down to their level? It would be a misjudgement to view this solitary example of university trained monks preaching in country parish churches as an isolated occurrence. Indeed, it appears as an exception only through the lack of surviving evidence; other accounts of scrupulous bailiffs would assuredly have reported similar incidents.

---

[47] The references for the five students follow the order in the text: WCM C.374; 375, 376; 377; 378; 379. All but Barnesley are in Emden, *BRUO*.

[48] WCM C. 383.

[49] E.g., at Bishop Wakefield's visitation, probably in May 1387 he ordered that a monk who was a master in theology, namely John Grene, was to give the sermon 'coram nobis clero et populo' (WCM Liber Albus fo 318ᵛ).

[50] WCM C.695; the prior and convent held the church of Bromsgrove and the adjacent chapel of King's Norton within the parish as well as lands and tithes there. (R.R. Darlington ed., *The Cartulary of Worcester Cathedral Priory*, the Pipe Roll Society, New Series, 38 (1968), item nos. 539 and 551).

[51] See Little and Pelster, *Op. cit.*, (n.18 above) 240-244 and Emden, *BRUO* for Bromwych's academic career, and for his Thomist position see J.I. Catto ed., *The Early Oxford Schools* (Oxford, 1984)513, i.e., the first volume in T.H. Aston ed., *The History of the University of Oxford* currently in progress. His recorded visits to Bromsgrove and King's Norton are on the accounts WCM C.544, 693, 693b, 694, and 695 (1334/5, when he preached).

Although Worcester monks were continuing to be sent to Oxford until the final years before the dissolution, there are only two fragments of evidence to indicate that they were still being employed as popular preachers in the sixteenth century.[52] Pointing toward a setting previously thought to have been outside the purview of the cathedral priory, these open up new insights into a sphere of activity hitherto unnoticed or, alternatively, into a change of policy in response to changing circumstances. In 1528 Brother Roger Neckham D.Th., was appointed custodian or perpetual chaplain of the charnel house which was situated on the north side of the cathedral.[53] It had been constructed by Bishop William de Blois in the early thirteenth century, attached to the sacrist's office in the late fourteenth century and refounded with new statutes in the mid-fifteenth century.[54] The statutes of Bishop Carpenter required the chaplain to have a university degree in order to ensure his competence in fulfilling the prescribed duties which included caring for the attached library, giving weekly lectures on the New Testament and preaching annually on Good Friday in the cathedral or at the cross in the churchyard outside.[55] All of Neckham's known predecessors in this office were secular priests, and it is most unlikely that he was the only suitable candidate available. The appointment of this senior monk to give regular public lectures and sermons may have been a move to attract more townspeople within the cathedral's sphere of influence at a time when the preaching of the friars in the diocese seems to have been gaining popularity.[56] Amidst the many preaching licences issued to the friars in this period there is only one to a Benedictine and that was to Neckham himself in February 1534; by it his mandate to preach in Latin or English was extended to all churches and other places within the city and diocese, and the scope of his influence on behalf of the cathedral chapter correspondingly enhanced.[57]

The successive generations of Worcester monks who received training at the university in the art of sermon preparation and preaching returned home to a cloister well stocked with reference works, biblical commentaries and an impressive collection of sermon materials and model sermons. The presence of some thirty-eight volumes of sermons, mostly of the thirteenth and fourteenth centuries, which have remained at Worcester to this day, bears silent witness to the monks' assessment of their priorities and to their enduring concern to develop their talents in the service of the Word.[58] Some of these

---

[52] There are five names of sixteenth century monk students in my biographical register, viz., John Blackwell, John Lawerne, Roger Neckham, Bartholomew Stoke and Humphrey Webley all of whom are noted by A.B. Emden in *A Biographical Register of the University of Oxford, A.D. 1501 to 1540.* (Oxford, 1974).

[53] HWRO b.716.093-BA.2648/9 (i) Reg. Geronimo Ghinucci p.82.

[54] For the foundation charter see Clement Price, *Op. cit.,* (n.30 above) item no.88 (2); for Bishop Wakefield's provisions in 1385 *Ibid.,* no.88 (3).

[55] HWRO b.716.093-BA.2648/6(ii) Reg. Carpenter 1, p.357-8.

[56] Between 1530 and 1534 there were more than thirty licences to friars entered in Ghinucci's register (n.53 above) pp.105-151.

[57] *Ibid.,* p.145. Neckham was still warden at this date (WCM C.415).

[58] See n.25 above; the list of sermon manuscripts in Worcester Cathedral Library is as follows: Mss. F.5, F.10, F.16, F.32, F.36, F.77, F.91, F.92, F.93, F.94, F.115, F.121, F.126, F.157; Q.3, Q.4, Q6, Q.9, Q.11, Q.12, Q.17, Q.19, Q.21, Q.45, Q.46, Q.53, Q.56, Q.57, Q.63, Q.64, Q.65, Q.67, Q.74, Q.77, Q.78, Q.87, Q.89, Q.100.

manuscripts are the works of well known preachers;[59] a few were copied on the spot by the monk students at Oxford who had the opportunity of hearing some of the foremost preachers, including friars; some were composed by the monks themselves; the majority, however are anonymous collections in which only a few of the sermons are ascribed to named individuals.[60]

While there are in these collections a few sermons intended for monastic or clerical audiences like the Benedictine Chapter meetings at Northampton, episcopal visitations of the priory or convocations of the clergy, most appear to have been intended for general use.[61] Although they are all written in Latin, apart from a very few exceptions, most of them must have been actually delivered in the vernacular.[62] Some of the Worcester manuscripts provide a series of sermons which follow the order of the liturgical year with every Sunday and other holy days included;[63] many have a large number of marginal annotations in contemporary or later hands and the worn folios are evidence of constant use. One medium sized but hefty volume entitled Sermones Variorum (Ms. Q.77) consists of many odd sizes and shapes of parchment - indeed, some of them appear to be scraps - bound together to form a very miscellaneous assortment.[64] Some of the pieces-converted-into-folios are small enough to have been tucked into the preacher's monastic habit and are covered with an illegible scrawl that suggests last minute haste or a sudden rush of divine inspiration, possibly both.

This examination of Worcester manuscripts and other relevant sources has uncovered convincing evidence of the cathedral chapter's educational policy, first with regard to the most talented members of its own community and secondly with concern for the larger community outside the cloister. In the last two and a half centuries before the dissolution this order prevailed; the monks were trained at the university to teach and to preach, and at Worcester enough evidence remains to show them performing both of these functions on a fairly regular basis. The exposure of the Worcester monk scholars' subsequent

[59] For example, they range from St. Augustine (Ms. Q.45) and Gregory the Great (Ms. Q.21), to the thirteenth century Dominican archbishop James de Voragine (Mss. F.115, Q.64) and the Franciscan Guibert de Tournai (Mss. F.36, F.77, Q.19, Q.57), to fourteenth century Englishmen such as William of Ockham (Ms. Q.74) and the Augustinian canon and bishop Philip Repingdon (Ms. F.121); there are also sermon collections of other friars, of Cistercians, and a volume containing the sermons of John Felton a fifteenth century vicar of St. Mary Magdalen's church, Oxford (Ms. Q.45).

[60] Ms. Q.64, for example, which contains Voragine's sermons may have been copied by John of St. Germans according to a note by Pantin in Floyer's Catalogue (n.19 above) and it has a table of contents compiled by Henry Fouke (see also the discussion in Little and Pelster (n.18 above, 245-6). John Lawerne's hand may be found in Ms. F.126 which is Sermones diversorum, as some folios bear a marked resemblance to his handwriting in the Bodley notebook (Ms.692). Ms.Q.89, a thirteenth century collection, and Ms. F.10, which is fifteenth century and contains a few English sermons, also have names probably of monk borrowers, on blank folios; and Ms. F.36 is inscribed Ricardus Hallowe habet istum librum.

[61] Sermons for monastic or clerical congregations are found in Mss. F.10 and Q.77, while Ms. Q.18, omitted from the list in n.58 above, is a collection of Collationes or conferences given by priors or other senior monks to their brethren.

[62] Sister Mary Aquinas Devlin, O.P., discusses this point in the introduction to her edition of The Sermons of Thomas Brinton, Bishop of Rochester (1373-1389), Camden Third Series, 85(1954), Vol. 1, xx-xxi. As G.R. Owst concludes, in Preaching in Medieval England (Cambridge, 1926) 225, it was common practice for preachers to write out Latin versions of all their sermons, for it was in this form that they were preserved and circulated. See also Katherine Walsh, A Fourteenth-Century Scholar and Primate: Richard Fitzralph in Oxford, Avignon and Armagh (Oxford, 1981) chap.III, 'The Preacher and his Sermon Diary'.

[63] Examples are Mss. F.5, F.16, F.92-94, F.115, F.157, Q.3, Q.4, Q.9, Q.21, Q.45, Q.53, Q.65.

[64] The smallest 'scrap' measures approximately four and one half inches by four inches.

careers - or, to use the more appropriate monastic term, vocation, which means that which they were called upon to do under obedience - has a significance which extends beyond Worcester to the other cathedral priories. A prolonged study of the university trained monks of Norwich, for example, has failed to reveal any record of public teaching or preaching assignments and only a few penitentiary appointments.[65] The lack of evidence at Norwich, and at other cathedral priories, can no longer be taken as proof that these activities were non-existent; rather, it is due to the loss of those records which might have enlightened us and to the silence of those which remain.

It is true that at Worcester the lecturing was confined to the cathedral precincts and much of the preaching also, although some of the preaching licences gave the monks a wider range within the diocese. These licences may have been requested only when the prior and chapter saw their normal activities being threatened by the friars who, as outsiders and constantly on the move, had to be equipped with a licence for their own protection and that of their audiences; the monks, by contrast, were resident and well known in the city and surrounding community.

This study raises a fundamental question. Would the Benedictines have expended their resources and manpower over a lengthy period if they had doubted that their activities were in accord with the Rule? They were well aware that the general precepts enunciated in the chapter on 'The Instruments of Good Works' were intended to have a practical application in the life of the community as a whole as well as in the life of the individual monk.[66] A fresh interpretation of several of these counsels was, one might say, thrust upon the monks in the mid-thirteenth century by the influx of the friars whose sole *raison d'être* was to teach and to preach. Confronted by the challenge of this new situation the Benedictine conscience was reawakened to the spiritual needs and welfare of the neighbour outside the convent gates. For the monks, in obedience to the Rule, it was a more restricted field of operation than for the friars; their neighbours were, in the main, those among whom they lived and with whom they came in frequent contact. As we have seen, these were the clergy and laity to whom they had been ministering before the advent of the friars, in accordance with papal directives and episcopal commissions; but the impetus to share in the benefits of a university training and to pass on these benefits to the community they already served owes much to the vision of Francis and Dominic which brought renewed zeal to the disciples of Benedict.

---

[65] See n.16 above.

[66] See the edition of *The Rule of St. Benedict* by Abbot Justin McCann (London, 1952) chapter 4. Dr. Dunbabin suggests that 'they got around more than strict adherence to the rule might seem to have permitted' but my interpretation here may not differ markedly from hers; see her chapter on 'Careers and Vocations' in J.I.Catto, *The Early Oxford Schools* (n.54 above) 604.

FROM 'ALMS' TO 'SPIRITUAL SERVICES':
The Function and Status of
Monastic Property in Medieval England
by
Benjamin Thompson

I t is a commonplace that landowners granted property to monasteries in the middle ages in order to secure a greater hope of salvation. So much is the undoubtedly correct assumption of all writers who touch on the subject.[1] What is not so clear is exactly how the making of the gift was to procure the desired spiritual benefits. It is assumed that endowments bought 'prayers', which on a general level is incontrovertible (although there is more to be said about spiritual activities themselves than that).[2] However, we ought to be able to describe the process of securing them more precisely and in greater detail, and to discover if it changed over the period we label the middle ages. For instance, the further assertion that such prayers may accurately be described as 'services' in the feudal sense is not equally self-evident and requires critical investigation.[3] The present paper attempts to contribute to that investigation by examining land granted to the church from the lay point of view, in terms of both its function - the objects for which it was given - and status - its place in the tenurial and legal world of the time. That time is the high and later middle ages in England, with particular reference to the transformation wrought in the century-and-a-half between the accession of Henry II and the death of Edward I.

The importance of the subject is that it can provide a basis for a general understanding of the lay attitude to ecclesiastical property in the middle ages. Unless we correctly comprehend what laymen thought they were doing each time they performed the common operation of granting land to churches, we shall not understand the basis of their attitude to ecclesiastical endowment in general. That act of donation, indeed, has left us with the most abundant source of evidence with which to investigate many aspects of medieval history, so that it is doubly important to do it the courtesy of understanding it clearly. Furthermore the frequent occurrence of the act shows that the attitudes to which charters bear witness were deep-rooted in the *mentalité* of the actors. From them

---

[1] E.G. in works relevant to this study, Elisabeth G. Kimball, "The judicial aspects of frank almoign tenure', *English Historical Review* xlvii (1932), 7: land was 'given to aid the salvation of the donor's soul'; Audrey W. Douglas, 'Frankalmoin and jurisdictional immunity: Maitland revisited', *Speculum* liii (1978), 26: 'the spiritual motives that prompted donations of land and revenues to churches'. But some writers play down spiritual motives in favour of secular, e.g. B.D. Hill, *English Cistercian Monasteries and their Patrons in the Twelfth Century* (Urbana, Illinois, 1968), 36-8, 40, 53-61. This will not concern us here: it is the author's opinion that grants to the church can only be explained in the first instance by spiritual motivation, as the charters say, and as even the recent dedication of the largest church in the world on the Ivory Coast shows.

[2] E.g. Kimball, 'Tenure in frank almoign and secular services', *English Historical Review* xliii (1928), 348: 'this salvation was to be aided by the prayers of the donee.'

[3] Douglas, 28: (of free alms tenure) 'the particular spiritual quality of its service'; 34 n. 20: 'marked by spiritual service'; Kimball, 'Tenure in frank almoin', 348: 'obligation of indefinite spiritual service'; F. Pollock & F.W. Maitland, *The History of English Law before the time of Edward I* (2nd edn., Cambridge 1898, reprinted 1968), i. 240: 'spiritual, as opposed to secular, service', also 242-3. These writers built upon each other, and Maitland relied upon Littleton, who referred to 'divine and spiritual service' done for donors in frankalmoin, *Littleton's Tenures*, bk. II, ch. vi, $135 (ed. Eugene Wambaugh, Washington, DC, 1903, p. 67).

were derived the attitudes to the church which had such a major role to play in medieval politics, and most of all at the point at which the middle ages are thought to have come to an end, at the Reformation. It is necessary, therefore, to return to the most essential form of evidence we have for the high middle ages, witnessing an important but common act, in order to begin to arrive at an understanding of lay assumptions in this respect.

We must take as a guide in this exploration the seminal account of the nature of 'frankalmoin' - or free alms - tenure by F.W. Maitland.[4] Although a number of writers have sought to elucidate and to elaborate - as well as in small matters to emend - Maitland's conclusions,[5] there are two particular directions in which they need to be further amplified and corrected. In the first place, Maitland's account of the legal and tenurial world of the twelfth century has been 'turned on its side' by the work of S.F.C. Milsom.[6] This paper is in part, therefore, an attempt to fill a gap by applying Milsom's account to ecclesiastical tenure, a subject on which he touches but does not examine systematically. Second, Maitland and subsequent writers concentrated their attention upon the status of ecclesiastical land without adequately taking into account its function. It seems to me that this process ought to be reversed: it is at least a fair *prima facie* assumption that the function of property logically precedes its status; the objects for which land was given ought in general to dictate the terms on which it was held. Therefore, we must first understand those objects before investigating the terms in their tenurial and legal setting. The passage of time, and in particular the survival of fixed but outmoded forms into eras which made different demands and imposed different standards, clouds the simplicity of this picture; but it is the correct assumption with which to begin, and the complexity should in any case follow from it.

First, therefore, we shall attempt to understand the objects which grants of land were intended to secure in high-medieval England, between the conquest and the early thirteenth century. Second, its status will come under the same scrutiny, which will necessitate a bibliographical excursus on work since Maitland. Third, we shall move into the later middle ages and investigate the changing demands of late-medieval donors in terms both of status and of function. And a postscript will take into account some of the complexity introduced into the picture by the transformation in the thirteenth century, and attempt to sum up the change and its importance.[7] The paper is intended as an essay rather than a comprehensive and fully researched account. It does not rest upon a

---

[4] Pollock & Maitland, i. 240-51; also in Maitland, *Collected Papers* (3 vols., Cambridge, 1911), ii. 205-22.

[5] See the works of Kimball and Douglas in nn. 1 & 2, and S.E. Thorne, 'The assize *Utrum* and canon law in England', *Columbia Law Review* xxxiii (1933), 428-36, R.C. Van Caenegem, *Royal Writs in England from the Conquest to Glanvill* (London, Selden Society lxxvii, 1959), 325-30.

[6] S.F.C. Milsom, 'Introduction' to the reprint of Pollock & Maitland (see n. 3), *The Legal Framework of English Feudalism* (Cambridge, 1976, hereafter *LF*), *Historical Foundations of the Common Law* (2nd edn., London, 1981, hereafter *HF*), see p. 146.

[7] There is only space here to see the lay point of view: elsewhere I have addressed some of the problems more generally from the ecclesiastical side, particularly through events around the reign of Edward I, and I hope in the future to present a more rounded picture; Benjamin Thompson, 'The statute of Carlisle, 1307, and the alien priories', *Journal of Ecclesiastical History* li (1990), 543-83, '*Habendum et Tenendum:* lay and ecclesiastical attitudes to the property of the church', in *Religious Belief and Ecclesiastical Careers in Late Medieval England*, ed. C. Harper-Bill (Woodbridge, 1991). The conflict between lay and ecclesiastical theories of property is missing here, therefore, and this may be to miss an important dimension in the story.

systematic investigation of all the available material (an enormous task, but one which I hope to undertake in the future) and in support of its suggestions I cite a limited range of evidence.[8] But I hope that by presenting my thoughts more boldly than the evidence here warrants to provide a clear starting-point for debate on the issues which seem to me to be important.

· · · · ·

In order to establish a 'control' against which to investigate gifts to the church, it is worth reflecting briefly upon what might be expected by donors in return for grants of land to laymen.[9] These may be broadly analysed into three groups, but for all of them a preliminary point needs to be made about tenure, in the historical context of England after the conquest but before 1290. The recipient usually became the tenant of the donor; that is to say, the grant created a relationship which was enshrined in the tenure which bound lord and vassal, and which, by its renewal in subsequent generations (for landed property does not die with people), might long outlast the original act of enfeoffment.[10]

In the first type of return which a grantor sought in making a grant, the bond between donor and recipient was originally a personal one between lord and man. The granting of lands by one to the other occurred within an already established relationship of service and protection, which was primarily based on loyalty and mutual trust - most obviously in the military context - rather than the bonds of tenure.[11] A lord both rewarded a follower for faithful service in the past, and looked forward to continued support in the future. This is clearly what William the Conqueror did in the years after 1066 when he distributed lands to those who had helped him conquer England, and who would continue to help him hold it.[12] This type of transaction is an example of what anthropologists have labelled 'gift-exchange'.[13] A gift is given not specifically in return for some other benefit of calculably equal value, but in the general expectation that it will be reciprocated by a gift in return. So, the household knight renders service to a lord in the hope and expectation of an ultimate reward in land, and the lord grants him the land partly in return for that service, and partly in the expectation of further service in the future.[14]

The donor of land might seek to purchase services more formally, we might say more commercially, by attaching specific conditions to the grant. The return which the

---

[8] More detail may be found in my 'The Church and the Aristocracy: lay and ecclesiastical landowning society in fourteenth-century Norfolk' (unpublished Ph.D. dissertation, Cambridge, 1989).

[9] See comments in Milsom, *LF*, 39, 112, 154-5 *HF*, 101-3.

[10] On the surprising rarity of grants by substitution, see n. 22.

[11] F.L. Ganshof, *Feudalism* (trans. P. Grierson, London, 1952).

[12] J.C. Holt, 'The introduction of knight service in England', *Anglo-Norman Studies* vi (1983), 89-106, J.H. Round, 'The introduction of knight service into England', in his *Feudal England* (London, 1909), 225-314.

[13] Marcel Mauss, *The Gift: forms and functions of exchange in archaic societies* (trans. Ian Cunnison, London, 1954); in the medieval context, Philip Grierson, 'Commerce in the dark ages: a critique of the evidence', *Transactions of the Royal Historical Society*, 5th ser. ix (1959), 137-9, Lester K. Little, *Religious Poverty and the Profit Economy in Medieval Europe* (London, 1978), 3-8, and further references in Miri Rubin, *Charity and Community in Medieval Cambridge* (Cambridge, 1987), 1-2.

[14] Even a work as late as 'Bracton' could see this, *Bracton on the Laws and Customs of England*, ed. G.E. Woodbine, trans. S.E. Thorne (4 vols., Camb., Mass., & Selden Society, London, 1968-77), ii. 72-3 (fo. 19b).

recipient was to render in return for enjoying the property was encoded in the tenurial contract, the terms under which he held it. This applies to many different forms of services, including the military services encapsulated in quotes of knights and days of castle guard which provided a lord with a body of soldiers for himself and protection for his fortresses.[15] The commercial element is perhaps starker at lower levels in the social and tenurial hierarchy, where the donor bought with his land the various services of tenants in socage, the farms of lessees, the rents of peasant husbandmen, and the manual labour of what came to be unfree serfs.[16]

Gift-exchange and commercial transactions are not mutually exclusive: the specification of services was not incompatible with the motive of reward and investment, particularly as it applies to military and serjeanty tenures.[17] Lords would naturally prefer to enfeoff their own tried followers. Moreover such enfeoffments were subject to the guidance of custom, which considerably limited the type and quantity of the return which a donor might seek on any particular occasion. It is therefore hard in practice to establish a distinction between vassals enfeoffed for notable loyalty, and those whose services were being bought on a more commercial basis.[18] In the lesser tenures, however, it is reasonable to assume that the services demanded for new grants were based more strictly on a commercial calculation by the donor of how much the land and its tenant could produce.[19] This is especially true of rents and farms in money, which both is the symptom and was the means of commercial calculation and valuation.[20] The donor equated the value of what was given with what he would get in return, and the elements of personal service and reward might have been entirely absent. In this relationship, incidents were the complement of services: if a tenant could not perform his services, for whatever reason, whether temporarily or permanently (and in the extreme case if he died), the lord got the tenement back, for as long as the incapacity lasted or until he re-granted it. He might have to retrieve it against a defaulting tenant through the customary processes of his own court, but this reinforced the recognition that he ought to have one or the other, the services he had purchased or his money back, in the form of the tenement which he given for them.[21]

The donor had a third option, for he might use his property in exchange not for

---

[15] Pollock & Maitland, i. 252-82, F.M. Stenton, *The First Century of English Feudalism* (Oxford, 1932), chs. iv-vi, C. Warren Hollister, *The Military Organization of Norman England* (Oxford, 1965), chs. iv-v.

[16] Pollock & Maitland, i. 291-3, E. Miller & J. Hatcher, *Medieval England: Rural Society and Economic Change, 1086-1348* (London, 1978), 111-33.

[17] See Pollock & Maitland on serjeanty, i. 283-90.

[18] Indeed we have been taught to think of the Conqueror's *servicia debita* as no more than rough indications of the size of the body of soldiers which each tenant-in-chief was to bring when serving the king, imposed under the exigencies of conquest; it is the mid-twelfth-century Exchequer which made us think that they were immutable services inseparable from the baronies which William created, Holt, 91, 99-106.

[19] See the increasing demands of lords in the thirteenth century, Miller & Hatcher, *Rural Society and Economic Change*, 45-9, 233-9.

[20] Peter Spufford, *Money and its Use in Medieval Europe* (Cambridge, 1988), esp. 240-63, 378-396, Little, *Religious Poverty*, 15-18.

[21] Milsom, *LF*, 8-35, 39-40, 112, 154-5, 160, Pollock & Maitland, i. 307-29, 351-6.

services within a tenurial framework, but for some form of payment altogether outside it, most obviously cash. He sold the tenement outright, thus converting a perpetual income in goods or services into a single payment; he converted one sort of capital into another, rather than using his capital to provide for future needs of matter and manpower. In tenurial terms, he might substitute the purchaser for himself as the new tenant of the land, in which case he himself dropped out of the tenurial framework altogether. But there were good legal reasons for preserving the forms by subinfeudating and taking a nominal service within the terms of tenure, such as a rose at midsummer, while receiving the real benefit of the sale outside it in the form of money.[22] In either form a sale was likely to be a commercial transaction, based on reciprocal calculation of market value and bound by contract. Nevertheless we must not ignore the potential for mixed exchange even here; the vendor might sell a tenement for less than its full market value, either in order to receive two types of commercial return by reserving some services from the land for the future, or to do a favour to the purchaser as a reward or informally to reserve to himself a residual obligation from him. Particularly in the emergent society of high medieval Europe, it is not at all surprising to find the elements of gift-exchange - more characteristic of the past - and commercial exchange - increasingly the model for the future - mixed together in any particular transfer of land, goods, and services.

When we compare these possibilities with the grants made to the church in the eleventh and twelfth centuries, we might bear in mind that the church too held land for military service or for rent, in other words by secular tenures.[23] Nevertheless, note this statement in the treatise known as Glanvill.[24]

> It should be noted that neither a bishop nor an abbot can alienate in perpetuity any part of his demesne without the assent and confirmation of the lord king, because their baronies are of the alms of the lord king and his ancestors.

Even those lands of bishoprics and monasteries existing in England in 1066, upon which the Conqueror so infamously imposed military service quotas,[25] *servicia debita*, were seen as *elemosina*, as if re-granted by the king as ecclesiastical benefactions. This is indeed the fundamental characteristic of early grants: they are gifts of alms to religious, and in particular to religious who are formally poor, and thereby worthy recipients of alms.

There is much variation in the drafting of charters until the later twelfth century, but

---

[22] Milsom, *LF*, 106-12, 146-53, *HF*, 114-15.

[23] H.M. Chew, *The English Ecclesiastical Tenants-in-Chief and Knight Service* (Oxford, 1932). Most ecclesiastical records concerning land illustrate rents owed, usually the result of purchases of land or grants burdened with secular service. While all these are essential to a complete understanding of monastic foundation in its social setting, they are not relevant to the theme here pursued.

[24] By which I shall refer to it: *Tractatus de legibus et consuetudinibus regni Anglie qui Glanvilla vocatur*, ed. G.D.G. Hall (London, 1965), vii. 1, p. 74. 'Notandum autem quod nec episcopus nec abbas, quia eorum baronie sunt de elemosina domini regis et antecessorum eius, non possunt de dominicis suis aliquam partem donare ad remanenciam sine assensu et confirmatione domini regis.' Translation slightly emended.

[25] Round, *Feudal England*, 249-52, 295-307, evidence accepted by Holt, 102 n. 85, and recited anew by R. Allen Brown, *Origins of English Feudalism* (London, 1973), 86-93, and the documents there cited and printed.

the charters of grant to ecclesiastical institutions exhibit two essential characteristics.[26] In the first place, lands and churches granted are increasingly described as 'alms'. or given 'in alms'. Peter Valoines, founding Binham priory in Norfolk in the 1080s or early 1090s, described the land he has given as 'beneficium et elemosinam', and similarly the Conqueror, in confirming William Warenne's first charter to Lewes, referred to the initial grant and other such grants made by his men as 'elemosina'.[27] Gradually, this hardened into the form 'in elemosinam', then 'in liberam, puram, et perpetuam elemosinam', through any combination of those adjectives.[28] Although this had become a formula, grants continued themselves to be seen as offerings of alms, as the passage quoted from Glanvill indicates and later charters and texts continue to show; and because they were offered freely - libera elemosina - we even describe them as free alms.[29] These gifts of land, therefore, continued to be thought of as retaining a fundamental common characteristic with the simple dropping of a penny into the lap of. a beggar.

The Binham charter continues: 'Quod beneficium et elemosinam specialiter facio pro anima domini mei Willelmi regis, qui Angliam adquisivit, qui mihi dedit illud manerium ...', and for the souls of Maud, his wife, William, his son, Henry the king, Maud the queen, and their sons, 'et pro meipso et uxore mea et filiis et fratribus propinquis meis, et pro animabus patris et matris mee ...', and so on. The gift of alms is made for the benefit of souls, a theme on which I hardly need enlarge. It is indeed the essence of such charters that the phrases 'pro anima' and 'pro animabus' (whatever the variety of the beneficiaries) qualifies the verbs 'do - dono - et concedo'. These lands were given to save souls.

How did they do this? What was the saving effect of giving alms to the church? If we take the charters literally we might extrapolate that, for the eleventh and twelfth centuries, there were in essence two ways in which grants were perceived to benefit the living and the dead. A gift of alms was quite simply in itself a good work which redounded to the credit of the donor. Maitland himself asserted that the term *elemosina* expressed 'rather the motive of the gift rather than a mode of tenure'.[30] Consider a later

---

[26] For a collection of charters see W. Dugdale, *Monasticon Anglicanum* (ed. J. Caley *et al.*, 6 vols in 8, London, 1817-30, hereafter *Monasticon*); also any cartulary, G.R.C. Davis, *Medieval Cartularies of Great Britain: A Short Catalogue* (London, 1958).

[27] *Monasticon*, iii. 345: the charter itself dates from the 1100s, V. H. Galbraith, 'Monastic foundation charters of the eleventh and twelfth centuries', *Cambridge Historical Journal* iv (1932-4), 220. *Early Yorkshire Charters*, viii. (ed. Charles Clay, Yorkshire Archaeological Society, 1949) 55: 'Hanc donationem ita concedo ut habeam eandem dominationem in ea quam habeo in ceteris elemosinis quas mei proceres faciunt meo nutu et hoc in ista habeam quod habeo in aliis'.

[28] See the excellent subject index to *Stoke by Clare Cartulary, BL Cotton Appx. xxi*, ed. Christopher Harper-Bill and Richard Mortimer (3 vols., Suffolk Records Society iv-vi, Woodbridge, 1982-4), at iii. 97, s.v. alms: the earliest to have the full form 'liberam, puram et perpetuam elemosinam' is no. 45 (mid-1170s); also no. 166, 'pure and perpetual and free' (1166x80).

[29] E.g. *Monasticon*, v. 63 (Bromholm), vi. 930 (Langley), 974-5 (Shouldham). See also references in the index to *Stoke by Clare Cartulary*, particularly those things to be held 'as freely as any alms'. Later, in 1293 Edward I said of Lenton priory 'quae de progenitorum nostrorum elemosinas est fundata', *Calendar of Close Rolls* (London, 1892-) *1296-1302*, 313, W. Prynne, *The History of King John, King Henry III, and the Most Illustrious King Edward I* (London, 1670), 570; and a confirmation of 1303 described a grant as 'elemosinas patris mei', Norfolk Record Office, Norwich Diocesan Archives SUN 8 (Cartulary of Coxford priory), fo. 60v (no. 527).

[30] Pollock and Maitland, i. 241.

grant to Binham, in which Roger Valoines quotes Theobald, archbishop of Canterbury, describing endowments as 'the alms which is interposed as a bridge between a man's father and paradise, by which the father may be able to pass over'.[31] We should in the first instance, therefore, simply take the terms of charters of foundation and donation at their face value. 'These alms I give for my soul' was the simplest expression of motive, but the variety of phraseology in charters reveals more: 'pro remedio et salute animarum', 'pro remissione peccatorum', and even (but spuriously) 'ut a Deo ipsa beata virgine intercedente peccatorum nostrorum nobis detur venia'.[32]

The church cannot be exonerated from encouraging the notion of a spiritual 'profit and loss' account amongst the lay aristocracy in the high middle ages. Although theologically only God can forgive sins, and that freely, the penitential system in which sinners made manifest their repentance by penance or other good works was easily perceived as a trade-off between guilt and its removal, a balancing act between sins and good works.[33] Bishop Ermenfrid of Sion imposed penance on those who had fought at Hastings and killed, at the rate of one year per man slain: but those who did not know how many they had killed were to do one day's penance per week for life.[34] He offered an alternative to this sentence, however, for the penitent could instead establish perpetual alms by founding a church or endowing one ('vel ecclesiam faciendo vel ecclesiam largiendo perpetua elemosina redimat'). The most significant result of this injunction, the Conqueror's own Battle abbey, was reported by its twelfth-century chronicler as having been founded for the souls of the slain, and for 'paying back for the blood shed there by an unending chain of good works'.[35]

The ambiguity inherent in the word 'elemosina' here points us towards the second redemptive mechanism: for not only is the thing given alms and given in alms, but it also establishes alms, by which is meant the good works and spiritual activities of the monks. Some of the early foundation charters record not just the donation of property to a church, but explicitly state that the donor has built the church and founded the monastery. Here is Roger Bigod: 'Ego...pro communi remedio et salute animarum nostrarum...dono domino Deo et [the Virgin, Peter and Paul] et ecclesie Cluniacensi ecclesiam quam apud Thetfordiam villam in honore Beate Virginis Marie construere et edificare coepi': I give the church which I have begun to build at Thetford (which became

---

[31] Printed and translated in Stenton, *English Feudalism*, 37-9, 259-60; 'elemosinam que quasi pons inter ipsum patrem et paradysum interponitur per quem pater transire valeat'.

[32] *Monasticon*, iii. 637 (Horsham St Faith), vi. 729 (Thetford canons).

[33] See Bishop Herbert Losinga of Norwich's comments in a sermon, based on Ecclesiasticus, iii. 33: 'Frequentate opera misericordiae. Vacate elemosinis. Quia sicut aqua extinguit ignem, ita elemosina extinguit peccatum', *The Life, Letters, and Sermons of Bishop Herbert de Losinga*, ed. E.M. Goulbourn & Henry Symonds (2 vols., Oxford & London, 1878), ii. 26, quoted in C. Harper-Bill, 'The struggle for benefices in twelfth-century East Anglia', *Anglo-Norman Studies* xi (1988), 113. See also *idem*, 'The piety of the Anglo-Norman knightly class', *Anglo-Norman Studies* ii (*Proceedings of the Battle Conference, 1979*), 63-6.

[34] *Councils and Synods with Other Documents relating to the English Church*, I (871-1204), ed. D. Whitelock, M. Brett and C.N.L. Brooke (2 vols., Oxford, 1982), i. 583.

[35] *The Chronicle of Battle Abbey*, ed. & trans. Eleanor Searle (Oxford, 1980), 66-7; 'quatinus iugi bonorum operum instantia commissa illic effusi cruoris redimerentur'.

the Cluniac priory there).[36] The gifts were intended to support monks, who, while being themselves poor and worthy recipients of alms, themselves gave alms and, more importantly in the Cluniac culture dominant in the eleventh century, devoted their lives to prayer.[37] Here is another East Anglian example:[38]

> since for the safety of their souls faithful men devoted to God perform many good works, and in particular it is thought that salvation depends upon the construction and endowment of holy mother church, for in churches the sins of the builders are diluted by the prayers of religious men and the mercy of God, the poor are sustained by alms and other benefits, and other offices of charity are administered: I, Robert Malet, hoping by a similar work to invoke the mercy of God, for the souls of [here follows the usual list], construct a church to the use of the monks at Eye and I place in it a convent of monks.

Both motives are here. The construction of a church (the foundation of a monastery) is itself a good work which will attract the mercy of God: but it also establishes good works to be performed by the monks in the form of prayers and alms, in which the founder shares vicariously although not himself directly performing them. Moreover these good works will continue after his death. Perhaps because of the increasing awareness that the works of the living continued to be of service to the dead who were still doing penance in purgatory,[39] donors usually emphasized that their gifts - and therefore the works which they supported - were to last for ever; they gave in perpetual alms.[40]

This sharing in the spiritual benefits which resulted from the monks' prayers and good works was known as fraternity.[41] It was generally recognized in the eleventh and twelfth centuries that the surest way to heaven was to become a religious; and if this was not compatible with an aristocratic life-style, it could be done as death itself approached.[42] The monastery was a half-way house to heaven, a foretaste of heaven on earth, as the

---

[36] *Monasticon*, v. 148; see also Horsham: 'edificavimus ecclesiam de Horsham', iii. 637.

[37] David Knowles, *The Monastic Order in England* (Cambridge, 1940), 29-30, 148-50, 'Cistercians and Cluniacs: the controversy between St Bernard and Peter the Venerable', *The Historian and Character* (Cambridge, 1963), 51-3, 67-8, 70, 74, Noreen Hunt, *Cluny under St Hugh* (London, 1967), 99-123, 139-40, C.J. Bishko, 'Liturgical intercession for the King-Emperors of Leon', *Studia Monastica* iii (1961), 53-76, Bede K. Lackner, *The Eleventh-Century Foundations of Cîteaux* (Washington, DC, 1972), 52-7.

[38] *Monasticon*, iii. 404-5.

[39] R.W. Southern, *Western Society and the Church in the Middle Ages* (Harmondsworth, 1970), 225-8, idem, 'Between Heaven and Hell', *Times Literary Supplement*, 18 June 1982, 651-2 (review of J. Le Goff, *La Naissance du Purgatoire*), Clive Burgess, ' "A fond thing vainly invented" : an essay on purgatory and pious motive in later medieval England', in *Parish, Church, and People: local studies in lay religion, 1350-1750*, ed. S.J. Wright (London, 1988), 59-64.

[40] See the index to the *Stoke by Clare Cartulary* (above, n. 28), in which most grants are mid-twelfth century or after, and most are perpetual.

[41] Rev. Preb. Clark-Maxwell, 'Some letters of confraternity', 'Some further letters of confraternity', *Archaeologia* lxxv (1926), 19-60, lxxix (1929), 179-216, H.E.J. Cowdrey, 'Unions and confraternity with Cluny', *Journal of Ecclesiastical History* xvi (1965), 152-62.

[42] Harper-Bill, 'Piety', 66, 69-76.

early Cluniac ideal had it and the Cistercians re-emphasized.[43] The next best thing to entering it was, therefore, as the Eye charter implies, to found a convent: in its good works the founder had a share as if he were a member of the community. Specifically, he could be buried in a place of honour in the chancel (closest to the vital operations, the liturgy, of the monks), the anniversary of his death was celebrated annually in masses, alms, and feasting, and his name might even have been mentioned daily in the canon of the mass at the consecration of the host.[44] At the end of the twelfth century, the Premonstratensian Ordinal and Statutes ordained that a founder was to have the same benefits at death as a canon dying in an abbey of the order, which included the circulation of his name in a mortuary roll through the whole order.[45] More generally, fraternity was granted in the phrase, 'so-and-so is admitted to a share in all benefits and prayers which are and shall be performed in this house for ever'.[46]

The high-medieval founder therefore both made a grant of alms, and performed alms at one remove by supporting the practitioners who were generally acknowledged to be the most effective exponents of spiritual works in the high middle ages, the religious. He exercised choice by selecting from among the increasing number of different types of the religious life on offer in the twelfth century.[47] One particular order or house would supply both monks and customs for his foundation, so that in making this choice he was selecting the emphasis of the good works which would save him. The Cluniacs offered primarily liturgy, the canons a greater element of pastoral work and almsgiving; and the Cistercians and Carthusians offered themselves as the 'pauperes Christi', hermits, who deserved to be supported for their own sake, and whose benefactors were therefore relying on the first redemptive mechanism - that they themselves were giving alms directly to the deserving poor - as much as on vicarious good works. Henry II stated that he had made grants to the Gilbertines 'ob religiosam conversationem et sanctum propositum' of the canons.[48]

If we now measure these grants against the types outlined at the beginning, we can see that these donors were, in the first place, attracting and rewarding followers with their grants of land. The foundations of the first generation after the conquest were established near the castles which were the barons' *capita honoris*, in part because they may have

[43] *Cluniac Monasticism in the Central Middle Ages*, ed. Noreen Hunt (London, 1971) 20-6, 32-43, G. Duby, *The Three Orders: feudal society imagined* (trans. Arthur Goldhammer, Chicago and London, 1980), 202, Knowles, *Monastic Order*, 207-24, esp. 222.

[44] Harper-Bill, 'Piety', 66, 'Struggle for Benefices', 114, *Stoke by Clare Cartulary*, 9-12, Cowdrey, 158-9, Lackner, 73-4, Penelope D. Johnson, *Prayer, Patronage and Power: the abbey of la Trinité, Vendôme, 1032-1187* (New York, 1981), 82, 90-1, Hunt, *Cluny under St Hugh*, 69, 132, Joan Evans, *Monastic Life at Cluny, 910-1157* (Oxford, 1931), 12, 20.

[45] H.M. Colvin, *The White Canons in England* (Oxford, 1951), 257-63.

[46] See Cowdrey, 154, for the Cluniac formula, and *Stoke by Clare Cartulary*, nos. 11, 14, 15 (i. 9, 11) for those adopted in final concords of the thirteenth century, of which the first may be taken as representative: 'prior recepit predictos ... in singulis beneficiis et oracionibus que de cetero fient in ecclesia sua imperpetuum'. Fines, unlike private charters, commonly recited fraternity as the return on grants, and this probably articulates the lay assumption: for the drafters of such an official document, it was important that something should have been given in return if there was nothing secular.

[47] David Knowles & R.N. Hadcock, *Medieval Religious Houses of England and Wales* (2nd edn., London, 1971), can be used as a useful survey; also *Monastic Order*, chs. vii, viii, x-xii, xxii.

[48] *The Book of St Gilbert*, ed. R. Foreville & Gillian Keir (Oxford, 1987), 162-3.

been intended directly to serve their founders' households in the castle chapels; the monks were conceived of as part of the lord's following.[49] Monastic benefactions had, however, little in common with the second and third types of transaction (grants for services and sales), with the exceptional feature that in tenurial terms, they, like sales, removed from the tenurial bargain the return which the donor received. But whereas in the one case land was given for a defined quantity of cash (as opposed to future services), in the other the return was spiritual benefits which could neither be enshrined in the tenurial relationship (like secular services) nor quantified outside it (like a once-for-all payment). These benefits were not services akin to quotas of knights and rents, which were formally purchased by the grant of land. Indeed, lawyers came to regard it as a cardinal principle of free alms tenure that that it was indefinite:[50] secular law was not competent to interpret and enforce monastic obligations to patrons, and there was therefore no binding relationship of reciprocity between the gift and the return on it.

It is important to be precise about this. In the first place it was not the case that benefactors did not, as a matter of fact, have general expectations of what the monks would do for them. They clearly expected one over-riding return, the salvation of their souls: 'pro anima mea'. But clearly this could not be the formal return on the grant, only the general end to which the alms were put. Equally, they knew that spiritual benefits were in part to be procured by the monks' prayers and alms, and it may be that in practice they thought of these works as services; the phrase 'free of all *secular* service' might indicate an assumption that there was some other return which they could equate with services.[51] But what was really important to them was the final result, the contribution to their salvation; it was precisely the monks' function to do this to the best of their ability as spiritual professionals who knew their own job. The monks were concerned for their own salvation, and what donors' gifts did was to secure them a share in the works performed to that end. Indeed, since donors relied both upon the simple fact that they had made a gift of alms and upon sharing generally in the monks' good works, it may have been important to them that the return on their gifts was not defined, for definition involves limitation. The donors wanted a share in all possible benefits flowing from all possible good works flowing from their own alms; the return which was expected was a general one. As far as the monks' activities are concerned, therefore, the charters, in so far as they mention spiritual activities at all, do not speak of them as services.[52]

---

[49] Brian Golding, 'The Coming of the Cluniacs', *Anglo-Norman Studies* iii (*Proceedings of the Battle Conference, 1980*), 68, Thompson, 'Statute of Carlisle', 575 n. 162, 'Church and Aristocracy', 36-7, Donald Matthew, *The Norman Monasteries and their English Possessions* (Oxford, 1962), 54-64; but see Marjorie Chibnall, 'Monks and Pastoral Work: a problem in Anglo-Norman History', *Journal of Ecclesiastical History* xviii (1967), 165-72.

[50] *Littleton's Tenures*, II. vi. $136.

[51] E.g. *Stoke by Clare Cartulary*, index, s.v. alms; *Monasticon*, iii. 404-5 (Eye), vi. 369 (Coxford), 419 (Buckenham). Later, 'prayers and alms' in general might be retained to the donor in such a clause, *Monasticon*, v. 69 (Normansburgh, end of twelfth century), reserving 'orationes', *Stoke by Clare Cartulary*, no. 293 (ii. 209-20), an early thirteenth century charter, 'absque omni servicio ad me vel ad heredes meos pertinente, preter elemosinas et oraciones'.

[52] With a few exceptions, it was not until the early thirteenth century that donors began to specify in particular cases the use to which their alms should be put (the poor, lights, or anniversaries); see *Stoke by Clare Cartulary*, iii. 12, nos. 572-646 *passim*, and index s.v. anniversary, lamps, and lights. But note that even these prove the rule to the extent that they were precisely the acts for which specific material provision was required (in the case of an anniversary the money was used for the pittance): the grant bought the materials, not the spiritual activities themselves, as they were later to do. The two twelfth-century exceptions in this cartulary are indeed exceptional, one (nos. 37, 71, 137) for the obit of the founder, the other (no. 538) for a man received into the community; both men would also have been general sharers in the benefits of the house, their anniversaries being but an additional special commemoration.

Nor, second, was it the case that, as a matter of fact, no specific acts would be performed for donors, particularly and specifically founders, to the general end of salvation. But the evidence, for instance of the Premonstratensian Ordinal, shows that what was actually done would have varied from order to order and from house to house, according to statute and custom;[53] these acts were defined by the religious themselves, and not by donors specifying what services were to be done in return for their grants. Some phrases show us that it was important to the religious that what they did they did freely;[54] indeed, it was simoniacal to sell sacraments for money.[55] Even if it was the natural assumption of laymen, therefore, that the monks were their tenants and their works services, the church in the twelfth century successfully counteracted the notion for a time, and prevented prayers and alms from becoming legally the purchase price of grants.[56]

The essential point is that the deeds of the monks which procured spiritual benefits had no binding contractual relationship with the grant of property and the continued tenure of that gift. They were not services built into tenurial relationships; and as a result they feature rarely in the charters which record grants. Moreover, when they do it is only in general statements in preambles, or in such a statement as that of Robert Malet that 'I make this grant because I hope to invoke the mercy of God'.[57] Gifts were made, in the terms of charters, to God himself and to various saints, *in the hope of* spiritual remuneration. Ecclesiastical benefactions should be seen as forms of gift-exchange, therefore, rather than as commercial transactions in which the return was contractually binding. Donors did not legally either demand or enforce the spiritual activities which would save them, as they would have done in a commercial transaction. Instead, they established their (clerical) followers in a monastery, or contributed to such a body, and relied upon the social convention that a gift demands a return - from the saints, as well as from the monks - to bring them to eternal bliss. They did not invest in their own salvation, so much as give freely of their goods to support religious men and spiritual activities, in the hope of spiritual benefits freely given in return. They gave, in fact, quite literally, free alms.

•   •   •   •   •

---

[53] See n. 45, and other monastic customaries, which, however, are far more concerned with dead brethren; e.g. *Udalrici Cluniacensis Monachi Consuetudines Cluniacenses*, in *Patrologia Latina* cxlix, 651-2, 767-78 (esp. 777-8), *Consuetudines Farfenses*, ed. Bruno Albers (Stuttgart, 1900), 192-206 (esp. 204-5), *The Monastic Constitutions of Lanfranc*, ed. M.D. Knowles (London, 1951), 120-32.

[54] Spiritual benefits and fraternity were cited as having been granted by the monks (reflecting the ceremony at which a layman was granted it in the chapter-house, *Constitutions of Lanfranc*, 114-15, Cowdrey, 'Unions and confraternity with Cluny', 157-8), rather than as the condition for a grant, even in final concords, see n. 46, and *Stoke by Clare Cartulary*, nos. 11, 14, 15, 289, 302, 321, 513, 540, 560. Even as late as 1276 the nuns of Marham addressed a benefactor thus: 'nos temporalia bona sua predicta nobis in hac parte collata spirituali remuneracione quantum in nobis est sibi recompensare volentes', Norfolk Record Office, Hare MS 1, fo. 68v. *Stoke by Clare Cartulary*, nos. 277 and perhaps 278 appear to be twelfth-century exceptions, the former indeed specifying fraternity and acceptance as a monk as 'hac condiscione'.

[55] *Conciliorum Oecumenicorum Decreta*, ed. J. Alberigo et al. (3rd edn., Bologna, 1973), 197 (1139, can. 2), 265 (1215, can. 66). Just at the point when the church was in practice to lose this point, Aquinas was trying to avoid the suggestion of simony by arguing that lands were given for the end of the increase of spiritual activities (final cause), and not directly in return for them (efficient cause); Susan Wood, *English Monasteries and their Patrons in the Thirteenth Century* (Oxford, 1955), 134, *Cistercian Statutes, 1256-88*, ed. J.T. Fowler (London, 1890), 30 n. 76, William Lyndwode, *Provinciale* (Oxford, 1679), 279.

[56] I hope to pursue the ecclesiastical view of the matter further elsewhere.

[57] *Monasticon*, iii. 404. Even when fraternity was seen as the return on a grant (see n. 54), this did not, apart from the act of acceptance into the confraternity, make any actual acts enforceable as services owed to the donor.

Such was the perceived function of monastic property in the high middle ages. What was its legal and jurisdictional status? In particular, what did free alms tenure mean, and what was the essence of this tenure?

This subject must take as its starting-point the seminal account by Maitland, who built upon the accounts in Littleton and Bracton.[58] He argued that tenure in free alms and the performance of secular services, particularly forinsec service owed to the grantor's lord, were not incompatible, so that freedom from secular service could not be the primary characteristic of this tenure.[59] Instead, he argued that those who made grants in free alms intended to place the land 'outside the sphere of merely human justice'. 'The land is subject to no jurisdiction other than the tribunals of the church', 'to the law and the courts of the church'.[60] This was why grants as recorded in charters were made not to men, but firstly and principally to God, and only secondarily to mortals.

Maitland's argument was based mainly on the assize *Utrum,* as it is revealed to us in the Constitutions of Clarendon of 1164 and in Glanvill. It purports to establish the boundary between secular and ecclesiastical jurisdiction. In it, Henry II apparently accepted that, barring a preliminary action before his own justiciar to establish the right to jurisdiction, land 'in alms' ('ecclesiastical fee' in Glanvill), was to be justifiable in the ecclesiastical forum, court christian.[61]

> If a dispute arises between a clerk and a layman, or a layman and a clerk, in respect of any tenement which the clerk wishes to establish as alms, the layman as lay fee, it shall be determined by a recognition of twelve lawful men, by the consideration of the king's chief justice and in his presence, *whether (utrum)* the tenement pertains to alms or to lay fee. And if it is recognized to pertain to alms, the plea shall be held in the ecclesiastical court, and if to lay fee, in the king's court [or the relevant seignorial court]; provided that he who was originally seised shall not lose his seisin until the plea has been settled.

This presents a problem of definition: which lands, precisely, were denoted by 'elemosina' in this and other texts? Elisabeth Kimball noticed an aspect of this problem when she attempted to define how land given in free alms was perceived in contemporary opinion, both clerical and lay. It was neither clearly 'lay fee'; nor was it land consecrated to God and therefore part of the church's 'spiritualities', as were the sites of churches. While recognizing the ambiguity of the material, Kimball tentatively assigned *elemosina* to the latter, and equated with it lands given to churches.[62] On this basis, the *prime facie*

---

[58] See nn. 3, 4; *Littleton's Tenures,* II. vi. $133-42 (ed. Wambaugh, 66-70), *Bracton,* ii. 93-4, iii. 329-34 (fos. 27b, 285b-287b).

[59] Pollock & Maitland, i. 244-6, *Bracton,* ii. 93-4.

[60] Pollock & Maitland, i. 244, 246-7, 251.

[61] Printed in *Select Charters and other Illustrations of English Constitutional History,* ed. W. Stubbs (9th edn., ed. H.W.C. Davis, Oxford, 1913), 165-7, translated in *English Historical Documents,* ed. D.C. Douglas & G.W. Greenaway (2nd edn., London, 1981), 769; also in Audrey Douglas, 'Maitland revisited', 29 & n. 5. My paraphrase.

[62] Kimball, 'Judicial aspects', 7-10.

evidence of *Utrum* had to be accepted: that lands held by the church in *elemosina* were justiciable only in its courts.

The problem, for both Kimball and Maitland, was that - certainly in the time of Bracton, and perhaps even in that of Glanvill - only land consecrated to God as the sites of churches and their dower lands actually did fall outside lay jurisdiction, and in almost all cases this involved parish churches only.[63] Land held by monasteries was the subject of litigation in secular courts and was clearly not barred from them, even if it had been given 'in liberam elemosinam'.[64] Moreover, as a matter of fact *Utrum* itself had removed jurisdiction over what was left to the king's court, except where clerks disputed such lands amongst themselves, because in disputes between a layman and a clerk it effectively decided the issue.[65] Bracton provided an explanation for this which depended upon a lay view of legal tenure: although lands given to churches were given primarily to God, those given to non-parochial churches were also given to men ('and the monks there serving God'), so that there are two different sorts of 'free alms', one more free than the other. The latter count as lay fee, so that monasteries can use the same legal remedies in the royal courts as laymen, relying on their own seisin and that of their predecessors.[66] The difficulty in accepting Maitland's conclusion is apparent. If land given in free alms was largely not subject to ecclesiastical jurisdiction even in the later twelfth century, the essence of this tenure cannot have been immunity from lay jurisdiction.

Bracton's explanation was a rationalization and not an historical account. It therefore avoids a central problem which Maitland's analysis throws up, and which he indeed tried to face. How did the church lose between Henry II and Bracton the jurisdiction, recognized in 1164, which it had apparently gained in the course of Stephen's reign?[67] *Utrum* is alleged 'gradually and silently' to 'have changed its whole nature', a process by which 'ecclesiastical tribunals suffered a severe defeat.'[68] Yet - and the subsidiary problem is indicated by those adverbs - the church at the time put up no resistance to the change

---

[63] Pollock & Maitland, i. 247-51, Thorne, 'Assize *Utrum*', 434-5, Van Caenegem, *Royal Writs*, 328-30, Douglas, 34-7, *Bracton*, iii. 329-32; the writ which Glanvill gives also envisages a rector, xiii. 24 (p. 163); but elsewhere his discussion does not imply a restriction, xii. 25, xiii. 24 (pp. 148, 163).

[64] E.g. Milsom, *LF*, 50-1, 91, 118; see also the Plea Rolls, listed in ibid., ix-x; but more detailed research needs to be done on these to establish precisely the kind of cases in which religious appear, in so far as the rolls will tell us (on which see ibid., 3-8 & *passim*).

[65] See n. 63.

[66] *Bracton*, ii. 52-3, 57-8, 59, 228-9, iii. 40, 127, 128, 331, iv. 175-6, 265-6. Unlike other ecclesiastical institutions, the possessions of a parish church belonged to God and that church, and not to the parson for the time being. Whereas, therefore, abbots, priors, and bishops could count on the seisin of their predecessors, and so litigate in royal courts using the writ of right, this remedy was not open to parsons. They therefore used *Utrum*, which became their 'writ of right', a 'singulare beneficium' introduced in their favour. For the author's confusion, see below n. 75.

[67] Samuel Thorne equally identified the problem, but simply admitted that he could not see how this had happened; still, he thought it had done so by the time of Glanvill, see n. 63.

[68] '[The *avitae leges*] conceded more than the church could permanently keep. If as regards criminous clerks the Constitutions of Clarendon are the high-water-mark of the claims of secular justice, as regards the title to lands they are the low-water-mark.' Pollock & Maitland, i. 247-8. Maitland (followed by the later writers) suggested that the lay court simply denied the use of *Utrum* to those who could use the royal remedies, and cited the writs of prohibition as the machinery for doing so, ibid., 251; but compare Douglas, 34 & n. 20.

of which we have any evidence.[69]

It it these problems which have led Audrey Douglas to re-open the fundamental question of what was intended by *elemosina* in the texts of the assize *Utrum*.[70] She argues that a distinction must be drawn between the different contexts of jurisdiction and tenure in which the term was used. First, in accordance with Bracton's conception of alms more free and free alms, *elemosina* was intended to denote spiritualities, the sites of churches and the dower land given them at their foundation, which were annexed to the church when the bishop consecrated and dedicated it.[71] It was episcopal action which gave to property its peculiarly ecclesiastical character, and which removed it from the sphere of lay jurisdiction. Land given 'in elemosina', on the other hand, in the sense of most of the land given to the church after 1066, was never intended to be exempt from the lay courts; this was a tenurial description. The church, therefore, was being offered much less in 1164 than has been thought: the lay power conceded jurisdiction only over spiritualities. In general, the church did not complain about clerics litigating in royal courts and using Henry II's new actions because it did not expect frankalmoin land to come under exclusive ecclesiastical jurisdiction. There was, therefore, no gradual and silent change, and the church lost little. The endowments of monasteries were always regarded as lay fee, and the church reflected this in referring to them as 'temporalities'.

The argument is undoubtedly illuminating, but it is not clear that it quite solves the problem. In the first place, the lack of a contemporary terminological distinction between the 'elemosina' which were annexed to a church by a bishop at consecration, and the 'elemosina' otherwise given to monasteries which we think of as lands in frankalmoin, is a weak point in Douglas' argument. If she is to be believed, throughout the twelfth century and beyond, the terms 'elemosina' and 'libera elemosina' were used, quite indiscriminately and without any differentiation, of two sorts of property between which lay a crucial jurisdictional distinction.[72] A more concrete problem is that, in criticizing Maitland for relying on Bracton, Douglas is in the end forced to rely on the same source to clinch her argument; for she has to explain the cases in which *Utrum* was used by religious houses in litigation about their lands, as opposed to those of parish churches which they held.[73] In doing so, she has to amplify what is comprehended in her jurisdictional *elemosina* to include not only the buildings, sites, and cemeteries of

[69] Kimball noticed this in the penultimate sentence of 'Judicial Aspects', 11: 'The English church apparently permitted this return to a state of affairs which had existed before the reign of Stephen without making any public objection.' The church did in fact resist *Utrum* itself, in the context of the Becket dispute, Douglas, 36.

[70] Douglas, 'Maitland Revisited'; see above, n. 1.

[71] Douglas, 33, 43-7; on things consecrated to God by priests, the dower of a church given at its dedication, its site, buildings and cemeteries, *Bracton*, ii. 40-1, 58, iii. 40, 60, 136, 331, 127 (things given at the time of dedication are more pure and free than those given afterwards), 128 (monastic buildings without which religious cannot serve a church are sacred), iv. 265-6 (even other appurtenances given to a monastery initially, such as common of pasture, count as dower).

[72] See above, n. 29, for the continued use of 'elemosina' for gifts to religious houses. The problem is if anything compounded by the terminology in *Glanvill*, who uses 'libera elemosina' and 'feodum ecclesiasticum' interchangeably, xii. 25, xiii. 24 (pp. 148, 163). If 'elemosina' had two different meanings according to whether it was being used in a context of jurisdiction or of tenure, it is surely the message of Milsom that such a distinction was hardly thinkable until the later twelfth century. See further below, 244.

[73] Douglas, 28, 33, 41-7, esp. 46: 'While the exact grounds for a decision for *elemosina* cannot be ascertained, recourse to Bracton again proves suggestive.'

churches, but also (with Bracton) the living-quarters of monasteries annexed to them, without which the religious would be unable to serve the church, and dower property given to the church at foundation and its appurtenances.[74] Apart from the possibility that the author of Bracton himself was inconsistent,[75] this throws up a problem for Douglas. For to include in *elemosina*-as-spiritualities both endowments given at the foundation of a house and things essential to the subsistence of the religious is to draw the net so wide as to lose the very precision desired. Under the first category, a substantial proportion of the property of religious houses would be categorized as spiritualities, because the first endowment made by the founder was so important and churches were often not dedicated until considerable endowments had been made;[76] under the second, even more could - tendentiously - be claimed, and the distinction between jurisdictional and tenurial *elemosina* all but disappears. Even if contemporaries in 1164 understood *elemosina* to denote this or anything like it, we are back where we started: religious did not in fact use *Utrum* for their lands and did use the royal courts, so that we have to accept that the church lost jurisdiction between 1164 and the early thirteenth century, as Maitland assumed. Whoever is right about what *elemosina* denoted in 1164, therefore, we still have to explain what happened in the following fifty years.

It is important to notice the circumstances of the disputes which actually went to the assize, as we find them on the plea rolls and elsewhere from the very end of the twelfth century.[77] In the first place they almost all involve parsons of parish churches, very rarely monasteries.[78] Second, where we have more than the barest statement of the facts in the common form of the plea rolls, it is clear that there is often a seignorial element in the dispute. One of the parties vouches a lord to warranty,[79] for instance, or the two parties turn out to be themselves lord and tenant.[80] This must alert us to the need to place the charters we are observing and the grants they record in a context different from that imagined by Maitland, the legal world of the twelfth century as re-drawn by Milsom.

Milsom sees the lord and his court as the focus of twelfth-century landholding society, until the reforms of Henry II - intending only 'to make the seignorial structure work according to its own assumptions', in the light of the difficulties over title caused by Stephen's reign[81] - in fact deprived them of their power and replaced them with the king's law, administered by his justices. The basis of Milsom's view is that title in the twelfth

---

[74] Ibid., 43, 46, *Bracton*, iii. 128, iv. 266; see n. 71.

[75] While including all these things amongst *res sacra* and therefore accepting that they are justiciable in court christian, he also categorically denies *Utrum* to abbots and priors on the grounds that they can use ordinary lay remedies, and therefore by implication denies them ecclesiastical jurisdiction; see n. 71.

[76] M. Brett, *The English Church under Henry I* (Oxford, 1975), 125, Galbraith, 'Monastic foundation charters', 214-22.

[77] Douglas, 37-41.

[78] Ibid., Van Caenegem 329-30; and see the indexes of plea rolls (under actions-Utrum) to find cases, e.g. *Curia Regis Rolls*, (London, 1922-), *Pleas before the King or his Justices, 1198-1212*, ed. D.M. Stenton (4 vols., Selden Society lxvii-viii, lxxxiii-iv, 1948-9, 1966-7), index to vol. iv.

[79] E.g. *Curia Regis Rolls*, i. 135, ii. 158, iii. 21, ii. 199, *Pleas*, iv. no. 4324.

[80] *Curia Regis Rolls*, iii. 229, 295, iv. 193; iv. 201; *Pleas*, iv. nos. 4134, 4248, 4283.

[81] Milsom, *LF*, 186, 177-9.

century was not derived from on high, in what he describes as a flat legal world of universal rights, in this case the law emanating from the crown which was common to all free men. It was derived from a lord, to whom a tenant did homage and by whom he was 'seised' of his tenement. In the early part of the century, there could be no other title but seignorial seisin, because there was no other guarantor of title than the lord from whom a tenant held. Tenure was a relationship between a donor and a recipient. There was, therefore, no distinction between title, tenure, and jurisdiction; the lord's court was the forum for the initial grant and the concomitant performance of homage and fealty, it governed the subsequent payment of the services, and it was the place for disputes about that tenure and those services. The presumption of this tenant's heir that he would be let in on the death of his father was not a right to inherit based on common universal rights, but simply a custom established in that lord's fee and therefore overseen by the court of his tenants, which tempered the naked operation of the lord's will; it was a prescriptive right against a lord to be seised. Equally, the lord could not bind his own successors to honour the grant by the force of an external authority, for his successors were themselves the only authority; it was simply the custom that a succeeding lord would honour his predecessors' grants, if they satisfied certain conditions of reasonableness, and all lords but the king had the added incentive that they themselves wished their own tenure to be renewed by their own lords, for themselves and their heirs.[82]

Milsom himself has offered only hints as to what his picture must do to our view of ecclesiastical tenure and jurisdiction, but it is possible to offer some suggestions here as to how it affects the question under review. In the first place, ecclesiastical tenure must be understood primarily as the interaction between two parties consequent upon a grant to (and perhaps the foundation of) a church. The foundation charters in the century after the conquest each record the establishment of a relationship between founder and monastery, lord and tenant, which was not primarily governed by external authorities. They describe a private series of local bargains, often bargains between a founder and a mother-church; hence the great variety in their terms up to the middle of the twelfth century. The tenant, a monastery or parish church, looked to its grantor (its lord) as the source and guarantor of its title, as was manifested later when parsons and monks vouched their lay lords to warranty in the king's court.[83] The king, indeed, is not entirely missing from the process, as we saw earlier in those charters which cited him as spiritual beneficiary. But he confirms grants not as king and source of the common law, but as the donor's lord and therefore the donor of the donor's fee, as Peter Valoines explicitly stated in his charter for Binham.[84] Since lords could not bind their successors under their own 'law', their grants to religious houses were not secured as perpetual endowments as far as secular justice - the lord's court - was concerned. Milsom suggests that from the lay point of view, grants in alms were understood as charitable subscriptions, which each lord must

---

[82] Milsom, *LF*, *HF*, chs. 5-6; also S.E. Thorne, 'English feudalism and estates in land', *Cambridge Law Journal* xvii (1959), 193-209. Milsom's view, derived from working with legal sources, must always be seen alongside the social fact of inheritance; see J.C. Holt, 'Feudal society and the family in early medieval England: I. The revolution of 1066', *Transactions of the Royal Historical Society*, 5th ser. xxxii (1982), 193-212,' II. Notions of patrimony', ibid., xxxiii (1983), 193-220.

[83] Milsom suggests that it may have been common for grantors in alms to act for their tenants, *LF*, 51.

[84] Above, n. 27 (and the Lewes example there), 232. For the lord's consent, see below, 254-255.

decide to continue or not.[85] They were one kind of charge upon the whole inheritance: Glanvill allows a landholder to make gifts in alms alongside marriage-portions and grants for services, as long as they amount only to a reasonable proportion of his free tenement.[86]

This accords with the use of the word 'elemosina', if we take it literally as I have tried to do above in understanding the motive of pious gifts. A gift of alms has a definitely voluntary quality about it. This was emphasized by the addition of the word 'libera' to qualify 'elemosina'; free alms freely given. Religious houses, like other tenants, depended upon the renewal of the relationship between them and their founders' and benefactors' heirs (although clearly it would be much less easy for an heir of a founder to remove his support from a religious house, and thus destroy the institution, than for the heir of a minor donor to do so). Since ecclesiastical tenants did not do homage to their lords, this might appear to differentiate them from tenants for secular service; but, on the analogy with family settlements, it is more likely to have resulted in a much looser obligation on the heir to renew than was true of grants sealed by homage, for such was the obligation which homage created.[87] Seen, therefore, as a temporary but renewable charitable subscription charged on the inheritance, but subject to the over-riding control of the current lord like other such charges, grants in alms must naturally be thought of as 'lay fee', as the later categories of the common law would have it.[88]

The original grantors, however, did attempt to impose obligations upon succeeding generations, in the first place by securing the consent and confirmation of their living heirs.[89] They also wrote their intentions into their charters. They sometimes indicated that the grant was to last for ever, to be held 'jure perpetuo', and this became enshrined in common form around the middle of the twelfth century as 'in perpetuam elemosinam'.[90] This is a plain statement about what donors expected of their heirs in the future. Furthermore, they occasionally specified that they expected no exaction or secular service to be taken from the tenements now given as alms, that they were to be held freely; such an intention was presumably inherent in the notion of 'free alms'.[91] The reason why the alms were free was quite simply that they were being devoted to spiritual rather than secular purposes. Another word appeared later to emphasize this freedom from secular burdens; 'pure' was taken by Bracton to indicate the definite absence of services owed by the ecclesiastical tenant to its lord.[92] Therefore, the phrase 'in liberam,

---

[85] *LF*, 91; also 120-1, 131-2, 145, *HF*, 112, 169-70, Thorne, 'Estates in land', 204-8. Some of the writs printed by Van Caenegem clearly show heirs taking back the lands their ancestors had given, *Royal Writs*, nos. 42, 47, 80, 128, 176. The lord's interest may be seen in ibid., nos. 35, 36, 38, 44a, 171, which may show lords further up the scale taking back lands which their tenants had granted in alms.

[86] *Glanvill*, vii. 1 (p. 69), 2 (74).

[87] Thorne, 'Estates in land', 196-208, Milsom, *HF*, 112, 170, *Glanvill*, ix. 2, *Bracton*, ii. 228-9.

[88] See n. 66.

[89] Thorne, 'Estates in land', 205-6, Milsom, *LF*, 131-2, and *Monasticon, passim*.

[90] *Monasticon*, vi. 73, 369; see n. 28.

[91] Ibid.; also *Monasticon*, iii. 330, 404-5, iv. 70-1, 206, v. 69, vi. 369, 729, etc.

[92] *Bracton*, iii. 93.

puram, et perpetuam elemosinam' may be thought of as part of the expression of intentions by donors. In describing the nature and motive of the gift, lords imposed obligations on their heirs about both the length and the terms of tenure, in an age when they could do so by no higher power than prescriptive force.

The fact that charters were drawn up at all, however, indicates that there was something more universal about these grants than the largely unrecorded enfeoffments to laymen. Charters announced grants to the world in general, and even to men of the future, because the parties to it were aware that the bargain was intended to reach beyond the temporally limited interaction between themselves, within the honour. In particular, the relationship between founder and monastery, unlike the same lord's grants to lay tenants, involved external authorities in the form of religious orders, mother-houses, and bishops.[93] Moreover, since charters were often drafted by the ecclesiastical recipients,[94] to a certain extent they may evince clerical rather than lay assumptions about grants in alms, although it is also true that the lay founders would have learnt about these matters from these very same monks, and therefore shared their assumptions. Ecclesiastical jurisdiction was indeed developing in the early twelfth century in the wake of papal reform, and canon law was staking its claim to control of ecclesiastical property.[95] The growth of ecclesiastical jurisdiction in England, in Stephen's reign in particular (in default of stable seignorial authority), provides the context in which bishops confirmed the properties of monasteries and judged disputes about ecclesiastical property.[96] In particular, it seems that when they annexed the sites of churches and their first endowments at consecration, they were held to have removed them from the lord's jurisdiction into the inalienable care of the church.[97]

Did the church claim jurisdiction over the sites and dower of churches only, or over all its property? The question which Douglas poses concerns the extent to which the church made a jurisdictional distinction between the two sorts of property. It is possible for us to identify a distinction between episcopal consecration and dedication of a church, and episcopal confirmation of all monastic property.[98] But not only is it not clear, for the reasons given above, where the boundary fell in the twelfth century,[99] but it is equally unproven that the church saw this as a distinction between property over which it

[93] Orders: e.g. Cluny, Knowles, *Monastic Order*, 154-8, Golding, 'Coming of the Cluniacs', 65-7, and note that the first endowments were often granted to the mother-house, e.g. Lewes, Thetford (Cluny), above nn. 27, 36. Mother-houses: the same is true, e.g. the Binham (St Alban's) and Horsham (Conques) charters quoted above, nn. 27, 36, and see Marjorie Morgan, *The English Lands of the Abbey of Bec* (Oxford, 1946), 10-13. Bishops: see n. 96.

[94] E.g. *Stoke by Clare Cartulary*, iii. 45.

[95] Thorne, 'Assize *Utrum*', 428-33, Brett, *English Church under Henry I*, 34-62, 91-100, 122-31, 141-61, F. Barlow, *The English Church, 1066-1166* (London, 1978), 145-76, A. Saltman, *Theobald Archbishop of Canterbury* (London, 1956), 15-18, 25-55, 133-64, 175-7.

[96] For episcopal confirmations, see any collection of episcopal *acta* (e.g. those being published by the British Academy, 1980-, and Saltman, *Theobald*, 187 n. 13), and *Stoke by Clare Cartulary*, nos. 69a-137 (esp. 70, 136-7), iii. 41-2.

[97] See n. 71.

[98] Douglas, 45, Kimball, 'Judicial aspects', 7.

[99] See above, 241. Douglas accepts that the indications are not clear, art. cit. 44-5, 46 & n. 63.

claimed jurisdiction and other types of property. Bishops and popes regularly confirmed all the possessions of monasteries throughout the twelfth century, as any collection of their *acta* reveals.[100] Confirmations explicitly undertook the duty of defending tenure of property, by pronouncing sentence of excommunication on those who violated it, and by taking a monastery and its possessions into explicit papal protection.[101] As a result, bishops and popes did continue to take cognizance of disputes concerning ecclesiastical property, even into the thirteenth century.[102] It is hard to avoid the conclusion that the church claimed jurisdiction over all its property, and that it exercised such jurisdiction in defence of it.

Claims and reality are different things, of course. The problem with grand disputes of which that involving Becket is such an outstanding example, is that they teach us to assume that conflict between jurisdictions is the norm. Certainly there was always that potential. But it is not unimportant that in this case the document defining jurisdictional boundaries was only drawn up because of the intransigence of the protagonists. In practice, as long as jurisdiction still represented real control and had not been reduced merely to financial opportunity, authorities often co-operated to secure the objects which their control was intended to implement. In the case of Henry II's reign, good order and just title had to be re-established after the disruption of the previous reign, something an endowed church will always find it necessary to support.[103] Indeed, churchmen in the middle ages constantly re-discovered the maxim that it was better to have lay authority on their side, because of their naked lack of protection if it was hostile. Hence the particular co-operation between Henry and Theobald, and the king's assumption that this would continue with Becket.[104]

Twelfth-century powers did not have the resources to be able to claim, in practice, to be exclusive; they had to use whatever means came to hand, and all princes used or tried to use the church.[105] Increasingly as powers and their resources grew more extensive and sophisticated, conflict arose and the boundaries of jurisdiction had to be defined, a process of which we see almost the beginning in the Constitutions of Clarendon. But such definition was a long process, and was mediated not only through the public quarrels of

---

[100] See n. 96, and for popes confirming and taking the possessions of religious houses into their protection, *Papsturkunden in England*, ed. Walther Holtzmann (3 vols., Berlin, 1930, 1935, 1952), *passim*, e.g. i. nos. 14, 346 (1119x23, 1194x8), which are both.

[101] N. above, and e.g. *Stoke by Clare Cartulary*, nos. 70-1, 136.

[102] Saltman, *Theobald*, documents nos. 20, 71, 103, 132, 134, 138, 144, 155, 169, 175, 206-8, 223, 212, 238, 277-8, *English Episcopal Acta, I: Lincoln 1067-1185*, ed. D.M. Smith (London, 1980), nos. 70, 137, 225, 229, 238, 264, 284, *IV: Lincoln 1185-1206*, ed. D.M. Smith (London, 1986), nos. 232, appendix II (31), *Acta Stephani Langton Cantuariensis Archiepiscopi A.D. 1207-1228*, ed. Kathleen Major (Canterbury & York Society, Oxford, 1950), xvii-xviii, no. 42. For disputes taken to Rome, Jane Sayers, *Papal Judges Delegate in the Province of Canterbury, 1198-1254* (Oxford, 1971), 179-83, 332-3, 351-3.

[103] Milsom, *LF*, 177-86; see the church's measures at the end of Stephen's reign, which relied copiously on royal support, W.L. Warren, *Henry II* (London, 1973), 426, Saltman, *Theobald*, 33-6.

[104] Warren, *Henry II*, 427-53, Saltman, *Theobald*, 164.

[105] This is indeed the trend of recent scholarship in this field, see Douglas, 27 n. 3, and Warren, *Henry II*, 399-446. Moreover, the bishop was himself a baron, and even a royal official or justice, so that he could himself hold two or three types of courts.

politicians, but also through the gradual but thorough practical experience of what worked best, and in particular of what litigants wanted. If we see the procedure proposed in 1164 and its *elemosina* in this light, less neat and satisfying though it is, we may be able to make more sense of the problem of frankalmoin and *Utrum*. The terminology of the clause may have been imprecise simply because the exact distinctions of jurisdiction and tenure which were later to emerge had not yet been worked out. From the royal point of view, the king was only just beginning to apply consistent categories to tenures, as the common law would later see them. While at either extreme the categories of lay fee owing secular service, and property annexed to churches as dower must have been fairly clear, land given in free alms was neither;[106] it was a grey area to contemporaries, just as it is now to historians, which is why they have found it so difficult to categorize it satisfactorily. As far as the church was concerned, the clause was consonant with its claims and its practice that bishops and popes had cognizance of lands held by ecclesiastical institutions.

The exercise of ecclesiastical jurisdiction is comprehensible in the context of the needs of founders and of ecclesiastical tenants. Jurisdictions appear more clearly as providing a range of not necessarily exclusive solutions when we look at them from the point of view of donors and recipients seeking protection. It is better to see them and their churches as looking for all the guarantees they could get from whoever was willing to give them, to which end they secured confirmations from lords including the king, heirs and other relatives, and bishops and popes.[107] The addition of ecclesiastical jurisdiction over a donation offered an external check - the only one available in the era of seignorial justice - on the untramelled authority of the donor's successors in their own lands. It thereby met the desire of a founder that his alms should be perpetual, that his heirs should not simply take endowments back and thereby deprive a house of its main means of support. It also gave tangible expression to the ideal of the monastery as the bridge between heaven and earth, as something set apart from other sites and other property. Equally, it offered monasteries themselves a second authority to which to turn in the event of a dispute about its property. This was important particularly when that dispute was with the lord and heir of the grantor, whether it was about the terms of tenure or about title; for his court would hardly be the most effective forum in which to seek redress.[108] In this context, the use of the free alms terminology for most grants to monasteries might even appear as a deliberate attempt to imitate the status of consecrated land, and to lend them an aura of difference which would both reinforce the prescriptive duty of the heir to renew the grant and offer tangible help in the event of trouble. Both parties were trying to have the best of both worlds, for the land was not removed from the control and protection of the lord's fee, but, being marked out as separate in intended function, thereby acquired the additional protection of ecclesiastical jurisdiction.

---

[106] See Henry II's statement in 1176 identifying lay fee with land owing secular service, which is the only type of land for which a clerk may be arraigned before a secular judge; Warren, *Henry II*, 538, Kimball, 'Judicial aspects', 10: 'excepto laico feodo, unde mihi vel alio domino saeculari laicum debetur servitium'. Henry also drew a simple contrast between military fees and the alms of churches, Van Caenegem, *Royal Writs*, 279 n. l.

[107] See nn. 84, 89, 96, 100.

[108] Hence the writs cited at n. 85. The case discussed by Douglas, 41-3, is of this sort. A complaint against an interloper, on the other hand, could be effectively pursued in the lord's court, as long as the lord wished to defend the house against external invaders. But ecclesiastical sanctions would have added weight to the action against them.

This was the situation which the expansion of royal justice gradually transformed. But we must try to be clear about what it actually did. 'Henry II and his advisers did great things, but they did not reach out from their own world'.[109] Henry's writs did not appear in a vacuum, but became available in addition to seignorial and ecclesiastical justice, and were indeed intended to enforce and regulate that justice. It is interesting that the very assize which is central here is, as far as our evidence goes, one of the first manifestations of the energy which Henry was to devote to the law.[110] We must note, however, that in 1164 Henry was purporting only to state the customs of the realm (and there is evidence that something like *Utrum* had been used under Stephen).[111] It is arguable, indeed that Henry intended the assize as a manifestation of co-operation, for in it he fully accepts ecclesiastical jurisdiction over *elemosina*. Moreover, the text clearly envisages only a preliminary action to define jurisdiction, and in the light both of seignorial power and of ecclesiastical claims it is possible to see why such was necessary. The fact that two or three authorities might settle disputes about land - the king, the lord, and the church - gave litigants plenty of scope for manipulation and manoeuvring. If one party cited the other to appear before a bishop, and the defendant refused to attend and to submit to the authority of the ecclesiastical judge, and moreover did not respond to ecclesiastical sanctions; or indeed if a church refused to submit itself to seignorial jurisdiction on the grounds that it was only liable before ecclesiastical judges; in these circumstances only a higher secular authority would be able to unjam the dispute by imposing a decision concerning jurisdiction. An ecclesiastical tenant with the support of its lord, against, for instance, a 'mere interloper', would not necessarily have needed to rely on other powers.[112] But neither a monastery whose lord had taken back the alms once granted by a predecessor,[113] nor a lay tenant of a tenement which a monastery, as lord, had itself taken into hand,[114] would have been helped by seignorial justice.[115] The recognition as we find it in 1164 can be envisaged as an offer of an action to parties to a dispute already under way, but whose progress had become stalemated by a dispute over jurisdiction. It was this which, Henry proposed, the royal court could sort out; he would arbitrate between seignorial and ecclesiastical jurisdictions.

---

[109] Milsom, *LF*, 3.

[110] Milsom suggests that the whole process of royal interference with seignorial justice began with the treaty between Henry and Stephen in 1153, promising to restore lands to those who lost them in the anarchy and their heirs, from which the regular procedure of the writ of right appeared, *LF*, 177ff., *HF*, 128-9. The evidence for the assizes comes from the mid-1160s and the 1170s, beginning with *Utrum* in 1164, ibid., 135, 138-9, Van Caenegem, *Royal Writs*, 82ff., 283-90.

[111] Best presented by Douglas, 29-32.

[112] See the cases at Milsom, *LF*, 50-1; see also *Curia Regis Rolls*, i. 161, in which a case involving the prior of Castleacre is put off *sine die* while the earl Warenne was with the king overseas: since the earl was the priory's patron, he had presumably been vouched to warranty.

[113] The case outlined by Douglas, 41-3, is of this sort.

[114] See e.g.s on the plea rolls, in which the use of 'mort d'ancester' makes explicit the tenurial orientation, *Pleas*, ii. nos. 98, 436, 483, 527, 626, 638; also *Curia Regis Rolls*, vii. 6 (St Benet's, Holm). Many of the cases on the plea rolls in which *Utrum* was used involved the lay tenants of parish churches, see n. 80.

[115] For these tenurial orientations, see the scheme in Milsom, *LF*, 71-102, and on novel disseisin, 8-35. The 'downward' claim, by a lay or ecclesiastical lord against a sitting ecclesiastical or lay tenant, would probably have had the same result, particularly before the availability of royal justice, because the lord would simply act, with or without due process of his court, leaving the tenant to bring legal action in some other way. The case at Milsom, *LF*, 91, however, shows the lay lord trying to get the land back through royal justice.

What *Utrum* certainly did not do, in the terms in which we have it, was to define exactly what was intended to fall to each forum, and therefore who could use it with any prospect of success.[116] Only by the decisions made by juries in actual recognitions, brought by litigants engaged in cases, would the practical boundary between lay fee and alms have become clear. Moreover, *Utrum* was buried in 1164 in a purported statement of customs produced in the heat of a dispute between the temporal and spiritual arms, not in a series of articles for an eyre. And its subsequent history suggests that it hardly played a major role in the history of Henry's law-giving; it does not re-appear, in fact, until the pipe rolls of the 1180s and Glanvill, where it is found being used by parsons.[117] On no reading of the facts, therefore, can the assize be allowed a very large role in the process of defining jurisdictions. The fact that it was used very occasionally later on by religious houses shows that it was not actually denied to monasteries concerning their lands, and supports the possibility that its terms were flexible and did not define *elemosina* closely.[118] It is therefore all the more true that the reason why the assize had no very significant effect was simply that it was not taken up by litigants. Whatever meaning was intended by Henry II in 1164, in practice *Utrum* did not contribute to the definition of the status of land in free alms.

Utrum is relatively unimportant because the other remedies offered by Henry II met the needs of litigants much better. Because lands held by the church had not been removed from the tenurial structure, and were not generally perceived to have been annexed to the exclusive competence of the ecclesiastical forum, their tenants were as able to take advantage of Henry's new actions as were lay landholders. To a certain extent, little had changed: in a dispute where the protection of the lord for a monastery was forthcoming (for instance against a mere interloper), the lord's court, and even his simple executive action, remained competent and effective.[119] What forced the tenant - as well as his lord - to royal justice was the rule, an accidental result of Henry's provisions, that the man in possession could not be challenged without a royal writ.[120] Even so, this need only have resulted in the purchasing of a writ of right patent addressed to the lord, by which the defendant would be forced to answer in the lord's court, although it also became possible to use novel disseisin before royal justices. In a dispute against the lord, however, a monastery now had available both novel disseisin, which took the case out of the lord's court, and the writ patent, which would do so if the lord's court failed to do justice to the demandant.[121] Glanvill's writ of right therefore has an option for a claim to hold of a lord in free alms.[122] It is not the case that the ecclesiastical authorities were not invoked by litigants, for we know of cases beyond the reign of Henry II which came

---

[116] The text of the Constitutions of Clarendon says the ecclesiastical party will be a 'clericus', but the Constitutions in general are not carefully drafted to specify all the different types of clergy, and in some clauses 'clergy' and even 'parsons' must have been intended to include religious, cc. i. iii, iv, xi, (*Select Charters*, 165-6). *Glanvill* has 'clerici', but in his actual writ, a parson.

[117] Van Caenegem, *Royal Writs*, 96, 329-30, *Glanvill*, xii. 25, xiii. 24 (148, 163).

[118] *Curia Regis Rolls*, iv. 291: see Douglas, 46-7, and 35 n. 25, 41-2.

[119] See n. 112.

[120] Milsom, *LF*, 46, 55-64 and *passim*.

[121] Ibid., 80-7 and *passim*.

[122] *Glanvill*, xii. 3 (p. 137).

before bishops and popes.[123] Nor, despite the fact that litigants themselves could buy writs of prohibition from the king, did the king use it on his own initiative to try to squeeze ecclesiastical jurisdiction.[124] But by and large more effective justice - that is, quicker and more surely implemented justice - was to be had in the king's court, so that it was thither that ecclesiastical landlords resorted.

It was this process which produced the classic Bractonian frankalmoin tenure. Royal justice imposed upon the divergent customs of lords' courts uniform practices and categories about both the processes of justice, and the terms of tenure and inheritance. The bargains once made between grantors and convents, and maintained by succeeding generations of lords and religious, now became subject to an external jurisdiction which could enforce, when requested to do so, its own view of the terms of those original deeds. This is why Bracton has to include a discussion of free alms tenure; but equally why he finds it extremely hard to discern consistent links between distinct categories of tenure and the words 'free', 'pure', 'perpetual', and 'alms'. [125] The object of perpetuity had indeed been met, but not by the insertion of the word 'perpetual': it was the fact that convents could now buy the writ of right and the assize of novel disseisin which prevented heirs from regarding their ancestor's grants as charitable subscriptions which they could choose not to renew. For the king would enforce tenure as perpetual unless it was specifically for a term. The words 'liberam et puram' were much harder for Bracton to make any sense of. 'Free' indeed denoted nothing consistent. And even the presumed meaning of 'pure', that no secular service was owed to the lord, could not remove the obligation for forinsec service to lords higher up the tenurial chain. Some grants, in any case, both used 'pure' and specified service![126] The spectacle of Bracton squirming so in order to define clear categories of tenure was the consequence of the application of royal justice to grants which had originally been the product of and subject to seignorial control.

The affect of the application of royal justice was to standardize the terms of charters even more than the strengthening of ecclesiastical jurisdiction had done in the mid-twelfth century. Grants from c. 1200 increasingly contained clearly defined tenure-clauses which specified the terms under which the grant was held in terms of who the lord was (usually the grantor and his heirs), what was owed to him, who was the tenant, and how long the grant was to last. A grant to a monastery might therefore have been 'to be held to the prior and convent and their successors of me and my heirs in free, pure, and perpetual alms, free of all secular service and claim whatsoever'.[127] These were phrases from which followed specific tenurial and judicial consequences, which were guaranteed by the jurisdiction of royal justice. Maitland's 'flat' legal world of the common law had arrived, and within its ambit fell the land held by monasteries.

•　　•　　•　　•　　•

---

[123] See n. 102.

[124] Van Caenegem. *Royal Writs*, 345.

[125] *Bracton*, ii. 93.

[126] Ibid.; Kimball, 'Frank almoign and secular services', 341-7.

[127] E.g. *Stoke by Clare Cartulary*, no. 221 (ii. 173): 'habendas et tenendas de me et heredibus meis predictis monachis tanquam liberam et perpetuam elemosinam, libere, quiete, absque omni servicio in perpetuum, salvo servicio domini regis, scilicet ...'.

The standardization resulting from the imposition of new standards and categories upon earlier practices was a symptom of the effect of the passage of time - of the strains resulting from the operation of changed circumstances on older forms of association. Such is the lot of the church in this fleeting world. And it is the lot of mankind too, for secular tenurial relationships also changed; by 1200, the personal relationship between lord and tenant which informed the original enfeoffment was no longer necessarily a living bond, which was nowhere more obviously manifested than in the relationship between the king and many of his tenants-in-chief. Magna Carta, indeed, was partly intended to secure for such barons the rights which the legal changes of the preceding half-century had brought to lesser tenants, notably the right to inheritance on defined terms, enforceable as a matter of course in royal courts.[128] Whereas, however, the extinction of families and the normal accidents of genealogy offered at least the chance of escheats, wardships, and marriages, and therefore of some turnover of families, perpetual ecclesiastical tenancies would never escheat for more than a vacancy.[129] Moreover those churches owed little or no enforceable service for their tenants. However, we need not imagine that in most cases this caused many problems: in general, the heirs of founders, and especially the direct heirs of the same lineage, did continue to foster their relationships with the houses on their fee, as patrons. They were even, by offering small gifts and favours, able to enjoy the position of spiritual beneficiaries.[130]

Nevertheless, the arrival of the common law continued to have its consequences for ecclesiastical tenure, in part imposed by the logic of legal development itself; having given law, kings were obliged continually to emend and refine it, in order to meet new cases, whether these arose from new circumstances or were generated by the development of the law itself and the ingenuity of lawyers deployed on behalf of their clients.[131] We must therefore observe further the effects of royal law upon the status and the function of ecclesiastical temporalities.

Consider a typical charter of donation of the later middle ages. In 1365 John Cheverston has granted to the prior and convent of Flitcham one quarter of the manor of Flitcham,[132]

> to be had and to be held to them and their successors of the chief lord of the fee for
> the services due and accustomed for ever, to find for John and his heirs for ever two
> suitable chaplains of the convent to celebrate masses and other divine services daily in
> the priory church for the good estate of John and his wife while they live and for their
> souls when they shall have died [and other names souls] ...

---

[128] Milsom, *LF*, 24-5, 162-3, J.C. Holt, *Magna Carta* (Cambridge, 1965), 207-23, 226-9. A new edition of this work is eagerly awaited, in which the plight of tenants-in-chief under the common law, in comparison with sub-tenants, will be more clearly described in the light of Milsom's work.

[129] On custody see Wood, *Monasteries and their Patrons*. 75-100.

[130] Thompson, 'Church and Aristocracy', 32-133.

[131] Milsom, *HF*, 3, 6-7, *LF*, 185-6.

[132] This is a paraphrased translation of Norfolk Record Office, FLI 65.

The essential elements in this and the many other similar charters of grant to the church of which it is representative are three-fold: that grants are made in return for celebrations and divine services for the souls of those persons specified; that they are often made directly to secular chaplains, or to a monastery to support such priests; and that the recipients are to hold by the usual services.

The crucial difference between these and earlier charters is the insertion of the purposive 'ad celebrandum' in front of 'pro anima mea'; the latter phrase no longer qualifies the verb of donation ('I give to X for my soul'), but describes what the recipient is actually to do (I give to X to celebrate for my soul'). The souls will benefit not so much from the act of giving as from the activities which are to be performed. In the later middle ages the daily mass in the form of a chantry was the most popular form of spiritual work purchased in this way by donors, and the same principle extended to other specified spiritual activities such as the saying of collects, antiphons and other prayers, the distribution of alms, and the performance of obits, lights and so on. The proliferation of grants to support such works was the practical outcome in late medieval popular religious practice of the development of the doctrine of purgatory.[133] The importance of these works here is that donors themselves defined what was to be done for their souls, rather than leaving the mechanics of the process of salvation to be arranged by their ecclesiastical tenants.

This process of specification transformed these spiritual activities into services. No longer were they the free return which the recipient chose to offer the donor in return for, but not in exchange for, the gift. They were particular acts specified by the donor; and they were defined in charters, often - as here - in the tenure clause introduced by 'habendum et tenendum', which described the terms upon which the land was to be held by the recipient. The charters therefore laid down a binding return on the grant. Unlike most grants to the church in the twelfth century, the relationship between land and the return on it was now contractually and quantifiably reciprocal.

This is made clear by the sanctions which were provided in the event of the contract not being fulfilled. John Cheverston's charter included a clause which allowed himself or his heirs to distrain on the land granted should the services specified fall into arrears. Distraint had been a normal initial remedy for default of secular services since at least the early thirteenth century, and its appearance in the context of spiritual activities emphasizes their transformation into services to be performed by recipients for property granted to them. There could be no enforcement where there were no services resulting from a grant.[134] Furthermore, this enforcement took place under the eye of secular, rather than ecclesiastical, justice; distraint began extra-judicially, but its operation was subject to the common law, and through the action of replevin often resulted in litigation in county and royal courts.[135]

---

[133] Burgess, '" A fond thing vainly invented"', 56-84; R.N. Swanson, *Church and Society in Late Medieval England* (Oxford, 1989), 296-308, cites the main literature.

[134] In the spiritual context see *Littleton's Tenures*, II. vi. §136-7, where the distinction between frankalmoin and tenure by divine service is quite clear.

[135] Pollock & Maitland, i. 353-5, 575-8, T.F.T. Plucknett, *Legislation of Edward I* (Oxford, 1949), 55-63, Milsom, *LF*, 8-11, 31-4, *HF*, 104-5, 142-3; and now Paul Brand, 'Lordship and distraint in thirteenth-century England', *Thirteenth-Century England* iii, ed. P.R. Coss & S.D. Lloyd (Woodbridge, 1991), 1-24.

Edward I's legislation went further than distraint in protecting donors. The following was laid down in the forty-first clause of the statute of Westminster II of 1285;[136]

> If a tenement is given for a chantry, lights, food for the poor, or to sustain other alms, but these alms [137] are withdrawn for two years, the donor or his heir has an action to recover the tenement in demesne.

The writ to initiate the action was known as *cessavit de cantaria* and was modelled upon clause twenty-one of the same statute (itself extending a provision in the statute of Gloucester), which gave to lords this same power over tenants defaulting on secular services.[138] The application of this secular writ to divine services makes crystal clear to us that these spiritual activities had acquired the status of secular services: not only were they defined by lay donors, but they were also now enforceable in lay justice, and were inexorably linked with the property which was given for them in a commercial and contractual relationship.

Clauses twenty-one and forty-one of the 1285 statute, however, had different pre-histories, which emphasize the transformation in the status of spiritual services. *Cessavit* for secular services restored to lords a right effectively lost in the early thirteenth century by the very introduction of the common law and its affect of securing the position of tenants even against what had once been the legitimate powers of their lords. In the seignorial world of the twelfth century, lords had been able to resume tenements from tenants who defaulted on their services, by due process in their own courts. Royal justice, and in particular novel disseisin, accidentally destroyed the power of the lord and his court, and left him only with the extra-judicial process of distraint and more lengthy proceedings at common law to enforce services.[139] This clause in the 1285 statute illustrates royal justice having to redress its own affects, for lords were now offered a swifter and more secure action for recovery of the land itself in the royal courts, to counterfeit the due process which they would have used in their own courts in the twelfth century. *Cessavit de cantaria,* on the other hand, reflected an entirely new situation: before this there had been no spiritual services within the compass of the secular law - seignorial or royal - on which ecclesiastical tenants could have defaulted. Only with the thirteenth-century increase in the number of grants being made for specific spiritual activities did it become thinkable to apply rules about secular services to ecclesiastical tenure. In doing so, therefore, clause forty-one was creating a novel possibility based on a change in attitude and practice on the part of the laity, rather than - as was the case with *cessavit* for secular services - restoring the twelfth-century status quo before the common law had interfered.[140]

---

[136] *Statutes of the Realm,* (11 vols. in 12, London, 1810-28), i. 91-2.

[137] Note this usage: it refers to the whole list of good works, not only to distributions of doles.

[138] *Statutes of the Realm,* i. 48, 82-3.

[139] Milsom, LF, 8-35, Plucknett, *Legislation of Edward I,* 56-8, 88-93, and see n. 135.

[140] The contrast is curiously exacerbated by another reflection, for which see note 160: *cessavit* for secular services could only be used for grants before 1290, because *Quia Emptores* prevented any more relations of lord and tenant from being created. *Cessavit de cantaria,* on the other hand, applied mainly to grants made thereafter, because so few grants before it were made for specific spiritual services.

The contrast in perceived function between land granted to the church in the high middle ages and that granted in the later is made clear by comparing the points at which sanctions operated in the two eras. For the nature of a sanction depends upon what it is designed to enforce. Consider the following statement of Henry II, addressing the pope about the Gilbertine lay brothers' revolt:[141]

> The fact that some of the brethren are attempting to lead a less disciplined life and break the Order's first requirements shocks us not a little, as well as those who have conferred gifts of alms upon these houses. ... both we ourselves and our barons will take back from the Order so changed our possessions and our estates, which we granted to these same houses *because of their religious life and holy purpose.* For whatever has been granted to these houses for those reasons may properly, we believe, be withdrawn when these same reasons fail to operate.

It was no good giving alms to holy men if they failed to remain holy; but Henry did not point, and could not have pointed, to specific works which those canons and lay brothers had failed to carry out. They were supported for the holy lives which they led, which made them worthy recipients of alms. The failure of such holiness constituted the reversal of the aims of the grant, so that it provided the occasion for Henry's threat of resumption. Later-medieval donors, on the other hand, were less concerned with the quality of the lives of those upon whom they conferred their patronage, and more with their ability to do certain specified acts - notably to say mass - and with the actual performance of the same. Such measures as were adopted, for instance, in the statutes of chantries and secular colleges, to secure suitable and modest-living chaplains, were primarily intended to ensure a continuous flow of masses, rather than to uphold the quality of spiritual life for its own sake.[142] The focus of sanctions, as in *cessavit*, was on the end product of the process, the performance of services. Monks and priests in receipt of such grants were being hired for the specific services which they uniquely could perform, rather than being supported simply for who they were and how they lived.

This change in the nature of grants to ecclesiastical institutions can be observed in the second feature of late medieval charters. Many dropped the clauses by which the grants were initially made to God and secondarily (as Bracton had it) to a particular church and those serving God there.[143] They were made directly to the institution itself, whether the prior and convent to support a monk or chaplain, the perpetual chaplain in his own name, or a body of such chaplains in the form of a chantry-college.[144] The transaction had become more recognizably an earthly contract, made between legal persons in this era for goods and services exchanged on a contractual basis. Gift-exchange, by which high medieval donors had made grants to God and the saints in the hope of heavenly reward, was no longer an acceptable mode of giving to an age increasingly imbued with

---

[141] *The Book of St Gilbert,* 162-3 (my italics). I am grateful to Professor Christopher Brooke for pointing out this reference to me.

[142] K.L. Wood-Legh, *Perpetual Chantries in Britain* (London, 1965), chs. iv, xi; e.g. the statutes for Rushworth College, founded by Edmund Gonville, *Monasticon,* vi. 1386-7.

[143] *Bracton,* ii. 52-3, 228-9.

[144] E.g. the charter under discussion, made to John, prior of Flitcham and the canons there, and Edmund Gonville's for Rushworth, printed at Thompson, *'Habendum et Tenendum',* 201.

the commercial mentality. It was preferable to make enforceable contracts with living parties on this earth to buy spiritual services which, under the developed doctrine of purgatory, quantifiably counted towards the penances which the beneficiaries must suffer and thereby reduced their days of purgation.[145]

The third change which can be observed in the charters concerns the status of land granted to the church in the later middle ages. John Cheverston's charter laid down that the manor was to be held, not of him in free alms, but of the lord from whom he had held it ('the chief lord of the fee') on the same terms as he had held it ('for the services due and accustomed', in this case half a knight's fee). This tenurial configuration was a result of the great statute of *Quia Emptores* of 1290, which, in effect, prohibited subinfeudation as a mode of conveyance and ensured that all subsequent grants would be made by substitution.[146] From that point onward, although grantors were given the freedom to alienate their property - and in particular to sell it, hence the title of the statute - to whomsoever they would, they could no longer create new tenures by subinfeudating land to recipients who would become their tenants, on terms agreed at the time of the grant.[147] Instead, they granted land to be held for the same services as they had held it, and they themselves dropped out of the tenurial chain altogether, leaving the donee as tenant of the lord. The effect of the statute was first to fix the tenurial system in the pattern in which it lay at the time of the statute, and then in the course of time to flatten it out as tenements escheated to lords for lack of heirs. It was thus to match more closely the flat jurisdictional world, which in many respects had been divorced from tenure a century earlier.

Quia Emptores is in part a compromise between the respective rights of lords and tenants in a system of dependent tenure subjected to the strains of changing circumstances. But it is also the end of one part of the story in which the intervention of the common law into the world of tenurial feudalism wrought havoc with the control of lords over their fees. In the twelfth century, lords exercised control over alienations by their tenants in so far as the services which their tenants owed them were affected.[148] Many subinfeudations were made by tenants precisely with the aim of supplying that service, but some grants, notably gifts to family-members and the church, and sales, diminished the tenant's resources without reserving services. If tenants alienated too much, their ability to perform their services was threatened, and this is what constituted the lord's interest. Seignorial control over alienation is manifested in the confirmations which founders of religious houses commonly, perhaps invariably, sought from their lords, up to and including the king, when they conveyed property to their churches.[149] The arrival of the common law, however, and in particular the assize of novel disseisin, made it much harder for lords to get out a tenant who had got in, and this lies behind the

---

[145] Burgess, ' "A fond thing vainly invented" ', 59-67.

[146] *Statutes of the Realm*, i. 106, Plucknett, *Legislation of Edward I*, 102-8, Milsom, *HF*, 113-16.

[147] It may not have intended this effect generally, but only in the context of sales of land for no or nominal service; but it was soon held to have prohibited subinfeudation completely; Milsom, *HF*, 116-17.

[148] Milsom, *LF*, 111-21, *HF*, 110-12.

[149] Milsom, *LF*, 120, Thorne, 'Estates in land', 205; *Monasticon, passim*; e.g. above, 232, 242.

complaint embodied in c. 39 of Magna Carta of 1217, which prohibited tenants from alienating so much of their tenements as to leave them without enough resources to fulfil their services.[150] But in this matter the future was with the freedom of alienation, as the common law gradually transformed tenants into owners. In 1290, therefore, lords exchanged recognition of such freedom for the protection of their own rights in the tenements, whose services were not to be changed by endless subinfeudations.

The effect of this on grants to the church was from the point of view of services, significant, for it prevented any further tenures in free alms from being created, except by the king.[151] From this point, ecclesiastical recipients had to accept responsibility for the services incumbent upon any particular tenement which they received. They might be able to persuade the lord of the land otherwise by buying him out, but they could not ignore him and his due and treat the transaction as only one between themselves and the donor. This marks the end of the development of free alms tenure, which began as a statement about the intention of a grant within a tenurial relationship, implying that the land was to be burdened with no secular return in so far as it could be avoided. Royal control produced the classic Bractonian frankalmoin, in which lands were immune from intrinsec services unless these were specified, and particularly if the grant was in pure alms, but under which burdens of forinsec service owed to higher lords could not be avoided if there were no other lands in the fee to support them. It was this subjection of ecclesiastical land to the demands of the tenurial structure within which it was situated that *Quia Emptores* made explicit, by removing one rung in the chain and forcing churches to accept secular burdens. But we must not over-emphasize the practical effect of this, for ecclesiastical tenants and their lords had always had to take account of their tenurial circumstances and the demands of lords paramount for services in their fees.[152] It was just that the statute revealed the situation more starkly; the receipt of 'temporal' property made ecclesiastical recipients explicitly liable for temporal services, and these were encoded in their title deeds.[153]

Although it had an important affect on ecclesiastical tenants in this respect, however, *Quia Emptores* was not primarily aimed at the threat to services. For between 1217 and 1290 changes in economic and military circumstances had combined to render services far less valuable than the actual income from the land which had been given to support them.[154] Inflation had rendered fixed rents grossly under-valued; military quotas were not exploited much in practice since they did not provide a practical basis for an army, and

[150] *Select Charters*, 343.

[151] *Littleton's Tenures*, II. vi. $140. As a matter of fact, the phrase was still used in some grants, which indicates two things: where a tenement carried no secular service - and advowsons commonly did not and were in fact the subjects of most grants given in free alms after 1290 - it made no difference to add a clause about free alms. Since, secondly, this was even done where there were services incumbent upon the tenement, it begs the old question of what free alms meant; and we must conclude that it was being used simply in the general sense of a gift to the church: it had no tenurial implications. See Thompson, 'Church and Aristocracy', 205-6 n. 56.

[152] See above, nn. 59, 126.

[153] There was a tangible practical effect: religious houses could no longer be immune from distraint upon their lords for services owed by those lords to their lords or the king, Kimball, 'Frank almoign and secular services', 352.

[154] Milsom, *HF*, 107-10, 112, *LF*, 111-113, 154-5; Miller & Hatcher, *Rural Society and Economic Change, 1086-1348*, 64-9, 173-8, 210-39, A.L. Brown, *The Governance of Late Medieval England, 1272-1461* (London, 1989), 85-7.

they had in any case been reduced in the course of the century. As a result, it was more important to hold land in demesne than to hold the seignory over it. The feudal incidents of escheat, wardship and marriage were more valuable than services because they accurately reflected the actual value of the land at the time the incident fell. We might add that the passage of time was likely to have rendered the relationship between lords and tenants a purely formal and economic one, rather than one of loyalty and trust, service and reward, which must have subsisted between their predecessors who had created the tenure. The lord's interest was therefore primarily economic rather than personal, and his primary economic interest was in incidents rather than services. The mischief which the thirteenth century had done him was to lengthen the tenurial chains by which lands were held of him each time lands were sold in that quickly-moving market or otherwise alienated.[155] As a result, when an escheat or wardship came to him, it often produced not tenure in demesne of the tenement held of him, but the seignory over the next tenant down the chain.[156] And if the tenure between tenant and sub-tenant was the result of a sale, the services were likely to have been purely nominal: wardship of a tenant of nine years of age would have produced not twelve years' enjoyment of the lands, nor even twelve years of rent, but twelve roses at midsummer. By preventing the further lengthening of the chain, the statute addressed this problem at least as far as future transactions were concerned.

This problem was even more relevant where ecclesiastical landholders were concerned, because the introduction of perpetual tenants into the tenurial chain removed all possibility of escheats ever coming to the lord.[157] The problem of mortmain was the most obvious mischief to the lord's incidents, and it was therefore the first to be tackled; *Quia Emptores,* which itself prohibited freedom of alienation to be extended to permit grants to the church, had been preceded by eleven years in the statute of Mortmain, on the basis of a protest twenty years before that in the Provisions of Westminster.[158] The statute *De viris religiosis* of 1279 simply prohibited further grants to the church, citing loss both of services and of incidents as its motives. If such grants were made, lords could simply retrieve the land in question into their own hands as forfeit, a provision which admirably matched their grievance. This was indeed the logical response to the problem, but it was not practical for the simple reasons that laymen and clerics wished to continue providing for their souls by making endowments, and the church was a good purchaser for those who wished to sell. The result was that land could be granted to the church under a licensing system which protected the rights of lords by allowing them to exact payment for their licences, by which they gave up the prospect of future incidents.[159]

---

[155] The reasons why sales were not made by substitution are given by Milsom, see n. 22.

[156] Plucknett, *Legislation*, 102-3.

[157] Plucknett, *Legislation*, 94-102, Milsom, *HF*, 113, *LF*, 112-21, J.M.W. Bean, *The Decline of English Feudalism* (Manchester, 1968), 49-66.

[158] *Select Charters*, 375, 393, 451-2. For the timing of the statute, P. Brand, 'The control of mortmain alienation in England, 1200-1300', *Legal Records and the Historian*, ed. J.H. Baker (London, 1978), 35-6, 40.

[159] Sandra Raban, *Mortmain Legislation and the English Church, 1279-1500* (Cambridge, 1982), 19-20, 38ff., 180-1, Plucknett, *Legislation*. 100-2, Thompson, 'Church and Aristocracy', 57-9.

Between them, therefore, Mortmain and *Quia Emptores* completed the transformation of the status of land which would come to the church, by subjecting it to the secular demands of the tenurial structure and to the control of temporal authority. It could no longer masquerade as 'free alms', whose roots lay in a tenurial relationship which was at once outside the normal run of secular relationships in owing no service, but nevertheless a real bond between lord and ecclesiastical tenant whose purposes the phrase 'free alms' expressed. Both these aspects of frankalmoin were reversed. In the first place, the church had to accept secular burdens incumbent on the land it received, in the form of the services due to the chief lord of the fee. It was, in fact, subjected to the demands of the tenurial structure. But this is not the same as saying that it was exposed to the realities of tenure, because this structure was no longer an organism of living bonds between lords and vassals; it had become a fossilized system of economic rights and dues in which lords and tenants took what they could in despite of each other. It was to this flattening system of ownership operating through the shell of tenure to which ecclesiastical property was not only subjected, but indeed in which it was more strictly regulated than other land by the royal authority which governed the even more flat legal world.

This is paralleled by the reversal of the second aspect of frankalmoin, for a grant to the church would no longer even create a relationship of tenure between the donor and recipient; the donor was obliged to drop out of the structure altogether. The personal living bond between founder and foundation, benefactor and monastery, of which the grant was itself both symptom and effect, would not now be reflected in a formal tenurial relationship. The anomaly of this is that it happened just at the point when ecclesiastical tenure, in terms of its function, had become like high medieval secular tenure; land was granted in return for specific services - of a spiritual nature - which were enforceable in contractual terms. Although, therefore, services became the main return on grants to the church in the later middle ages, they did not exist within tenure. Tenure had to be counterfeited between donor and recipient and their successors, for instance in the explicit provision for distraint in charters of grant, and the availability of *cessavit de cantaria* after 1285.[160] Spiritual services were owed, as was John Cheverston's chantry, to one who became by the very act of donation no longer a party to the tenure of the land granted. They were equivalent not to rent-service, but to rent-charge. Grants of land to the church in the later middle ages were, therefore, even more clearly commercial and contractual than before. They were purchases of commodities made between two contracting parties.

Indeed, it is probably the case that the prohibition of the tenurial bond stimulated the process of specification of spiritual services, since there was no tenure to hold the relationship together after the grant, nor which might be used as a basis for sanctions in the absence of specific provision.[161] The effects of the statute of Westminster II probably

---

[160] By an unexplained chance, c. 21 of the statute of Westminster II (to enforce secular services) was drafted for use between lords and tenants, and thus became irrelevant to grants made after 1290, whereas c. 41, for default of spiritual services, was drafted for use between donors and recipients, and therefore continued to be relevant after the passage of *Quia Emptores* five years later; *Statutes of the Realm*, i. 82-3, 91-2, and see also the writs in *Novae Narrationes*, ed. E. Shanks & S.F.C. Milsom (Selden Society lxxx, London, 1963), liv, lix, 242-5, *Early Registers of Writs*, ed. E. de Haas & G.D.G. Hall (Selden Society lxxxvii, London, 1970), 297-9.

[161] For instance, the provision of the statute of Westminster II, c. 41, that land alienated by an ecclesiastical tenant could be recovered in demesne by the donor or his heirs (for which see below, n. 165), could not apply to grants made after 1290, whose makers would therefore have had to rely exclusively upon *cessavit de cantaria*, and therefore upon having made provision for specific spiritual services.

tended in the same direction; and the beginnings of the specification of spiritual services are to be found at the point where lords were losing control within their fees to royal justice, in the course of the thirteenth century. All these things stimulated them to specify what ecclesiastical recipients were to perform in return for their grants, and to provide measures for enforcing these. In the twelfth century a grant had created a relationship of tenure subject primarily to the control of the donor himself, as lord, which was flexible in that it was not based upon specified services, but on the personal spiritual bonds between a lord and his family monastery. Now a grant divorced status and function and created two separate relationships which were defined and regulated, one in respect of secular economic obligations inextricably incumbent upon the property, the second for the spiritual services, a relationship which was not now even based on tenure, but upon contract.

. . . . . .

As a postscript, we are obliged to take account not just of the contrast in terms of status and function between land granted to the church in the high middle ages and that granted in the later period. For the earlier grants created permanent tenurial relationships which generally survived into the fourteenth and fifteenth centuries: monasteries rarely escheated, so that the terms under which they held could rarely be changed.[162] There were, therefore, in the later middle ages two forms of ecclesiastical tenure, one characteristic of the period, the other surviving from the previous; and because so much land had been granted to the church in the eleventh and twelfth centuries, the outmoded but extant terms of free alms tenure probably applied more commonly to property held by ecclesiastical institutions than those of specific spiritual services.[163] Lawyers recognized the distinction, and categorized the two as tenure in free alms, an indefinite tenure, and the definite tenure by divine service.[164]

The difference was also clearly understood in the statute of 1285. Clause forty-one itself matched *cessavit* (which provided an action for the enforcement of tenure by divine services) with a second remedy for lords of land held in frankalmoin: if land once so given to a religious house was subsequently alienated, the donor or his heir had an action (*contra formam collacionis*) to recover it in demesne.[165] The crucial wrong which lords might suffer under this tenure was held to be the alienation of the tenement which they or their ancestors had given. Because in free alms tenure, the clause may be glossed as saying, there are no services temporal or spiritual, there can be no default on them through which lords may recover the land. But if a grant of land is reversed by alienation, it both ceases to be a perpetual gift, and can no longer support the vicarious penances in

---

[162] For some examples of such updating of spiritual services in the context of refoundations, see Thompson, 'Church and Aristocracy', 60 n. 43, 110-12.

[163] Even more common was the tenure by barony of those churches which had been in existence at the conquest, because the land in the church's hand at that point was probably not matched by the accretions of the rest of the middle ages; see Raban, *Mortmain Legislation*, 130ff. I also ignore a hybrid form between the two discussed here, when lands had been granted for specific spiritual services, but before *Quia Emptores* had removed the possibility of a relationship of lord and tenant between the parties. It partakes of the status of the earlier type of tenure, but in function matches the later, and what is said here about those two matters applies to each accordingly.

[164] *Littleton's Tenures*, II. vi. $133-42 (ed. Wambaugh, 66-70).

[165] *Statutes of the Realm*. i. 91-2; this applied equally to land granted for specific spiritual services, which would have applied to the hybrid in n. 163.

which the founders are the participants; it therefore subverts the original purposes of the gift. Since we have no jurisdiction to enforce those penances, we must therefore protect at least the fact of the original gift, the grant of land. Alms alienated are no longer alms.[166] The same assumption may be found in the mouth of the fourteenth-century magnates and commons.[167] The church in England had been endowed by the ancestors of the king and lords for the purposes of ministering to them and to the people; but papal provisions and taxation of English monasteries by foreign mother-houses alienated and misapplied these endowments, which could therefore be rectified by resumption by the donors. This was to apply to the whole church in England the assumptions concerning alienation and misuse of alms which lay behind *contra formam collacionis*. Whereas, therefore, *cessavit de cantaria* protected one side of the equation, the spiritual services incumbent on land where there were such, *contra formam collacionis* protected tenure of the land itself, because it was the basis of the relationship between lord and tenant; it was alms.

It is interesting to observe what were the antecedents of this provision, since we have seen that *cessavit de cantaria* was a new remedy, albeit one based on high medieval seignorial practice for secular services which was itself replicated in *cessavit*. Although canon law also prohibited the alienation of property by churches, the roots of *contra formam collacionis* probably did not lie there.[168] Rather, like *cessavit* but unlike *cessavit de cantaria*, it was intended to counterfeit a power which twelfth-century lords enjoyed in their own jurisdiction. We have already seen that these lords expected to exercise some control over alienations by their tenants, but this was particularly because of the threat to their services.[169] That this control was also exercised over ecclesiastical tenants is suggested by Glanvill's explicit statement that ecclesiastical tenants-in-chief could not alienate their lands without royal consent and confirmation, because they were 'of the alms of the lord king'.[170] The fact that Bracton widened the scope of the prohibition to include all patrons suggests that Glanvill was articulating the common assumption about tenants in alms.[171] They were not to alienate because their lands were literally alms from their donors. If this is so, it is likely to be the case that in practice lords lost the power of controlling alienations by their ecclesiastical tenants just as they did over those by lay tenants, namely in the course of the thirteenth century by the intervention of the common

---

[166] This gloss is to some extent supported by a gloss of Edward I, who restricted the availability of the writ to founding families and their heirs, and excluded from it land 'postmodum adquisitis': the distinction seems to be between lands given in alms by founders, and lands bought later by the house, for which they had already rendered a return in cash, or even secular services, and against their alienation of which there was no particular interest. (This leaves out the possibility of donors other than from the founding family giving land in alms for spiritual purposes, although if they gave for specific spiritual services they would have been protected by *cessavit de cantaria*.) *Councils and Synods with Other Documents relating to the English Church, II, 1205-1313*, ed. F.M. Powicke & C.R. Cheney (2 vols., Oxford, 1964), ii. 966 [5].

[167] Thompson, 'Statute of Carlisle', 546-8, 550-3, 'Habendum et Tenendum', 218-221.

[168] *Glanvill*, ed. Hall, 185-6.

[169] Above, n. 148.

[170] *Glanvill*. vii. 1 (p. 74): see above, n. 24. This is at first sight curious, because ecclesiastical tenants-in-chief which were in existence before 1066 were the one group of monasteries to be burdened significantly with secular services, and thereby precisely those whom we would expect to alienate (by subinfeudation) in order to satisfy their service-quotas. However, it may be that they still required royal assent for such alienations; it was just that they would get it. And by Glanvill's time they had already done this, *The Red Book of the Exchequer*, ed. Hubert Hall (3 vols., Rolls Series, London, 1896), i. 186-445.

[171] *Bracton*, ii. 52.

law.[172] In the secular tenures, this process issued in *Quia Emptores* which protected the lord's residual economic rights in the form of services and incidents, in return for accepting the reality of free alienation within the tenurial structure.

Contra formam collacionis, however, pre-empted *Quia Emptores* by five years. Just, in fact, at the point when laymen (apart from tenants-in-chief) were formally released from seignorial control over their freedom to alienate, ecclesiastical tenants were formally re-subjected to such control. The reason for the difference is instructive. On the one hand, lords allowed their lay tenants freely to change places in the tenurial chain with whomsoever they wished, and thereby gave up any attempt to control who their tenants were; it was possible to impose any new secular tenant upon a lord, as long as he held by the same services. This was because the course of time had both rendered services so much less valuable than incidents, and in most cases stripped the relationship between the lord, the tenant, and the services to be performed of those personal elements of mutual loyalty and co-operation which informed the original establishment of the relationship. On the other hand, it was still of considerable moment that the tenurial connection between each particular family and its churches be kept alive. The family maintained the institution to which it had given alms because the identity of each over many generations was bound up in the other, and it could therefore not accept free alienation of those alms. Nor could it allow the arrival of a different tenant on that land, for the land owed no services; it was only of any use in the hands of the family monastery, or back in the hands of the family itself. Indeed, the fact that under the terms of foundation the land had no services incumbent upon it made it even more vital to maintain a personal relationship in an era which had come to expect a return of specific spiritual services from ecclesiastical endowments. In the absence of legal leverage over the monastery's activities, patrons were only left with the shell of free alms tenure to exploit as a point of contact and obligation, in order to retain their position as participants in and beneficiaries of the spiritual activities performed by the religious.[173] Patronal families had both to lock their monasteries into a perpetual tenurial relationship with them, and actively to ensure that their alms, in terms both of their resources and of the activities which these supported, were not diminished.

• • • • •

The period between the mid-twelfth and the early fourteenth centuries - that bounded by the reigns of the great lawgivers, Henry II and Edward I - witnessed a transformation of the tenurial and legal world; a three-dimensional society based on the real power of lordship was flattened out into one based on ownership regulated by the common law, which was the tool of royal jurisdiction. The realities of dependent tenure were reduced to a lifeless shell for the exploitation of residual services and incidents. Lands held by the church were not immune from these developments, in particular in that they were both regulated in the royal courts and by royal legislation. But just as in the twelfth century ecclesiastical tenure differed from secular, so did it in the latter middle ages in both the forms in which it then existed.

---

[172] Milsom, *LF*, 103-21, 146-53; also Wood, *Monasteries and their Patrons*, 155-6. In c. 1220 a founder explicitly forbade alienation by the religious of the new house, perhaps because it was precisely at that time that it was becoming thinkable for ecclesiastical tenants to do so without reference to their lords, *A Cartulary of Creake Abbey*, ed. A.L. Bedingfeld (Norfolk Record Society xxxv, Norwich, 1966), no. 2.

[173] Thompson, 'Church and Aristocracy', 65-77, 90-133.

Both forms - free alms tenure, and tenure by divine services - were antiquated, even deliberately so, in that they not only preserved elements of dependent tenure which characterized the secular tenure of the high middle ages, but also had to counterfeit the elements they did not have. To put it at its simplest, 'free alms' had tenure but no services, and 'divine services' had services but no tenure. In frankalmoin, the ancient vertical relationship between patron and monastery as lord and tenant endured, whereas tenure by divine service replicated the exchange of land for a specific and enforceable return in the form of services. Lords in free alms, therefore, in an era which expected a return of specific spiritual services from ecclesiastical tenure, had to ensure that they remained the beneficiaries of the spiritual activities which were performed, but over which they had no legal leverage, by deliberately keeping the relationship alive. Equally, lords in divine services had to create a counterfeit tenure (through distraint and *cessavit*) because they could not re-create the tenurial pattern of vertical relationship. Sanctions preserved the lord's interest in each of the two cases. *Cessavit de cantaria* focused upon the services which were the object of grants for divine services; and *contra formam collacionis*, in providing against alienation of the land itself, thereby sought to preserve the tenurial relationship existing between patron and monastery in free alms tenure. And to those grants made for specific spiritual services but before 1290, both sanctions applied.[174] Both sides of the equation, the land itself and the objects it supported, were taken into account.

Ecclesiastical tenure preserved and counterfeited these antiquated elements precisely at the time that they were becoming irrelevant to secular tenure, at the very point when it was recognizing that tenurial feudalism had lost its inherent reality, and was recognizing the replacement of tenure by a flat legal world of contract and rights, and the more flexible social and political bonds of 'bastard feudalism'.[175] Free alms preserved tenurial relationships when tenure had become merely a framework of exploitation in the secular sphere; divine services replicated tenure for services when lords had all but lost interest in secular services for their own sakes. The tenure by which ecclesiastical institutions held in the later middle ages was, therefore deliberately old-fashioned, in part preserving features of tenurial feudalism, in part counterfeiting them where they were missing. This was because monasteries still had something to offer which, unlike the secular forms of exchange, could still be comprehended in terms of tenure and services. At one level this reveals that ecclesiastical tenure had been forced into secular modes of tenure, and the laity had thereby made inroads into the separateness of the church and its control of its own spiritual function: such was the ecclesiastical complaint in 1285 in response to the statute of Westminster II.[176] This aspect of the story has not been examined here because the ecclesiastical point of view is essential to it. But we may suspect that, on a larger view, the claims of the twelfth-century church were but a brief intrusion into the control over the resources of society by those who govern it. In the early middle ages, lay lords exercised de facto control of ecclesiastical property; by the later they had exchanged this for a control inscribed in law, for royal control of jurisdiction and status, and their own control of function.

---

[174] See n. 165.

[175] For which see now Christine Carpenter, *Locality and Polity: Landed Society in Warwickshire, c. 1401-1499* (Cambridge, 1991).

[176] *Councils & Synods II*, ii. 964 [5]; 'in quo videtur ecclesie et prelatis graviter preiudicari, ad quos pertinet cognitio et compulsio ut, stante collatione, suppleatur defectus'.

NUNNERY FINANCES IN
THE EARLY FIFTEENTH CENTURY
by
Jackie Mountain

edieval nunneries were not only religious institutions; they were also landholders. Their economic activities, as well as their religious ones, were supervised by the diocesan bishop. At visitations he, or his appointee, would examine the financial state of the house, while also investigating its spiritual health. The visitor would ask to see the most recent set of accounts and listen to the complaints of those nuns, who felt that their superior had been ill-advised, corrupt or incompetent. This system has ensured the survival of a great deal of material concerning nunnery finances. The problem for the historian is its lack of uniformity. Visitations had a standard procedure, but individual testimony was not recorded in a set form. The interpretation of the evidence, given its biased nature, is also difficult. Accounts, on the surface, present fewer problems and comparison should be more straightforward. Each head of house was required to compile an annual account. Although this task seems to have been neglected in many houses under many superiors, a diligent bureaucracy, external prompting from the bishop or a crisis produced records.[1] This paper attempts to compare three sets of accounts. These were selected not simply because they are all in print and chronologically close to one another but also because they originated in geographically and socially different institutions. The economic circumstances can, therefore, be compared.

Romsey, in Hampshire was founded in c. 907 and reconstituted in 967, with royal patronage. Its location, on the Solent, made it an ideal stopping off place for travellers to Normandy. In 1412/13, the year of the account, its temporal income was £404. 6s. 4d.[2] Catesby, in Northamptonshire, was a more modest house. Founded in c. 1175 by a local knight, its income for 1414/15 was £98. 3s. 6d. including spiritualities.[3] Marrick, meanwhile was a remote house on the North Yorks Moors.[4] It was wealthier than many Yorkshire houses and had an income of £79. 12s. 6d. in 1415/16.

Catesby's accounts give the most complete picture of its economic position; manorial, household and religious accounts are combined and the grangers and stock accounts are included. For Marrick the manorial and household accounts are combined and the sacrist

1. Power, Eileen *English Medieval Nunneries* (Cambridge 1922) pp 217-226. I am grateful to Brenda Bolton for providing the inspiration for this paper, to Emma Mason for her constant encouragement and support and to Joan Greatrex for expert help with the movements of Henry Beaufort.

2. Knowles and Hadcock *Medieval Religious Houses* (London 1971) pp 255, 264 *Living Records of Romsey Abbey* (Winchester 1906) p 194 reprinted in Coldicott, Diana K. *Hampshire Nunneries* (Chichester 1989) p. 127 based on PRO SC6 981/21

3. Knowles and Hadcock op cit. pp 253, 272-273. Baker, George *History of Northampton* (London 1822-30) vol 1 pp 278-285

4. Tillotson, John H. *Marrick Priory: A Nunnery in Late Medieval Yorkshire*. Borhtwick Paper no. 75.

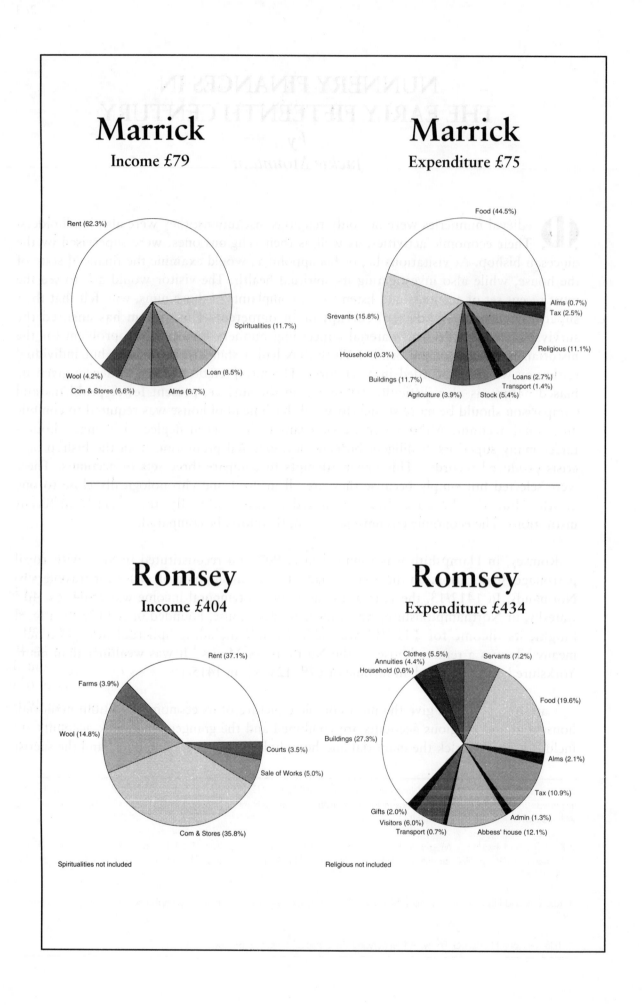

Marrick
Income £79

- Rent (62.3%)
- Spiritualities (11.7%)
- Loan (8.5%)
- Alms (6.7%)
- Com & Stores (6.6%)
- Wool (4.2%)

Marrick
Expenditure £75

- Food (44.5%)
- Alms (0.7%)
- Tax (2.5%)
- Religious (11.1%)
- Loans (2.7%)
- Transport (1.4%)
- Stock (5.4%)
- Agriculture (3.9%)
- Buildings (11.7%)
- Household (0.3%)
- Srevants (15.8%)

Romsey
Income £404

- Rent (37.1%)
- Farms (3.9%)
- Wool (14.8%)
- Courts (3.5%)
- Sale of Works (5.0%)
- Com & Stores (35.8%)

Spiritualities not included

Romsey
Expenditure £434

- Clothes (5.5%)
- Annuities (4.4%)
- Household (0.6%)
- Servants (7.2%)
- Food (19.6%)
- Buildings (27.3%)
- Alms (2.1%)
- Tax (10.9%)
- Gifts (2.0%)
- Admin (1.3%)
- Visitors (6.0%)
- Transport (0.7%)
- Abbess' house (12.1%)

Religious not included

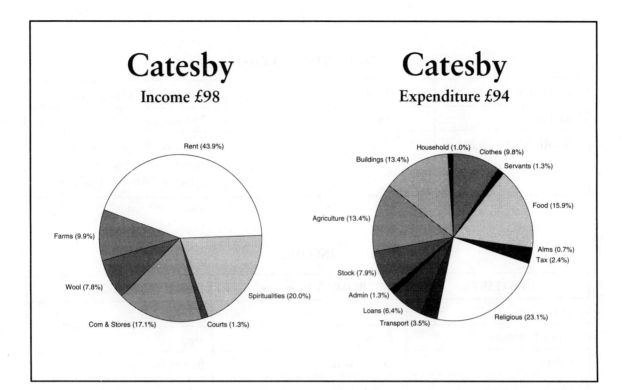

Catesby

Income £98

Rent (43.9%)
Farms (9.9%)
Wool (7.8%)
Com & Stores (17.1%)
Courts (1.3%)
Spiritualities (20.0%)

Catesby

Expenditure £94

Household (1.0%)
Buildings (13.4%)
Clothes (9.8%)
Servants (1.3%)
Agriculture (13.4%)
Food (15.9%)
Stock (7.9%)
Alms (0.7%)
Tax (2.4%)
Admin (1.3%)
Loans (6.4%)
Transport (3.5%)
Religious (23.1%)

EXPENDITURE

CATESBY	ROMSEY	MARRICK
rents resolute	convent	general
petty	abbess	money
houses	extra conventual	buildings
household	various	iron
necessary	repairs	weeding and harvest
carts		servants
livestock		
customary payments		
purchase of corn		
rewards		
in the year past: tedding and making of hay; autumnal expenses; stubble		
costs of the mill		
mowing making and tedding hay; autumnal expenses; stubble; thrashing and winnowing corn		
servants stipend		

ACCOUNTS EXAMINED

CATESBY	1414/5	Elizabeth Swynford, Prioress
ROMSEY	1412/13	Not Known
MARRICK	1415/16	Cecily de Blayston, Bursar Agnes Gower, Sacrist Agnes de Wenslaw, Granger

INCOME

CATESBY	ROMSEY by manor	MARRICK
rent	rent	rent by place
farms & pensions	farms	alms
oblations	sale of works	foreign receipts
issues of the manor	sale of wool	
perquisites of courts & fines	sale of corn & stores	
	courts	

and grangers accounts are appended. The Romsey document includes no spiritualities and is a summary of manorial accounts combined with a summary of expenditure. Thus all three documents combine estate and household accounts but they do not cover the identical areas. Without a stock and grangers account, a full description of consumption cannot be constructed. Purchase of stock, for instance, could represent an agricultural investment or acquisition of food on the hoof. Only one stock account has survived and a strict comparison of the three houses is not, therefore, feasible. The position is further complicated by the different formats used by the three houses: both headings and their contents vary. The layout of the main cash accounts is as follows.

Thus the compilers have produced very different documents. These reflect different aims, different bureaucracies and the differing social mileaux of the houses. A comparison should attempt to identify these differences. None of the documents record the impetus for their compilation but they all provide clues.

The Catesby account is one of a series of six. It is very idiosyncratic and its usefulness would probably be limited to comparing each year with the last. The main account was not strictly cash. The farms and pensions section includes tithes, paid in kind, recorded in the form "And for two quarters of peas received by the year as appears elsewhere", ie in the grangers account, but although no cash value is shown it has been included in the total for that section. The expenditure section is very detailed; the amount of wax purchased, the new altar cloth and its fringe, "the ale about the carriage of the peas to the sheepcote" are all listed. Yet the headings provide no guide to type of outgoing. For instance procurations to the pope are included with the stewards fee under "rents resolute". A payment for amercements to the bailiff of Badby and a letter to the clerk to the bishop to excuse the house from the tenth are under "petty expenses" along with sheep shearing costs. The expenses of collecting rents and provision of forty hurdles are under "necessary expenses". This heading also includes 4 skins of parchment and 2 stirrups and stirrup leathers. It is difficult to see any logic in this arrangement and it must merely reflect organic growth.

At Marrick there was a major problem of rent arrears. The layout of the receipts in three columns: amount received; source and nature of payment; amount still owing, suggests a well organised if struggling steward. £22 of arrears had built up over several years. The actual rental income was £36 although a 1456 rental gives it as £33. This is presumably because Marrick was a victim of the withdrawal from agricultural exploitation of marginal lands.[5] The expenditure section is well organised and suggests that separate tallies were kept for household expenditure, payments of money by the steward, capital expenditure, the blacksmith's bill and agricultural expenditure. Life was very spartan. here is no record of the purchase of clothes, parchment or paper. 1s. was spent on visitors and 15d. on spices.

In contrast, Romsey had three kitchens. The coquina and percoquina (one of which would have been for meat) served the convent, while the abbess and her guests were catered for separately. The nuns were provided with clothes and issued with pittances.

5. A recent paper on this subject is Bailey, Mark The concept of the margin in the Medieval English Economy Economic History Review Series 2 vol 42 (1989) pp 1-17.

Whereas Catesby and Marrick had a single steward, the division of the receipts into six manors, although land was held in sixteen places, suggests six stewards, whose performance was being monitored. The expenditure section also appears to be a summary of accounts from officials. The stewards from the manors presumably supplied the cost of "repairs of the houses and other expenses there" for each manor. The cellaress and Wardrobe mistress would have supplied the expenses of the convent, while the extra-conventual expenses appear, with one exception, to be those of the clerks. This item is the "repair of the houses at Romsey mills" for which the amount has been changed but the old amount has been used in the addition.

The two sections for the abbess and "various" are more confused. The first seems to represent money which she paid out directly, since it includes her own household expenses and the fees of the servants. The liveries are combined as one item with spices for the guesthouse, and this suggests a common source. She also accounted for gifts of £8 12s. but, interestingly, a gift of £10 to Lord Henry Bishop of Winchester is listed under "various" along with wine for nobles visiting the abbess, and the shoeing of horses for the lady's household. The document was possibly compiled as a hurried response to a visitation; the gift to the bishop would have been usual in such circumstances, while the entry for the repairs at Romsey mills and the splitting of the abbess' expenditure was due to a hurried assembling of data from several sources. The hierarchy of accounts may explain the lack of specific agricultural items. Even with villein services, which existed in sufficient numbers on some manors for the surplus to be sold, and which would have provided heriots etc there would have been a need for casual labour at harvest and new stock. The heading "repairs to the houses and other expenses there" for each accounting manor probably represents the total cash investment.

Catesby was a cistercian house and enjoyed not only the profits of vileinage but also the free labour of four lay brothers and a lay sister. This was a considerable addition to the wealth of a house. At Marrick, where all labour had to be paid for, the servants are listed individually; a shepherd, a swineherd, a cowman, nine other outdoor labourers, a kitchenmaid, a maid in the bakehouse and dairy and a maid in the sacristy were paid between 2s and 26s for their labour. Thus houses in what had been the Danelaw had a financial burden because of the lack of vileinage and Cistercian houses, which included many male houses famed for their wealth, would have had considerable advantages. Catesby, certainly seems to have spent very little on servants, although the entries are somewhat confused, since the names of those receiving cash payments are not the same as those receiving payment in kind. This illustrates a problem which sometimes occurs in series of accounts, the failure to update names. The payments are usually fairly accurate.

At Marrick the nuns financial position was further weakened by their inability to grow wheat. One third of their income was spent on it and they combined it with the cheaper maslin when baking bread, which only took place once a fortnight. The lack of a stock account makes judging other consumption difficult but only 14d of pork and 3s. 5d. of hens and geese were bought. Perhaps surprisingly 45s was spent on butter and eggs. In contrast Catesby spent nothing on wheat and the Winter meat and egg bill was 33s while that in the Summer was £7. Lent and Advent will partly account for the difference but the house also ate its own stock. During the year 5 oxen, 20 cows, 1 stirk, 5 calves, 14 sheep, 14 ewes, 40 hogs, 1 boar and 12 pigs were sent to the larder. The size of the element of inaccuracy that can enter valuations and which has previously been discussed by a recent author in a paper on the domestic economy of small religious houses, is clear.[6] Of course, as Christopher Dyer has established, a house with a high income such as Romsey had higher liabilities as well.[7] Thus Romsey was the only house paying tax (41) and this may have contributed to their deficit. The link between taxation and debt has been noted, particularly at St Albans.[8] Certainly the King as patron was using the house as a source, rather than an object, of patronage. Annuities went to the kings clerks. Additionally guests would expect wine rich food and gifts.

The breakdown of sources of income and the expenditure patterns of the three houses can be illustrated by pie charts. For each house the catagories of income used at Romsey have been used, since the other accounts are detailed enough to allow items to be assigned accurately. For expenditure, modern catagories have been imposed because the organisation of the originals was not informative. However the differing headings and item descriptions do cause problems. For instance, at Catesby clothes for the nuns and liveries for the servants are treated as a single item.

Thus the diagrams are not strictly comparable and should not be directly compared.

At Romsey, it can be seen, over half the income derived from direct exploitation of land. Its position on good communication links and the availability of plentiful free labour may have made this more profitable than leasing land. Internal sales may have been included, it is impossible to tell without the stock and grangers accounts. The lack of spiritualities suggests that, as at Marrick, the sacristan accounted separately. The largest item of expenditure was on building repairs. At all three houses this takes a substantial slice of the outgoings. This demonstrates that maintenance was a continual drain and, perhaps, why complaints about the lack of it featured so strongly in visitation reports. At Marrick the amount of it has been artificially inflated by the construction of a new barn. Professor John Tillotson who has analysed the account in detail suggests that the loan in the income chart was for this purpose.[9] The nuns of Marrick also needed alms to balance their books but they managed to fulfil their obligations to give alms to others, even though the amount given was tiny. The dominance of food and servants in their budget as indicated above is clearly illustrated. In contrast, the nuns at Romsey spent relatively lavishly on alms, oblations and gifts, demonstrating how expectations varied with income. At Catesby the dominant item, nearly a quarter of the budget, was religious expenditure. There is a close correlation between this and the income from spiritualities, as at Marrick, and this contradicts many suppositions that have been made about the use of advowsons. Food was a relatively small expense but of course agricultural spending was higher as a consequence.

Spending patterns, as the diagrams show, were determined not only by income but also

---

6.Jack, Sybil of poverty and pigstyes: The small religious houses on the eve of the dissolution. Paregon vol 1 (1983) pp 69-91.

7. Dyer, Christopher Standards of Living in the Later Middle Ages. Social Change in England c.1200-1520 (Cambridge 1989) Chaps 1-4.

8. Biddick, Kathleen Power in early English Development Comparitive Studies in Society and History vol. 32 no 1 (1990) pp 3-23.

9. Tillotson op cit p 12.

perceived liabilities, social customs, geographical and topographical factors and inherited buildings. Single accounts provide only snapshots, without a series it is impossible to define the exceptional and the usual. The next stage of this work is to analyse the other five Catesby accounts before moving on to look at as many from other houses as possible. In the past the desires to generalise or to concentrate on only one house have dominated discussion. The standard work in this area remains Eileen Powers English Medieval Nunneries, published in 1922 but based mainly on a thesis submitted in 1916[10]

In 1981 Coburn Graves, who was studying Stixwold in the twelfth century commented

"Indispensable as Miss Power's work is for all students of the history of the woman religious in medieval England . . . .. she has assimilated material from all kinds of nunneries from diverse regions and varying periods of time to produce a composite that offers many problems for the study of a particular nunnery's history. With reference to financial difficulties Miss Power indicated the nunneries were, like the monasteries, beset with poverty, which she attributed to causes beyond the control of the nuns (such as natural disasters and intrusion of external lay and ecclesiastical authorities). In addition she adduced substantial evidence to support her interpretation that nuns were guilty of bad management and incompetence, concluding that because of these deficiencies the nuns contributed largely to their own misfortune . . . .Power was the historian of the decline"[11]

The thrust of this critique is entirely convincing but the last sentence is a measure of the esteem in which Power is held. Recent studies of individual nunneries and an exceptional general study have contradicted her views but Power has prevailed.[12] Yet seventy years have passed since her pioneering work. During that time there have been fierce debates about the economic history of the period in some of which Power herself participated. Her judgement that "Nuns were never very good businesswomen" appears a harsh and gross generalisation in the light of recent studies of general attitudes to investment and agricultural decisions[13] It has recently been pointed out that the system of double accountability, to the convent and the bishop, made the religious houses conservative in their agricultural and lordship practices.[14]

The corporate nature of the landholdings can, however, lead to a neglect of the importance of individuals. During the period covered by Medieval English Nunneries their were over to thousand heads of house. Their competence and honesty varied. Some did have financial management removed from their hands. This happened at Catesby in 1442 for reasons detailed below. Others were dynamic and innovative. The work of John Wiggenhall at Crabhouse, who in the 1420s organised the virtual rebuilding of the house,

---

10. Power op cit. The original thesis was Power, E.E. Some Chapters on Medieval Nuns (unpublished MA thesis London 1916)

11. Graves, Coburn V. Stixwold in the Market Place in Distant Echoes ed Nichols, John A. and Shank, Lillian T. Medieval Religious Women vol 1. Cistercian Studies No. 71 (Kalamazoo 1984).

12. Tillotson op cit. Graves op cit. Levett A.E. The accounts of the nunnery of St Mary Pre (Pray) in Studies in Medieval History ed by Cam, H.M., Coate M., Sutherland, L.S. (Oxford 1938) pp 287-300. The exception is Jack op cit.

13. Power op cit. p228

14. Swanson R.N. Church and Society in Late Medieval England (Oxford 1989) chapter 4.

was noted by Power.[15]

The visitation system encouraged the recording of internal dissent and debt. Power's view of debt is certainly simplistic. All three houses examined here were technically in debt but the reasons differ. At Marrick it was due in part to capital investment and their vulnerability to price rises. At Romsey taxation, which was levied, as now, on the previous year but not predictably caused a deficit. Only at Catesby, where a loan existed but the reason is unknown, could incompetence be a factor. Certainly Catesby could also claim to be a victim of fate. During the year they lost 12 ewes, 3 sheep, 3 wethers, 23 lambs, 1 boar and 2 hilts to the Murrain. This represents a substantial loss.

While they provide a lot of detailed information these accounts cannot be used as more than a basis for discussion. The way in which things could change is illustrated by events at this last house.

The Catesby account may be disorganised but it gives no hint of the situation which was to prevail in 1442 when William Alnwick, Bishop of Lincoln visited. The house, which had had only six nuns in 1415, now had four separate households. There was no chaplain, although they had been paying the substantial sum of £22 for one in 1415. The communion cup had been pawned and the unnamed prioress was "in debt to the convent for three quarters of the year".[16] Clearly there had been great upheaval. The episodic nature of the surviving documentation makes the explanation of such changes speculative at best. Generalisation about one house seems impossible.

Geography and regional variations in social structures complicate the national picture. Life at Marrick, one of many poor Yorkshire houses, may have been grim but in 1536 when 102 Yorkshire nuns were given the option of moving to other, wealthier houses, or living a celibate life "in the community" 99 opted to stay.[17] This says something about the lot of single gentle women in Yorkshire at that time. Within five years there was to be no choice!

The nunneries and the way, they were endowed were a response to particular social and economic structures. The pre-conquest foundations were royal in origin and provided initially for royal ladies. With the exception of Syon, post conquest foundations were much humbler. In areas such as Yorkshire the desire to found a nunnery may have outstripped the ability to endow it adequately. The general economic problems of the later period exacerbated the problems. Local society however responded to those needs with help. The same may not have been true further South. The concern of bishops with the financial situation of those seeking to become anchorites has been documented.[18] Applicants were required to show that they had sufficient funds as well as a vocation.

---

15. Power op cit. pp. 90-95.

16. Thompson A.H. Visitations of Religious Houses in the Diocese of Lincoln part 2. 1 pp 46-46-53 Canterbury and York Series vol. xxiv (London, 1919)

17. Woodward G. The exemption from suppression of certain Yorkshire Priories English Historical Review vol 76 no 300 (1961) pp 385-401.

18. Warren A.K. Anchorites and their Patrons in Medieval England (University of California Press 1985) chapters 2 and 3.

The nunneries were permanent institutions and bishops inherited their problems. While amalgamation might have solved many problems, mortmain and the feudal rights of patrons prevented it in all but one case, Stamford and Wythorpe, where the patronal family was common to both. Certainly the nuns should not be seen as entirely responsible for the poor financial health of many nunneries in the medieval period.

LOOKING FOR MEDIEVAL WOMEN:
AN INTERIM REPORT ON THE PROJECT "WOMEN'S RELIGIOUS LIFE AND COMMUNITIES, A.D. 500-1500"

by
Mary Martin McLaughlin

"Looking for medieval women" may strike some readers as a rather too encompassing title for a fairly brief report on a project concerned with women associated with the religious life and its orders and communities between 500 and 1500.[1] These women were, after all, a small minority of their sex, though one varying considerably in size at different times and places. Yet our title seems justified both by the purposes of our work and by its results so far. When we embarked on this project, we hoped to contribute particularly to basic research needs in two fields of growing interest to medievalists: monastic and religious history and the history of women. As far as we know, ours remains the most comprehensive research project at present under way in both of these large fields, and we are finding, too, that our work offers scholarly possibilities even more varied than those that we initially envisaged. By emphasizing the scope of our project, as well as its focus on both the individual and the collective experience of medieval religious women, we wish to suggest its affinities with the interests of prosopographers and the ways in which it may serve, and foster, their studies, along with the concerns of medievalists in various other fields.

In pursuing primarily the minority who were religious women, and the communities to which its members belonged, we are indeed finding many other women of diverse social ranks and conditions, sometimes more informally or indirectly related to the religious life. Regarding the scope of our enterprise, it is worth noting that the social and religious functions of female communities, significantly different from those of their male counterparts, make this minority far more consequential in the larger history of medieval women than mere numbers might suggest. Of primary importance in this respect are the sources which are an essential concern of this project. For the surviving records of women's religious life and of individual communities also constitute the most substantial and coherent body of materials available for the study of European women before 1500. These records document the experience and activities during many centuries of considerable numbers of women who, though by no means fully representative of all women in their diverse societies, do in many ways reflect, and illumine, a wide social spectrum.

Women associated with religious life were married and widowed as well as celibate; they entered this life at widely varying ages, from childhood to late maturity. As wives and widows, mothers and daughters, sisters, cousins, aunts, and nieces, they belonged to families at nearly every level of medieval society, from royal and aristocratic to those of decidedly lower status in towns and countryside. By no means all of them were professed nuns; many communities also included lay sisters or *conversae,* as well as female servants

---

[1] This project and publication have been supported by the National Endowment for the Humanities, a federal agency which supports study in such fields as history, philosophy, literature and languages.

and sometimes lay "boarders" or corrodians. Women founders and benefactors, who were numerous during this period, often remained closely attached to the communities they supported. Some of them became members and heads of these communities; we shall meet an example shortly in Countess Ela of Salisbury. Especially in later medieval centuries, many pious laywomen of diverse social status in different parts of Europe embarked informally on a communal life. Often these communities of women, known variously as beguines or *mantellate or pinzochere,* eventually became institutionalized as beguinages or as monasteries or convents of recognized orders. Further extending the social range of women associated with the religious life were the houses of repentant prostitutes established in many late medieval towns and cities. Still another category of religious women, of varying social status and especially numerous in England, were those who abandoned the world or monastic communities for the solitary life of recluses or anchoresses.

Similarly documented by the records we explore are the often striking diversities in character, size, and activities of women's religious communities and their members. These few examples are intended merely as suggestive. Shaftesbury Abbey, the largest and richest of English female communities, housed 120 nuns in the early fourteenth century; Wilton and Romsey numbered 80 or 90. But most were considerably smaller, closer in size, if not in wealth, to our exemplary Lacock, which numbered usually between 14 and 17. Like others of their kind, the abbesses of Shaftesbury and similar abbeys were great landholders, with all of the political and social rights and responsibilities that this position entailed. Their communities and many others were also engaged in extensive economic enterprises, such as Lacock's sheep-raising and cloth-production. The manufacture of ecclesiastical vestments and fine tapestries was often a specialty of women's communities in various parts of Europe; many beguinages supported themselves by working in the lowlier processes of the great cloth industry of Flemish and other Northern towns.

Beyond their specifically religious functions, the most common activities of religious women were educational and caritative. English nuns, for example, were notably active in the teaching of young children, especially girls but also boys; and the care of the sick and poor, particularly through the direction and staffing of hospitals, was an important social function in England and elsewhere during the later Middle Ages. As individuals, nuns and other religious women were saints, mystics and reformers, writers, scholars and teachers, scribes and illuminators; a few, like the fifteenth-century printer-nuns of S.Jacopo di Ripoli in Florence, were engaged in less familiar occupations which, among other things, the work of our project is discovering.

Briefly put, the long-term purpose of this computer-assisted project is to produce three comprehensive and coordinated instruments of research: 1) a Repertory of female religious communities existing in the Latin West before 1500; 2) a Biobibliography of notable women associated with these communities as founders, benefactors, heads and other administrators, or members in some way distinguished as spiritual leaders, teachers, writers, and artists; included here also are important religious women, anchoresses and others, who were not members of communities; and 3) an International Bibliography of modern studies of women's religious life in the Middle Ages. The first two works will be produced as a series of fascicles devoted to major European regions, e.g., the British Isles,

Italy, Spain, the Low Countries, each accompanied by appropriate maps; the third, based upon the other two, will be published as a single volume, organized chronologically, topically, and geographically.

In this pioneering enterprise, we ourselves have necessarily undertaken research efforts of sometimes daunting dimensions. This is particularly the case because we are committed to providing more precise and substantial information than that commonly supplied by works of this kind. This commitment requires extensive investigation of both published and unpublished sources, especially archival records, far beyond the minimal need to identify these sources for bibliographical purposes. Limited as we are in personnel, accomplishing this research is our most difficult task. Indeed, the success of our project depends a great deal on the collaboration of our colleagues. For this reason we welcome most especially the opportunity to present this report to the readers of *Medieval Prosopography* and *MONASTIC STUDIES* and to invite the contributions of prosopographers and other medievalists in areas of their special interests. [2]

Supported by grants from the National Endowment for the Humanities and sponsored by Barnard College, the project has been under way since 1982, when we began work on the Monastic Repertory and Biobibliography for Italy. This has proved to be a formidable task, given the numbers of communities, the riches of many Italian archives, and the state of scholarship in this field. More recently, while continuing work on Italy, we have turned our attention also to the British Isles, where the scholarly foundations are considerably better laid and where, therefore, we can advance more rapidly in every aspect of our enterprise. Much of what I have to say about the potential uses of the project will be illustrated by the work accomplished so far on these two important European regions.

Much of this report is based also on the results of a major effort of our research team during the first phase of the project. This is our development of a data base program for the production of our Monastic Repertory and Biobibliography, which are cross-linked in various ways, and eventually our general bibliography. For this program we have employed the data base management system Condor 3.2.11.10, for use on an IBM personal computer. We have thus created, in effect, another research instrument, a cumulative data base which has given us much greater flexibility in our research design and procedures than we would otherwise have had. It has, in particular, made possible the achievement of a primary goal of the project: the development of a dynamic profile of a religious community, reflecting in significant and precise detail important aspects of its changing life.

Since the format and content of our data records are explained at length in the following pages, I note here only some general features of our program. As our examples

---

[2] For the use of potential contributors whose work is concerned with particular individuals, communities, or areas, we are happy to provide "report forms" for the Monastic Repertory and the Biobibliography and for research in unpublished sources. These forms, which are tailoreed to our needs, define specifically the kinds of substantive and bibliographical information we are seeking. Inquiries and coorespondance regarding the project should be directed to Mary McLaughlin, R. D. 3, Box 422, Valley Farm Road, Millbrook, NY 12545, or to Suzanne Wemple, Department of History, Barnard College, Columbia University, New York, NY 10027. As a full time editor and research scholar, Heath Dillard has been a member of our research group since its inception. Constance Berman joined the project as a research scholar in May 1985. Eleanor Riemer was a member of the project from 1983-1985 and Susan Adler has served as a student assistant for the past two years.

show, our designations for categories ("fields") and substantive data are not "coded" in the strict sense of the term. We use English language abbreviations for categories, e.g. DC for "document," DT for "date," and for common items of identification or information, e.g., "abs" for "abbess," "prp" for "property," "lnd" for "land"; we also employ unabbreviated words and phrases when necessary. In addition to a comprehensive Logbook explaining our procedures and abbreviations, we have prepared a short list of abbreviations to accompany print-outs of our data records. Supporting the abbreviated entries in the bibliographies of our Repertory and Biobibliography records is a General Bibliography in which all references are stored in full. (A sample page appears at the end of this report.) For research purposes, and for the coordination of information for entry in our data base, we also use written report forms permitting more detailed recording of data; we employ similar forms to record examination of unpublished sources. Copies of these forms are available for the use of contributors to the work of this project.

Making possible the continual revision and updating of our computer records, our data base program enables us to incorporate the results of successive phases of research. Through Condor's "report-writing" feature, combined with a sophisticated word-processing program such as *NOTA BENE*, we plan to produce, in narrative form, the completed entries in our Monastic Repertory and Biobibliography. As our records accumulate, our data base also enables us to generate quantitative data on a number of important topics, and it permits interim circulation of our results, pending completion of major phases of our work. We can, for example, serve the needs of current scholarship by supplying print-outs of bibliography, data on specific orders, communities, and individuals, and topically selected lists.

Since our data base for the Repertory and Biobibliography represents both the current stage of our work and its continuing, cumulative character, to explain our computer records is also to indicate the kinds of information we are seeking and to suggest their uses for other scholars. Illustrating here both our research design and its possibilities are completed entries for a particular community in our monastic repertory (MONREP) and for two individuals in our biobibliography (BIO), one of them associated with our exemplary community. For the MONREP record, which is divided into eight parts, three containing data and five for bibliography, we have chosen the English abbey of Lacock in Wiltshire. For our purposes, it should be said, a community is defined as an institutional entity with a continuing life of at least fifty years; encompassed by our definition are not only canonically recognized institutes such as abbeys, priories, and convents, but also more informal entities such as beguinages and hospitals, if the latter were staffed primarily by women.

Beginning with MONREP 1, Main Entry: Lacock Abbey, like every other community (CN) in our repertory, is identified by its unique number, indicating the country and province or county to which it belongs. It is further identified geographically again by province or county (PR), in this case Wiltshire, by diocese (DI), Salisbury, and by place name, (PN), Lacock. Still more specific identification is provided in the following "fields": the community's status (S), i.e., whether abbey, priory, convent, or hospital; its common name, in this case identical with place; its alternate and/or later names; its dedication, to St. Mary and St. Bernard; its location, between the village of Lacock and the Avon river, in the meadow called "Snaylesmeade." Also indicated are previous or later locations, including its present location, in this case still in the village of Lacock, 1/2 mile east of the Melksham-Chippenham road A350.

Details concerning its foundation, order and rule are contained in the next group of fields, beginning with the date of foundation (FDT) and of its end (FIN) or continuing existence, which would be signified by the abbreviation X. Lacock was suppressed in 1539, one of the last English female houses to be dissolved. The circumstances of its foundation are indicated in the field (FD), which informs us that Lacock was founded by Ela (Isabella), countess of Salisbury, who gave her manor and village of Lacock for a female community to be called "locus beate Marie." The two earliest extant documents relating to the community, with their dates, are noted in the fields, DC 1 and 2; DT 1 and 2. The first in Lacock's case, as in so many others, was the charter of donation from the founder (or earliest benefactor), granting the land on which the abbey was built; the grant was confirmed by Ela's eldest son, William Longespee, in a charter of 1229, now surviving in a copy. Confirming this grant, the second document is a royal charter dated 31 January 1230; it was followed by another dated 26 February 1230, giving Ela express permission to assign her manor for the building of an abbey. The abbey church was actually dedicated in 1232.

If a community received the privilege of papal exemption, which Lacock did not, this would be indicated in (PX) with the name of the pope and the date. The final group of fields in this main entry provides information regarding the community's order, congregation, and rule. Because female communities were often inclined to changes of order, we have allowed for two changes. In this case we learn that -- despite Ela's original intention to found a Cistercian community, as its dedication suggests -- Lacock was and remained Augustinian (OSA), following the Rule of St. Augustine (RI RA). Special information or controversial points not covered by other fields may be indicated in (NB): here noted is the existence of an early fifteenth-century copy of the Augustinian Rule, and the fact that the nuns, actually canonesses, observed obedience and chastity, but took no vows and were not strictly enclosed.

In the second part of our MONREP entry we record information concerning the character and development of a community, its organization, activities and relationships with other communities and with external authorities. Here a first group of fields indicates relationships with other communities involving incorporation and dependency; these, in the case of Lacock, did not exist. Data concerning ecclesiastical jurisdictions and visitations, noted in (ECC), here include visitations by the bishop of Salisbury, for which evidence exists but no reports; the bishop enjoyed rights of nominating novices in the fourteenth century. Lacock was subject to visitation also by representatives of the general chapter of Augustinian canons in England. At its suppression (FIN), the community was reported in good order.

The large category (SEC) encompasses relationships with secular authorities and various aspects of monastic economy. In the first field is noted litigation with a local family, the Bluets, and with royal authority over knight service, along with resistance to royal intrusions. Lacock's assets (ASSETS) included landed property, rights in churches, a quarry, a fishery, a coal mine in Gloucestershire, and, as the bases of its sheep-raising and cloth-producing enterprise, a flock of over 2000 sheep, along with fulling-mills and a gig-mill. (A gig-mill is a machine consisting of rotary cylinders covered with wire teeth for raising the nap on woolen cloth.) Lacock's income (INCOME) was derived from its sheep and cloth-producing enterprise, from rents and other revenues, including those added by its market rights and annual fairs. Under (VALUES) are recorded various estimates of the abbey's wealth and/or income, suggesting its apparently stable prosperity to its end; the value of its property was assessed for tax purposes in 1291 (the taxation of Pope Nicholas IV) at £102+; later assessments, based on net annual income or taxable revenue, were £120 in 1476 *(Status Compoti),* and in 1535 *(Valor Ecclesiasticus)* more than £168, revised in 1536 to £194.

In the categories (ART), artistic and architectural works, and (REM), physical remains, we identify, as far as possible, surviving works of art and architecture, including existing remains of monastic buildings. Here, in the field (ART), we note two seals of which only impressions survive: the thirteenth-century conventual seal and the seal of Abbess Ela, which bears an image of the Virgin and Child under a canopy. Among English female communities Lacock is probably the richest in physical remains. These are largely incorporated in successive alterations of the imposing house owned since the eighteenth century by members of the Talbot family. Remains of Lacock were subjects of the earliest successful photographs by William Henry Fox Talbot who made here the very first photographic negative. Because these remains are so extensive, we refer in CN STUDIES to Pevsner (Wiltshire) and note in (REM) only the most significant; the north wall of the thirteenth-century church, the fifteenth-century cloister and vault with thirteenth-century doors, and important parts of the monastic ground storey, left substantially intact by the builder and re-builders of the house. These include the undercroft, the vaulted sacristy, the chapter house, and the "warming-room" with large hooded fireplace (the only room in which the nuns would have had a fire). Lacock Abbey became part of the National Trust in 1944.

Another field in this section of our entry provides for information regarding the caritative and educational activities (CAR) of the community; at least one Lacock charter refers in general to the "demands of charity," which included feeding the local poor, especially during Lent. Here are indicated also notable (NOT) features and additional data which do not find a place in other categories. Noted in abbreviated form are significant surviving manuscripts from Lacock's library, including the "Annals" and pre-1357 "Book" of Lacock (British Library), a copy of William Brito's *Dictionary* and a collection of Anglo-French poems (Lacock), and a thirteenth-century Psalter (Oxford, Bodleian, MS Laud lat. 114). Note-worthy also are the following items: two fragments of a late thirteenth-century cellaress's roll (surviving as binding-leaves of Brito's *Dictionary*), an account-roll of 1346-47 (used as binding-leaves of two cartularies) which records consumption of food week by week, along with total quantities received and expended during the year, and a record of the expenses for clothing a nun in 1395-96.

Likely to be of particular interest to prosopographers is the third part of our monastic record, encompassing information regarding individual members of the community. Entries for documented heads, abbesses or prioresses, and other noteworthy individuals will be found in the Biobibliography. This part of the community entry begins with data concerning the social status and origins of its members (MEM). In defining social status, we follow the commonly accepted divisions of a particular society. In the case of England,

"N" (noble) and "N+" signify the baronage and higher aristocracy; "N-", those of knightly or gentry status; "M", "M+" and "M-" signify the middle ranks from higher to lower, or richer to poorer. Lacock's nuns came mostly from the Wiltshire nobility in the thirteenth century, and later also from prosperous gentry and burgess families of southern England.

The abbey's numbers at different dates for which evidence survives are recorded in the next group of fields. Here we have numbers for four dates between 1230 and 1473, and for a fifth, the date of suppression (see OTH), suggesting that the membership of the community remained quite small and stable, normally between fourteen and seventeen, though at times somewhat larger. Its patronage (PTR), belonging for more than a century to the founder's family, eventually descended to the house and duchy of Lancaster, thence in 1399 to the Crown. The founder (FDR) is again identified as Countess Ela, who became a nun under the first prioress and then first abbess. Among the abbey's benefactors (BEN) are noted, first, kings and noblemen, including John de Bluet, who endowed the Lady Chapel in 1313. Women benefactors are noted in a separate category; these include, among other noble-women, Amice, Countess of Devon, as well as the founder and her family, notably her great-grand-daughter and heir, Margaret de Lacy.

In the fields (HDH) and (HD2), we have space to identify only a few notable heads of house among the seventeen abbesses listed in the pertinent volume of the Victoria County History and also in our own BIO, where entries for some of them will be found. Here we refer to Wymarca, the first prioress, the foundress who was also the first abbess, and a number of others. In the field (NNS), again space permits the identification of a few nuns notable for various reasons, among them the founder and two of her granddaughters. In many cases, individuals mentioned here would also merit an entry in the BIO. The field (OTH) lets us enter significant information not provided for elsewhere: here we note the numbers for a fifth date, 1539, and officials of the abbey, including three chaplains and a confessor, for whom we have evidence.

The remaining sections of our MONREP records are devoted to bibliographical data: the first and second to unpublished and the third to published sources, the fourth and fifth to modern studies and briefer references. Here, limitations of space have sometimes pushed us to particular feats of compression, especially in identifying unpublished sources, e.g., in the Public Record Office or other archives. One solution to our problems has been the division of the listing into two columns, the first (U) a general entry, the second (T), a brief identification of contents, especially in the case of manuscripts. For Lacock, two cartularies of the thirteenth and fourteenth centuries survive at the abbey itself (U1) -- these were edited (strictly speaking, abstracted) and published by Kenneth Rogers in 1979 (P14) -- along with a large collection of deeds in the Public Record Office, and others in local archives.

Since all published works, both sources and studies, are cited in full in a separate general bibliographical file, they are cited here only by short titles, also listed separately. All published studies of Lacock, and brief references, are noted in the two sections of "Studies and References." To indicate the relationship between our short titles and our fuller bibliography, we provide a sample page of the latter.

Illustrating our Biobibliography (BIO) records, doubtless of special interest to prosopographers and other scholars pursuing individuals rather than communities, are two examples. The subject of the first is Countess Ela of Salisbury, founder and first abbess of Lacock, suggesting relationships between our MONREP and BIO records for a single community and its members. For our second example, which illustrates more fully certain features of our BIO records, we turn to Italy and St. Catherine of Bologna (Caterina Vegri). To introduce them with a few general remarks: in creating the BIO record, our goal was a format linked with the pertinent MONREP record, a format that would permit us to enter and retrieve as much substantive information about the lives and activities of individuals as possible and at the same time leave space for important bibliographical data. As in the MONREP record, these include unpublished and published sources, significant modern studies, and entries in authoritative reference works encompassed in BIOBIBLIOGRAPHY 2: Sources and Studies.

In our data file, BIO 1, essential identification is contained in the first group of fields, which again begin with a unique ID number, and go on, in this case, to relate the founder and first abbess of Lacock to the regions, towns, and places with which she was most closely associated: Wiltshire (PR), Salisbury (TN), and Lacock (PN). Then our individual is identified by her name or names (N), her social status (SS), here, high nobility; the names of her father (F), William, Earl of Salisbury, and mother (M), probably Eleanor de Vitré, her husband (H), William Longespée (an illegitimate son of Henry II), and other family members (FM), of her eight children, her eldest son, also William, and two younger sons, one a bishop and another a canon of Salisbury.

Beginning with dates of birth (BD) and death (DD), further biographical details are noted in the next group of fields. Born sometime between 1187 and 1191, Ela of Salisbury died in 1261. If our individual attained the honor of sainthood or beatification -- as did Catherine of Bologna, our second example -- this is recorded in (S) and (B); official canonization or beatification are indicated by their dates, popular veneration by an appropriate abbreviation, with her feast day and date of canonization or beatification, if pertinent. Succeeding fields record information regarding her early life (EL), education (ED), and religious life (RL): with her husband she contributed extensively to the building of Salisbury Cathedral, and after his death she was for two years Sheriff of Wiltshire, the only woman ever to hold that office there. Having realized her plans for the foundation of Lacock by 1232, she herself entered the community as a nun in 1237 and became its first abbess in 1239, resigning the office in 1257, as we note in the next group of fields (ABS C1: 1239-57). These pertain to the communities with which an individual may have been associated and with official or distinctive positions held by her as abbess (ABS), founder (FDR), benefactor (BEN), or "other" (OTH); the order or orders to which she belonged are indicated by (ORI), etc. Both these and a final group of categories pertaining to the individual's distinctive activities and achievements are better illustrated in our second example, the BIO record of St. Catherine of Bologna (Caterina Vegri).

Concerning this fifteenth-century Italian saint, abbess, mystical writer, and artist, we may note first of all the province, Emilia-Romagna, and the two cities, Bologna and Ferrara, where she spent her life, and her social status, which with respect to her father's family was upper middle class, though her mother apparently belonged to a patrician family of Bologna. As a result of very recent study (Foletti, 1985) of archival materials pertaining to the prosperous Vegri family in Ferrara and other records, significant details have been added to our knowledge of Catherine's family background; her father, if he was the Giovanni to whom her paternity is traditionally ascribed, was probably a diplomat in the service of the Este court. Her mother, we learn, received in 1459 a papal concession for reception in her seventies as a lay member of Corpus Domini, Bologna, where Catherine was abbess.

Her own name, with variants of the patronymic, and the names of her father and mother follow, then the dates of her birth and death, and in the field (S), the date of her canonization, which did not occur until 1712, and her feast-day, March 9. In succeeding fields we have compressed the salient data concerning her early life, her education and religious life. Her childhood in Bologna was followed by the years she spent in Ferrara with her mother, several of them, apparently, as a companion to the young Margherita d'Este, at the Este court, where her education made her proficient in Italian and, to some extent, in Latin. In 1426, at thirteen or thereabouts, Catherine entered the lay community that would, after much travail and internal conflict, become the monastery of Clarisse, Corpus Domini, in 1431.

Again, recent research has added substantially to our knowledge of the early history of Corpus Domini, which began as a community of pious laywomen or *pinzochere* and as something of a nursery of spiritual reform. Emerging from its inner divisions were two monastic communities: Sant 'Agostino, following the Augustinian rule, as well as Corpus Domini itself. There Catherine was a nun and, later, novice mistress until 1455 when, as we note in the next group of fields, she returned to Bologna, where she founded a community of Clarisse, also called Corpus Domini, which she ruled as abbess until her death in 1463.

Her exceptional gifts, spiritual, literary, and artistic, are all indicated in the appropriate fields, along with the proficiencies in art and music of this patron saint of artists. As a writer (WRI), she used the vernacular in religious and mystical works, Latin in a collection of sermons for her nuns. In the field (SO), intended to identify spiritual or devotional orientation, she is described as an ascetic and visionary especially devoted to the imitation of Christ, and in (MY) we indicate references to her writings in the bibliography. Extant manuscripts written and illuminated by her are noted in (ART), and in (MU) her skill in performing on the viola is noted; A final field (IC) is provided for "iconography," significant portrayals of the individual in contemporary and later works of art.

In the bibliography, her own writings, both published and unpublished, are indicated in the fields (USI) and (PSI), their counterparts (US2) and (PS2) referring to contemporary works about her. Here a word of explanation about abbreviations for repositories of unpublished sources is in order. These accompany the general bibliography for a country and its regional divisions, provinces, and cities. In the case of Catherine of Bologna, (US1) AAB signifies the arch-episcopal archives (Archivio Arcivescovile) in Bologna; ABC the large collection of documents contained in the Archivio della Beata Caterina. Contained in 56 "cartoni," this collection includes both works by Catherine (US1) and unpublished works, contemporary and later, about her (US2). Important materials, recently studied, also exist in the Archivio Arcivescovile (AAF) and Archivio di Stato

(ASF) in Ferrara, and in the archives of the convent of Corpus Domini in that city.

As the example of Catherine suggests, in contrast to that of Ela of Salisbury, for some individuals the bibliography, especially of modern works, is so extensive as to require considerable selectivity and critical judgment. The hagiographical process that would ultimately contribute to the canonization of Catherine of Bologna was already at work in the first "life," the *Specchio de Illuminazione*, published in 1469; it was written by Illuminata Bembo, a nun of Corpus Domini, Bologna, who knew her abbess well. But Catherine has also been a subject of intensive recent study, and her case significantly illustrates the effects of close examination of unpublished sources in removing such saintly personages from the embrace of pious hagiography to the realm of critical historical investigation. Her case exemplifies as well, therefore, the processes of continuous updating essential to our work, which must take account, for example, of new and important studies like that accompanying Cecilia Foletti's recently published critical edition of St. Catherine's major treatise: Santa Caterina Vegri, *Le sette armi spirituali* (Padova: Editrice Antenore, 1985).

Through experimentation and revision we have enlarged our format to make possible the inclusion of six modern studies, significant books or articles, and six briefer references. Even so, particularly with respect to studies, our choices must be carefully made, and we try to include both "classic" and more recent works, though we are not always so fortunate in our guidance as we are here in Foletti's study and in Serena Spano's earlier and fundamental "Per uno studio su Caterina da Bologna" (*Studi Medievali*, 3 ser., 12 [1971], 713-59).

If our three exemplary records have conveyed some sense of the structure and uses of our data base, other possibilities, especially its collective uses, may be less obvious. In noting a few of these, I hope to suggest how it may open larger perspectives, questions, and lines of inquiry in the religious life of medieval women, along with other facets of their experience. Beginning with numbers, quantitative data of various kinds, our data base -- and ultimately our published repertory and biobibliography, for Italy and for other major regions -- will aim to encompass as completely as possible all female communities from the earliest foundation to ca. 1500. These include the various kinds of institutional entities noted earlier. Obviously, not all of the communities founded during this millenium will have remained in existence until 1500. Some, especially earlier foundations, will have disappeared; others will have merged in one way or another with other communities, as they tended rather often to do; some will have been suppressed in medieval or modern times; some still exist today. So our totals will not represent absolute numbers; the nearly 370 communities we have identified in medieval Tuscany were never all in existence at the same time.

Our data base will, however, enable us to provide figures for the number of communities existing during any century or half-century between 500 and 1500, or during longer periods, for example, before and after 1200. We can, eventually, also supply figures for the numbers of communities in every province, town, or city of those countries on which we have completed work, and in different monastic and religious orders; we can also provide data on their location, whether urban or rural. We shall also be able to retrieve substantial data on the relative size of communities at various times and places, about their origins and the circumstances of their foundation, their benefactors, female as well as male, including their relative numbers, their family ties, and the relationships between female and male communities (as dependencies, for example, or in so-called "double" monasteries). Other categories for which data can be provided include endowments and relative wealth or poverty, economic, caritative, and educational activities, and other important aspects of their histories and functions: for example, on questions of special interest to some scholars, the numbers of communities of *repentite* or repentant prostitutes, the numbers of hospitals, etc. With respect to individuals, collective data can be supplied for those involved in particular activities, such as teachers, writers, scribes, artists, musicians, or representing varieties of devotional practice or spiritual achievement, such as visionaries and mystics, saints and *beate*, including contemporary writings by or about these individuals.

Besides its other uses, this diverse quantitative information should, we hope, make possible the more accurate testing and fruitful replacement of a number of rather fragile current generalizations regarding women's religious life during the medieval centuries. It will also open fresh lines of inquiry, raising and helping to answer new questions, and new possibilities of comparative study in various areas. To point to just one example, we may compare the number of communities we have identified in a single Italian province, 370 in Tuscany, with the total, 150 (excluding hospitals) for England as a whole in the thirteenth century and thereafter. These figures, along with others, pertaining, for example, to the size of individual communities, raise questions meriting closer study. In England, where there were only nine abbeys and a few other communities surviving before the Conquest, the great period of expansion was the twelfth century, with more than eighty new communities founded during a short period, 1135-65. In Italy, by contrast, massive expansion occurred in the thirteenth and fourteenth centuries, with especially large numbers of mendicant convents, of which only four survived in England.

How are we to account for these and other striking differences between women's religious life in England and that in Italy and other continental regions? How, more specifically, are we to explain the relatively modest appeal of this life, except in the twelfth century, to Englishwomen? Are answers to be found in sex ratios, in differing marriage patterns and practices (relating, perhaps, to dotal and inheritance customs), in differences between urban and rural settings, in the distinctive character of English religious culture, in which the anchorite's solitary life, with its proportionately larger appeal to women, represented the highest form of spirituality? These are questions demanding the attention of demographers and of students of the history of women, the family, and social and economic history, as well as monastic and religious history. I mention them simply to illustrate the kinds of inquiry that may be generated and supported by our data base and the works it will produce. I mention them, too by way of suggesting once again why, in our view, a major goal of our project is "looking for medieval women" in general as well as for religious women and their communities in particular.

MONASTIC REPERTORY 1: MAIN ENTRY

CN 2C004   PR WIL   TN SALISB   DI SALISB   PN Lacock   DUP 06/16/86

NMM   Lacock   S AB
NMA   S.M. and S. Bernard
NML   S.M. /locus beate Marie, FDT/Beate Marie S. Bernardi, seal, 13-16C
DED   S.M. / Bernard
LC.   bnet. vil. PN & Avon Riv. in meadow called Snaylesmeade; completed, 1285C
LCP

FDT   1229   FIN 1539
FD.   FDR don. her manor&ch. Lacock for fm. locus beate M:meant as CIS, U/1 ^nuns, 1232
DC1   don.1nd:fd.charte   DT1 1229
DC2   roy.cnf.DC1: Hen3   DT2 1230   PX

ORI   OSA, 1230   R1 RA
OR2   R2
OR3
CGR   NB R1:cnf.Bp.TN,1230; in French, 1400A

MONASTIC REPERTORY 2: DEVELOPMENTS

CN 2C004   PR WIL   TN SALISB   DUP 06/16/86
INC

Iby
DEP

Dof

ECC   visBpTN,14-15C:nx.acta;Abp1332;chap.OSA,1392,1450C,1518/Bp.nms.novs14C
SEC   1tg.fam.Bluet:chs&water,13-4C/1tg.knt.srv/resists roy.intrusions,14-5C
         ASSETS 1nd/chs/quarry/fishery/2000sheep1476:graze rgts;fulling mill
         INCOME rnts/fairs,PN,1237,57/mkts.PN,1242,60/feudal rgts,jur/wool
         VALUES StofIN/val.L101+yr,1291/L120C,later/+des,fire,1447/L168+,FIN
ART   seal impressions:FDR,13C;CN,13C-16C,may show FDR
REM   much relid/ch.wall,13C/cloister&vault,15C/doors13C/sacristy/warming room
CAR   charity:feed loc.poor,esp.Lent,Maundy,All Souls:L9+yrFIN
NOT   MSS:Annals/Psalter/2carts/Cls.accts/prp.rolls/Anglo-Fr.poems/R,in Fr:nx.X

MONASTIC REPERTORY 3: INDIVIDUALS

CN 2C004   PR WIL   TN SALISB   DUP 05/28/86

MEM   N,1300B/1oc.N-&M,1300A   NO1 15   YR1 1230   NO2 22   YR2 1395
PTR   famFDR>DkLAN>BlkPr>J.Gaunt>roy 1399   NO3 17   YR3 1445   NO4 14   YR4 1473
FDR   Ela,Isabella,Cts.Salisbury(1186-1261),nun under 1 ^prs.,then 1 ^Abs:ID,2C004
BEN   K.Hen3,1246,47,64&K.Ed1,1285:aid bld/Humphrey dBohun,El.HER&ESS,1274/ J.dRip
         ariis,13C/J.de Bluet:Lady Chapel,1313/oth.loc.N-
WMB   Constance dleghFDT/AmiceCtsDEV1261A/da&gr.dasFDR:Marg.dLacy,Cts.LIN, DD1309
HDH   Wymarca:1 ^Prs.FDT-1239/FDR;1 ^Abs.1239-57/Beatrice oiKent,dKancia:FDR chose/
         Alice:1^elc/Juliana/Agnes/J.dMontfort/K.leCras/
HD2   S.dSainteCroix/dMontfort/A.dBrymesden/F.Selyman/A.dWyke/E.dMontfort/A.Frary
NNS   Alicia Garinges:1 ^canoness,1232:fr.2VOO4GoringOXF.OSA/gr.das.FDR.Kath&Loric
         a/da.AmiceWMB/MarieDenys,Prs.2Coo2Kington,OSB,1535
LAY   Eleanor deMonfort,minor:incustody Abs.Elena dM,1426/roy.&oth.corrodies
OTH   cura:Wm.Cirencester,OP,1303/conversi,13C/NO5:17+3nov;4cpls;38srvs=9wm.FIN

CN BIBLIOGRAPHY

UNPUBLISHED SOURCES

CN 2C004   PR WIL   TN SALISB   DUP 06/16/86

NMM   Lacock 1

U1   PRO:E 40/9244,9364,10899,11183,11184;135/442,ff.33,33v;   T1
U2   -179/52/65,66,71C;315/420,f.120/SC 12/33/27,37;   T2
U3   -SC 6/Hen3/3985,m .23d,24d,25,26d,27,30d,31,32,33d;   T3
U4   -DL 5/6,f.205;7/1,no.61a;30/127/1907   T4
U5   SALISB:Regs.Mortival2,f.3v;Aiscough,f.14v;Beauchamp 1,   T5
U6   -f.142;Erghum.ff.21,23,23v;Metford,f.132;Hallam.f.22/   T6
U7   BL:Harl.5019.ff.222seq./Harl.Roll.I,14/Add.Ch.47145/   T7
U8   -Cotton MS.Vit.A.VIII,ff.113seq.SeeBowles&Nichols(1835)   T8 Annals,13C;Bk,14C
U9   WILTSHIRE RO:Deed 132/3/OXFORD:Bodl,MS Laud:lat.114   T9/Psalterium,13-6C

XT

CN BIBLIOGRAPHY

UNPUBLISHED SOURCES.

CN 2C004   PR WIL   TN SALISB   DUP 03/11/86

NMM   Lacock 2

U1   PRO:Wards 2/94B/3,3a,4,9,11,24,27,28,34,55,56,60,67,69 T1
U2   -75,84-7,120,122,125,137,140-1,143,150,152-5;2/94C/6.   T2
U3   -7,9;2/94E/19,20,24,25,27,31-3,48,55-6,59,60,63,66,71,   T3
U4   -73,77,78,87,89,91,92,96,97,113/   T4
U5   LACOCK ABBEY:Older Cartulary (OC)Newer Cartulary (NC)   T5 2carts 1242A /1304A
U6   -MS Mrs.A.D.Burnett-Brown,Wm.Brito,Dictionary   T6 Dictionary,14-15C
U7   T7
U8   T8
U9   T9

XT

CN BIBLIOGRAPHY

PUBLISHED SOURCES

CN2C004   PR WIL   TN SALISB   DUP 06/17/86

NMM   Lacock

P1   Dugdale 6:501-10/Taxatio:186,189,192-3,214,237/
P2   Cal.Pat.(1232-47)287;(1307-13)511;(1313-17)126;(1330-4)
P3   -332;(1338-40)297;(1358-61)109;(1385-8)109;(1396-9)447.
P4   -482;(1401-5)223,241;(1429-36)289(1446-52)86(1461-7)527
P5   Cal.Ch.R(1226-57)225,230,274,332,460(1257-1300)25-6.29/
P6   Cal.Lib.R(1226-40)332(1245-51)69,139/
P7   Cal.CloR(1259-61)22-3(1261-4)335(1279-88)311(1341-3)209
P8   -k(1360-64)156(1381-85)90/Cal.IPM9:93/Val.Ecc.2:115seq/
P9   Hun.R2,268,270,277/Blk.Prince Reg4:180,183-4,400,405/
P10   Reg.Gandavo2:860/Bk.Fees2:737,742,1305/Som.Med.Wills,19
P11   -:287,299,411/Cal.InqMiscl:243;3:408/Cal.Anct.D.4:A8877
P12   -A9357,A9378,A9397;5:A13651/Reg.J.Gaunt(1397)20,924/
P13   Bowles&Nichols(1835)/Parl.R2:182-3/Ch&Doc.SAL(1891)251
P14   Rogers (1979)/L&P,Hen8,9:47;13(2):177;14(1):40,43;15:
P15   -296,479,613;17:567j,1012;18(1)543;20(2)323;21(1)693/

XT   Col.Pap.Reg2:17;5:327seq/Clark-Maxwell(1902,1904,1905)

STUDIES AND REFERENCES

CN 2C004   PR WIL   TN SALISB
NMM Lacock 1

DUP 05/06/86

ST1 Talbot (1895)	ST2 Elphinstone-Fyffe(1942)47
ST3 Brakspear(1900a)	ST4 Brakspear(1900b)
ST5 Brakspear(1900c)	ST6 VCH,WIL2:99,303-16

REF1 K&H 229/Power 689	REF2 Davis(1958)59
REF 3 Ker(1964)107;idem,Report	REF4 Dugdale 6:500-1
REF5 Savine(1909)108	REF6 Aubrey(1862)92
REF7 Somerville(1953)1:287-9	REF8 -411/Salter(1920):139,193
REF9 Fletcher(1937)66	REF10 Clarke(1896)288-9,310

XT

SELECTED LACOCK BIBLIOGRAPHY
alphabetically by abbreviation

ABBREVIATION: Bowles&Nichols,1835

Bowles, W. L. and J. B. Nichols, eds., *Annals and Antiquities of Lacock Abbey* (London, 1835).

ABBREVIATION: Brakspear, 1900b

Brakspear, Harold, "Lacock Abbey Church," *Archaeological Journal*, 57 (1900), 1-9.

ABBREVIATION: Cal.Pap.Reg.

Bliss, William Henry and J.A. Twemlow, eds., *Calendar of Entries in the Papal Registers Relating to Great Britain and Ireland: Papal Letters (1198-1492)*, 14 vols. (London: H.M.S.O, 1893-1960).

ABBREVIATION: Clark-Maxwell,1905

Clark-Maxwell, William G., ed., "Earliest Charters of the Abbey of Lacock," *Wiltshire Archaeological and Natural History Society Magazine*, 35 (1905), 191-201.

ABBREVIATION: Reg.J.Gaunt, 1911.

Armitage-Smith, Sydney,ed.,*John of Gaunt's Register (1371-5)* Camden Society, 3rd ser., 20 and 21, 2 vols. (1911).

ABBREVIATION: Rogers, 1979

Rogers, Kenneth H.,ed., *Lacock Abbey Charters*, Wiltshire Record Society, 34 (for 1978), 145.+ (Devizes, 1979).

BIOBIBLIOGRAPHY 1: DATA FILE

DUP 06/16/86

ID 2C004   PR WIL   PR2   TN SALISB   TN2   PN Lacock

N Ela, Isabella, Cts.Salisbury   SS N+
F William,El.Salisbury,DD1196   M Prob.EleanordeVitre?
H wid.Wm.Longespee.so.K.Hen2:DD1226   FM 8cdn:Nich.BpTN:Rich,canonTN/3das.
BD 1187/91 DD 8/24/1261   S   B
El sole heir of F/sheriff,PR,1226-8   ED
RL FDR,C7=C1,1229,as widow/ent.C1 as nun,1237: HDH=Wyhmarca, Prs/ID=1
^Abs1239/rsg.1257&names 2 ^Abs/bur.ch.CN,as also 2 sons,oth.kin

TTLS Countess/Founder,C7=C1/Abbess,C1   OR1 OSA   OR2   OR3

HDH1 2C004	C1 1239-57rsg.lacock	HDH2	C2	
NUN1	C3	NUN2	C4	
BEN1	C5	BEN2	C6	
FDR1 2C004	C7 1229,lacock	FDR2	C8	
OTH				

SP only woman sheriff,PR
WR1   MY   SO
ART   MU   IC

BIOBIBLIOGRAPHY 2: SOURCES AND STUDIES

DUP 06/16/86

ID 2C004   PR WIL   PR2   TN SALISB   TN2   PN Lacock

N Ela/Isabella, Cts.Salisbury

US1

US2 PRO:Lacock deeds (see CN 2C004)

PS1

PS2 Rogers (1979)/Bowles & Nichols (1835)

ST1 Clark (1905)	ST2
ST3	ST4
ST5	ST6

REF1 VCH,WIL2:303-16	REF2 ComPeer,11,378-379
REF3	REF4
REF5	REF6

BIOBIBLIOGRAPHY 1: DATA FILE

DUP 08/04/86

LID 1EO15   PR ER   PR2   TN FERRAR   TN2 BOLOGN   PN Ferrara/Bologna

N Caterina Vegri/Vigri   SSm+/nQpatQ
F Vegri, Giovanni (see Foletti.1985)   M Mammolini, BenvenutaTN2
H   FM
BD 1413Se8 DD1463Mr9   S 1712Mr9   B
EL chdTN2,movTN,1420Q/crt.dEste1424Q   ED hum.crt.dEste/1+V&L/art/mus
RL ent.lay cn.1426>C1,OFM,1431:portress Q,novice-mistress/fd.C2,OFM,TN2,1455/abs1
456-63

TTLS Abs.C2   OR1 OFM   OR2   OR3

HDH1	C1	HDH2 1E208	C2 1456-63,CorpusDominiTN2	
NUN1 IE154	C3 1431-55, Corpus Domini TN	NUN2	C4	
BEN1	C5	BEN2	C6	
FDR1 1E208	C7 1455,CorpusDomini TN2	FDR2	C8	
OTH				

SP patronS/artists
WRI V/rel,mys/L/sermons   MY US1,PS1   SO asc/vis/imit.Christi
ART ilmss:C2/ms=Oxf Bod.   MU viola,perf.   IC

BIOBIBLIOGRAPHY 2: SOURCES AND STUDIES

DUP 08/04/86

ID 1EO15   PR ER   PR2   TN FERRAR   TN2 BOLOGN   PN Ferrara/Bologna

N Caterina Vegri/Vigri

US1 BOLOGN:AAB:(ABC),cart.25,26,28,35/C2:mss,incl.il.Breviario(autogr)/Rosarium metricum
      de mysteriis Passionis Christi Domini/oth.
US2 BOLOGN:AAB:(ABC)cart.156/FERRAR:ASF:arch.nct.ant./arch.op.pia/BCAriostea:arch.
      Pasi/coll.Antonielli.868/cl.I.354,356/C1:arch.

PS1 Le sette armi,ed.Foletti(1985)/Sermones ad sacras virgines (1522,1635)

PS2 !!luminata Bembo, Vita:Specchio de Illuminazione (1469,1797)

ST1 Spanò(1971)	ST2 Foletti(1985)
ST3 Alberigo(1963-1965)	ST4 Samaritani(1973)
ST5 Stienon du Pré(1949)	ST6 Nuñez.(1911-1912)

REF1 DB125:381-3	REF2 BS3:980-02
REF3 DS2.1:288-90	REF4 DHGE11:1505-06
REF5	REF6

STUDIES AND REFERENCES

CN 2C004   PR WIL   TN SALISB
NMM   Lacock 1

DUP 05/06/86

ST1 Talbot (1895)	ST2 Elphinstone-Fyffe(1942)47
ST3 Brakspear(1900a)	ST4 Brakspear(1900b)
ST5 Brakspear(1900c)	ST6 VCH,WIL2:99,303-16

REF1 K&H 229/Power 689	REF2 Davis(1958)59
REF 3 Ker(1964)107;idem,Report	REF4 Dugdale 6:500-1
REF5 Savine(1909)108	REF6 Aubrey(1862)92
REF7 Somerville(1953)1:287-9	REF8 -411/Salter(1920):139,193
REF9 Fletcher(1937)66	REF10 Clarke(1896)288-9,310

XT

SELECTED LACOCK BIBLIOGRAPHY
alphabetically by abbreviation

ABBREVIATION: Bowles&Nichols,1835
Bowles, W. L. and J. B. Nichols, eds., *Annals and Antiquities of Lacock Abbey* (London, 1835).

ABBREVIATION: Brakspear, 1900b
Brakspear, Harold, "Lacock Abbey Church," *Archaeological Journal*, 57 (1900), 1-9.

ABBREVIATION: Cal.Pap.Reg.
Bliss, William Henry and J.A. Twemlow, eds., *Calendar of Entries in the Papal Registers Relating to Great Britain and Ireland: Papal Letters (1198-1492)*, 14 vols. (London: H.M.S.O, 1893-1960).

ABBREVIATION: Clark-Maxwell,1905
Clark-Maxwell, William G., ed., "Earliest Charters of the Abbey of Lacock," *Wiltshire Archaeological and Natural History Society Magazine*, 35 (1905), 191-201.

ABBREVIATION: Reg.J.Gaunt, 1911.
Armitage-Smith, Sydney,ed.,*John of Gaunt's Register (1371-5)* Camden Society, 3rd ser., 20 and 21, 2 vols. (1911).

ABBREVIATION: Rogers, 1979
Rogers, Kenneth H.,ed., *Lacock Abbey Charters*, Wiltshire Record Society, 34 (for 1978), 145.+ (Devizes, 1979).

BIOBIBLIOGRAPHY 1: DATA FILE

DUP 06/16/86

ID 2C004   PR WIL   PR2   TN SALISB   TN2   PN Lacock

N   Ela, Isabella, Cts.Salisbury   SS   N+
F   William,El.Salisbury,DD1196   M   Prob.EleanordeVitre?
H   wid.Wm.Longespee.so.K.Hen2:DD1226   FM   8cdn:Nich.BpTN:Rich,canonTN/3das.
BD 1187/91 DD 8/24/1261   S   B
El sole heir of F/sheriff,PR,1226-8   ED
RL FDR,C7=C1,1229,as widow/ent.C1 as nun,1237: HDH=Wyhmarca, Prs/ID=1
^Abs1239/rsg.1257&names 2 ^Abs/bur.ch.CN,as also 2 sons,oth.kin

TTLS Countess/Founder,C7=C1/Abbess,C1		OR1 OSA	OR2	OR3
HDH1 2C004	C1 1239-57rsg.lacock	HDH2	C2	
NUN1	C3	NUN2	C4	
BEN1	C5	BEN2	C6	
FDR1 2C004	C7 1229,lacock	FDR2	C8	
OTH				

SP only woman sheriff,PR
WR1   MY   SO
ART   MU   IC

BIOBIBLIOGRAPHY 2: SOURCES AND STUDIES

DUP 06/16/86

ID 2C004   PR WIL   PR2   TN SALISB   TN2   PN Lacock

N Ela/Isabella, Cts.Salisbury

US1

US2 PRO:Lacock deeds (see CN 2C004)

PS1

PS2 Rogers (1979)/Bowles & Nichols (1835)

ST1 Clark (1905)	ST2
ST3	ST4
ST5	ST6

REF1 VCH,WIL2:303-16	REF2 ComPeer,11,378-379
REF3	REF4
REF5	REF6

BIOBIBLIOGRAPHY 1: DATA FILE

DUP 08/04/86

LID 1EO15   PR ER   PR2   TN FERRAR   TN2 BOLOGN   PN Ferrara/Bologna

N Caterina Vegri/Vigri   SSm+/nQpatQ
F Vegri, Giovanni (see Foletti.1985)   M Mammolini, BenvenutaTN2
H   FM
BD 1413Se8 DD1463Mr9   S 1712Mr9   B
El chdTN2,movTN,1420Q/crt.dEste1424Q   ED hum.crt.dEste/1+V&L/art/mus
RL ent.lay cn.1426>C1,OFM,1431:portress Q,novice-mistress/fd.C2,OFM,TN2,1455/abs1
456-63

TTLS Abs.C2		OR1 OFM	OR2	OR3
HDH1	C1	HDH2 1E208	C2 1456-63,CorpusDominiTN2	
NUN1 1E154	C3 1431-55, Corpus Domini TN	NUN2	C4	
BEN1	C5	BEN2	C6	
FDR1 1E208	C7 1455,CorpusDomini TN2	FDR2	C8	
OTH				

SP patronS/artists
WRI V/rel,mys/L/sermons   MY US1,PS1   SO asc/vis/imit.Christi
ART ilmss:C2/ms=Oxf Bod.   MU viola,perf.   IC

BIOBIBLIOGRAPHY 2: SOURCES AND STUDIES

DUP 08/04/86

ID 1EO15   PR ER   PR2   TN FERRAR   TN2 BOLOGN   PN Ferrara/Bologna

N Caterina Vegri/Vigri

US1 BOLOGN:AAB:(ABC),cart.25,26,28,35/C2:mss,incl.il.Breviario(autogr)/Rosarium metricum de mysteriis Passionis Christi Domini/oth.
US2 BOLOGN:AAB:(ABC)cart.156/FERRAR:ASF:arch.nct.ant./arch.op.pia/BCAriostea:arch. Pasi/coll.Antonielli.868/cl.I.354,356/C1:arch.
PS1 Le sette armi,ed.Foletti(1985)/Sermones ad sacras virgines (1522,1635)

PS2 Illuminata Bembo,Vita:Specchio di Illuminazione (1469,1797)

ST1 Spanò(1971)	ST2 Foletti(1985)
ST3 Alberigo(1963-1965)	ST4 Samaritani(1973)
ST5 Stienon du Pré(1949)	ST6 Nuñez.(1911-1912)

REF1 DB125:381-3	REF2 BS3:980-02
REF3 DS2.1:288-90	REF4 DHGE11:1505-06
REF5	REF6